SSAT
核心词汇速记

李涛 ◎ 编著

机械工业出版社

本书中的词汇均是 SSAT 考试中的必备核心词汇，选自历年真题及各类官方出版物。每个词条都提供该单词在真题中的词性和中文释义；"变"一栏提供该单词的相关变体，便于考生对比记忆；"记"一栏采用联想、词根、词缀、谐音等各种方法帮助考生记忆单词；"考"一栏将该单词在 SSAT 考试中的"同义""类比"词对挑出来，让考生可以更加有目的性地去记忆。每个词条都按照星级标注了单词的难易程度和重要程度，让考生做到有的放矢。本书既可以作为 SSAT 考生的自学用书，也可以作为各类 SSAT 课程的配套教材。

图书在版编目（CIP）数据

SSAT 核心词汇速记 / 李涛编著 . —北京：机械工业出版社，2019.11
ISBN 978 - 7 - 111 - 64155 - 1

Ⅰ.①S… Ⅱ.①李… Ⅲ.①英语-词汇-高中-入学考试-美国-自学参考资料 Ⅳ.①G634.413

中国版本图书馆 CIP 数据核字（2019）第 251645 号

机械工业出版社（北京市百万庄大街 22 号　邮政编码 100037）
策划编辑：苏筛琴　　　　责任编辑：苏筛琴
版式设计：张文贵　　　　责任印制：张　博
三河市宏达印刷有限公司印刷
2020 年 1 月第 1 版・第 1 次印刷
184mm×240mm・26.25 印张・585 千字
标准书号：ISBN 978 - 7 - 111 - 64155 - 1
定价：66.00 元

电话服务	网络服务
客服电话：010 - 88361066	机　工　官　网：www.cmpbook.com
010 - 88379833	机　工　官　博：weibo.com/cmp1952
010 - 68326294	金　书　网：www.golden-book.com
封底无防伪标均为盗版	机工教育服务网：www.cmpedu.com

前　言

我从 2013 年开始接触 SSAT 考试，于 2016 年开始着手写这本书，前后历经 3 年时间才按照自己的心愿把这本书完全整理了出来。现在回头看，有些时候铆足了劲儿去做一件前途未卜的事情，还是挺需要耐心和毅力的。

SSAT 的全称是 Secondary School Admission Test，简单地说就是"美国中考"，是打算去美国、加拿大私立中学读书的孩子必须参加的一个考试。由于种种原因，美国只有私立中学才可以接收外国留学生持长期有效签证就读，直至高中毕业考入大学。但是，基本上美国私立中学都要求留学生必须参加 SSAT 考试。只有顺利通过 SSAT 考试，才能进入优质的私立中学就读。

在 SSAT 考试中，词汇部分应该是最令中国孩子头疼的一个方面。首先，SSAT 的单词是真的难，某些词汇的难度甚至和 SAT 或者 GRE 持平；其次，SSAT 单词的涉及面非常广，你可能知道"马"的英文单词是 horse，但是你知道"公马""母马""小马驹"用英文怎么说吗？最后，因为考生年龄的原因，SSAT 词汇里面很多类比对孩子是很难理解的，这些问题可能高中生、大学生稍加思考就明白，但是对于小孩子来说理解起来还是有一些困难的。

针对这些情况，这本书就应运而生了。首先，本书按照单词的难易程度和重要程度把单词按照星级来划分，最难的且重要的单词标注三颗星（★★★），一般难度的标注两颗星（★★），相对简单的标注一颗星（★），让学生做到有的放矢；其次，本书最后整理出了"类别词"，把常考的类比关系词对整理了出来，让学生更容易按照整体关系来记忆单词；另外，书中出现的每个单词的后面也都说明了类比词对之间的关系，以便于年纪小一些的孩子可以更加快速和高效地理解。

最后，感谢身边的朋友对本书的支持。在此感谢杭州新东方胡玲老师和上海新东方高宇琪老师的引荐；感谢我的好朋友解晓琦和阿里巴巴员工沈泽凡对这本书做出的贡献，没有你们的帮助肯定没有现在这本书。

李　涛

2019 年 10 月 31 日于杭州

本书使用说明

SSAT考试必备核心词汇

根据星级来划分单词，让学生明白单词的难易程度和重要程度

这个单词在SSAT考试中的词性，很多单词在SSAT考试中词性会变

将本单词和其相关单词的变体放在一起，便于学生对比记忆

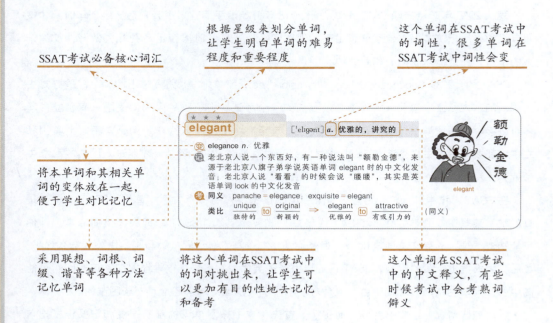

采用联想、词根、词缀、谐音等各种方法记忆单词

将这个单词在SSAT考试中的词对挑出来，让学生可以更加有目的性地去记忆和备考

这个单词在SSAT考试中的中文释义，有些时候考试中会考熟词僻义

目 录

前言
本书使用说明

List 01	1		List 28	111
List 02	5		List 29	115
List 03	9		List 30	119
List 04	13		List 31	123
List 05	17		List 32	128
List 06	21		List 33	132
List 07	25		List 34	136
List 08	30		List 35	140
List 09	35		List 36	144
List 10	39		List 37	148
List 11	43		List 38	152
List 12	47		List 39	156
List 13	51		List 40	160
List 14	55		List 41	164
List 15	59		List 42	168
List 16	63		List 43	172
List 17	67		List 44	176
List 18	71		List 45	181
List 19	75		List 46	185
List 20	79		List 47	190
List 21	83		List 48	195
List 22	87		List 49	199
List 23	91		List 50	203
List 24	95		List 51	207
List 25	99		List 52	211
List 26	103		List 53	215
List 27	107		List 54	219

List 55 224	List 78 319
List 56 229	List 79 323
List 57 233	List 80 327
List 58 237	List 81 331
List 59 242	List 82 335
List 60 246	List 83 339
List 61 250	List 84 344
List 62 255	List 85 348
List 63 259	List 86 352
List 64 263	List 87 356
List 65 267	List 88 361
List 66 271	List 89 365
List 67 275	List 90 369
List 68 279	List 91 373
List 69 283	List 92 377
List 70 287	List 93 381
List 71 291	List 94 385
List 72 295	List 95 389
List 73 299	List 96 393
List 74 303	List 97 397
List 75 307	类别词 401
List 76 311	索引 407
List 77 315	

SSAT词汇 List 01

★★★ elegant
['elɪgənt] *a.* 优雅的，讲究的

变 elegance *n.* 优雅

记 老北京人说一个东西好，有一种说法叫"额勒金德"，来源于老北京八旗子弟学说英语单词 elegant 时的中文化发音；老北京人说"看看"的时候会说"瞜瞜"，其实是英语单词 look 的中文化发音

考 同义 panache = elegance；exquisite = elegant

类比 unique 独特的 to original 新颖的 ⇒ elegant 优雅的 to attractive 有吸引力的 （同义）

elegant

★ foible
['fɔɪbl] *n.* 弱点，小缺点

记 缺点（foible）导致失败（fail）

考 同义 foible = weakness

★ villain
['vɪlən] *n.* 坏人，恶棍

记 远方的村（village）中有一个恶棍（villain）

考 类比 hero 主角 to villain 坏人 ⇒ protagonist 主角 to antagonist 敌手 （反义）

★ grizzly
['ɡrɪzli] *n.* 灰熊

记 NBA 中 "孟菲斯灰熊" 队英文即为 Memphis Grizzlies

考 类比 grizzly 灰熊 to bear 熊 ⇒ mint 薄荷 to herb 草 （种属）
hammerhead 锤头鲨 to grizzly 灰熊 ⇒ shark 鲨鱼 to bear 熊 （纵向）

grizzly

★★ embellish
[ɪm'belɪʃ] *v.* 装饰

变 embellishment *n.* 装饰

记 em- + bell 铃铛 + -ish：用铃铛（bell）来装饰（embellish）美丽的圣诞节

考 类比 cosmetics 化妆品 to embellish 装饰 ⇒ ornament 装饰品 to adorn 装饰 （事物及其用途）

☆ elegant   ☆ foible   ☆ villain   ☆ grizzly   ☆ embellish embellishment (装饰) — to — decorative (装饰性的) ⇒ circumlocution (累赘说法) — to — indirect (不直接的)　（同义）

注　关于"装饰"的单词在 SSAT 的习题中有很多，如：decorate，ornament，garnish。

wan
[wɒn] *a.* 苍白的

记　跑完马拉松，获得（won）冠军，但是脸色苍白（wan）
考　同义　wan = pale

indicate
[ˈɪndɪkeɪt] *v.* 表明，指出

变　indication *n.* 暗示，表明
记　in- + dic- 说话 + -ate：话中有话，好像在表明（indicate）什么
考　同义　indicate = signify；indicate = signal；indicate = point out
　　类比　lapse (失误) — to — error (错误) ⇒ inkling (暗示) — to — indication (表明)　（<程度）

pilot
[ˈpaɪlət] *n.* 飞行员

考　类比　driver (司机) — to — car (车) ⇒ pilot (飞行员) — to — airplane (飞机)　（人物及其对象）
　　　　　pilot (飞行员) — to — airplane (飞机) ⇒ captain (船长) — to — ship (船)　（人物及其对象）

gong
[gɒŋ] *n.* 锣

记　发音就是模拟敲锣的声音
考　类比　gong (锣) — to — mallet (锣槌) ⇒ drum (鼓) — to — stick (鼓槌)　（动作及其对象）
　　　　　bell (铃) — to — clapper (铃舌) ⇒ gong (锣) — to — striker (锣槌)　（事物及其部分）

panicky
[ˈpæniki] *a.* 恐慌的，惊慌的

记　这个单词来自 panic
考　同义　panicky = alarmed

athlete
[ˈæθliːt] *n.* 运动员

考　类比　tutor (老师) — to — pupil (学生) ⇒ coach (教练) — to — athlete (运动员)　（人物及其对象）
　　　　　athlete (运动员) — to — trophy (奖品) ⇒ soldier (士兵) — to — medal (勋章)　（人物及其对象）

valediction
[ˌvælɪˈdɪkʃn] *n.* 告别演说

记　vale 拉丁词根"再见" + diction "说话"，再见时说的话即为告别演说
考　类比　valediction (告别演说) — to — commencement (毕业典礼) ⇒ dedication (献词) — to — opening (开业)　（空间）

stanza ★★★
['stænzə] *n.* 诗节

记 斯坦（Stan）在认真书写每一个诗节（stanza）

考 类比
- novel to chapter → ballad to stanza （组成）
  小说　　章节　　　歌谣　　诗节
- stanza to poem → act to opera （组成）
  诗节　　诗　　　幕　　歌剧
- prose to paragraph → poetry to stanza （组成）
  散文　　段落　　　诗歌　　诗节
- stanza to poem → paragraph to essay （组成）
  诗节　　诗　　　段落　　文章
- stanza to poem → cup to dishware （组成）
  诗节　　诗　　　杯子　　餐具
- stanza to line → paragraph to sentence （组成）
  诗节　　行　　　段落　　句子
- stanza to poem → verse to song （组成）
  诗节　　诗　　　韵文　　歌曲
- epoch to era → stanza to paragraph （同义）
  时代　　时代　　诗节　　段落

friction ★★
['frɪkʃn] *n.* 摩擦

记 小说（fiction）中一定要有人物之间的摩擦（friction）

考 类比
- discontent to rebellion → friction to spark （因果）
  不满　　叛逆　　　摩擦　　火花
- rub to friction → squeeze to pressure （因果）
  摩擦　　摩擦力　　挤压　　压力

insect ★★★
['ɪnsekt] *n.* 昆虫

变 insecticide *n.* 杀虫剂

考 类比
- larva to insect → embryo to mammal （动物）
  幼虫　　昆虫　　　胚胎　　哺乳动物
- throng to people → swarm to insects （同义）
  人群　　人　　　一群虫子　　昆虫
- pun to joke → termite to insect （种属）
  双关语　笑话　　　白蚁　　昆虫
- bat to mammal → butterfly to insect （种属）
  蝙蝠　　哺乳动物　蝴蝶　　昆虫
- rose to flower → bee to insect （种属）
  玫瑰　　花　　　蜜蜂　　虫子
- butterfly to insect → cardinal to bird （种属）
  蝴蝶　　昆虫　　　红衣凤头鸟　鸟
- dragon fly to insect → dragon to myth （种属）
  蜻蜓　　飞虫　　　龙　　神话
- mosquito to insect → soccer to sport （种属）
  蚊子　　虫　　　足球　　体育运动
- triangle to shape → ant to insect （种属）
  三角形　形状　　　蚂蚁　　昆虫

hoe 锄头	to	weed 草	→	insecticide 杀虫剂	to	pest 害虫	（事物及其对象）
pesticide 杀虫剂	to	insect 昆虫	→	money 钱	to	employee 员工	（事物及其对象）
pesticide 杀虫剂	to	insect 昆虫	→	antiseptic 防腐剂	to	germ 细菌	（事物及其对象）

★ formidable   [ˈfɔːmɪdəbl] a. 强大的，令人可畏的

记 for + mid-中间 + -able 能：为了能站在舞台中间，他做出了巨大的（formidable）努力
考 同义   formidable = powerful

★ rancid   [ˈrænsɪd] a. 恶臭的

记 鸡蛋过期了，发出又酸（acid）又臭（rancid）的味道
考 类比   stale 馊的 to bread 面包 → rancid 恶臭的 to meat 肉 （修饰）
注 关于"恶臭的"的单词在 SSAT 的习题中有很多，如：malodorous, stinking, fetid, noisome, putrid。

★★ recipe   [ˈresəpi] n. 食谱

记 著名的"食之秘餐厅"英文即为 Secret Recipe
考 类比   blueprint 蓝图 to house 房子 → recipe 菜单 to cake 蛋糕 （事物及其用途）
　　　　cookbook 烹饪书 to recipes 食谱 → manual 手册 to instructions 说明 （组成）
　　　　recipe 食谱 to ingredient 原材料 → speech 演讲 to word 话 （组成）

★★ laconic   [ləˈkɒnɪk] a. 简洁的，简短的

记 这个单词来自 Laconia（拉哥尼亚），是希腊南部的一个王国。拉哥尼亚人以语言简练而闻名。传说希腊北部的马其顿国王菲利普想占领拉哥尼亚，他曾经写了一封信威胁拉哥尼亚人，说："If we come to your city, we will raze it to the ground.（假如我们到了你们的城市，就会把你们的城市夷为平地。）"很快，马其顿国王就收到回信，上面只有一个词 IF。
考 类比   money 钱 to miserly 吝啬的 → word 话语 to laconic 简洁的 （缺乏）
注 关于"简洁的"单词在 SSAT 的习题中有很多，如：brief, terse, concise, succinct。

★ fledgling   [ˈfledʒlɪŋ] n. 初出茅庐者

记 fledge 一词是"长羽毛"的意思
考 同义   fledgling = newcomer
　　　　类比   fledgling 初出茅庐者 to beginner 新人 → backer 支持者 to supporter 支持者 （同义）

SSAT词汇 List 02

★★ boundary
['baʊndri] n. 边界

- 变 boundless a. 无限的，无边无际的
- 记 bound 范围 + -ary
- 考 同义 boundary = limit；boundary = edge
- 类比 boundless 无限的 to space 空间 ⇒ bottomless 无底的 to pit 坑 （修饰）

★ equitable
['ekwɪtəbl] a. 公平的，公正的

- 记 判决很公正（equitable），原告、被告双方都很平静（equable）
- 考 同义 equitable = fair

★ augment
['ɔːgment] v. 增加

- 记 律师的合理论据（argument）增加（augment）了自己辩护人胜诉的概率
- 考 同义 augment = increase

★★★ aqueduct
['ækwɪdʌkt] n. 导水管

- 变 aquatic a. 水的，水生的
- 记 aque- 水 + duct- 引导
- 考 类比
  - aqueduct 导水管 to water 水 ⇒ pipeline 管道 to gas 天然气 （空间）
  - electricity 电 to wire 电线 ⇒ water 水 to aqueduct 导水管 （空间）
  - arboreal 树栖的 to tree 树 ⇒ aquatic 水的 to water 水 （同义）
  - aquatic 水的 to water 水 ⇒ terrestrial 陆地的 to land 土地 （同义）
  - aquatic 水生的 to fish 鱼 ⇒ slithery 滑溜的 to snake 蛇 （事物及其特点）

★★★ investigate
[ɪn'vestɪgeɪt] v. 调查

- 变 investigation n. 调查，研究

记 联邦调查局 FBI 就是 Federal Bureau of Investigation
考 同义 investigation = inquiry；investigate = examine

类比
flexibility 灵活 to agility 敏捷 → sleuth 侦查 to investigate 调查 （同义）
author 作者 to write 写 → detective 侦探 to investigate 调查 （人物及其动作）
alibi 不在场证明 to criminal 罪犯 → investigation 调查 to police 警察 （人物及其对象）

malady ['mælədi] *n.* 弊病，疾病

记 得病（malady）的人要多听音乐（melody）来减缓病情
考 同义 malady = illness

convince [kən'vɪns] *v.* 说服

变 conviction *n.* 坚定信念
考 类比
remind 使记得 to remember 记起 → convince 说服 to believe 相信 （因果）
conviction 信念 to opinion 观点 → reverence 尊敬 to admiration 羡慕 （程度）

contemporary [kən'temprəri] *a.* 当代的，同代的

考 同义 contemporary = modern

iconoclast [aɪ'kɒnəklæst] *n.* 偶像破坏者

记 icon 偶像 + clast（blast）爆炸：偶像破坏者（iconoclast）即为炸掉（blast）偶像（icon）的人
考 类比
iconoclast 偶像破坏者 to convention 传统 → anarchist 无政府主义者 to government 政府 （人物及其对象）

iconoclast

encumber [ɪn'kʌmbə] *v.* 阻塞，妨碍

记 这个记者遭遇（encounter）坏人的妨碍（encumber）
考 同义 encumber = burden

dedication [ˌdedɪ'keɪʃn] *n.* 题词

考 类比
valediction 告别演说 to commencement 毕业典礼 → dedication 题词 to opening 开业 （空间）
注 dedication 这个单词"奉献"的意思我们是很熟悉的，此处是熟词僻义。

bolster ['bəʊlstə] *v.* 支持

记 手枪皮套（holster）的作用就是去支撑（bolster）手枪

考 同义 bolster = support

sentence ★★★
['sentəns] n. 句子；判刑

考 类比 （事物及其用途）（事物及其用途）（组成）（组成）（组成）（组成）（种属）

furnish ★
['fɜːnɪʃ] v. 提供，供应

考 同义 furnish = supply

expunge ★★
[ɪkˈspʌndʒ] v. 擦去，删掉

记 ex- 朝外 + punge 谐音 "胖子"：朝外删除（expunge）掉一个胖子
考 同义 expunge = erase；expunge = obliterate
类比 expunge to remove → scrutinize to inspect （同义）
删除　　移除　　　　检查　　　检测
注 关于 "擦去，删除" 的单词在 SSAT 的习题中有很多，如：efface, eradicate, expurgate, bowdlerize。

cavern ★★
['kævən] n. 洞穴

变 cavernous a. 洞穴状的
记 这个本身就包含单词 cave
考 同义 chasm = cavern
类比 canal to river → mine to cavern （同类：人工和自然）
运河　河流　　　矿　　洞穴
cavernous to hollow → calamitous to unfortunate （同义）
洞穴状的　空的　　　灾难的　　　　不幸的

fascinate ★★★
['fæsɪneɪt] v. 着迷，入迷

变 fascinating a. 有趣的
考 同义 enthrall = fascinate；intrigue = fascinate；fascinating = intriguing
类比 dominate to influential → fascinate to interesting （同义）
统治　　有影响力　　　　着迷　　　有趣的

interesting to fascinating ⇒ scary to terrifying （同义）
有趣的　　　有趣的　　　可怕的　　　害怕的

★★★ frugal ['fruːgl] *a.* 节俭的，朴素的

变 frugality *n.* 节俭，朴素
记 谐音：腐乳过；仅靠腐乳来过日子，真的挺节俭的（frugal）
考 同义 economical ＝ frugal；frugal ＝ husbandry

类比
frugal to spending ⇒ unruly to obedient （反义）
节俭的　　花费的　　不守规矩的　听话的
terse to language ⇒ frugal to money （缺乏）
简洁的　　语言　　　节俭的　　钱
prudent to indiscretion ⇒ frugal to wastefulness （反义）
谨慎的　　轻率　　　　节俭的　　浪费
feral to domestication ⇒ crude to refinement （反义）
野生的　　驯养　　　　原始的　　精炼
generous to frugal ⇒ philanthropist to miser （反义）
大方的　　节俭的　　慈善家　　　　　小气鬼
frugality to stingy ⇒ pride to haughty （同义：正反向）
朴素　　　小气的　　自豪　　傲慢的
frugal to miserly ⇒ confident to arrogant （同义：正反向）
节俭的　　吝啬的　　自信的　　傲慢的

注 关于"节俭的"单词在 SSAT 的习题中有很多，如：thrifty, sparing, stingy, abstemious.

★ cork [kɔːk] *n.* 软木塞

记 开红酒最核心（core）的步骤就是成功移除那个软木塞（cork）
考 类比 box to cover ⇒ bottle to cork （事物及其部分）
　　　　盒子　　盖子　　　瓶子　　木塞

★★ exhort [ɪɡˈzɔːt] *v.* 忠告，劝诫

变 exhortation *n.* 劝告，训诫
记 注意区分 exhort "劝告" 和 extort "勒索"
考 同义 exhort ＝ urge
类比 exhortation to urge ⇒ eulogy to praise （事物及其目的）
　　　训诫词　　　敦促　　赞歌　　表扬

注 exhort 这个单词的英文释义为：to try very hard to persuade someone to do something。

List | 01 words ★ 复习一下学过的单词！

☐ athlete	☐ formidable	☐ insect	☐ recipe
☐ elegant	☐ friction	☐ laconic	☐ stanza
☐ embellish	☐ gong	☐ panicky	☐ valediction
☐ fledgling	☐ grizzly	☐ pilot	☐ villain
☐ foible	☐ indicate	☐ rancid	☐ wan

SSAT词汇 List 03

★ reproach
[rɪ'prəʊtʃ] v. 责备

记 罗密欧反复接近（approach）敌人的女儿朱丽叶，受到自己父亲的责备（reproach）
考 同义 reproach＝blame

★ dissonance
['dɪsənəns] n. 不和谐声音，不一致

记 dis- ＋ son-（sound）＋ -ance
考 同义 cacophony＝dissonance

★★★ catastrophe
[kə'tæstrəfi] n. 灾难

记 cata- 掉 ＋ astro-（star）＋ -phe：老话说天空中有星星掉下来，地上就要有灾难（catastrophe）
考 同义 catastrophe＝disaster；catastrophe＝fiasco；catastrophe＝calamity
catastrophe＝havoc；catastrophe＝disarray

类比
hungry 饥饿 to starvation 饿死 ⇒ defect 缺陷 to catastrophe 灾难 （＜程度）
catastrophe 灾难 to problem 问题 ⇒ bliss 极乐 to pleasure 快乐 （＞程度）
Martin Luther King Jr. 马丁·路德·金 to peace 和平 ⇒ Hitler 希特勒 to catastrophe 灾难 （人物及其特点）

★ visage
['vɪzɪdʒ] n. 容貌

记 vis- 看 ＋ age
考 同义 visage＝face；visage＝appearance

★ warrant
['wɒrənt] v. 保证，担保

变 warranted a. 保证的
记 沃伦（Warren）·巴菲特担保（warrant）这只股票肯定会涨

warrant

考 类比　overblown　to　exaggerated　⇒　warranted　to　justified　（同义）
　　　　过分渲染的　　　夸张的　　　　　保证的　　　保证的

anguish
['æŋgwɪʃ] n. 极度痛苦；v. 使极度痛苦

记 谐音：俺跪屎：俺跪在屎里面了，觉得好痛苦（anguish）
考 同义　anguish = agonize；anguish = suffering
　 类比　sadness　to　anguish　⇒　joy　to　exultation　（＜程度）
　　　　伤心　　　极度痛苦　　　快乐　　极度喜悦

gimmick
['gɪmɪk] n. 小把戏

记 gimm-（gimme = give me）+ -ick（trick）= give me trick
考 同义　gimmick = devious trick

barometer
[bə'rɒmɪtə] n. 气压计

记 baro- 大气压力 + -meter 测量：测量大气压力的东西即为气压计（barometer）
考 类比　barometer　to　pressure　⇒　ruler　to　length　（事物及其对象）
　　　　气压计　　　压力　　　　　尺子　　长度
　　　　protractor　to　angle　⇒　barometer　to　pressure　（事物及其对象）
　　　　量角器　　　角度　　　　　气压计　　　压力
　　　　speedometer　to　velocity　⇒　barometer　to　pressure　（事物及其对象）
　　　　测速仪　　　　速度　　　　　气压计　　　压力
　　　　barometer　to　pressure　⇒　odometer　to　mileage　（事物及其对象）
　　　　气压计　　　压力　　　　　里程表　　　英里数
　　　　pressure　to　barometer　⇒　temperature　to　thermometer　（事物及其对象）
　　　　压力　　　气压计　　　　　温度　　　　　温度计

astronomy
[ə'strɒnəmɪ] n. 天文学

变 astronomer n. 天文学家
记 astro- 星星 + -nomy 学科：研究星星的学科，现在称为天文学（astronomy）
考 类比　astronomer　to　stars　⇒　biologist　to　life　（人物及其对象）
　　　　天文学家　　　星星　　　生物学家　　生命
　　　　chemistry　to　alchemy　⇒　astronomy　to　astrology　（同义：新旧之称）
　　　　化学　　　　炼金术　　　　天文学　　　占星术

iron
['aɪən] n. 铁

考 类比　wood　to　decay　⇒　iron　to　rust　（事物及其动作）
　　　　木材　　腐烂　　　　铁　　生锈
　　　　abrasive　to　skin　⇒　corrosive　to　iron　（事物及其特点）
　　　　粗糙的　　皮肤　　　　腐蚀的　　　铁
　　　　iron　to　metal　⇒　granite　to　rock　（种属）
　　　　铁　　金属　　　　　花岗岩　　岩石

steel / 钢 — to — metal / 金属 ⇒ iron / 铁 — to — ore / 矿石 （纵向）

注 这个题的思路有些复杂：用 iron 可以炼出 steel，用 ore 可以炼出 metal。

cooper
★

['kuːpə] n. 制桶工人

记 库珀（Cooper）是一个制桶工人（cooper）
考 类比 coopers / 桶匠 — to — barrel / 桶 ⇒ cartographer / 制图人 — to — map / 地图 （人物及其对象）

supplement
★

['sʌplɪmənt] n. 增补，补充

记 你的父母会持续给你提供（supply）补给（supplement）
考 同义 supplement = addition

unicorn
★★

['juːnɪkɔːn] n. 独角兽

记 uni- 一 + -corn（horn 角）：只有一个角的动物即为独角兽（unicorn）
考 类比 myth / 神话 — to — history / 历史 ⇒ unicorn / 独角兽 — to — horse / 马 （纵向）
unicorn / 独角兽 — to — mythological / 神话的 ⇒ horse / 马 — to — realistic / 现实的 （事物及其特点）

prod
★

[prɒd] v. 刺激

记 因为过于骄傲（proud），所以受到同行的打击和抨击（prod）
考 同义 goad = prod

coat
★

['kəʊt] n. 外套

考 类比 woolen / 羊毛的 — to — coat / 大衣 ⇒ cotton / 棉质的 — to — sheet / 被单 （修饰）
sidewalk / 人行道 — to — concrete / 水泥 ⇒ coat / 外套 — to — cloth / 布 （事物及其用途）
coat / 大衣 — to — jacket / 夹克 ⇒ chair / 椅子 — to — stool / 凳子 （种属）

incision
★

[ɪnˈsɪʒn] n. 切口，切开

变 incisive a. 深刻的，敏锐的
记 医生决定（decision）在孕妇的身体上切个口子（incision）进行剖腹产
考 同义 incision = open wound; incisive = trenchant

nimble
★★★

['nɪmbl] a. 敏捷的，灵巧的

变 nimbleness n. 敏捷

谐音：宁波：宁波人民身手敏捷（nimble）

同义 nimble = deft；agile = nimble；dexterous = nimble；nimble = quick
dexterity = nimbleness；agility = nimbleness

类比
| nimble 敏捷的 | to | coordination 协调 | → | articulate 清晰的 | to | pronunciation 发音 | （修饰） |
| adroit 敏捷的 | to | nimbleness 敏捷 | → | crooked 弯曲的 | to | hook 钩子 | （同义） |

★★ maxim

['mæksɪm] *n.* 格言，座右铭

记 格言（maxim）可以把语言的能力最大化（maximum）表现出来

同义 maxim = proverb；adage = maxim

★★ irk

[ɜːk] *v.* 使烦恼

记 新买的衣服沾上了墨水（ink），很是烦恼（irk）

类比
| irk 使烦恼 | to | enrage 激怒 | → | nudge 轻推 | to | thrust 用力刺入 | （＜程度） |
| irk 使烦恼（反义） | to | soothing 安慰的 | → | support 支持 | to | undermining 暗中破坏的 | |

irk

★★★ insolent

['ɪnsələnt] *a.* 无礼的，傲慢的

变 insolence *n.* 无礼，傲慢

记 有些人就是既懒惰（indolent）又傲慢（insolent）

同义 insolent = impertinent

类比
recalcitrant 叛逆的	to	obedience 听话的	→	insolent 傲慢的	to	respect 尊敬	（反义）
insolence 无礼	to	brazen 厚颜无耻	→	obedience 顺从	to	dutiful 顺从的	（同义）
flippancy 轻浮	to	jollity 快乐	→	insolence 傲慢	to	pride 自豪	（同义：正反向）

List | **02** words　　　　　　　　　　　　　　★ 复习一下学过的单词！

□ aqueduct	□ contemporary	□ equitable	□ furnish
□ augment	□ convince	□ exhort	□ iconoclast
□ bolster	□ cork	□ expunge	□ investigate
□ boundary	□ dedication	□ fascinate	□ malady
□ cavern	□ encumber	□ frugal	□ sentence

SSAT词汇 List 04

★★ ramble
['ræmbl] v. 漫步，漫游
- 变 rambling a. 杂乱无章的
- 记 大量 (ample) 闲人在街上漫步 (ramble)
- 考 同义 rambling = amorphous
  类比 drift/漂移 to move/移动 → ramble/漫步 to walk/走路 （种属）

★ waver
['weɪvə] v. 抽出，摇摆
- 记 左右挥手 (wave) 摇摆不定 (waver)
- 考 同义 fluctuate = waver; vacillate = waver
  类比 hesitate/犹豫 to waver/犹豫 → loathe/讨厌 to detest/厌恶 （同义）

★ assimilate
[ə'sɪməleɪt] v. 吸收，同化
- 记 as- + simil- (similar) + -ate：把相似的 (similar) 东西放在一起，即为吸收 (assimilate)
- 考 同义 assimilate = incorporate

★★ agitation
[ˌædʒɪ'teɪʃn] n. 搅动，煽动
- 记 在车站 (station) 有人用谣言来煽动 (agitation) 群众
- 考 同义 agitation = commotion; agitation = disturbance

★★ represent
[ˌriːprɪ'zent] v. 代表
- 变 representation n. 代表，表示
- 考 同义 representation = symbol
  类比 emissary/使者 to represent/代表 → guard/守卫 to protect/保护 （人物及其特点）
  picture/图片 to representation/表现 → perfume/香水 to fragrance/香味 （事物及其用途）

☆ ramble　☆ waver　☆ assimilate　☆ agitation　☆ represent

13

pebble

['pebl] *n.* 鹅卵石

记 把鹅卵石 (pebble) 放在桌子 (table) 上

考 类比 stream 小溪 to drop 水滴 ⇒ boulder 大石头 to pebble 鹅卵石 （>程度）
   pebble 鹅卵石 to rock 石头 ⇒ drop 水滴 to liquid 液体 （种属）

accede

[əkˈsiːd] *v.* 同意

记 同意 (accede) 接受 (accept) 对方提出的要求

考 类比 accept 接受 to accede 同意接受 ⇒ ostracize 驱逐 to deport 驱逐 （同义）

isolate

[ˈaɪsəleɪt] *v.* 隔离，绝缘

变 isolation *n.* 隔离，绝缘

考 同义 sequester = isolate；segregate = isolate；isolation = quarantine

weave

[wiːv] *v.* 编织

变 weaver *n.* 编织工

记 编织 (weave) 工人离开 (leave) 工厂

考 类比 weave 编织 to fabric 布料 ⇒ write 写 to text 文本 （动宾）
   book 书 to writer 作家 ⇒ cloth 衣服 to weaver 编织工 （人物及其对象）

cherub

[ˈtʃerəb] *n.* 小天使

记 中东学者丢尼修发表的《天阶序论》将天使分成九类，智天使 (cherub) 排名第二，而我们常说的 angle 仅排名第九

考 同义 cherub = angel

   类比 cherub 天使 to wings 翅膀 ⇒ imp 小恶魔 to horns 角 （人物及其特点）

elaborate

[ɪˈlæbəreɪt] *a.* 精心制作的；[ɪˈlæbərət] *v.* 详述

变 elaboration *n.* 精心制作

记 e- 朝外 + labor 努力 + -ate：朝外付出努力，即为精心制作的 (elaborate)

考 同义 elaborate = develop；elaborate = demonstrate；elaboration = explanation

commend

[kəˈmend] *v.* 称赞，赞扬

变 commendatory *a.* 赞赏的；commendation *n.* 赞扬

记 因为新书被人赞扬（commend），所以他到处跟人推荐（recommend）自己的书
考 同义 commendation = acclamation；commend = compliment
　　　　eulogy = commendation；extol = commend

类比 converge 汇合 to disperse 分散 → denigrate 诋毁 to commend 表扬 （反义）
　　 reprimand 训斥 to commend 表扬 → loathe 厌恶 to adore 羡慕 （反义）
　　 condolence 哀悼 to grief 悲痛 → commendation 赞扬 to success 成功 （因果）
　　 enthusiastic 热情的 to mania 狂热 → commendatory 赞赏的 to eulogy 颂扬 （<程度）

★★
quiver
['kwɪvə] v. 颤抖；n. 箭筒

记 看到满屋子的银子（silver），惊得自己浑身颤抖（quiver）
考 类比 blossom 开花 to bloom 开花 → quiver 震颤 to vibrate 震动 （同义）
　　　arrow 箭 to quiver 箭筒 → water 水 to canteen 水箱 （空间）
注 关于"颤抖"的单词在 SSAT 的习题中有很多，如：tremble, shudder。

★★
confer
[kən'fɜː] v. 给予，协商

记 开会（conference）时大家可以相互协商（confer）
考 同义 confer = grant；confer = bestow；confer = exchange opinions
注 关于"给予"的单词在 SSAT 的习题中有很多，如：endow, bequeath。

★★★
expel
[ɪk'spel] v. 驱逐，开除

记 ex- 朝外 + -pel（pull）：朝外推，即为开除（expel）
考 同义 expel = ostracize；expel = cast out；expel = eject

类比 exile 放逐 to country 国家 → expel 驱逐 to school 学校 （空间）
　　 consume 消耗 to devour 吞食 → suspend 暂停工作 to expel 驱逐 （<程度）
　　 notice 注意 to warning 警告 → suspension 暂停职务 to expel 开除 （<程度）

注 关于"放逐"的单词在 SSAT 的习题中有很多，如：exile, banish, expulse。

★
safeguard
['seɪfɡɑːd] n. 保护，保卫

记 safe 安全的 + guard 保卫
　 我们常用的"舒肤佳"英文即为 Safeguard
考 同义 precaution = safeguard

☆ quiver　　　☆ confer　　　☆ expel　　　☆ safeguard

15

semantics [sɪˈmæntɪks] *n.* 语义学

记 语义学（semantics）是一门浪漫的（romantic）学科

考 类比 semantics 语义学 — to — meaning 意思 ⇒ phonetics 语音学 — to — sound 发音 （事物及其用途）

impudent [ˈɪmpjʊdənt] *a.* 无耻的，不礼貌的

记 注意区分 impudent "没礼貌的" 和 imprudent "轻率的，鲁莽的"
考 同义 flippant = impudent
注 关于"没礼貌的"单词在 SSAT 的习题中有很多，如：churlish, impolite, impertinent。

extraordinary [ɪkˈstrɔːdnrɪ] *a.* 非凡的

考 同义 miraculous = extraordinary；incredible = extraordinary；phenomenal = extraordinary

torsion [ˈtɔːʃn] *n.* 转矩

记 转动转矩（torsion）需要拉力（tension）
考 类比 elongate 拉伸 — to — tension 张力 ⇒ rotate 扭转 — to — torsion 转矩 （因果）
torsion 转矩 — to — rotate 扭转 ⇒ torque 转矩 — to — twist 扭转 （因果）
torsion 转矩 — to — rotate 扭转 ⇒ gravity 重力 — to — pull 拉 （事物及其动作）

List | 03 words ★ 复习一下学过的单词！

□ anguish	□ cooper	□ irk	□ reproach
□ astronomy	□ dissonance	□ iron	□ supplement
□ barometer	□ gimmick	□ maxim	□ unicorn
□ catastrophe	□ incision	□ nimble	□ visage
□ coat	□ insolent	□ prod	□ warrant

SSAT词汇 List 05

★ levity
['levɪti] *n.* 轻浮，轻率
- 记：老人普遍沉稳（gravity），年轻人普遍轻浮（levity）
- 考：同义　levity = improper gaiety

★ aberration
[ˌæbə'reɪʃn] *n.* 异常，越轨
- 记：ab- 远离 + err（error）+ -ation：朝着错误的方向发展，引申为异常（aberration）
- 考：同义　aberration = deviation

★★ truce
[truːs] *n.* 休战
- 记：据可靠（true）消息，战斗双方会暂时休战（truce）
- 考：同义　truce = pause；truce = cease-fire；armistice = truce

★★ emissary
['emɪsəri] *n.* 使者，密使
- 记：使者（emissary）的任务（mission）就是朝外传递信息
- 考：类比
  - emissary 使者 to represent 代表 → guard 守卫 to protect 保护 （人物及其特点）
  - emissary 使者 to message 消息 → paperboy 报童 to newspaper 报纸 （人物及其对象）

★ urgency
['ɜːdʒənsi] *n.* 紧急情况
- 考：同义　urgency = exigency

★★ vegetarian
[ˌvedʒɪ'teəriən] *n.* 素食主义者
- 记：素食主义者（vegetarian）只吃蔬菜（vegetable）
- 考：类比
  - vegetarian 素食者 to meat 肉 → pacifist 和平主义者 to war 战争 （人物及其对象）
  - vegetarian 素食者 to meat 肉 → pacifist 和平主义者 to violence 暴力 （人物及其对象）

☆ levity　☆ aberration　☆ truce　☆ emissary　☆ urgency
☆ vegetarian

apathy ★★★
[ˈæpəθi] n. 冷漠，无兴趣

变 apathetic a. 冷漠的；pathetic a. 可怜的，悲哀的
记 我对你充满同情（sympathy），你却对我如此冷漠（apathy）
考 同义 apathy = indifference

类比
pathetic 可怜的 to pity 可怜 → awesome 令人敬畏的 to amazement 惊异 （同义）
apathy 冷漠 to phlegmatic 迟钝的 → zeal 热情 to enthusiastic 热心的 （同义）
indifference 冷漠 to apathy 冷漠 → vexed 焦急的 to anxiety 焦虑 （同义）
apathetic 冷漠的 to phlegmatic 迟钝的 → enthusiastic 热情的 to passionate 热心的 （同义）

注 关于"冷漠的"单词在 SSAT 的习题中有很多，如：aloof，detached，impassive，nonchalant。

counterfeit ★★
[ˈkaʊntəfɪt] a. 伪造的；n. 假货

记 counter- 反 + -feit 做：反向做即为伪造
考 类比
money 钱 to counterfeit 假币 → genuine 真迹 to art forgery 伪造 （反义）
perjury 伪证 to testimony 证词 → counterfeit 假币 to money 钱 （反义）

lung ★
[lʌŋ] n. 肺

记 谐音：狼：狼心狗肺（lung）
考 类比
gill 鳃 to fish 鱼 → lung 肺 to mammal 哺乳动物 （事物及其部分）
exhale 呼出 to lung 肺 → perspire 呼吸 to skin 皮肤 （事物及其用途）

baton ★★
[ˈbætɒn] n. 指挥棒，警棍

记 用警棍（baton）打蝙蝠（bat）
考 类比
baton 指挥棒 to conductor 指挥 → brush 刷子 to painter 粉刷匠 （人物及其工具）
tractor 拖拉机 to farmer 农民 → baton 指挥棒 to conductor 指挥 （人物及其工具）

abhor ★★★
[əbˈhɔː] v. 痛恨，憎恶

变 abhorrence n. 痛恨
记 ab- 离开 + hor (horror)：因为憎恶（abhor）恐怖的东西，所以远离
考 同义 abhor = detest

类比　abhor 痛恨 → to → dislike 不喜欢　⇒　adore 崇拜 → to → fondness 喜爱　（＞程度）
　　　hate 讨厌 → to → abhorrence 痛恨　⇒　pleasure 快乐 → to → enjoyment 享受　（同义）

注　关于"痛恨，憎恶"的单词在 SSAT 的习题中有很多，如 despise, loathe。

☆ decode [ˌdiːˈkəʊd] *v.* 解码

记　de- 否定 + code 密码
考　类比　decode 解码 → to → encoded 编码的　⇒　purity 纯洁 → to → contaminated 污染的　（反义）
　　　　　indecipherable 难以解码的 → to → decoded 解码的　⇒　unmanageable 难以管理的 → to → controlled 控制的　（反义）

☆ implement [ˈɪmplɪmənt] *n.* 工具

记　干活的工具（implement）不够，需要补充（complement）
考　同义　implement = instrument

☆ impregnable [ɪmˈpreɡnəbl] *a.* 无法攻破的，不受影响的

记　im- 否定 + pregna（pregnate）+ -able：不能（im）怀孕（pregnant），因为无法攻破（impregnable）
考　同义　impregnable = secure
　　类比　impregnable 无法攻破的 → to → penetration 刺入　⇒　inscrutable 不可理解的 → to → understanding 理解　（反义）

☆ dilettante [ˌdɪlɪˈtænti] *n.* 业余爱好者，浅尝辄止者

记　这个单词属于我早期见过特别奇怪但又特别可以拿出来炫耀的单词，请同学们多念几遍，然后在不经意的场合拿出来 show 几次
考　同义　dilettante = amateur

☆☆ inept [ɪˈnept] *a.* 笨拙的

变　ineptly *ad.* 笨拙地
记　有人擅长（adept）做这个，有人就不擅长（inept）做这个
考　同义　ungainly = inept
　　类比　botched 搞砸了的 → to → ineptly 笨拙地　⇒　perfect 精通的 → to → expertly 熟练地　（同义）

☆☆☆ erratic [ɪˈrætɪk] *a.* 古怪的，不稳定的

记　因为不稳定（erratic），所以总犯错（error）
考　同义　erratic = unpredictable；erratic = inconsistent

类比　erratic / 不可预测的　to　predictable / 可预测的　⇒　exorbitant / 过高的　to　reasonable / 合理的　（反义）

limerick
[ˈlɪmərɪk] n. 五行打油诗

记　源于爱尔兰的一座城市利默里克 Limerick 的一群诗人，他们创造了当地一首民歌，把其中一句 "Will you come up to Limerick?" 连续重复了五遍

考　类比　limerick / 五行打油诗　to　epic / 史诗　⇒　ditty / 小曲　to　opera / 歌剧　（＜程度）
　　　　limerick / 五行打油诗　to　poem / 诗　⇒　lampoon / 讽刺　to　satire / 讽刺文学　（种属）
　　　　skit / 滑稽短剧　to　play / 戏剧　⇒　limerick / 五行打油诗　to　poem / 诗　（种属）
　　　　limerick / 五行打油诗　to　poem / 诗　⇒　catch / 上口的小调　to　song / 歌曲　（种属）

devious
[ˈdiːvɪəs] a. 弯曲的，不光明正大的

记　魔鬼（devil）只走偏僻的（devious）小路
考　同义　devious = cunning；devious = tricky
　　类比　devious / 弯曲的　to　circuitous / 绕行的　⇒　yield / 屈服　to　submit / 服从　（同义）

hag
[hæg] n. 老太婆

记　戴帽子（hat）的老太婆（hag）
考　同义　hag = crone

List | 04 words　　　　　　　　　　　　★ 复习一下学过的单词！

- accede
- agitation
- assimilate
- cherub
- commend
- confer
- elaborate
- expel
- extraordinary
- impudent
- isolate
- pebble
- quiver
- ramble
- represent
- safeguard
- semantics
- torsion
- waver
- weave

SSAT词汇 List 06

ordinance ★★
[ˈɔːdɪnəns] *n.* 条例，法令
记 这是一个对普罗大众（ordinary）都有强制性的法令（ordinance）
考 同义 decree = ordinance；ordinance = rule

juggler ★
[ˈdʒʌɡlə] *n.* 变戏法的人
记 变戏法的人（juggler）在丛林（jungle）里练习手上功夫
考 类比 dancer 舞蹈家 to feet 脚 ⇒ juggler 变戏法者 to hands 手 （人物及其工具）

thermometer ★★★
[θəˈmɒmɪtə] *n.* 温度计
记 thermo- 热 + -meter 测量：测量热度的东西即为温度计（thermometer）
考 类比 clock 表 to time 时间 ⇒ thermometer 温度计 to temperature 温度 （事物及其对象）
scale 天平 to weight 重量 ⇒ thermometer 温度计 to temperature 温度 （事物及其对象）
pressure 压力 to barometer 气压计 ⇒ temperature 温度 to thermometer 温度计 （事物及其对象）

flock ★★★
[flɒk] *n.* 羊群，鸟群
记 羊群（flock）的圈在外面被锁上（lock）了
考 同义 swarm = flock
类比 wolf 狼 to pack 狼群 ⇒ bird 鸟 to flock 鸟群 （组成）
school 鱼群 to fish 鱼 ⇒ flock 鸟群 to bird 鸟 （组成）

stove ★★
[stəʊv] *n.* 炉子
记 冬天到了，我要去商店（store）里买个炉子（stove）
考 类比 weaving 织布 to loom 织布机 ⇒ cooking 做饭 to stove 炉子 （事物及其用途）

☆ ordinance　　☆ juggler　　☆ thermometer　　☆ flock　　☆ stove

| gas | to | vehicle | ⇒ | wood | to | stove | （事物及其用途）|
| 汽油 | | 车辆 | | 木头 | | 炉子 | |

★ torturous

[ˈtɔːtʃərəs] *a.* 折磨人的，痛苦的

记 这个单词来自于 torture "折磨"
考 类比

| torturous | to | bothersome | ⇒ | breathtaking | to | nice | （＞程度）|
| 痛苦的 | | 烦人的 | | 令人激动的 | | 不错的 | |

★★ harass

[ˈhærəs] *v.* 骚扰

变 harassment *n.* 骚扰
记 har- (her) + ass：她的 (her) 屁股 (ass) 被摸，说明受到骚扰 (harass)
考 同义 harass = vex
类比

| harassment | to | anger | ⇒ | disappointment | to | sorrow | （因果）|
| 骚扰 | | 生气 | | 失望 | | 悲伤 | |

★ profit

[ˈprɒfɪt] *n.* 利润

变 profitable *a.* 有利可图的
考 同义 gainful = profitable
类比

| lottery | to | luck | ⇒ | company | to | profit | （事物及其对象）|
| 彩票 | | 运气 | | 公司 | | 利润 | |

★ wail

[weɪl] *v.* 哭泣

记 坐船远行 (sail) 离开妈妈，哭 (wail) 得一塌糊涂
考 类比

| sleep | to | doze | ⇒ | wail | to | sob | （＞程度）|
| 睡觉 | | 打瞌睡 | | 哭泣 | | 啜泣 | |

wail

★★★ malign

[məˈlaɪn] *v.* 诽谤，污蔑；*a.* 恶意的，有害的

变 malignant *a.* 恶性的，恶意的
记 肿瘤有良性的 (benign) 也有恶性的 (malign)
考 同义 malign = slander; malign = harmful; malignant = evil

★ bore

[bɔː] *n.* 钻孔

考 类比

| drill | to | bore | ⇒ | blade | to | cut | （事物及其用途）|
| 钻子 | | 钻孔 | | 刀片 | | 切 | |

注 bore 这个单词"无聊"的意思我们是很熟悉的，此处是熟词僻义。

★★★ chisel

[ˈtʃɪzl] *n.* 凿子；*v.* 雕刻，凿

记 起司 (cheese) 太硬，必须用凿子 (chisel) 凿

考 同义 chisel = inscribe
类比 sculptor [to] chisel (人物及其工具)
雕刻家　　　凿子
chisel [to] carving → blender [to] mixing (事物及其目的)
凿子　　　雕刻　　　　搅拌机　　　混合
spatula [to] clay → chisel [to] marble (事物及其对象)
抹刀　　　黏土　　　凿子　　　大理石
chisel [to] marble → trimmer [to] hedge (事物及其对象)
凿子　　　大理石　　　修剪机　　　树篱

★★★ manager ['mænɪdʒə] n. 经理

变 unmanageable a. 难管理的，难处理的
考 同义 incorrigible = unmanageable
类比 principal [to] teacher → manager [to] cashier (人物及其对象)
校长　　　老师　　　　经理　　　收银员
manager [to] store → administrator [to] hospital (人物及其对象)
经理　　　商店　　　　管理者　　　医院
indecipherable [to] decoded → unmanageable [to] controlled (反义)
难以解码的　　　解码的　　　难以管理的　　　控制的

★★★ permeate ['pɜːmɪeɪt] v. 渗透，弥漫

变 permeable a. 可渗透的；impermeable a. 难以渗透的
记 per- 到处 + -meate（meat）：妈妈做饭香，屋里到处（per）都弥漫着（permeable）肉（meat）味
考 同义 permeate = imbue；permeable = porous
类比 fluid [to] impermeable → light [to] opaque (缺乏)
流动的　　　难以渗透的　　　光　　　不透明的

★ proliferate [prə'lɪfəreɪt] v. 激增，增值

记 pro- 朝前 + life：美国 20 世纪 50 年代激增出（proliferate）很多生命（life）
考 同义 proliferate = increase

★ morgue [mɔːg] n. 停尸房

记 罗马神话中的死神是莫尔斯（Mors），所以由它引申出一系列与死亡有关的单词，morgue 就是其中之一，这个词在法语中原指"辨认尸体的地方"
考 类比 surgeon [to] hospital → coroner [to] morgue (空间)
医生　　　医院　　　验尸官　　　停尸房

★ leery ['lɪri] a. 机敏的，机警的

记 谐音：李尔：莎士比亚笔下的李尔王是个机警的（leery）人
考 同义 leery = suspicious

winsome

['wɪnsəm] *a.* 迷人的，吸引人的

记 因为胜利（win），所以迷人（winsome）

考 同义 winsome = charming

类比 winsome (迷人的) to attractive (有吸引力的) （同义）

fathom

['fæðəm] *n.* 英寻；*v.* 测量深度

记 感觉自己的父亲（father）深不可测（fathom）

考 类比 foot (英尺) to length (长度) ⇒ fathom (英寻) to depth (深度) （事物及其用途）

fathom (测量深度) to depth (深度) ⇒ appraise (评价) to value (价值) （动宾）

meteorology

[ˌmiːtɪəˈrɒlədʒi] *n.* 气象学

变 meteorologist *n.* 气象学家

记 meteor 流星 + -ology 学科：气象学（meteorology）即为根据流星（meteor）来判断天气的学科（ology）

考 类比 botany (植物学) to plants (植物) ⇒ meteorology (气象学) to weather (天气) （事物及其对象）

weather (天气) to meteorologists (气象学家) ⇒ vegetation (植被) to botanist (植物学家) （人物及其对象）

List | 05 words ★ 复习一下学过的单词！

- aberration
- abhor
- apathy
- baton
- counterfeit
- decode
- devious
- dilettante
- emissary
- erratic
- hag
- implement
- impregnable
- inept
- levity
- limerick
- lung
- truce
- urgency
- vegetarian

SSAT词汇 List 07

★★★ document
['dɒkjʊmənt] *n.* 文本，文档

记 我们电脑中常见的 word 文档扩展名 doc. 代表的即为 document

考 类比
- archive 档案馆 to documents 文件 ⇒ warehouse 仓库 to merchandise 货品 （空间）
- outline 大纲 to document 文件 ⇒ sketch 略图 to picture 图画 （事物及其部分）
- postscript 附言 to letter 信件 ⇒ addendum 附录 to document 文件 （事物及其部分）

★★★ lethargic
[lɪ'θɑːdʒɪk] *a.* 昏昏欲睡的，无生气的

变 lethargy *n.* 昏睡，倦怠

记 神话传说中，人死之后要过鬼门关，经黄泉路，在黄泉路和冥府之间，由忘川河划分为界，喝了忘川河水的人就会忘记前生，忘川的英文即为 Lethe，所以 lethargic 本意是指"健忘的"，后来引申为"无生气的"

考 同义 lethargic = torpid；lethargic = drowsy；lethargic = listless

类比
- lethargic 倦怠 to energy 能量 ⇒ brazen 厚颜无耻的 to tact 机智 （缺乏）
- trivial 琐碎的 to consequential 重要的 ⇒ robust 强健的 to lethargic 无生气的 （反义）

★★★ material
[mə'tɪərɪəl] *a.* 物质的，实质的

变 materialize *v.* 成形，使具体化；immaterial *a.* 非物质的，不重要的

考 同义 materialize = take form

类比
- material 物质的 to matter 物质 ⇒ legal 合法的 to law 法律 （同义）
- immaterial 不重要的 to relevance 相关的 ⇒ superficial 肤浅的 to profundity 深刻 （反义）

★★ corridor
['kɒrɪdɔː] *n.* 走廊

记 corri-（carry）+ -dor（dog）：经过走廊（corridor），顺道把狗（dog）带走（carry）

☆ document　　☆ lethargic　　☆ material　　☆ corridor

考 类比 tunnel 隧道 — to — mine 矿 ⇒ corridor 走廊 — to — building 建筑物   (空间)

palatial 壮丽的 — to — space 地方 ⇒ labyrinthine 复杂的 — to — corridor 走廊   (修饰)

★★ rebel   [rɪˈbel] v. 反叛

变 rebellious a. 叛逆的；rebellion n. 叛逆
记 re- 相反 + -bel（词根来自战争女神 Bellona，她的丈夫是战神 Mars）
考 同义 rebel = maverick；insurgent = rebellious

类比 discontent 不满 — to — rebellion 叛逆 ⇒ friction 摩擦 — to — spark 火花 (因果)

★ henchman   [ˈhentʃmən] n. 追随者

记 hench-（bench）+ man：明星的追随者（henchman）是一群无论明星在哪儿都会搬个小凳子（bench）去看的人（man）
考 同义 henchman = follower

★ mar   [mɑː] v. 破坏

记 我把地图上被敌人破坏（mar）的地方都标记了（mark）一下
考 同义 mar = spoil；mar = damage
注 关于"破坏"的单词在 SSAT 的习题中有很多，如：distain, contaminate。

★ thread   [θred] n. 线

记 因为受到威胁（threat），所以命悬一线（thread）
考 同义 filament = thread

类比 thread 线 — to — cloth 衣服 ⇒ pulp 纸浆 — to — paper 纸 (组成)

needle 针 — to — thread 线 ⇒ truck 卡车 — to — trailer 拖车 (同类)

★★★ digress   [daɪˈgres] v. 离题

变 digression n. 离题；digressive a. 离题的
记 di- 朝外 + gress 走路：朝外走向不同的地方即为离题（digress）
考 类比 veer 转向 — to — course 路线 ⇒ digress 离题 — to — subject 主题 (事物及其动作)

digression 离题 — to — topic 话题 ⇒ detour 绕道 — to — itinerary 旅途 (事物及其动作)

aberrant 异常的 — to — standard 标准 ⇒ digressive 离题的 — to — topic 话题 (事物及其动作)

course 跑道 — to — swerve 转弯 ⇒ topic 话题 — to — digress 离题 (事物及其动作)

toady

['təʊdi] *n.* 谄媚者

记 今天（today）你谄媚（toady）了吗

考 类比 fib/撒小谎 —to— liar/骗子 ⇒ flatter/奉承 —to— toady/谄媚者 （人物及其特点）

bowling

['bəʊlɪŋ] *n.* 保龄球

考 类比 bowling/保龄球 —to— lane/保龄球道 ⇒ soccer/足球 —to— field/球场 （空间）

wreck

[rek] *v.* 破坏

变 wreckage *n.* 残骸

记 自己的脖子（neck）在事故中遭到破坏（wreck）

考 同义 debris = wreckage

类比 carcass/尸体 —to— animal/动物 ⇒ wreck/失事船只 —to— ship/船 （同义）

salvage/营救 —to— wreck/失事船只 ⇒ excavate/挖掘 —to— ruin/废墟 （动宾）

audacious

[ɔːˈdeɪʃəs] *a.* 大胆的，鲁莽的

记 谐音：all day：趁着妈妈不在家，大胆的（audacious）孩子在外面玩了一整天 all day

考 同义 audacious = bold

类比 audacious/胆大的 —to— boldness/胆大 ⇒ sanctimonious/假装虔诚的 —to— hypocrisy/虚伪 （同义）

注 关于"胆大的"单词在 SSAT 的习题中有很多，如：insolent, bold, foolhardy, daredevil。

amuse

[əˈmjuːz] *v.* 娱乐

变 amusing *a.* 搞笑的；amusement *n.* 消遣

考 同义 amusement = mirth；amuse = divert

类比 vex/使烦恼 —to— fret/烦恼 ⇒ amuse/娱乐 —to— divert/娱乐 （同义）

ruse/诡计 —to— deceive/欺骗 ⇒ diversion/消遣 —to— amuse/娱乐 （事物及其用途）

vendor/小商贩 —to— sell/卖 ⇒ entertainer/演艺人员 —to— amuse/娱乐 （人物及其动作）

amusing/搞笑的 —to— uproarious/喧闹的 ⇒ interesting/有趣的 —to— mesmerizing/令人着迷的 （＜程度）

★★★ caprice

[kə'pri:s] n. 反复无常，任性

变 capricious a. 任性的，反复无常的
记 ca-（car）+ price：车的价格反复无常（caprice）
考 同义 caprice = whim；caprice = fickle

★★ cultivate

['kʌltɪveɪt] v. 培养，种植

记 cultivate 和 culture 长得很像，动词意思也相同
考 同义 cultivate = nurture；culture = cultivate

类比 arable 可耕种的 —to→ cultivation 种植 ⇒ navigable 可航行的 —to→ sailing 航行 （同义）

★★★ jubilant

['dʒu:bɪlənt] a. 高兴的

记 登上木星（Jupiter）很高兴（jubilant）
考 同义 jovial = jubilant

类比 doubt 怀疑 —to→ hesitant 犹豫的 ⇒ happiness 快乐 —to→ jubilant 快乐的 （同义）

注 关于"高兴的"单词在 SSAT 的习题中有很多，如：jaunty，exultant，jocular，overjoyed。

★ consecrate

['kɒnsɪkreɪt] a. 神圣的

记 con- + secr-（sacred 神圣的）+ -ate
考 同义 holy = consecrate

★★ merit

['merɪt] v. 应得，值得

记 即使结过一次婚（married），他依然值得（merit）拥有一份真挚的爱情
考 同义 merit = deserve

类比 bonanza 意外之财 —to→ windfall 意外之财 ⇒ earn 赚的 —to→ merit 值得 （同义）

注 merit 这个单词"优点"的意思我们很熟悉，此处是熟词僻义。

★★ scissor

['sɪzə] n. 剪刀

考 类比
saw 锯 —to→ branch 树枝 ⇒ scissor 剪刀 —to→ paper 纸 （事物及其对象）
knife 刀 —to→ butter 黄油 ⇒ scissor 剪刀 —to→ paper 纸 （事物及其对象）
buttress 扶壁 —to→ support 支撑 ⇒ scissor 剪刀 —to→ cut 切 （事物及其用途）

scissors to cut ⇒ shovel to excavate （事物及其用途）
剪刀   切   铁铲   挖掘

scissors to cut ⇒ shovel to scoop （事物及其用途）
剪刀   切   铁铲   舀

scissors to trim ⇒ scales to weigh （事物及其用途）
剪刀   修剪   天平   称重

tailor to scissor ⇒ surgeon to scalpel （人物及其工具）
裁缝   剪刀   医生   手术刀

tailor to scissor ⇒ explorer to compass （人物及其工具）
裁缝   剪刀   探险家   指南针

barber to scissor ⇒ surgeon to scalpel （人物及其工具）
理发师   剪刀   医生   手术刀

saw to carpenter ⇒ scissors to tailor （人物及其工具）
锯   木匠   剪刀   裁缝

List | 06 words　　　　　　　　　　★ 复习一下学过的单词！

- □ bore
- □ chisel
- □ fathom
- □ flock
- □ harass
- □ juggler
- □ leery
- □ malign
- □ manager
- □ meteorology
- □ morgue
- □ ordinance
- □ permeate
- □ profit
- □ proliferate
- □ stove
- □ thermometer
- □ torturous
- □ wail
- □ winsome

SSAT词汇 List 08

★★★ terrestrial
[tɪˈrestrɪəl] *a.* 地球的，陆地的

记 我们常说的 ET（外星人）的全称就是 extra-terrestrial

考 类比
- earth 陆地 to terrestrial 陆地的 → planet 行星 to celestial 天上的 （空间）
- terrestrial 陆地的 to earth 陆地 → celestial 天上的 to heaven 天堂 （同义）
- sun 太阳 to solar 太阳的 → earth 陆地 to terrestrial 陆地的 （同义）
- aquatic 水生的 to water 水 → terrestrial 陆地的 to land 陆地 （同义）

★ roe
[rəʊ] *n.* 鱼卵

记 鱼卵 roe 排成排 row

考 类比
- roe 鱼卵 to salmon 鲑鱼 → egg 鸡蛋 to chicken 鸡 （事物及其部分）

★★★ loom
[luːm] *n.* 织布机；*v.* 隐约出现

记 织布机（loom）放在屋子（room）里

考 类比
- loom 隐约出现 to appear 出现 → seem 看上去好像 to be 是 （＜程度）
- weaving 织布 to loom 织布机 → cooking 做饭 to stove 炉子 （事物及其用途）

★ sully
[ˈsʌli] *v.* 玷污，弄脏

记 萨莉（Sally）喜欢玷污（sully）别人的名声

考 类比
- tarnish 失去光泽 to silver 银器 → sully 玷污 to reputation 名声 （动作及其对象）

☆ terrestrial　　☆ roe　　☆ loom　　☆ sully

plagiarize ★★

[ˈpleɪdʒəraɪz] v. 剽窃，抄袭

变 plagiarism n. 剽窃，抄袭
记 单词 plagiarize 在拉丁语中本是"绑架"之意，在 1660 年进入英文中时依旧保持该意，随后随着词义的改变，才有了今天的"剽窃"之意
考 同义　plagiarism = thievery

类比　money 钱 — to — steal 偷　⇒　idea 主意 — to — plagiarize 剽窃　（动宾）

platform ★

[ˈplætfɔːm] n. 站台

考 类比　platform 站台 — to — passenger 乘客　⇒　classroom 教室 — to — student 学生　（空间）

bland ★★★

[blænd] a. 平淡的

记 在中国这片平淡的（bland）土地（land）上，诞生了很多名人
考 类比　bland 平淡的 — to — taste 味道　⇒　green 无经验的 — to — experience 经验　（缺乏）

　　　safe 安全的 — to — dangerous 危险的　⇒　bland 平淡的 — to — spicy 辛辣的　（反义）

　　　infinite 无限的 — to — limitless 无限的　⇒　bland 平淡的 — to — boring 无趣的　（同义）

hypothesis ★★

[haɪˈpɒθəsɪs] n. 假设

变 hypothesize v. 假设
记 hypo-（hippo 犀牛）+ thesis 论文：论文（thesis）里提出了一个对于犀牛的假设（hypothesis）
考 同义　speculate = hypothesize

类比　hypothesis 假设 — to — test 测试　⇒　cake 蛋糕 — to — bake 烤　（动宾）

　　　hypothesis 假设 — to — scientist 科学家　⇒　proof 证据 — to — mathematician 数学家　（人物及其对象）

hypothesis

bake ★★★

[beɪk] v. 烘烤

变 baker n. 面包师；bakery n. 面包店
考 类比　oven 炉子 — to — kiln 窑　⇒　baker 面包师 — to — potter 制陶工人　（纵向）

　　　coffee 咖啡 — to — brew 煮　⇒　bread 面包 — to — bake 烘烤　（动宾）

hypothesis 假设	to	test 测试	⇒	cake 蛋糕	to	bake 烤	（动宾）
bread 面包	to	bakery 面包店	⇒	beer 啤酒	to	bar 酒吧	（空间）
map 地图	to	cartographer 地图编辑者	⇒	cake 蛋糕	to	baker 烘焙师	（人物及其对象）
baker 烘焙师	to	bread 面包	⇒	sculptor 雕刻家	to	statue 雕塑	（人物及其对象）
baker 烘焙师	to	bread 面包	⇒	jeweler 珠宝商	to	pendant 挂坠	（人物及其对象）

★★ barrel

[ˈbærəl] n. 桶

记 酒吧（bar）里放着一个桶（barrel）
考 同义 barrel = keg

类比	cooper 桶匠	to	barrel 桶	⇒	cartographer 制图人	to	map 地图	（人物及其对象）

★★ molt

[məult] v. 换毛

记 大雪融化（melt），蛇开始脱皮（molt）

考 类比	molt 脱皮	to	skin 皮肤	⇒	shed 脱毛	to	hair 头发	（动宾）
	overthrow 推翻	to	oust 驱逐	⇒	shed 脱毛	to	molt 换毛	（时间先后）

★ coordination

[ˌkəʊɔːdɪˈneɪʃn] n. 协调

记 co-共同 + ordin-（order）+ -ation：两个要求（order）在一起，要保证相互协调（coordination）

考 类比	nimble 敏捷的	to	coordination 协调	⇒	articulate 清晰的	to	pronunciation 发音	（修饰）

★ tower

[ˈtaʊə] n. 塔

变 towering a. 高耸的

考 类比	towering 高耸的	to	height 高度	⇒	hulking 巨大的	to	size 型号	（修饰）
	tower 塔	to	airport 机场	⇒	lighthouse 灯塔	to	shoreline 海岸线	（空间）

★★★ console

[kənˈsəʊl] v. 安慰

变 consolation n. 安慰；inconsolable a. 无法安慰的

记 给仇人的家属送去慰问（console），所以得到了仇人的宽恕（condone）
考 同义 console = comfort；consolation = comfort
类比 hysterical 歇斯底里的 to concerned 关心的 → inconsolable 极度沮丧的 to blue 忧郁的 （＞程度）
unhappy 不快乐的 to inconsolable 无法安慰的 → uncertain 不确定的 to doubtful 怀疑的 （＜程度）

cognizant
[ˈkɒɡnɪzənt] *a.* 认知的

记 cogn- "认识，知道"，是 know 的变体
考 类比 cognizant 认知的 to awareness 意识 → restive 不安宁的 to impatience 急躁 （同义）

poodle
[ˈpuːdl] *n.* 狮子狗

记 狮子狗（poodle）爱吃面（noodle）
考 类比 poodle 狮子狗 to dog 狗 → Hereford 赫里福种的食用牛 to cattle 牛 （种属）

idle
[ˈaɪdl] *a.* 懒惰的，不活跃的

记 你的偶像（idol）其实很懒（idle），一年只拍一部戏
考 同义 idle = inactive
类比 sufficient 充足的 to plentiful 足够的 → inactive 不活跃的 to idle 懒惰的 （同义）
idle 闲置的 to employed 被占用的 → graceful 优雅的 to clumsy 笨拙的 （反义）

articulate
[ɑːˈtɪkjʊleɪt] *v.* 清晰发音，明确表达
[ɑːˈtɪkjələt] *a.* 口齿清晰的

变 inarticulate *a.* 口齿不清晰的；articulateness *n.* 口齿清晰
记 出口（articulate）成章（article）
考 同义 inarticulate = tongue-tied；articulate = enunciate
类比 articulate 口齿清晰的 to speaking 说话 → legible 清晰易辨的 to writing 书写 （修饰）
articulateness 口齿清晰 to speech 演讲 → legibility 易读 to handwriting 书写 （修饰）
articulate 清晰发音 to clearly 清楚地 → shout 叫喊 to loudly 大声地 （修饰）
articulate 口齿清晰的 to speech 演讲 → graceful 优雅的 to movement 动作 （修饰）
nimble 敏捷的 to coordination 协调 → articulate 清晰的 to pronunciation 发音 （修饰）

☆ cognizant　☆ poodle　☆ idle　☆ articulate

speech 演讲	to	articulate 发音清晰的	→	sound 声音	to	euphonious 悦耳的	（修饰）
adroit 敏捷的	to	motion 行动	→	articulate 口齿清晰的	to	speech 演讲	（修饰）
articulate 雄辩的	to	orator 演讲者	→	agile 灵活的	to	acrobat 杂技演员	（人物及其特点）

★ bibliography [ˌbɪblɪˈɒɡrəfi] n. 参考书目

记 biblio-（Bible）+ graph- 写 + y：写《圣经》（Bible）需要一系列参考书目（bibliography）
考 同义 bibliography = lists of books

★ swivel [ˈswɪvl] v. 旋转

记 单词打乱顺序构成 wives 和 l，可以想象成妻子们（wives）围着钢管（l）旋转（swivel）
考 同义 swivel = pivot

List | 07 words   ★ 复习一下学过的单词！

□ amuse	□ corridor	□ jubilant	□ rebel
□ audacious	□ cultivate	□ lethargic	□ scissor
□ bowling	□ digress	□ mar	□ thread
□ caprice	□ document	□ material	□ toady
□ consecrate	□ henchman	□ merit	□ wreck

☆ bibliography   ☆ swivel

SSAT词汇 List 09

★ assault [əˈsɔːlt] v. 进攻

记 因为受到侮辱（insult），所以要进攻（assault）

考 类比 forward/向前的 to backward/向后的 ⇒ assault/攻击 to retreat/撤退 （反义）
       onslaught/攻击 to assault/攻击 ⇒ assail/攻击 to attack/攻击 （同义）

★★★ prose [prəʊz] n. 散文

记 散文（prose）写得过于华丽，像一朵玫瑰花（rose）

考 类比 poetry/诗歌 to prose/散文 ⇒ sonata/奏鸣曲 to etude/练习曲 （同类）
       prose/散文 to paragraph/段落 ⇒ poetry/诗歌 to stanza/诗节 （组成）
       florid/绚丽的 to prose/散文 ⇒ ornate/华丽的 to building/建筑物 （修饰）

★ refuse [rɪˈfjuːz] v. 拒绝，不愿

考 同义 refuse = deny
   类比 lazy/懒惰的 to inert/惰性的 ⇒ resist/抵制 to refuse/拒绝 （同义）

★ ridiculous [rɪˈdɪkjʊləs] a. 荒谬可笑的

记 这个单词在口语中常被故意发成 ri-donkeyl-ous，不知道跟驴有啥关系
考 同义 inane = ridiculous；ludicrous = ridiculous

★ concur [kənˈkɜː] v. 同意

记 既然事情已经发生（occur），那我就勉强同意（concur）吧
考 同义 concur = agree

☆ assault   ☆ prose   ☆ refuse   ☆ ridiculous   ☆ concur

★★★ pure

[pjʊə] *a.* 纯净的

变 purify *v.* 纯净，净化；purity *n.* 纯净
考 同义 immaculate = pure

类比
- emend 修订 → faulty 有错的 ⇒ purify 净化 → contaminated 污染的 （缺乏）
- purify 净化 → clean 干净的 ⇒ explain 解释 → clear 清楚的 （动作及其目的）
- attract 吸引 → repel 排斥 ⇒ purify 净化 → contaminate 污染 （反义）
- feeble 虚弱的 → vigor 精力 ⇒ adulterated 掺杂的 → purity 净化 （缺乏）
- decode 解码 → encoded 编码的 ⇒ purify 净化 → contaminated 污染的 （反义）
- condense 压缩 → compact 紧凑的 ⇒ refine 精炼 → pure 纯的 （同义）

★ lunge

[lʌndʒ] *v.* 刺入

记 剪刀刺（lunge）入肺（lung）中
考 同义 lunge = thrust

★★ decay

[dɪˈkeɪ] *v.* 衰退，腐烂

变 decadent *a.* 颓废的，衰败的
记 因为推迟（delay）把剩饭菜放入冰箱，所以食物腐烂（decay）了
考 类比
- wood 木材 → decay 腐烂 ⇒ iron 铁 → rust 生锈 （事物及其动作）
- decadent 腐烂的 → decayed 腐烂的 ⇒ lacerated 撕裂的 → tore 撕开的 （同义）

★★ beseech

[bɪˈsiːtʃ] *v.* 恳求，哀求

记 这个单词可以看作 be seen，可以理解为：因为做坏事被看到（be seen），所以恳求（beseech）对方不要透露出去
考 同义 beseech = implore；beseech = entreat；beseech = plead

★★ plow

[ˈplaʊ] *v.* 犁地；*n.* 犁

记 老实的农民伯伯犁地（plow），不切实际的人却在吹（blow）牛
考 类比
- saw 锯 → carpenter 木匠 ⇒ plow 犁 → farmer 农民 （人物及其工具）
- gardener 园丁 → dig 挖 ⇒ farmer 农民 → plow 犁地 （人物及其动作）

erect ★

[ɪˈrekt] *a.* 竖直的，竖立的

记 e- 朝外 + -rect 正，直

考 类比 vertical 垂直的 to horizontal 水平的 ⇒ erect 竖直的 to prone 俯卧的 （空间）

lament ★★★

[ləˈment] *v.* 哀悼，悔恨

变 lamentation *n.* 悲哀，哀悼

记 哀悼（lament）自己跛了的（lame）腿

考 同义 lamentation = remorse；lament = regret；lament = moan
deplore = lament；lament = rue

horde ★★

[hɔːd] *n.* 一大群

记 每天一大群（horde）人对着上帝（lord）说："Oh My God."

考 同义 horde = swarm；horde = multitude

类比 horde 一群 to throng 一群 ⇒ hurl 投掷 to throw 扔 （同义）

split ★★

[splɪt] *v.* 分裂；*n.* 分裂

记 老外吃完饭之后 AA 制就会说："Let's split the bill."，你可千万别伸手就把账单给撕了

考 同义 dissociate = split off；rend = split；split = cleft

censor ★★

[ˈsensə] *v.* 审查

变 censorious *a.* 挑剔的，批评的；censorship *n.* 审查制度

记 检查人员审查（censor）出不合格的内容，作者受到责备（censure）

考 类比 censor 审查 to accept 接受 ⇒ reject 拒绝 to welcome 欢迎 （反义）

credulous 轻信的 to believe 相信 ⇒ censorious 挑剔的 to criticize 批评 （＞程度）

libertarian 自由论者 to censorship 审查制度 ⇒ pacifist 和平主义者 to violence 暴力 （人物及其对象）

encroach ★

[ɪnˈkrəʊtʃ] *v.* 蚕食，侵占

记 en-（in）+ croach-（reach）：到达（reach）并进入（in）别人的地盘即为侵占（encroach）

考 同义 impinge = encroach

subtract [səbˈtrækt] v. 减

- 记 sub- 下 + -tract 拉：朝下拉即为减少（subtract）
- 考 同义 subtract = deduct

类比 divide/除 to multiply/乘 ⇒ subtract/减 to plus/加 （同类）

pretext [ˈpriːtekst] n. 借口

- 记 pre- 提前 + text 文本：借口（pretext）就是需要提前（pre）想好的文本（text）
- 考 同义 pretext = excuse

astute [əˈstjuːt] a. 机敏的，狡猾的

- 记 虽然形势严峻（austere），但是当事人机敏（astute）应对
- 考 同义 astute = shrewd；astute = sharp；perceptive = astute；astute = clever

relieve [rɪˈliːv] v. 减轻，释放

- 记 心中有信仰（believe），即使有压力也会很容易释放（relieve）
- 考 同义 relieve = ease

List | 08 words ★复习一下学过的单词！

articulate	cognizant	loom	roe
bake	console	molt	sully
barrel	coordination	plagiarize	swivel
bibliography	hypothesis	platform	terrestrial
bland	idle	poodle	tower

☆ subtract　　☆ pretext　　☆ astute　　☆ relieve

SSAT词汇 List 10

★★ liberate
['lɪbəreɪt] *v.* 解放，使自由

记 这个单词即为我们熟悉的"自由女神像（the Statue of Liberty）"中 liberty 的动词形式
考 同义 liberate = free； liberate = release

★★ vacillate
['væsɪleɪt] *v.* 摇摆，犹豫

记 家长犹豫（vacillate）是否该给孩子接种疫苗（vaccinate）
考 同义 vacillate = waver； vacillate = fluctuate； vacillate = change

★★ assemble
[ə'sembl] *v.* 集合，聚集

记 我们常说的"流水线"即为 assembly line，其中的 assembly 是 assemble 的名词形式
考 同义 assemble = convene； assemble = gather； construct = assemble
注 关于"集合，聚集"的单词在 SSAT 的习题中有很多，如：muster, congregate。

★★ sterilize
['sterəlaɪz] *v.* 消毒，杀菌

记 用化肥（fertilizer）来杀菌（sterilize）
考 类比 wash 洗 to dirt 尘土 ⇒ sterilize 杀菌 to bacterium 细菌 （动宾）
　　　 sterilize 杀菌 to germ 细菌 ⇒ scour 洗涤 to grime 污垢 （动宾）

★★★ sphere
[sfɪə] *n.* 球体

考 类比 helix 螺旋 to spring 弹簧 ⇒ sphere 球体 to baseball 棒球 （事物及其特点）
　　　 sphere 球体 to round 圆形 ⇒ honeycomb 蜂巢 to hexagonal 六边形 （事物及其特点）
　　　 cube 立方体 to square 正方形 ⇒ sphere 球体 to circle 圆形 （事物及其特点）

☆ liberate　　☆ vacillate　　☆ assemble　　☆ sterilize　　☆ sphere

gratis
['grætɪs] *a.* 免费的

记 grat- (great) + is：伟大的 (great) 东西都是 (is) 免费的 (gratis)
考 同义 gratis = without charge

emulate
['emjʊleɪt] *v.* 模仿

记 emulate 和 imitate 不仅意思相同，长得也很相似
考 同义 emulate = imitate
类比 emulate (模仿) to person (人) ⇒ mimic (模拟) to gesture (姿势) （动宾）

sparse
[spɑːs] *a.* 稀疏的，瘦弱的

记 做个 spa 希望自己可以变瘦 (sparse)
考 同义 meager = sparse；sparse = thin

emaciated
[ɪ'meɪʃɪeɪtɪd] *a.* 瘦弱的，憔悴的

记 e- 朝外 + mac- (MAC) + iated：苹果公司推出 e 的 MAC 系列越来越瘦 (emaciated) 了
考 同义 frail = emaciated；emaciated = thin
类比 frail (脆弱的) to emaciated (瘦弱的) ⇒ robust (强健的) to invigorated (精力充沛的) （同义）

pertinent
['pɜːtɪnənt] *a.* 相关的，中肯的

变 impertinent *a.* 无礼的，粗鲁的
记 各个大洲 (continent) 之间都是有关系的 (pertinent)
考 同义 applicable = pertinent；impertinent = presumptuous；insolent = impertinent
类比 pertinent (相关的) to relevant (相关的) ⇒ ignorant (无知的) to unknowing (不知的) （同义）

synthesis
['sɪnθəsɪs] *n.* 综合

记 syn- (same) + thesis：我的论文 (thesis) 内容就是好多相同 (same) 内容的综合 (synthesis)
考 同义 synthesis = combination

avoid
[ə'vɔɪd] *v.* 避免

变 avoiding *a.* 避免的
考 同义 avoid = avert；avoiding = abstinent

☆ gratis　　☆ emulate　　☆ sparse　　☆ emaciated　　☆ pertinent
☆ synthesis　　☆ avoid

razor ★★

[ˈreɪzə] n. 剃刀

记 用剃刀（razor）将一片土地夷为平地（raze）

考 类比 rudder 船舵 to steering 操纵 → razor 剃刀 to shaving 刮胡子 （事物及其动作）

scalpel 手术刀 to razor 剃刀 → surgeon 外科医生 to barber 理发师 （纵向）

harsh ★★

[hɑːʃ] a. 严厉的，严酷的

记 尽管题目很难 hard，但老师依然严格（harsh）要求学生

考 同义 harsh = grim；harsh = severe；harsh = raucous；harsh = strident

steel ★★

[stiːl] n. 钢铁

记 偷（steal）铁（steel）小组

考 类比 bread 面包 to moldy 发霉的 → steel 钢铁 to rusty 生锈的 （修饰）

steel 钢 to metal 金属 → iron 铁 to ore 矿石 （纵向）

注 这个题的思路有些复杂：用 iron 可以炼出 steel，用 ore 可以炼出 metal。

recess ★★

[rɪˈses] n. 凹处；休息

记 recess 在日常生活中很常见：除了我们常见的"凹处"之外，开会时候的"休会"或者法庭上的"休庭"都可以说 recess；其名词形式 recession 常用到的场合 economic recession 指的是"经济衰退"

考 类比 half time 半场休息 to soccer 足球 → recess 休息 to school 学校 （事物及其部分）

table 桌子 to altar 祭坛 → recess 凹处 to alcove 凹室 （种属）

注 recess 这个单词作"凹处"讲的时候英文释义为：part of a wall which is built further back than the rest of the wall。

engage ★

[ɪnˈgeɪdʒ] v. 从事，使用

考 同义 engage = employ

humid ★★

[ˈhjuːmɪd] a. 潮湿的

变 humidifier n. 加湿器；humidity n. 湿度

记 hu 湖 + mid 中间：湖中间当然很潮湿（humid）了

考 同义 humid = muggy

☆ razor　　☆ harsh　　☆ steel　　☆ recess　　☆ engage
☆ humid

类比　desert／沙漠　to　arid／干旱的　⇒　rainforest／雨林　to　humid／潮湿的　（事物及其特点）
　　　humidifier／加湿器　to　moisture／湿度　⇒　furnace／炉子　to　heat／热度　（事物及其用途）
　　　mileage／英里数　to　odometer／里程表　⇒　humidity／湿度　to　humidiometer／湿度计　（事物及其用途）

★ locomotive　[ˌləʊkəˈməʊtɪv]　n. 火车头

记　火车头（locomotive）的移动（locomotion）是火车前进的动力（motive）

考　类比　bus／公车　to　road／道路　⇒　locomotive／火车头　to　track／轨道　（空间）
　　　　heat／热　to　sun／太阳　⇒　steam／蒸汽　to　locomotive／火车头　（事物及其特点）

★ agnostic　[æɡˈnɒstɪk]　n. 不可知论者

记　大夫的诊断结论（diagnostic）是：他是一个不可知论者（agnostic）

考　同义　agnostic = non-believer

agnostic

List | 09 words　　★ 复习一下学过的单词！

□ assault	□ decay	□ lunge	□ refuse
□ astute	□ encroach	□ plow	□ relieve
□ beseech	□ erect	□ pretext	□ ridiculous
□ censor	□ horde	□ prose	□ split
□ concur	□ lament	□ pure	□ subtract

42　　☆ locomotive　　☆ agnostic

SSAT词汇 List 11

★ tornado
['tɔː'neɪdəʊ] *n.* 龙卷风，飓风

记 多伦多（Toronto）在刮飓风（tornado）
考 类比 tremor（震动）to earthquake（地震）⇒ wind（风）to tornado（龙卷风）（＜程度）

★★ mischievous
['mɪstʃɪvəs] *a.* 淘气的

记 mis- 否定 + -chievous（achieve）成就：没有任何成就是因为很淘气（mischievous）
考 同义 mischievous = impish；mischievous = troublemaking
类比 adept（熟练的）to unskilled（不熟练的）⇒ mischievous（淘气的）to obedient（顺从的）（反义）

★★★ vary
['veəri] *v.* 变化

变 variable *a.* 可变的；invariable *a.* 不变的；varied *a.* 多变的
记 这个人非常（very）善于变化（vary）
考 同义 variable = changeable
类比 defend（防守）to untenable（站不住脚的）⇒ modify（修改）to invariable（不变的）（反义）
varied（多变的）to identical（同一的）⇒ collaborative（合作的）to unilateral（单边的）（反义）

★ lackluster
['læklʌstə] *a.* 无光泽的，平凡的

记 lack 缺乏 + luster 光泽
考 同义 lackluster = dull

★ snoop
[snuːp] *v.* 窥探

记 史努比小狗（Snoopy）喜欢到处去窥探（snoop）
考 类比 snoop（窥探）to look（看）⇒ eavesdrop（偷听）to listen（听）（同义：正反向）

truncate

[trʌŋˈkeɪt] v. 截断，缩短

- 变 truncated a. 截断了的
- 记 trunc- (truck) + -cate (cut)：一辆卡车 (truck) 把树干截断 (truncate)，切 (cut) 成两半
- 考 同义 truncate = shorten

类比 amenable 顺从的 —to→ agreeable 愉快的 ⇒ truncated 截断的 —to→ shortened 截断的 （同义）

(amenable 这个单词的英文释义为：If you are amenable to something, you are willing to do it or accept it; agreeable)

itinerary

[aɪˈtɪnərəri] n. 旅程，路线

- 变 itinerant a. 巡回的，流动的
- 记 我们通过国外网站购买机票，打印出来的机票行程单上方就写着 ITINERARY
- 考 同义 itinerant = nomadic; itinerant = traveling

类比
- digression 离题 —to→ topic 话题 ⇒ detour 绕道 —to→ itinerary 路线 （缺乏）
- itinerary 路线 —to→ journey 旅行 ⇒ program 程序 —to→ concert 演唱会 （事物及其用途）
- itinerary 路线 —to→ travel 旅行 ⇒ agenda 议程 —to→ meeting 会议 （事物及其用途）
- food 食物 —to→ expiry date 有效期 ⇒ airline ticket 机票 —to→ itinerary 路线 （事物及其部分）

swelter

[ˈsweltə] v. 闷热

- 变 sweltering a. 热的，难受的
- 记 夏天穿毛衣 (sweater) 不热 (swelter) 才怪
- 考 类比
  - funny 好笑的 —to→ hilarious 滑稽的 ⇒ hot 热的 —to→ sweltering 大汗淋漓的 （＜程度）
  - sweat 出汗 —to→ sweltering 热的难受的 ⇒ whimper 啜泣声 —to→ weep 哭泣 （＜程度）

shelter

[ˈʃeltə] n. 避难所；v. 庇护

- 记 对于蜗牛来说，壳 (shell) 就是它的避难所 (shelter)
- 考 同义 shelter = refuge

类比
- raucous 刺耳的 —to→ quiet 安静的 ⇒ shelter 庇护 —to→ exposure 暴露 （反义）
- bee 蜜蜂 —to→ pollinate 授粉 ⇒ roof 房顶 —to→ shelter 庇护 （事物及其用途）

drudgery ★

[ˈdrʌdʒəri] *n.* 苦工，苦差事

记 在药（drug）店做事真的是个苦差事（drudgery）
考 同义 drudgery = toll

drudgery

affable ★

[ˈæfəbl] *a.* 友好的

记 注意区分 affable "友好的" 和 effable "可表达的"
考 同义 affable = friendly
注 关于"友好的"单词在 SSAT 的习题中有很多，如：amiable, genial, gentle, courteous, amicable, intimate。

accentuate ★★

[əkˈsentʃueɪt] *v.* 强调

变 accentuated *a.* 强调的
记 用不同的口音（accent）来强调（accentuate）
考 同义 emphasize = accentuate; emphatic = accentuated; accentuated = highlighted; accentuated = underlined; accentuated = forceful

detest ★★

[dɪˈtest] *v.* 厌恶

记 学生都很厌恶（detest）考试（test）
考 同义 abhor = detest

类比 hesitate 犹豫 to waver 犹豫 ⇒ loathe 讨厌 to detest 厌恶 （同义）
detest 厌恶 to cherish 珍惜 ⇒ subdue 抑制 to embolden 使大胆 （反义）

注 关于"厌恶"的单词在 SSAT 的习题中有很多，如：despise, loathe。

animosity ★

[ˌænɪˈmɒsəti] *n.* 憎恨，敌意

记 因为小时候被狗咬了，所以他对动物（animal）充满深深的敌意（animosity）
考 同义 hostility = animosity; animosity = hatred

类比 friend 朋友 to animosity 敌意 ⇒ hypocrite 伪君子 to sincerity 真诚 （缺乏）

breed ★

[briːd] *n.* 一个品种的动物

记 一个品种的动物（breed）流着相同的血（bleed）
考 类比 breed 一种狗 to dog 狗 ⇒ flavor 味道 to ice cream 冰淇淋 （事物及其部分）

注 breed 这个单词"喂养"的意思我们很熟悉，此处是熟词僻义。

★★★ poverty

['pɒvəti] n. 贫穷

记 poverty 这个单词的形容词形式即为我们常见的 poor
考 同义 distress = poverty；penury = poverty；need = poverty（need 这个单词的英文释义为 a condition of poverty or misfortune）

类比 famine 饥荒 to abundance 大量 ⇒ poverty 贫穷 to wealth 财富 （反义）

★ alchemy

['ælkəmi] n. 炼金术

记 古代的炼金术士们总想将低贱的金属变为金子，古埃及人将他们所研究的炼金术连同其命名 al-kimia 一起传入欧洲变成炼金术（alchemy），最后成为今天的化学（chemistry）。

考 类比 chemistry 化学 to alchemy 炼金术 ⇒ astronomy 天文学 to astrology 占星术 （同义：新旧之称）

★★ diminish

[dɪ'mɪnɪʃ] v. 减少，变小

记 di- 加强 + mini 小 + -ish
考 同义 diminish = reduce；diminish = decrease；diminish = wane

类比 adjust 适应 to adapt 适应 ⇒ belittle 贬低 to diminish 减少 （同义）

electrify 使兴奋 to excitement 兴奋 ⇒ diminish 减少 to reduction 减少 （同义）

★ dock

['dɒk] n. 码头

记 一只狗（dog）被锁（lock）在码头（dock）
考 同义 dock = wharf

类比 dock 码头 to boat 船 ⇒ hangar 机库 to airplane 飞机 （空间）

★★ verify

['verɪfaɪ] v. 核实，查证

记 我们在用支付宝付钱的时候会出现 verify payment 的字样，需要我们确认付款
考 同义 verify = prove true；verify = corroborate；verify = authenticate

---

List | 10 words　　　　　　　　　　　　　　　　★ 复习一下学过的单词！

□ agnostic	□ engage	□ locomotive	□ sphere
□ assemble	□ gratis	□ pertinent	□ steel
□ avoid	□ harsh	□ razor	□ sterilize
□ emaciated	□ humid	□ recess	□ synthesis
□ emulate	□ liberate	□ sparse	□ vacillate

☆ poverty　　☆ alchemy　　☆ diminish　　☆ dock　　☆ verify

SSAT词汇 List 12

★★★ stubborn ['stʌbən] *a.* 顽固的，倔强的

记 英语中说人"倔"会说 as stubborn as a mule
考 同义　stubborn = headstrong；adamant = stubborn；stubborn = refractory；
　　　　obstinate = stubborn；stubborn = recalcitrant
　　类比　abstract 抽象的 to concrete 具体的 ⇒ stubborn 倔强的 to flexible 灵活的 （反义）
注 关于"坚定的，顽固的"的单词在 SSAT 的习题中有很多，如：adamant, determined, rigid, resolute, unyielding。

★★ altruism ['æltruɪzəm] *n.* 利他主义

变 altruistic *a.* 利他的，无私心的
记 altru 谐音 all true：因为他对待别人都是完全（all）真实的（true），所以说他是无私心的（altruistic）
考 同义　altruism = generosity
　　类比　altruistic 利他的 to selfish 自私的 ⇒ sensitive 敏感的 to ignorant 无感的 （反义）

★★★ arid ['ærɪd] *a.* 干旱的

记 干旱的（arid）季节突然袭击（raid）英国
考 同义　arid = dry
　　类比　bankrupt 破产的 to fund 资金 ⇒ arid 干旱的 to rain 雨 （缺乏）
　　　　desert 沙漠 to arid 干旱的 ⇒ rainforest 雨林 to humid 潮湿的 （事物及其特点）
　　　　desert 沙漠 to arid 干旱的 ⇒ swamp 湿地 to humid 潮湿的 （事物及其特点）
　　　　desert 沙漠 to arid 干旱的 ⇒ swamp 湿地 to wet 湿的 （事物及其特点）
　　　　moist 潮湿的 to arid 干旱的 ⇒ sublime 崇高的 to deserted 被抛弃的 （反义）
　　　　famished 非常饥饿的 to hungry 饥饿的 ⇒ arid 干旱的 to dry 干的 （＞程度）

arid 干旱的 to dry 干的 ⇒ glacial 冰冷的 to cold 寒冷的 （＞程度）

identical
[aɪˈdentɪkl] *a.* 相同的

记 同卵双胞胎（identical twins）拥有相同的（identical）身份（identity）
考 同义 duplicate = identical
类比 comparable 可比较的 to identical 相同的 ⇒ different 不同的 to antithetical 对立的 （＜程度）

square
[skweə] *n.* 正方形

考 类比 oval 椭圆 to oblong 长方形 ⇒ circle 圆形 to square 正方形 （纵向）
cube 立方体 to square 正方形 ⇒ sphere 球体 to circle 圆形 （事物及其特点）
circle 圆形 to ball 球形 ⇒ square 正方形 to cube 立方体 （事物及其特点）

desire
[dɪˈzaɪə] *v.* 渴望，欲望；*n.* 渴望

考 同义 yearn = desire
类比 condense 压缩 to expand 扩张 ⇒ desire 欲望 to reject 拒绝 （反义）
desire 欲望 to need 需求 ⇒ strength 力量 to force 力量 （同义）
ask 问 to demand 询问 ⇒ desire 欲望 to need 需求 （同义）

conjecture
[kənˈdʒektʃə] *n.* 猜测

记 ISEE、老 SAT 和 GRE 考试中有填空题，主要就是根据连接词（conjunction）来大胆猜测（conjecture）句子之间的逻辑关系
考 同义 conjecture = guess

proximity
[prɒkˈsɪmɪti] *n.* 接近，靠近

记 proximity 和 approximate 一起记忆
考 类比 neighbor 邻居 to proximity 接近 ⇒ adversary 反对者 to opposition 反对 （人物及其特点）

impromptu
[ɪmˈprɒmptjuː] *a.* 即兴的

记 Winston Churchill 的一句名言：I'm just preparing my impromptu remarks.
考 类比 impromptu 即兴的 to preparation 准备 ⇒ reckless 鲁莽的 to caution 谨慎 （缺乏）

spontaneous 即兴的 —to→ calculated 有计划的 ⇒ impromptu 即兴的 —to→ scheduled 已安排好的 （反义）

★ homily

['hɒmɪli] *n.* 说教

记 成天在家（home）里听妈妈的说教（homily）
考 同义　homily = lecture

★ entreat

[ɪn'triːt] *v.* 恳求

记 恳求（entreat）大夫好好治疗（treat）你的病
考 同义　entreat = beg; beseech = entreat

★ herculean

[ˌhɜːkjʊ'liːən] *a.* 力大无比的

记 Herculean 赫拉克勒斯是希腊神话中的英雄，传说他神勇无比、力大无穷，完成了 12 项被誉为"不可能完成"的任务，除此之外，他还解救了被缚的普罗米修斯。在今天的西方世界，赫拉克勒斯一词已经成为大力士和壮汉的同义词
考 同义　herculean = exceptional power or strength

★★★ scoop

[skuːp] *v.* 用勺舀

记 用勺舀（scoop）汤（soup）
考 同义　scoop = gouge
　　类比　ruler 尺子 —to→ measure 测量 ⇒ spoon 勺子 —to→ scoop 舀 （事物及其用途）
　　　　　scissors 剪刀 —to→ cut 切 ⇒ shovel 铁铲 —to→ scoop 舀 （事物及其用途）

★ guffaw

[gə'fɔː] *n.* 大笑，狂笑

记 谐音：寡妇。听到前女友变成寡妇的消息后，他开始大笑（guffaw）
考 类比　chill 使寒冷 —to→ freeze 结冰 ⇒ giggle 咯咯笑 —to→ guffaw 大笑 （<程度）

★★★ lamp

[læmp] *n.* 灯

记 用灯（lamp）照的热度来做烤全羊（lamb）
考 类比　key 钥匙 —to→ lock 锁 ⇒ switch 开关 —to→ lamp 灯 （事物及其用途）
　　　　　handcuff 手铐 —to→ arrest 逮捕 ⇒ lamp 灯 —to→ light 点灯 （事物及其用途）
　　　　　radiator 暖气 —to→ heat 热 ⇒ lamp 灯 —to→ light 光亮 （事物及其对象）
　　　　　fire 火 —to→ heat 热 ⇒ lamp 灯 —to→ light 光亮 （事物及其对象）

mountain 山 → to → vantage point 有利位置 ⇒ lighthouse 灯塔 → to → lamp 灯 （事物及其部分）

★ ardor

['ɑ:də] *n.* 热情，狂热

记 教练命令（order）球员，用自己的热情（ardor）去好好踢球
考 同义 ardor = passion

★★ congenial

[kən'dʒi:niəl] *a.* 意气相投的

记 这两兄弟天生（congenital）意气相投（congenial）
考 同义 congenial = agreeable；congenial = amiable；congenial = pleasant

类比 congenial 意气相投的 → to → agreeable 令人愉快的 ⇒ stoical 禁欲的 → to → unemotional 不移动感情的 （同义）

注 congenial 这个单词的英文释义为：pleasant in a way that makes you feel comfortable and relaxed。

★★ pristine

['prɪsti:n] *a.* 原始的，淳朴的

记 淳朴的（pristine）牧师（priest）
考 同义 immaculate = pristine

类比 clean 干净的 → to → pristine 结晶的 ⇒ happy 开心的 → to → ecstatic 狂喜的 （＜程度）

★ irrigate

['ɪrɪgeɪt] *v.* 灌溉，冲洗

记 洗车的时候不小心冲洗（irrigate）了别人家晾晒的床单，激怒（irritate）了对方
考 同义 irrigate = flush

类比 irrigate 灌溉 → to → dry 干 ⇒ smooth 使光滑 → to → coarse 粗糙的 （缺乏）

irrigate 灌溉 → to → water 水 ⇒ ventilate 通风 → to → air 空气 （事物及其用途）

★ garble

['gɑ:bl] *v.* 混淆，断章取义

记 总是将大理石（marble）和其他石头混淆（garble）
考 同义 garble = confuse

List | **11** words ★ 复习一下学过的单词！

☐ accentuate	☐ detest	☐ lackluster	☐ swelter
☐ affable	☐ diminish	☐ mischievous	☐ tornado
☐ alchemy	☐ dock	☐ poverty	☐ truncate
☐ animosity	☐ drudgery	☐ shelter	☐ vary
☐ breed	☐ itinerary	☐ snoop	☐ verify

SSAT词汇 List 13

indulge
[ɪnˈdʌldʒ] *v.* 沉溺，放纵

- 考 谐音 in door：在学校表现得像个好学生似的，一进家门（in door）就开始沉溺于（indulge）游戏
- 考 同义 indulge = pamper

clarinet
[ˌklærɪˈnet] *n.* 单簧管

- 记 clari-（clear）+ net：这首单簧管（clarinet）独奏曲在网上（net）的版本不那么清晰（clear）
- 考 类比 brass 黄铜乐器 to cornet 短号 ⇒ woodwind 木管乐器 to clarinet 单簧管 （种属）
  woodwind 木管乐器 to clarinet 单簧管 ⇒ percussion 打击乐器 to cymbal 铙钹 （种属）

skeptic
[ˈskeptɪk] *n.* 怀疑论者

- 变 skeptical *a.* 怀疑的
- 记 古希腊哲学家皮洛主张：对一切事物都保持淡定，不要轻易做出判断。皮洛门徒们自称为 Skeptikoi，该词来自希腊语 skeptesthai "察看，深思"
- 考 同义 skeptic = doubter；incredulous = skeptical

fatigue
[fəˈtiːg] *n.* 劳累

- 考 fatigued *a.* 疲乏的
- 记 fat + i + -gue（que）缺：因为胖子（fat）缺乏锻炼，所以容易劳累（fatigue）
- 考 同义 fatigued = jaded；fatigue = weariness
  类比 boredom 无聊 to variety 多样性 ⇒ fatigue 劳累 to vigorousness 朝气 （缺乏）

query
[ˈkwɪəri] *n.* 疑问

- 记 quer-（question）+ y
- 考 同义 question = query

☆ indulge　☆ clarinet　☆ skeptic　☆ fatigue　☆ query

aghast [əˈɡɑːst] a. 吓呆的

记 大白天见到一个（a）鬼（ghost），吓呆了（aghast）
考 同义 aghast = shocked

muscle [ˈmʌsl] n. 肌肉

变 muscular a. 肌肉发达的
考 同义 brawny = muscular；burly = muscular
类比 muscle 肌肉 to weightlifting 举重 → vision 视力 to reading 阅读 （事物及其用途）
muscle 肌肉 to movement 运动 → battery 电池 to watch 表 （事物及其用途）

sidestep [ˈsaɪdstep] v. 回避

记 往边上（side）走一步（step）即为回避（sidestep）
考 同义 evade = sidestep
类比 strive 力争 to attain 达到 → sidestep 回避 to avoid 避免 （同义）

artificial [ˌɑːtɪˈfɪʃl] a. 人造的

记 我们常说的人工智能（AI）英文即为 Artificial Intelligence
考 同义 affected = artificial
类比 artificial 人工的 to synthetic 合成的 → adorn 装饰 to decorate 装饰 （同义）
artificial 人工的 to authentic 真正的 → gorgeous 华丽灿烂的 to dreary 枯燥的 （反义）
nature 自然 to nurture 养育 → authentic 真正的 to artificial 人工的 （纵向）

sunder [ˈsʌndə] v. 切开

记 周日（Sunday）早上没事干，切（sunder）个西瓜吃
考 同义 sunder = separate

debunk [diːˈbʌŋk] v. 揭穿，拆穿

记 de- 否定 + -bunk（bank）：拆穿（debunk）这家银行（bank）的真实面目
考 同义 debunk = disclose
类比 refute 反驳 to argument 言论 → debunk 拆穿 to myth 神话 （动宾）

placate

[pləˈkeɪt] *v.* 安慰

- 变 implacable *a.* 无法安抚的
- 记 大难发生，他受到朋友安慰（placate）后才略显平静（placid）
- 考 同义 abate = placate；soothe = placate

administrator

[ədˈmɪnɪstreɪtə] *n.* 管理人

- 记 administrator 的名词为 administration（管理），对应的就是 MBA（= Master of Business Administration 工商管理学硕士）中"管理"这个词
- 考 类比 manager (经理) to store (商店) ⇒ administrator (管理人) to hospital (医院) （人物及其对象）

confine

[kənˈfaɪn] *v.* 限制

- 变 confinement *n.* 限制
- 记 con- + fin- (finish) + e：走到哪儿都是结束，说明限制（confine）重重
- 考 同义 confine = restrict

  类比 confine (限制) to prisoner (囚犯) ⇒ detain (拘留) to suspect (嫌疑犯) （动宾）

  escape (逃跑) to confinement (限制) ⇒ run (跑) to danger (危险) （因果）

miserly

[ˈmaɪzəli] *a.* 吝啬的

- 变 miser *n.* 守财奴
- 记 吝啬的（miserly）人其实都是很聪明的（wisely）
- 考 类比 money (钱) to miserly (吝啬的) ⇒ word (话语) to laconic (简洁的) （缺乏）

  frugal (节俭的) to miserly (吝啬的) ⇒ confident (自信的) to arrogant (傲慢的) （同义：正反向）

  philanthropic (仁慈的) to benevolence (仁慈) ⇒ miserly (吝啬的) to stinginess (吝啬) （同义）

  generous (大方的) to frugal (节俭的) ⇒ philanthropist (慈善家) to miser (小气鬼) （反义）

  sage (圣人) to judicious (明智的) ⇒ miser (小气鬼) to stingy (吝啬的) （人物及其特点）

  burglar (盗贼) to stealth (鬼鬼祟祟) ⇒ miser (吝啬鬼) to greed (贪婪) （人物及其特点）

  profligate (放荡的) to moral (道德) ⇒ miser (小气鬼) to generous (大方的) （反义）

  hedonist (享乐主义的) to pleasure (快乐) ⇒ miser (守财奴) to money (钱) （人物及其对象）

miser 小气鬼 to generous 大方的 ⇒ benefactor 捐赠者 to stingy 吝啬的 （人物及其特点）

generous 大方的 to philanthropist 慈善家 ⇒ stingy 小气的 to miser 守财奴 （人物及其特点）

★★ paramount
[ˈpærəmaʊnt] *a.* 最重要的

记 美国电影公司"派拉蒙"公司的英文单词即为 paramount
考 同义 paramount = supreme
类比 important 重要的 to paramount 至高无上的 （＜程度）

★★ exploit
[ɪkˈsplɔɪt] *v.* 利用，开发；*n.* 英勇行为

考 同义 exploit = use；utilize = exploit
类比 exploit 英勇行为 to adventure 胆大行为 ⇒ safari 旅行 to expedition 远足 （同义）

★ stature
[ˈstætʃə] *n.* 身高，身材

记 自由女神像（statue）身材（stature）高大
考 同义 stature = height

★★ somber
[ˈsɑːmbə] *a.* 忧郁的

记 分手的人都喜欢让自己醉，因为一清醒（sober）就很忧郁（somber）
考 同义 gloomy = somber；somber = melancholy；somber = sad

★★ immaculate
[ɪˈmækjʊlət] *a.* 完美的

记 im- 否定 + maculate 污点的
考 同义 immaculate = pure；immaculate = pristine；immaculate = flawless
类比 immaculate 无瑕的 to dirt 尘土 ⇒ innocent 清白的 to guilt 罪 （缺乏）

List | **12** words ★复习一下学过的单词！

☐ altruism	☐ desire	☐ homily	☐ pristine
☐ ardor	☐ entreat	☐ identical	☐ proximity
☐ arid	☐ garble	☐ impromptu	☐ scoop
☐ congenial	☐ guffaw	☐ irrigate	☐ square
☐ conjecture	☐ herculean	☐ lamp	☐ stubborn

☆ paramount   ☆ exploit   ☆ stature   ☆ somber   ☆ immaculate

List 14

skit
[skɪt] *n.* 滑稽短剧

记 这个滑稽短剧（skit）中的男演员穿了一条裙子 skirt

考 类比 skit／滑稽短剧 to play／戏剧 ⇒ limerick／五行打油诗 to poem／诗 （种属）

intrigue
[ɪn'tri:g] *v.* 使感兴趣；*n.* 阴谋诡计

变 intriguing *a.* 有趣的

记 in + trig-（trick）+ -ue：用恶作剧（trick）把你吸引进来（in），让你感兴趣（intrigue）

考 同义 intrigue = plot；intrigue = fascinate；fascinating = intriguing

bombard
[bɒm'bɑ:d] *v.* 轰炸，炮击

记 用炸弹（bomb）去轰炸（bombard）敌人

考 同义 bombard = attack

clandestine
[klæn'destɪn] *a.* 秘密的

记 clan 部落 + destined 命中注定的 = clandestine 秘密的：三个词都很有神秘感

考 同义 clandestine = secret；surreptitious = clandestine

注 关于"秘密的"单词在 SSAT 的习题中有很多，如：covert，stealthy，furtive。

haughty
['hɔ:ti] *a.* 傲慢的

记 我就讨厌那种又淘气（naughty）又傲慢的（haughty）家伙

考 同义 arrogant = haughty；haughty = contemptuous

类比 frugality／节俭 to stingy／小气的 ⇒ pride／自豪 to haughty／傲慢的 （同义：正反向）

compel
[kəm'pel] *v.* 强迫，迫使

变 compelled *a.* 强迫的；compelling *a.* 强制的

☆ skit ☆ intrigue ☆ bombard ☆ clandestine ☆ haughty
☆ compel

记 com- + -pel（pull）：大家一起推动（pull）即为强迫（compel）
考 同义 compel = coerce; compel = force; compelled = forced; compelling = impelling

antithesis
[ænˈtɪθəsɪs] *n.* 对立面

记 anti- 相反 + thesis 论点
考 同义 antithesis = opposite

adjacent
[əˈdʒeɪsnt] *a.* 邻近的

记 谐音：a Jason 的：一个叫 Jason 的家伙住在我家附近（adjacent）
考 同义 adjacent = neighboring

类比 adjacent 邻近的 to neighboring 邻近的 ⇒ tranquil 安静的 to quiet 安静的 （同义）

fake
[feɪk] *a.* 假的

考 同义 fake = spurious; fake = bogus

manufacture
[ˌmænjʊˈfæktʃə] *v.* 制造，加工

记 manu- (many) + -facture (factory)：很多（many）产品都是在工厂（factory）制造（manufacture）出来的
考 同义 manufacture = make

flourish
[ˈflʌrɪʃ] *v.* 繁荣，兴旺

记 flour- (flower) + -ish：花（flower）开正旺（flourish）
考 同义 flourish = prosper; burgeon = flourish

anonymous
[əˈnɒnɪməs] *a.* 匿名的

变 anonymity *n.* 匿名
记 an- 否定 + onym- (name) + -ous
考 同义 anonymity = namelessness

类比 anonymous 匿名的 to name 名字 ⇒ amorphous 无形的 to shape 形状 （缺乏）
single-handed 单枪匹马的 to assistance 帮助 ⇒ anonymous 匿名的 to authorship 作者身份 （缺乏）

feasible
[ˈfiːzəbl] *a.* 可行的，可实现的

记 在春节（festival）的时候选择节食不可行（feasible）
考 同义 feasible = practical; feasible = executable
注 关于"可行的"单词在 SSAT 的习题中有很多，如：presumptive, plausible, possible.

feasible

dominate

['dɒmɪneɪt] *v.* 支配，控制

变 dominion *n.* 主权，统治权
记 domin 在拉丁词根中是"房子"的意思，引申的意思为"支配"
考 同义 jurisdiction = dominion

类比 dominate/统治 to influential/有影响力 → fascinate/着迷 to interesting/有趣的 （同义）

disperse

[dɪ'spɜːs] *v.* 分散，散开

记 dis- 朝外 + -perse（purse）钱包：钱包里的钱朝外（dis）分散（disperse）开来
考 同义 disperse = dispatch；disperse = discharge；distribute = disperse

类比 converge/汇合 to disperse/分散 → denigrate/诋毁 to commend/表扬 （反义）

clot/凝块 to dissolved/溶解的 → crowd/人群 to dispersed/分散的 （修饰）

tile

[taɪl] *n.* 瓷砖

记 这次购进瓷砖（tile）的数量已经计入文档（file）
考 类比 tile/瓷砖 to floor/地板 → book/书 to shelf/书架 （空间）

tile/瓷砖 to mosaic/马赛克 → musician/音乐家 to orchestra/管弦乐队 （组成）

collage/拼贴画 to painting/绘画 → mosaic/马赛克 to tile/瓷砖 （组成）

apogee

['æpəʊdʒiː] *n.* 最高点，远地点

记 apo-（apple）+ -gee（fee）：苹果（apple）手机的价格（fee）在手机里是最高的（apogee）
考 类比 pinnacle/顶峰 to mountain/山 → apogee/最高点 to orbit/轨道 （空间）

anxiety

[æŋ'zaɪəti] *n.* 焦虑，渴望

记 这个单词的形容词形式是 anxious
考 同义 anxiety = phobia

类比 indifference/冷漠 to apathy/冷漠 → vexed/焦急的 to anxiety/焦虑 （同义）

trek

[trek] *v.* 艰苦跋涉

记 著名电影《星际迷航》的英文即为 Star Trek
考 同义 trek = trail

☆ dominate　　☆ disperse　　☆ tile　　☆ apogee　　☆ anxiety
☆ trek

类比 erase/抹去 to delete/删除 ⇒ trek/艰苦跋涉 to hike/远足 （同义）

★ neophyte ['ni:əfaɪt] n. 新手

记 neo- 新 + -phyte (fight)：初生 (neophyte) 牛犊不怕虎，到处跟人去比武 (fight)
考 同义 novice = neophyte

List | 13 words   ★ 复习一下学过的单词！

☐ administrator	☐ debunk	☐ miserly	☐ sidestep
☐ aghast	☐ exploit	☐ muscle	☐ skeptic
☐ artificial	☐ fatigue	☐ paramount	☐ somber
☐ clarinet	☐ immaculate	☐ placate	☐ stature
☐ confine	☐ indulge	☐ query	☐ sunder

SSAT词汇 List 15

sweatpants
['swetpænts] *n.* 长运动裤

记 sweat 汗 + pants 裤子：长运动裤（sweatpants）就是可以吸汗（sweat）的裤子（pants）

考 类比 drawstring 拉绳 to sweatpants 长运动裤 ⇒ laces 鞋带 to shoes 鞋 （事物及其部分）

virtually
['vɜːtʃʊəli] *ad.* 几乎，差不多

考 同义 virtually = nearly

mob
[mɒb] *n.* 暴民

记 鲍勃（Bob）是个暴民（mob），总是去抢劫（rob）别人

考 类比 din 喧闹 to sound 声音 ⇒ mob 暴民 to people 人 （种属）

类比 din 喧闹 to loud 吵闹的 ⇒ mob 暴民 to unruly 不守规矩的 （同义）

banal
[bə'nɑːl] *a.* 陈腐的，平庸的

记 腐烂了的（banal）香蕉（banana）
政府下令禁止（ban）那些陈腐的（banal）东西

考 同义 banal = commonplace

类比 insipid 清淡的 to food 食物 ⇒ banal 平庸的 to conversation 谈话 （修饰）

注 关于"陈腐的"单词在 SSAT 的习题中有很多，如：trite, dull, cliché, prosaic。

asset
['æset] *n.* 资产

记 评价（assess）别人的资产（asset）情况

考 类比 amateur 外行 to nonprofessional 外行 ⇒ asset 资产 to valuable thing 财富 （同义）

asset 资产 to black 黑色 ⇒ debit 借贷 to red 红色 （同义）

注 这个题的思路有些复杂：一般公司盈利会用黑色笔来书写，而亏钱则会用红色笔来写。所以才有了我们常说的"财政赤字"。

☆ sweatpants ☆ virtually ☆ mob ☆ banal ☆ asset

★ rend

[rend] v. 撕裂

记 把借（lend）钱的账单撕破（rend）
考 同义 rend = split

★★ advance

[əd'vɑːns] v. 发展，前进

变 advanced a. 高级的
考 同义 advanced = highly evolved; advanced = precocious
类比 shelve 搁置 to forward 向前 ⇒ hold 搁置 to advance 发展 （纵向）

★★★ sage

[seɪdʒ] n. 圣人，贤人；a. 明智的

记 这个圣人（sage）上了年纪（age）
考 同义 judicious = sage; sage = wise
类比
sage 圣人 to judicious 明智的 ⇒ miser 小气鬼 to stingy 吝啬 （人物及其特点）
sage 圣人 to wisdom 智慧 ⇒ mechanic 机修工 to dexterity 灵巧 （人物及其特点）
grumpy 脾气坏的 to malcontent 不满的 ⇒ prudent 谨慎的 to sage 明智的 （因果）
seer 预言家 to prophecy 预言 ⇒ sage 圣人 to wisdom 智慧 （人物及其特点）

★★ rotate

[rəʊ'teɪt] v. 旋转

记 安卓手机从上往下滑动就会出现"旋转"一栏，对应英文即为 rotate
考 同义 rotate = revolve
类比
elongate 拉伸 to tension 张力 ⇒ rotate 扭转 to torsion 转矩 （因果）
torsion 转矩 to rotate 扭转 ⇒ torque 转矩 to twist 扭转 （因果）
torsion 转矩 to rotate 扭转 ⇒ gravity 重力 to pull 拉 （事物及其动作）

rotate

★★ hockey

['hɒki] n. 冰球

记 谐音：好奇：我一直很好奇冰球（hockey）是怎么玩的
考 类比
December 十二月 to year 年 ⇒ hockey 冰球 to winter sports 冬季运动 （种属）
puck 冰球 to hockey 冰球运动 ⇒ ball 球 to soccer 足球 （事物及其部分）
soccer 足球 to field 球场 ⇒ hockey 冰球 to rink 冰球场 （空间）

★★★ blizzard

['blɪzəd] n. 暴风雪

记 曾推出过《魔兽争霸》《星际争霸》以及《暗黑破坏神》的著名游戏公司"暴雪娱乐"的英文即为 blizzard

考 类比
flurry to blizzard → drizzle to downpour （<程度）
阵风   暴风雪   毛毛雨   大雨

blizzard to snowflake → hurricane to breeze （>程度）
暴风雪   雪片   飓风   微风

blizzard to snow → flood to rain （>程度）
暴风雪   雪   洪水   下雨

sprinkle to deluge → flurry to blizzard （<程度）
喷洒   洪水   小风   暴风雪

rain to flood → snow to blizzard （<程度）
雨   洪水   雪   暴风雪

decorate [ˈdekəreɪt] v. 装饰

考 同义 adorn = decorate

类比
garnish to salad → decorate to cake （动宾）
装饰   沙拉   装饰   蛋糕

decorate to plain → cook to raw （动宾）
装饰   普通的   煮   生的

artificial to synthetic → adorn to decorate （同义）
人工的   合成的   装饰   装饰

scrutinize [ˈskruːtɪnaɪz] v. 仔细检查

记 家长仔细检查（scrutinize）他涂改过的卷子，他觉得自己死定（screwed）了

考 同义 inspect = scrutinize；scrutinize = examine carefully

类比
expunge to remove → scrutinize to inspect （同义）
删除   移除   检查   检测

espy to scrutinize → harm to obliterate （<程度）
看到   仔细检查   伤害   消灭

consider to contemplate → examine to scrutinize （<程度）
考虑   沉思   检查   仔细检查

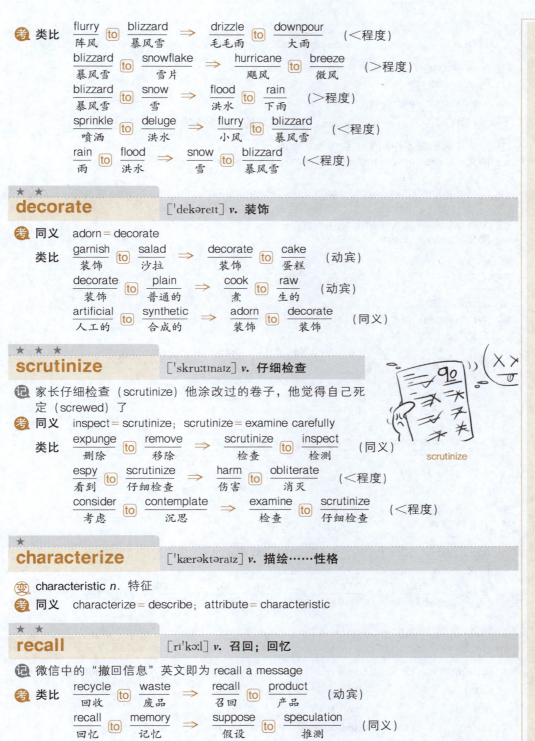
scrutinize

characterize [ˈkærəktəraɪz] v. 描绘……性格

变 characteristic n. 特征
考 同义 characterize = describe；attribute = characteristic

recall [rɪˈkɔːl] v. 召回；回忆

记 微信中的"撤回信息"英文即为 recall a message

考 类比
recycle to waste → recall to product （动宾）
回收   废品   召回   产品

recall to memory → suppose to speculation （同义）
回忆   记忆   假设   推测

★ concord
[ˈkɒnkɔːd] n. 和睦，一致

记 con- + -cord（core）核心
考 同义 reconcile＝concord

★★ supreme
[suːˈpriːm] a. 最高的，最重要的

记 这个单词被很多中国学生看作 super me
考 同义 supreme＝paramount；supreme＝ultimate

★ yearn
[jɜːn] v. 渴望

记 小孩子们都渴望（yearn）过年（year）
考 同义 yearn＝desire

★★★ felon
[ˈfelən] n. 重罪犯

变 felony n. 重罪
记 海伦（Helen）是个重罪犯（felon）
考 同义 criminal＝felon

类比
- felon 重罪犯 to crime 犯罪 ⇒ physician 医生 to cure 治疗 （人物及其动作）
- measles 麻疹 to disease 疾病 ⇒ felony 重罪 to crime 犯罪 （种属）
- tremor 震动 to earthquake 地震 ⇒ misdemeanor 轻罪 to felony 重罪 （＜程度）
- misdemeanor 轻罪 to felony 重罪 ⇒ drizzle 毛毛雨 to snowstorm 暴风雪 （＜程度）
- misdemeanor 轻罪 to felony 重罪 ⇒ jaywalker 乱穿马路者 to criminal 罪犯 （＜程度）

★ equal
[ˈiːkwəl] v. 等于，比得上

变 unequaled a. 独一无二的，无与伦比的；equivalent a. 等价的，相等的
考 同义 peer＝equal；unique＝unequaled

类比 discrepancy 差别 to difference 不同 ⇒ equivalent 相等的 to equal 相等的 （同义）

List | 14 words　　　★ 复习一下学过的单词！

□ adjacent	□ bombard	□ fake	□ manufacture
□ anonymous	□ clandestine	□ feasible	□ neophyte
□ antithesis	□ compel	□ flourish	□ skit
□ anxiety	□ disperse	□ haughty	□ tile
□ apogee	□ dominate	□ intrigue	□ trek

SSAT词汇 List 16

endure
[ɪnˈdjʊə] v. 忍耐,容忍

变 endurance n. 忍耐力

考 同义 endure = last; endure = stick with

类比
- flexibility 灵活性 to bend 弯曲 → stamina 持久力 to endure 容忍 (动作及其目的)
- stoicism 禁欲主义 to endurance 忍耐 → awe 敬畏 to astonishment 惊讶 (同义)
- sprint 快跑 to speed 忍耐力 → marathon 马拉松 to endurance 忍耐力 (事物及其特点)
- endurance 忍耐力 to lethargic 无生气的 → cunning 狡猾的 to naive 单纯的 (反义)

mileage
[ˈmaɪlɪdʒ] n. 英里数

记 mile 英里 + -age

考 类比
- mileage 英里数 to odometer 里程表 → humidity 湿度 to humidiometer 湿度计 (事物及其用途)
- barometer 气压计 to pressure 压力 → odometer 里程表 to mileage 英里数 (事物及其用途)

abbreviate
[əˈbriːvieɪt] v. 缩写,使简短

记 ab- + brevi- (brief) 简短的 + -ate

考 类比
- abbreviate 缩短 to shorten 缩短 → retract 撤退 to withdraw 回撤 (同义)
- abbreviate 缩短 to short 短的 → fortify 加强 to strong 强壮的 (因果)
- abbreviate 缩短 to delete 删除 → moisten 弄湿 to flood 淹没 (<程度)
- prune 修建 to eradicate 根除 → abbreviate 缩短 to delete 删除 (<程度)

trust
[trʌst] v. 信任

变 distrust v. 不信任; trusting a. 信任的

☆ endure ☆ mileage ☆ abbreviate ☆ trust

考 同义 distrust = suspicion

类比
- dishonesty (不信任) : to : distrust (不信任) → strange (奇怪的) : to : odd (奇怪的) （同义）
- lull (哄骗) : to : trust (相信) → cajole (欺骗) : to : compliance (顺从) （动作及其目的）
- compliant (顺从的) : to : servile (奴性的) → trusting (信任的) : to : gullible (易受骗的) （＜程度）
- taciturn (不太说话的) : to : quiet (安静的) → trusting (信任的) : to : gullible (易受骗的) （＜程度）

★ forswear

[fɔː'sweə] v. 发誓放弃

记 swear 本身就有"发誓"的意思
考 同义 forswear = give up

★ resilient

[rɪ'zɪlɪənt] a. 能复原的，坚强的

记 re- + -silient (silent) 安静的；坚强的 (resilient) 人就是在偃旗息鼓 (silent) 后又能重 (re) 出江湖的人
考 同义 resilient = tough

★ blemish

['blemɪʃ] v. 玷污，弄脏

变 unblemished a. 无缺点的
记 女生常用的 BB 霜英文即为 blemish balm
考 类比
- desecrate (玷污) : to : sanctity (尊严) → blemish (耽误) : to : reputation (名声) （动宾）
- impeccable (无瑕疵的) : to : fault (缺点) → unblemished (无缺点的) : to : imperfection (不完美) （反义）

★★ appropriate

[ə'prəʊprɪət] a. 合适的；v. 占用，拨出

变 inappropriate a. 不合时宜的
记 有些人觉得随便占用 (appropriate) 别人的东西也是合适的 (appropriate)
考 同义 untimely = inappropriate；appropriate = suitable；appropriate = applicable
preempt = appropriate（preempt 这个单词的英文释义为：to appropriate, seize, or take for oneself before others）

★ helmet

['helmɪt] n. 头盔

记 hel- (hell) + met (meet)：骑车不带头盔 (helmet)，那咱就只能地狱 (hell) 见 (met) 了
考 类比
- gauntlet (金属手套) : to : glove (手套) → helmet (头盔) : to : hat (帽子) （种属）
- cap (帽子) : to : baseball (棒球) → helmet (头盔) : to : cycling (骑车) （事物及其部分）

★ reciprocal

[rɪ'sɪprəkl] a. 互惠的，相互的

记 我们数学中"倒数"的英文单词即为 reciprocal

考 同义 shared = reciprocal

immobile ★★★
[ɪˈməʊbaɪl] *a.* 稳定的，不变的

变 mobility *n.* 移动性；mobilize *v.* 调动，集合
考 同义 mobilize = activate；immobile = stationary

类比
vision 视力 to lens 镜片 → mobility 移动 to crutches 拐杖 （事物及其用途）
glasses 眼睛 to sight 景象 → cane 手杖 to mobility 移动 （事物及其用途）
active 活泼的 to mobile 可移动的 → sedentary 久坐的 to immobile 不可移动的 （同义）

passion ★★
[ˈpæʃn] *n.* 激情，感情

变 passionate *a.* 热情的；dispassionate *a.* 不带感情的，平心静气的
记 pass- 词缀来自于希腊神话中的 Pan（潘神），传说此神生性好色，所以以这个词缀构成的单词均与"感情"有关
考 同义 ardor = passion

类比
apathetic 冷漠的 to phlegmatic 迟钝的 → enthusiastic 热情的 to passionate 热心的 （同义）
dispassionate 平心静气的 to partisanship 党派偏见 → intemperate 放纵的 to moderation 节制 （反义）

eerie ★★
[ˈɪəri] *a.* 可怕的，怪异的

记 一个含有 5 个字母的单词，竟然出现了 3 个 e，真的够可怕的（eerie）
考 同义 eerie = uncanny；eerie = frightening

glance ★★
[glɑːns] *v.* 一瞥，扫视

记 谐音：格兰仕：眼睛一扫视（glance），看到了"格兰仕"这个牌子
考 类比
whisper 低语 to scream 尖叫 → glance 扫视 to stare 凝视 （＜程度）
period 句号 to exclamation point 感叹号 → glance 扫视 to stare 凝视 （＜程度）

verbose ★
[vɜːˈbəʊs] *a.* 冗长的，啰嗦的

记 verb-（word）+ bose-（boss）：老板（boss）话（word）太多，显得很啰嗦（verbose）
考 类比
discursive 离题的 to focus 集中 → verbose 冗长的 to brevity 简洁 （缺乏）
verbose 啰嗦的 to wordy 冗长的 → brief 简短的 to short 短的 （同义）

conspicuous ★★★
[kənˈspɪkjuəs] *a.* 显著的，显眼的

记 con + spic- 看 + uous：因为大家都看，所以非常显眼（conspicuous）
考 同义 obvious = conspicuous；prominent = conspicuous；conspicuous = plain as day（显

类比: plausible (可信的) to believe (相信) ⇒ conspicuous (明显的) to notice (注意) （同义）
眼的，非常明显）
authoritative (权威的) to acceptance (接受) ⇒ conspicuous (显眼的) to attention (注意力) （事物及其特点）

★
spurious
['spjʊərɪəs] *a.* 伪造的，假的

记 一枚伪造的（spurious）马刺队（spur）的总冠军戒指
考 同义 fake = spurious
类比 spurious (假的) to authenticity (真实性) ⇒ laughable (可笑的) to seriousness (严肃) （反义）

★★
tribute
['trɪbjuːt] *n.* 礼物，颂词

记 雷锋的贡献（contribute）我来歌颂（tribute）
考 同义 eulogy = tribute；tribute = praise
类比 tribute (礼物) to emperor (皇帝) ⇒ tax (税) to government (政府) （人物及其对象）

★
rotten
['rɒtn] *a.* 腐烂的

记 我得到（gotten）的说法是，苹果如果不放在冰箱里就容易腐烂（rotten）
考 类比 wood (木头) to rotten (腐烂的) ⇒ bread (面包) to moldy (发霉的) （修饰）
apple (苹果) to rotten (腐烂的) ⇒ metal (铁) to rusty (生锈的) （修饰）
fresh (新鲜的) to rotten (腐烂的) ⇒ pill (药) to poison (毒药) （反义）

★
distress
[dɪ'stres] *n.* 不幸，贫困

记 因为压力（stress）太大，所以感觉很不幸（distress）
考 同义 distress = poverty

List | **15** words　　　　　　　　　　　　　　★ 复习一下学过的单词！

- advance
- concord
- mob
- scrutinize
- asset
- decorate
- recall
- supreme
- banal
- equal
- rend
- sweatpants
- blizzard
- felon
- rotate
- virtually
- characterize
- hockey
- sage
- yearn

SSAT词汇 List 17

★★ entice
[ɪnˈtaɪs] *v.* 诱使，怂恿

- 变 enticement *n.* 诱惑
- 记 这个孩子怂恿（entice）整个（entire）班级的学生跟老师作对
- 考 同义 lure = enticement；entice = tempt
- 类比 entice 诱惑 to tempt 诱惑 ⇒ consent 赞成 to agree 同意 （同义）

★ juxtapose
[ˌdʒʌkstəˈpəʊz] *v.* 并置

- 记 juxta-（next）+ pose 拜访：往旁边（next）摆放，即为并置（juxtapose）
- 考 同义 juxtapose = place side by side

★ hue
[hjuː] *n.* 色彩

- 记 苏（Sue）喜欢不同的颜色（hue）
- 考 同义 hue = color

★ lethal
[ˈliːθl] *a.* 致命的

- 记 神话传说中，人死之后要过鬼门关，经黄泉路，在黄泉路和冥府之间，由忘川河划分为界，喝了忘川河水的人就会忘记前生，这对于有情感的人类可谓是致命的打击。忘川的英文即为 Lethe，所以"致命的"英文为 lethal
- 考 同义 lethal = fatal

★★★ pinnacle
[ˈpɪnəkl] *n.* 顶点

- 记 pin 大头针 + -nacle（uncle）：叔叔（uncle）第一个到了山峰（pinnacle），奖品是个大头针（pin）
- 考 同义 peak = pinnacle；pinnacle = summit；pinnacle = acme
  pinnacle = top；apex = pinnacle
- 类比 pinnacle 顶峰 to mountain 山 ⇒ apogee 最高点 to orbit 轨道 （空间）

descent : nadir → ascent : pinnacle （纵向）
下降 : 低点 → 上升 : 顶点

注 关于"顶点"的单词在 SSAT 的习题中有很多，如：crest，zenith。

★★ pilfer
['pɪlfə] v. 偷窃

记 小偷小摸（pilfer）毁人一生（life）

考 类比
filch : pilfer → fidget : squirm （同义）
偷窃 : 偷窃 → 坐立不安 : 蠕动

swipe : pilfer → provoke : vex （同义）
偷窃 : 偷窃 → 激怒 : 使烦恼

（swipe 这个单词的英文释义为 to steal；filch）

★ gown
[gaʊn] n. 长袍

记 孩子长大（grown）了，旧的衣服（gown）不适合他了

考 类比
kimono : gown → wader : boot （种属）
和服 : 长袍 → 长筒防水靴 : 靴子

★ shard
[ʃɑːd] n. 碎片

记 即使你已心碎（shard），也不会有人和你分享（share）这份悲痛

考 类比
rubble : stone → shard : glass （事物及其部分）
碎石 : 石头 → 碎片 : 玻璃

★ racket
['rækɪt] n. 球拍

记 球拍（racket）不能用来发射火箭（rocket）

考 类比
racket : bat → tennis : baseball （纵向）
球拍 : 球棒 → 网球 : 棒球

racket : tennis → glove : box （事物及其对象）
球拍 : 网球 → 手套 : 拳击

★★ ceremonious
[ˌserɪ'məʊnɪəs] a. 隆重的，正式的

变 unceremoniousness n. 随意

记 这个单词来自 ceremony

考 类比
ceremonious : informal → clerical : secular （反义）
正式的 : 不正式的 → 牧师 : 世俗的

brusque : unceremoniousness → obstinate : intractability （同义）
唐突 : 随意 → 顽固的 : 难驾驭

★★★ obliterate
[ə'blɪtəreɪt] v. 消灭，消除

记 ob- 相反 + liter- (letter) 字母 + -ate：没有字母，即消除（obliterate）了文化

考 同义 obliterate = annihilate；obliterate = erase；obliterate = destroy；expunge = obliterate

类比
espy : scrutinize → harm : obliterate （<程度）
看到 : 仔细检查 → 伤害 : 消灭

注 关于"消除"的单词在 SSAT 的习题中有很多，如：efface, eradicate, expurgate, bowdlerize。

court ★★★

[kɔːt] *n.* 法院，球场；*v.* 求爱

变 courtship *n.* 求爱

考 类比
flirt (调情) to courtship (求爱) → banter (开玩笑) to conversation (交流) （同类）
actor (演员) to theater (剧院) → lawyer (律师) to court (法庭) （空间）
lawyer (律师) to court (法庭) → cook (厨子) to kitchen (厨房) （空间）
training center (培训中心) to practice (练习) → court (法庭) to judge (裁判) （空间）
track (跑道) to horse racing (赛马) → court (球场) to tennis (网球) （空间）

eavesdrop ★★

['iːvzdrɒp] *v.* 偷听，窃听

记 eaves 屋檐 + drop 掉落：站在屋檐（eaves）下，偷听（eavesdrop）雨滴跌落（drop）声

考 类比
snoop (窥探) to look (看) → eavesdrop (偷听) to listen (听) （同义：正反向）

feeble ★★★

['fiːbl] *a.* 虚弱的，无效的

变 enfeeble *v.* 使衰弱无力

记 他非常虚弱（feeble），所以不能（able）跑步

考 同义 feeble = rickety；feeble = ineffective；debilitate = enfeeble

类比
feeble (虚弱的) to vigor (精神) → adulterated (掺杂的) to purity (纯度) （缺乏）
feeble (虚弱的) to vigor (精神) → awkward (笨拙的) to grace (优雅) （缺乏）

注 feeble 这个单词"虚弱的"意思我们很熟悉，但有时候 SSAT 会考到这个单词"无效的"意思。

odometer ★★

[əʊ'mɒɪtə] *n.* 里程表

记 odo 希腊语词根"道路"+ -meter 测量：测量道路的工具为"里程表 odometer"

考 类比
odometer (里程表) to distance (距离) → scale (秤) to weight (重量) （事物及其用途）
barometer (气压计) to pressure (压力) → odometer (里程表) to mileage (英里数) （事物及其用途）
mileage (英里数) to odometer (里程表) → humidity (湿度) to humidiometer (湿度计) （事物及其用途）

deciduous ★

[dɪ'sɪdjʊəs] *a.* 落叶的

记 落叶的（deciduous）树木决定（decide）秋天已经开始

考 类比
deciduous (落叶的) to leaves (树叶) → evergreen (常青的) to needles (针叶) （修饰）

command ★★ [kəˈmɑːnd] v. 命令，指挥

变 commander n. 司令官，长官
记 苹果电脑左下角的第四个按键即为 command 键
考 类比
whisper 低语 to bellow 轰鸣 ⇒ suggest 建议 to command 命令 （<程度）
commander 长官 to decree 命令 ⇒ principal 校长 to discipline 纪律 （人物及其对象）

geriatrics ★ [ˌdʒeriˈætrɪks] n. 老年病学

记 这个单词是 1901 年由澳大利亚医生 Ignatz L. Nascher 首创，模仿了 pediatrics 这个单词（在古希腊语中 ger- 指的是 old age），其实 Ignatz 当年是把这个词拼写成 gerontiatrics 的
考 类比
geriatrics 老年病学 to aged 年老的 ⇒ pediatrics 儿科 to children 儿童 （人物及其对象）
senior citizens 老人 to geriatrics 老年病学 ⇒ children 儿童 to pediatrics 儿科 （人物及其对象）

innovation ★ [ˌɪnəˈveɪʃn] n. 创新

考 同义 innovation = novelty
类比 trailblazer 开拓者 to innovation 创新 ⇒ hermit 隐士 to solitude 孤独 （人物及其特点）

merchandise ★★ [ˈmɜːtʃəndaɪz] n. 商品，货物

记 我们身边的招商银行（China Merchants Bank），其中的 merchant 意思为"商人"，其变体 merchandise 即为"商品，货物"

merchandise

考 类比
menu 菜单 to food 食物 ⇒ catalog 目录 to merchandise 货物 （空间）
archive 档案馆 to documents 文件 ⇒ warehouse 仓库 to merchandise 货品 （空间）

List | 16 words ★ 复习一下学过的单词！

- abbreviate
- appropriate
- blemish
- conspicuous
- distress
- eerie
- endure
- forswear
- glance
- helmet
- immobile
- mileage
- passion
- reciprocal
- resilient
- rotten
- spurious
- tribute
- trust
- verbose

SSAT词汇 List 18

★ valet
['væleɪ] *n.* 贴身男仆

记 我的贴身男仆（valet）偷走了我的钱包（wallet）
考 同义 valet = manservant

★★ wrap
[ræp] *v.* 包装

记 注意这个单词的首字母 w 不发音，所以这个单词发音和 rap 是一样的
考 同义 wrap = envelope
类比 announce to inform ⇒ wrap to conceal （动作及其目的）
　　 宣布　　　 通知　　　　 包装　　　 隐藏
　　 preserve to store ⇒ wrap to conceal （事物及其用途）
　　 保存　　　 贮藏　　　　 包装　　　 隐藏

★ efficient
[ɪˈfɪʃnt] *a.* 有效的

考 同义 efficient = efficacious；efficient = effective

★ arduous
[ˈɑːdjuəs] *a.* 努力的，费劲的

记 这项任务很费劲（arduous），所以单靠热情（ardor）是不够的
考 同义 difficult = arduous

★★★ spark
[spɑːk] *n.* 火花

记 公园（park）起火，火花（spark）四射
考 类比 lightening to spark （事物及其特点）
　　　 闪电　　　　 火花
　　　 uprising to revolution ⇒ spark to fire （＜程度）
　　　 起义　　　 革命　　　　 火花　　 火
　　　 discontent to rebellion ⇒ friction to spark （因果）
　　　 不满　　　　 叛逆　　　　 摩擦　　　 火花

☆ valet　　☆ wrap　　☆ efficient　　☆ arduous　　☆ spark

ruse ★★

[ruːz] *n.* 策略，计谋

记 安抚生气的女朋友的策略（ruse）之一就是买玫瑰花（rose）
考 同义 ruse = trick
类比 ruse 诡计 to deceive 欺骗 ⇒ diversion 消遣 to amuse 娱乐 （事物及其用途）

drab ★

[dræb] *a.* 单调的，无聊的

记 被人拖（drag）着做那些单调无聊的（drab）事
考 同义 drab = dull

muddle ★★★

['mʌdl] *v.* 使糊涂，使困惑

记 站在吵架的婆媳之间（middle），越听越觉得困惑（muddle）
考 类比 muddle 使困惑 to reasoning 说理 ⇒ babble 乱说 to speech 演讲 （同义：正反向）
floundering 乱动 to movement 移动 ⇒ muddle 乱弄 to reasoning 讲理 （同义：正反向）
muddle 使困惑 to confusion 困惑 ⇒ cheer 使高兴 to confidence 自信 （同义）
（cheer 这个单词的英文释义为：a feeling of happiness and confidence）
muddle 使困惑 to confusion 困惑 ⇒ boost 推动 to courage 勇气 （同义）
（boost 这个单词的英文释义为：something that helps or encourages sb./sth.）

incidental ★

[ˌɪnsɪ'dentl] *a.* 附带的，偶然的

记 这个事件（incident）的发生纯属偶然（incidental）
考 同义 incidental = minor

bassinet ★

[ˌbæsɪ'net] *n.* 摇篮

记 bassi-（basket）+ net 网：由网（net）织成的篮子（basket）即为摇篮（bassinet）
考 类比 bassinet 摇篮 to crib 婴儿床 ⇒ car 汽车 to taxicab 出租车 （同义）

firmament ★

['fɜːməmənt] *n.* 天空

记 注意区分 firmament "天空" 和 filament "灯丝"
考 同义 firmament = sky
类比 star 星星 to firmament 天空 （空间）

amulet
['æmjʊlət] *n.* 护身符

记 护身符（amulet）是个很有趣的（amusing）东西
考 同义 amulet = talisman

amulet

infamous
['ɪnfəməs] *a.* 臭名昭著的

记 注意这个单词是"臭名昭著的"意思，不是"没有名气的"意思
考 同义 notorious = infamous

类比 infamous 臭名昭著的 to corruption 贪污 ⇒ admirable 令人羡慕的 to nobility 高尚 （因果）

loathe
[ləʊð] *v.* 讨厌，厌恶

记 我很讨厌（loathe）誓言（oath）这类虚伪的东西
考 类比 loathe 极其厌恶 to dislike 不喜欢 ⇒ pulverize 粉碎 to break 打破 （>程度）

hesitate 犹豫 to waver 犹豫 ⇒ loathe 讨厌 to detest 厌恶 （同义）

reprimand 训斥 to commend 表扬 ⇒ loathe 厌恶 to adore 羡慕 （反义）

注 关于"厌恶"的单词在 SSAT 的习题中有很多，如：abhor, despise。

bellicose
['belɪkəʊs] *a.* 好战的，好斗的

记 bell 来自战争女神 Bellona（她的丈夫是战神 Mars）
考 同义 belligerent = bellicose；bellicose = combative

类比 swift 快的 to fast 快的 ⇒ bellicose 好战的 to warlike 好战的 （同义）

chandelier
[ˌʃændə'lɪə] *n.* 枝形吊灯

记 钱德勒（Chandler）正站在梯子上，安装枝形吊灯（chandelier）
考 类比 chandelier 枝形吊灯 to ceiling 房顶 ⇒ bat 蝙蝠 to cave 洞穴 （空间）

ceiling 枝形吊灯 to chandelier 房顶 ⇒ puppeteer 操纵木偶者 to puppet 木偶 （空间）

prototype
['prəʊtətaɪp] *n.* 原型，标准

记 proto- 最初，原始 + type 类型
考 同义 prototype = model；prototype = paradigm

★★★ ravenous

['rævənəs] *a.* 贪婪的

记 一只贪婪的（ravenous）的大乌鸦（raven）
考 同义 ravenous＝gluttonous；ravenous＝voracious

类比
ravenous 贪婪的	to	hunger 饥饿	⇒	furious 狂怒的	to	indignation 愤慨	（＞程度）
ravenous 贪婪的	to	hunger 饥饿	⇒	parched 非常口渴的	to	thirsty 口渴的	（＞程度）
ravenous 贪婪的	to	hungry 饥饿的	⇒	stingy 小气的	to	thrifty 节约的	（＞程度）
ravenous 贪婪的	to	hungry 饥饿的	⇒	jubilant 喜气洋洋的	to	happy 快乐的	（＞程度）
livid 非常生气的	to	anger 生气	⇒	ravenous 贪婪的	to	hungry 饥饿的	（＞程度）
ravenous 贪婪的	to	famished 饥饿的	⇒	dismayed 难过的	to	distressed 痛苦的	（同义）
fanatic 狂热者	to	devoted 忠诚的	⇒	gourmet 美食家	to	ravenous 贪吃的	（人物及其特点）

★ nebulous

['nebjʊləs] *a.* 星云的，模糊的

记 nebul-（nebula）星云的 + -ous
考 同义 vague＝nebulous；nebulous＝opaque

★ covert

['kʌvət] *a.* 隐蔽的，秘密的

记 闭（cover）嘴，这是个秘密的（covert）事
考 同义 covert＝undercover
注 关于"秘密的"单词在 SSAT 的习题中有很多，如：stealthy, clandestine, surreptitious, secretive。

List | 17 words

★ 复习一下学过的单词！

☐ ceremonious	☐ entice	☐ innovation	☐ odometer
☐ command	☐ feeble	☐ juxtapose	☐ pilfer
☐ court	☐ geriatrics	☐ lethal	☐ pinnacle
☐ deciduous	☐ gown	☐ merchandise	☐ racket
☐ eavesdrop	☐ hue	☐ obliterate	☐ shard

☆ ravenous   ☆ nebulous   ☆ covert

SSAT词汇 List 19

★ dissemble
[dɪˈsembl] *v.* 掩饰，隐藏
记 难以掩饰（dissemble）两个双胞胎长得很像（resemble）这个事实
考 同义　dissemble = guise

★ oath
[əʊθ] *n.* 誓言，誓约
记 律师在法庭上要求证人必须说实话的时候会说："You are under oath."
考 同义　oath = vow

★ zenith
[ˈzenɪθ] *n.* 顶峰，顶点
记 谐音：让你撕：让你在顶峰（zenith）撕纸
考 同义　zenith = summit
注 关于"顶点"的单词在SSAT的习题中有很多，如：crest, pinnacle, acme。

★ inkling
[ˈɪŋklɪŋ] *n.* 暗示
记 墨水（ink）痕迹暗示（inkling）他是个舞文弄墨的人
考 同义　inkling = hint
类比　lapse (to) error ⇒ inkling (to) indication　（<程度）
　　　过失　　错误　　　暗示　　指示

★★★ impervious
[ɪmˈpɜːviəs] *a.* 不受影响的，无法入侵的
记 im- 否定 + pervi- (pervade) 遍及，弥漫 + -ous
考 同义　impervious = sealed
类比　invincible (to) subdued ⇒ impervious (to) damaged　（反义）
　　　战无不胜的　被制服的　　不受影响的　破坏的
　　　insatiable (to) satisfied ⇒ impervious (to) penetrated　（反义）
　　　不知足的　　满意的　　　无法入侵的　刺穿的
　　　obstruct (to) impede ⇒ impenetrable (to) impervious　（同义）
　　　妨碍　　　阻碍　　　不能通过的　　无法入侵的

☆ dissemble　　☆ oath　　☆ zenith　　☆ inkling　　☆ impervious

gloomy ★★
['gluːmi] *a.* 忧郁的，黑暗的

记 新郎（groom）因为没钱给新娘买戒指，显得非常忧郁（gloomy）
考 同义 gloomy = murky; gloomy = somber
类比 gloomy 忧郁的 to lugubrious 悲哀的 ⇒ pleasant 快乐的 to ecstatic 狂喜的 （<程度）

liaison ★
[lɪˈeɪzn] *n.* 联络，联合

记 li-李 + ai-艾 + son：离婚之后，儿子（son）是老李家和老艾家的唯一联系（liaison）了
考 同义 association = liaison

liaison

cast ★★
[kɑːst] *n.* 全体演员

记 全体演员（cast）请在城堡（castle）门口集合
考 类比 choir 合唱队 to singer 歌手 ⇒ cast 全体演员 to actor 演员 （组成）
cast 全体演员 to actor 演员 ⇒ staff 全体员工 to member 成员 （组成）
conductor 指挥 to orchestra 管弦乐队 ⇒ director 导演 to cast 全体演员 （人物及其对象）

tractor ★★
[ˈtræktə] *n.* 拖拉机

记 tract- 拉 + -or：拉（tract）着你动的东西即为拖拉机 tractor
考 类比 tractor 拖拉机 to farmer 农民 ⇒ baton 指挥棒 to conductor 指挥 （人物及其工具）
tractor 拖拉机 to farmer 农民 ⇒ plane 飞机 to aviator 飞行员 （人物及其工具）
tractor 拖拉机 to farmer 农民 ⇒ joke 笑话 to comedian 喜剧演员 （人物及其工具）

pungent ★★★
[ˈpʌndʒənt] *a.* 辛辣的，刺激性的，刺鼻的

记 孕妇（pregnant）不能吃辛辣的（pungent）食物
考 同义 pungent = smelly
类比 pungent 辛辣的 to flavor 口味 ⇒ poignant 尖锐的 to criticism 批评 （修饰）
pungent 刺激性的 to flower 花 ⇒ poignant 辛酸的 to emotion 情感 （修饰）
pungent 刺激性的 to flower 花 ⇒ poignant 辛酸的 to speech 演讲 （修饰）
pungent 刺鼻的 to odor 味道 ⇒ intense 强烈的 to emotion 情感 （修饰）

property

[ˈprɒpəti] *n.* 财产，地产

记 选择去投资合适的（proper）财产（property）
考 同义　property = chattel
类比　rent 组 to property 地产 ⇒ hire 雇用 to employee 员工 （动宾）
　　　impound 扣押 to property 财产 ⇒ imprison 囚禁 to person 人 （动宾）
　　　trespasser 侵入者 to property 财产 ⇒ invader 入侵者 to nation 国家 （人物及其对象）

repugnant

[rɪˈpʌgnənt] *a.* 讨厌的，敌对的

记 re- + pugnant（pregnant）：收入不高的妻子再次（re）怀孕（pregnant），觉得挺烦（repugnant）
考 同义　offensive = repugnant；repugnant = disgusting

livid

[ˈlɪvɪd] *a.* 非常生气的

记 男女明星隐私照片被拍得栩栩如生（vivid），让明星很生气（livid）
考 同义　livid = furious
类比　livid 非常生气的 to anger 生气 ⇒ radiant 容光焕发的 to happiness 快乐 （>程度）
　　　livid 非常生气的 to anger 生气 ⇒ ravenous 贪婪的 to hungry 饥饿的 （>程度）

adjoin

[əˈdʒɔɪn] *v.* 连接，毗邻

记 因为加入（join）所以毗邻（adjoin）
考 同义　adjoin = connect

instruction

[ɪnˈstrʌkʃn] *n.* 指示，说明

变 instruct *v.* 指导
记 我们购买的很多物品外包装上都有这个单词，对应的翻译是"说明书"
考 同义　paternalism = parent instruction
类比　cookbook 烹饪书 to recipes 食谱 ⇒ manual 手册 to instructions 说明 （组成）
　　　atlas 地图集 to maps 地图 ⇒ manual 手册 to instructions 说明 （组成）

repeal
[rɪˈpiːl] v. 废除，撤销

记 被告上诉（appeal）成功，法官撤销（repeal）第一次的审判

考 类比 repeal/撤销 to enact/颁布 ⇒ splice/拼接 to separate/分开 （反义）
　　　 retract/撤销 to statement/言论 ⇒ repeal/废除 to legislation/立法 （动宾）

wither
[ˈwɪðə] v. 枯萎

记 天气（weather）不好，花都枯萎（wither）了
考 同义 wither = fade

headstrong
[ˈhedstrɒŋ] a. 倔强的

记 倔强的（headstrong）人都头（head）脑简单、四肢发达（strong）
考 同义 headstrong = stubborn

slippery
[ˈslɪpəri] a. 滑的

变 slipper n. 拖鞋
记 slip 滑 + pery
考 同义 lubricant = slippery
　　类比 slipper/拖鞋 to feet/脚 （空间）

trophy
[ˈtrəʊfi] n. 奖品

记 因为胜利（triumph），所以获得奖品（trophy）
考 类比 remuneration/报酬 to labor/劳动 ⇒ trophy/奖品 to victory/胜利 （事物及其对象）
　　　 contestant/竞争者 to trophy/奖品 ⇒ student/学生 to honor/荣誉 （人物及其对象）

List | 18 words ★ 复习一下学过的单词！

□ amulet	□ covert	□ infamous	□ ravenous
□ arduous	□ drab	□ loathe	□ ruse
□ bassinet	□ efficient	□ muddle	□ spark
□ bellicose	□ firmament	□ nebulous	□ valet
□ chandelier	□ incidental	□ prototype	□ wrap

☆ repeal　　☆ wither　　☆ headstrong　　☆ slippery　　☆ trophy

SSAT词汇 List 20

★★
colossus [kəˈlɒsəs] *n.* 巨像

变 colossal *a.* 巨大的
记 这个单词来自 colosseum，原指"古罗马巨大的斗兽场"
考 同义 colossal = gigantic；enormous statue = colossus
类比 enormous/巨大的 to colossal/巨大的 ⇒ fundamental/基础的 to rudimentary/基础的 （同义）

★★★
bouquet [bʊˈkeɪ] *n.* 花束

记 宴会（banquet）上放了很多花束（bouquet）
考 同义 bouquet = nosegay
类比 bouquet/花束 to flower/花 ⇒ chain/链条 to link/一个链条 （组成）
bouquet/花束 to flower/花 ⇒ forest/森林 to tree/树木 （组成）
daisy/雏菊 to bouquet/花束 ⇒ grape/葡萄 to bunch/一串葡萄 （组成）

★
oblivious [əˈblɪviəs] *a.* 遗忘的，健忘的

记 很明显（obvious）他是个健忘的（oblivious）人
考 同义 oblivious = forgetful

★
debilitate [dɪˈbɪlɪteɪt] *v.* 使……衰弱，使……虚弱

记 de- 否定 + bilitate（ability）：让你失去能力，即为 debilitate
考 同义 debilitate = enfeeble；weaken = debilitate

★★★
solution [səˈluːʃn] *n.* 解决方案；溶液

考 类比 fossil/化石 to petrified/石化的 ⇒ solution/溶液 to dissolved/溶解的 （修饰）
riddle/谜语 to solution/解决方案 ⇒ question/问题 to answer/答案 （事物及其对象）

☆ colossus　　☆ bouquet　　☆ oblivious　　☆ debilitate　　☆ solution

$\dfrac{\text{clue}}{\text{线索}}$ to $\dfrac{\text{solution}}{\text{解决方案}}$ ⇒ $\dfrac{\text{signpost}}{\text{路标}}$ to $\dfrac{\text{destination}}{\text{终点}}$ （＜程度）

tenacious
[tɪ'neɪʃəs] *a.* 顽强的

- 记 tenacious 和 pertinacious 这两个单词不仅长得像，意思也类似
- 考 同义 persistent = tenacious；tenacious = unyielding
- 注 关于"顽强的"单词在 SSAT 的习题中有很多，如：perseverant，unswerving，steadfast。

understate
[ˌʌndə'steɪt] *v.* 保守的说，轻描淡写

- 变 understated *a.* 轻描淡写的，微妙的
- 记 under 下面 + state 陈述
- 考 同义 understated = subtle；understate = downplay

chemist
['kemɪst] *n.* 化学家

- 考 类比 $\dfrac{\text{beaker}}{\text{烧杯}}$ to $\dfrac{\text{chemist}}{\text{化学家}}$ ⇒ $\dfrac{\text{hammer}}{\text{锤子}}$ to $\dfrac{\text{geologist}}{\text{地质学家}}$ （人物及其工具）

  $\dfrac{\text{chemistry}}{\text{化学}}$ to $\dfrac{\text{alchemy}}{\text{炼金术}}$ ⇒ $\dfrac{\text{astronomy}}{\text{天文学}}$ to $\dfrac{\text{astrology}}{\text{占星术}}$ （同义 新旧之称）

inter
[ɪn'tɜː] *v.* 埋葬

- 变 interment *n.* 埋葬
- 记 这个失误埋葬（inter）了这个实习生（intern）的工作前景
- 考 同义 interment = burial

  类比 $\dfrac{\text{inter}}{\text{埋葬}}$ to $\dfrac{\text{tomb}}{\text{坟墓}}$ ⇒ $\dfrac{\text{deposit}}{\text{存钱}}$ to $\dfrac{\text{bank}}{\text{银行}}$ （空间）

steady
['stedi] *a.* 稳定的

- 考 同义 imperturbable = steady

replica
['replɪkə] *n.* 复制品

- 记 老板，你卖给我的是仿真品（replica），你总得给我个合理的答复（reply）吧
- 考 同义 copy = replica

roar
[rɔː] *v.* 咆哮

- 记 边划桨（oar）边嚎叫（roar），希望船队赶快到
- 考 类比 $\dfrac{\text{rustle}}{\text{沙沙作响}}$ to $\dfrac{\text{roar}}{\text{咆哮}}$ ⇒ $\dfrac{\text{walk}}{\text{走路}}$ to $\dfrac{\text{run}}{\text{跑步}}$ （＜程度）

★★ mundane

[mʌnˈdeɪn] *a.* 世俗的，常见的

记 明天又是一个日复一日（mundane）的周一（Monday）
考 同义　mundane = common；mundane = boring；mundane = routine

★★★ auspicious

[ɔːˈspɪʃəs] *a.* 吉利的，幸运的

变 inauspicious *a.* 不详的，不吉利的
记 胆大的（audacious）孩子都有一个幸运的（auspicious）前程
考 同义　auspicious = favorable；auspicious = opportune；ominous = inauspicious

类比　$\dfrac{\text{auspicious}}{\text{吉利的}}$ to $\dfrac{\text{ominous}}{\text{恶兆的}}$ ⇒ $\dfrac{\text{timely}}{\text{及时的}}$ to $\dfrac{\text{inopportune}}{\text{不适当的}}$ （反义）

★ jollity

[ˈdʒɒlɪti] *n.* 高兴

记 能吃到果冻（jelly）就很高兴（jollity）
考 同义　jollity = merriment

类比　$\dfrac{\text{flippancy}}{\text{轻浮}}$ to $\dfrac{\text{jollity}}{\text{快乐}}$ ⇒ $\dfrac{\text{insolence}}{\text{傲慢}}$ to $\dfrac{\text{pride}}{\text{自豪}}$ （同义：正反向）

★★ ink

[ɪŋk] *n.* 墨水

考 类比　$\dfrac{\text{brick}}{\text{砖头}}$ to $\dfrac{\text{wall}}{\text{墙}}$ ⇒ $\dfrac{\text{ink}}{\text{墨水}}$ to $\dfrac{\text{painting}}{\text{图画}}$ （事物及其用途）

$\dfrac{\text{ink cartridge}}{\text{墨盒}}$ to $\dfrac{\text{printer}}{\text{打印机}}$ ⇒ $\dfrac{\text{seat}}{\text{椅子}}$ to $\dfrac{\text{theater}}{\text{剧院}}$ （空间）

$\dfrac{\text{heater}}{\text{加热器}}$ to $\dfrac{\text{hot tub}}{\text{热水浴缸}}$ ⇒ $\dfrac{\text{ink}}{\text{墨水}}$ to $\dfrac{\text{printer}}{\text{打印机}}$ （空间）

★ furl

[fɜːl] *v.* 卷起，折叠

变 unfurl *v.* 展开
记 偷猎者卷起（furl）手中的动物皮（fur），打算悄悄过海关
考 同义　furl = roll up；unfurl = spread out

★★★ bloom

[bluːm] *v.* 开花

变 blooming *a.* 开花的
记 用扫帚（broom）扫去昨晚的残花（bloom）
考 类比　$\dfrac{\text{blossom}}{\text{开花}}$ to $\dfrac{\text{bloom}}{\text{开花}}$ ⇒ $\dfrac{\text{quiver}}{\text{震颤}}$ to $\dfrac{\text{vibrate}}{\text{震动}}$ （同义）

$\dfrac{\text{river}}{\text{河流}}$ to $\dfrac{\text{flow}}{\text{流动}}$ ⇒ $\dfrac{\text{flower}}{\text{花}}$ to $\dfrac{\text{bloom}}{\text{开花}}$ （事物及其动作）

$\dfrac{\text{blooming}}{\text{开花的}}$ to $\dfrac{\text{rose}}{\text{玫瑰花}}$ ⇒ $\dfrac{\text{ripe}}{\text{成熟的}}$ to $\dfrac{\text{tomato}}{\text{番茄}}$ （修饰）

☆ mundane　　☆ auspicious　　☆ jollity　　☆ ink　　☆ furl
☆ bloom

★★ universe

['juːnɪvɜːs] *n.* 宇宙

记 uni- 一个 + -verse 转：世间万物都围绕着一个（uni）宇宙（universe）在转（verse）

考 类比 $\frac{hand}{手}$ to $\frac{body}{身体}$ ⇒ $\frac{star}{星星}$ to $\frac{universe}{宇宙}$ （空间）

$\frac{pandemic}{大流行病}$ to $\frac{endemic}{地方性疾病}$ ⇒ $\frac{universe}{宇宙}$ to $\frac{aboriginal}{当地}$ （＞程度）

★ deft

[deft] *a.* 灵巧的，机敏的

记 左（left）撇子一般都比较灵巧（deft）
考 同义 deft = skillful

List | **19** words   ★ 复习一下学过的单词！

□ adjoin	□ impervious	□ oath	□ slippery
□ cast	□ inkling	□ property	□ tractor
□ dissemble	□ instruction	□ pungent	□ trophy
□ gloomy	□ liaison	□ repeal	□ wither
□ headstrong	□ livid	□ repugnant	□ zenith

SSAT词汇 List 21

★★ phlegmatic [flegˈmætɪk] *a.* 冷淡的，迟钝的

记 phlegm 本意为"黏液"，古人认为黏液多的人不易激动，行动较迟缓（phlegmatic）

考 类比 apathy (冷漠) to phlegmatic (迟钝的) ⇒ zeal (热情) to enthusiastic (热心的) （同义）
apathetic (冷漠的) to phlegmatic (迟钝的) ⇒ enthusiastic (热情的) to passionate (热心的) （同义）

注 关于"冷漠的"单词在 SSAT 的习题中有很多，如：aloof, detached, indifferent, impassive, nonchalant。

★★★ reluctant [rɪˈlʌktənt] *a.* 不情愿的

变 reluctance *n.* 不情愿
记 谐音：驴拉个坦克：你让驴拉个坦克，它肯定不情愿（reluctant）
考 同义 loath = reluctant

类比 reluctance (不情愿) to willing (愿意) （反义）
dauntless (胆大的) to fear (恐惧) ⇒ eager (渴望的) to reluctance (不情愿) （反义）
reluctant (不情愿的) to eager (渴望的) ⇒ timid (胆小的) to courageous (勇敢的) （反义）

★★★ ecstatic [ekˈstætɪk] *a.* 狂喜的

记 ecstatic 的名词形式是 ecstasy，因为有"狂喜"的意思，所以在美国 ecstasy 是毒品的代名词

考 类比 ecstatic (狂喜的) to happy (快乐的) ⇒ servile (奴性的) to submissive (顺从的) （＞程度）
eager (渴望的) to fervent (强烈的) ⇒ pleased (开心的) to ecstatic (狂喜的) （＜程度）
clean (干净的) to pristine (极其洁净的) ⇒ happy (开心的) to ecstatic (狂喜的) （＜程度）
scalding (滚烫的) to tepid (微温的) ⇒ ecstatic (狂喜的) to satisfied (满意的) （＞程度）
gloomy (忧郁的) to lugubrious (悲哀的) ⇒ pleasant (快乐的) to ecstatic (狂喜的) （＜程度）

☆ phlegmatic　　☆ reluctant　　☆ ecstatic

circumspect
['sɜːkəmspekt] *a.* 细心的，慎重的

- 变 circumspection *n.* 慎重，细心
- 记 circum- 环绕 + -spect 看：因为到处去看，所以显得很慎重（circumspect）
- 考 同义 caution = circumspection

类比 circumspect 慎重的 → to wary 谨慎的 ⇒ reckless 鲁莽的 → to foolhardy 有勇无谋的 （同义）

expropriate
[eks'prəuprieit] *v.* 没收

- 记 合适的（appropriate）东西可以保留，非法的东西必须没收（expropriate）
- 考 同义 expropriate = confiscate

boulder
['bəuldə] *n.* 大石头

- 记 肩（shoulder）上扛个大石头（boulder）
- 考 类比 stream 小溪 → to drop 水滴 ⇒ boulder 大石头 → to pebble 鹅卵石 （＞程度）

fecund
['fekənd] *a.* 肥沃的，多产的

- 记 谐音：因为非（常）肯（努力），所以有成果（fecund）
- 考 同义 fecund = fruitful

perspire
[pə'spaiə] *v.* 流汗，出汗

- 变 perspiration *n.* 出汗，流汗
- 记 per- 始终 + spire（Sprite）雪碧：因为始终出汗（perspire），所以想喝雪碧（Sprite）冷静一下
- 考 类比 exhale 呼出 → to lung 肺 ⇒ perspire 呼吸 → to skin 皮肤 （事物及其用途）
  perspiration 出汗 → to nervous 紧张 ⇒ shivering 颤抖 → to cold 冷的 （因果）

arable
['ærəbl] *a.* 可耕种的

- 记 Arab 阿拉伯 + le 乐：看到沙漠中可耕种的（arable）绿洲，阿拉伯人乐了
- 考 类比 arable 可耕种的 → to cultivation 耕作 ⇒ navigable 可航行的 → to sailing 航行 （同义）

claw
[klɔː] *n.* 爪子

- 记 法律（law）规定色狼不要将爪子（claw）伸向女乘客
- 考 类比 cat 猫 → to claw 爪 ⇒ eagle 鹰 → to talon 爪 （事物及其部分）
  person 人 → to fingernail 指甲 ⇒ eagle 鹰 → to claw 爪 （事物及其部分）
  lion 狮子 → to horse 马 ⇒ claw 爪子 → to hoof 蹄子 （纵向）

agile ★★★ [ˈædʒaɪl] *a.* 敏捷的

- 变 agility *n.* 敏捷，灵敏
- 记 他虽然身体很脆弱（fragile），但是依然身手敏捷（agile）
- 考 同义 agile = nimble; agile = adept; agile = quick; agility = nimbleness

类比
- agile 敏捷的 to brisk 敏锐的 ⇒ monitor 监控 to check 检查 （同义）
- agility 敏捷 to gymnastics 体操 ⇒ strength 力气 to weight-lifting 举重 （事物及其特点）
- articulate 雄辩的 to orator 演讲者 ⇒ agile 灵活的 to acrobat 杂技演员 （人物及其特点）

default ★ [dɪˈfɔːlt] *v.* 拖欠，不履行

- 记 拖欠（default）别人的钱是个错误（fault）
- 考 同义 renege = default

deplete ★ [dɪˈpliːt] *v.* 耗尽，耗干

- 记 因为总删除（delete）资源，所以最终资源耗尽（deplete）
- 考 同义 deplete = reduce

salutary ★ [ˈsæljʊtri] *a.* 有益的，有好处的

- 记 谐音：仨六：揭牌时候连续揭到仨六，对自己赢牌大有好处（salutary）
- 考 同义 beneficial = salutary

relinquish ★ [rɪˈlɪŋkwɪʃ] *v.* 放弃

- 记 re- 回 + -linquish（lingual）语言的：不说（re）自己的语言（lingual）即为放弃（relinquish）
- 考 同义 relinquish = surrender; relinquish = give up; relinquish = concede

quarry ★★★ [ˈkwɒri] *n.* 采石场

- 记 在采石场（quarry）和别人吵架（quarrel）
- 考 类比
  - stone 石头 to quarry 采石场 ⇒ fruit 水果 to orchard 果园 （空间）
  - rock 石头 to quarry 采石场 ⇒ coal 煤 to mine 煤矿 （空间）
  - marble 大理石 to quarry 采石场 ⇒ ore 矿石 to mine 矿藏 （空间）

foolhardy ★★ [ˈfuːlhɑːdi] *a.* 有勇无谋的

- 记 有勇无谋的（foolhardy）人就像个傻子（fool）一样，再难（hard）的事情都会上
- 考 类比 foolhardy 蛮干的 to recklessness 鲁莽 ⇒ serene 安静的 to tranquility 安静 （同义）

circumspect —to→ wary ⇒ reckless —to→ foolhardy （同义）
慎重的　　　　谨慎的　　　鲁莽的　　　　有勇无谋的

注 关于"胆大的"单词在 SSAT 的习题中有很多，如：bold, audacious, insolent。

keen

[ki:n] *a.* 敏锐的

变 keenness *n.* 敏锐，锐利
记 保持（keep）敏锐（keen）
考 同义 keen = sharp; keenness = acumen

score

[skɔː] *n.* 乐谱；比分

考 类比
score —to→ composer ⇒ prescription —to→ doctor （人物及其对象）
乐谱　　作曲家　　　　药方　　　　医生

architect —to→ blueprint ⇒ composer —to→ score （人物及其对象）
建筑师　　　蓝图　　　　作曲家　　　乐谱

composer —to→ score ⇒ author —to→ book （人物及其对象）
作曲家　　　乐谱　　　作者　　　书

director —to→ script ⇒ conductor —to→ score （人物及其对象）
导演　　　脚本　　　指挥家　　　乐谱

actor —to→ script ⇒ musician —to→ score （人物及其对象）
演员　　剧本　　　音乐家　　　乐谱

score —to→ game ⇒ egg —to→ chicken （事物及其对象）
比分　　比赛　　鸡蛋　　鸡

canvas

[ˈkænvəs] *n.* 帆布，画布

记 我们常说的匡威（converse）鞋，其实是一种帆布（canvas）鞋

考 类比
paper —to→ novel ⇒ canvas —to→ portrait （空间）
纸　　小说　　画布　　肖像画

billboard —to→ advertisement ⇒ canvas —to→ painting
广告牌　　　　广告　　　　画布　　　绘画
（事物及其用途）

leather —to→ belt ⇒ canvas —to→ jeans （事物及其用途）
皮革　　皮带　　帆布　　牛仔裤

canvas

List | 20 words　　　　★ 复习一下学过的单词！

- auspicious
- bloom
- bouquet
- chemist
- colossus
- debilitate
- deft
- furl
- ink
- inter
- jollity
- mundane
- oblivious
- replica
- roar
- solution
- steady
- tenacious
- understate
- universe

86　　☆ keen　　☆ score　　☆ canvas

SSAT词汇 List 22

★★★ lens
[lenz] *n.* 镜头，镜片

记 我把我的单反镜头 (lens) 借 (lend) 给你

考 类比
- lens 镜片 to glass 玻璃 ⇒ sweater 毛衣 to wool 羊毛 （组成）
- pane 窗格 to window 窗户 ⇒ lens 镜片 to spectacles 眼镜 （组成）
- vision 视力 to lens 镜片 ⇒ mobility 移动 to crutches 拐杖 （事物及其用途）
- lens 镜片 to spectacles 眼镜 ⇒ mirror 镜子 to dresser 梳妆台 （事物及其部分）
- lens 镜片 to glasses 眼镜 ⇒ engine 发动机 to truck 卡车 （事物及其部分）
- stamen 雄蕊 to flower 花 ⇒ lens 眼睛里的晶状体 to eye 眼睛 （空间）

注 lens 这个单词的意思是：the part behind the pupil that focuses light and helps you to see clearly。

★★ witness
['wɪtnəs] *n.* 目击者；*v.* 目击

记 骗子说，只有智慧 (wit) 的人才能看到 (witness) 皇帝的新衣

考 类比
- witness 目击者 to trial 审判 （空间）
- discern 识别 to perceptive 感知 ⇒ see 看见 to witness 目击 （同义）
- spectator 观众 to tournament 锦标赛 ⇒ witness 目击者 to crime 犯罪 （人物及其对象）
- testimony 证词 to witness 目击者 ⇒ proof 证据 to theorist 理论家 （人物及其对象）

★★★ exaggeration
[ɪɡˌzædʒəˈreɪʃn] *n.* 夸张

变 exaggerated *a.* 夸张的

记 exag- (exact) +-geration (generation)：上下两代人

exaggeration

☆ lens ☆ witness ☆ exaggeration

（generation）长相精确到（exact）一模一样，真夸张（exaggeration）

考 同义　exaggeration = aggrandizement；exaggeration = hyperbole
　　　　　hyperbole = exaggerated expression

类比　hyperbole 夸张 to exaggeration 夸张 ⇒ ornament 装饰 to decoration 装饰　（同义）

　　　overblown 过分渲染的 to exaggerated 夸张的 ⇒ warranted 保证的 to justified 保证的　（同义）

altimeter
['æltɪmɪtə] n. 测高仪，高度计

记　alt- 高 + meter- 测量

考　类比　weight 重量 to scale 天平 ⇒ altitude 高度 to altimeter 测高仪　（事物及其对象）

　　　　　altimeter 测高仪 to height 高度 ⇒ speedometer 测速仪 to velocity 速度　（事物及其对象）

veto
['viːtəʊ] v. 否决

记　你支持（vote）而我反对（veto）
考　同义　veto = reject

terse
[tɜːs] a. 简洁的

记　用一个短语（term）来概括一篇文章，真够简洁的（terse）
考　同义　terse = aphoristic

类比　terse 简洁的 to language 语言 ⇒ frugal 节俭的 to money 钱　（缺乏）

注　关于"简洁的"单词在 SSAT 的习题中有很多，如：brief, concise, laconic, succinct。

whim
[wɪm] n. 奇想，心血来潮

变　whimsical a. 异想天开的
记　他（him）突然心血来潮（whim）想要学习英语
考　同义　caprice = whim；whim = impulse；whimsical = fanciful；whimsical = fickle

paltry
['pɔːltri] a. 微小的，不重要的

记　家禽（poultry）对于城里人来说是不重要的（paltry）
考　同义　paltry = worthless；paltry = meager；paltry = unimportant
　　　　　paltry = trifling；insignificant = paltry

recollect
[ˌrekə'lekt] v. 回忆，想起

变　recollection n. 回忆

考 同义 reminisce = recollect；recollect = remember；reminiscence = recollection

★ stool
[stuːl] n. 凳子

记 她站在（stood）凳子（stool）上演讲
考 类比 coat/外套 to jacket/夹克 → chair/椅子 to stool/凳子 （同义）

★★ autobiography
[ˌɔːtəbaɪˈɒɡrəfi] n. 自传

记 auto- 自己 + bio- 生命 + graph- 写 + y：写关于自己生命的东西
考 类比 autobiography/自传 to literature/文学 → ballad/歌谣 to song/音乐 （种属）
autobiography/自传 to author/作者 → self-portrait/自画像 to artist/画家 （人物及其目的）

★★★ jovial
[ˈdʒəʊviəl] a. 快乐的

记 来源于主神朱庇特（jupiter），他被人认为是快乐的源泉
考 同义 jovial = happy；jovial = jubilant；jovial = cheerful
类比 jaunt/短途旅游 to jovial/快乐的 → odyssey/长途跋涉 to suffering/苦难的 （纵向）

★ avocation
[ˌævəˈkeɪʃn] n. 副业

记 a- 否 + vocation 职业
考 同义 avocation = side job

★ sojourn
[ˈsɒdʒən] v. 逗留，停留

记 谐音：so John（约翰）的女朋友在问他：So, John. You wanna sojourn here?
考 同义 sojourn = visit

★ ornery
[ˈɔːnəri] a. 坏脾气的

记 一个很普通（ordinary）、脾气却很大（ornery）的人
考 同义 ornery = cranky

★ salvage
[ˈsælvɪdʒ] v. 打捞，救助

记 salva-（save）+ age
考 同义 salvage = save
类比 salvage/营救 to wreck/失事船只 → excavate/挖掘 to ruin/废墟 （动宾）

☆ stool ☆ autobiography ☆ jovial ☆ avocation ☆ sojourn
☆ ornery ☆ salvage

satiate ★★
['seɪʃIeɪt] v. 充分满足

- 变 satiated a. 充分满足的
- 记 satiate 和 satisfy 相同，都含有词根 satis- "足够的"
- 考 同义 satiate = fill

类比 satiate 使满足 —to→ satisfy 满足 ⇒ gregarious 社交的 —to→ social 社交的 （同义）

satiated 满足的 —to→ hunger 饥饿 ⇒ adroit 敏捷的 —to→ clumsiness 笨拙 （反义）

badger ★
['bædʒə] v. 烦扰

- 记 bad + -ger (girl): 坏女孩 (bad girl) 总是让人烦恼 (badger)
- 考 同义 badger = vex

quill ★
[kwɪl] n.（豪猪身上的）刚毛

- 记 qu 去 + ill: 用刚毛 (quill) 去 (qu) 扎你，你就会生病 (ill)
- 考 类比 scent 味道 —to→ skunk 臭鼬 ⇒ quills 刚毛 —to→ porcupine 豪猪 （事物及其部分）

thorn 刺 —to→ rose 玫瑰 ⇒ quill 刚毛 —to→ porcupine 豪猪 （事物及其部分）

combative ★
['kɒmbətɪv] a. 好战的

- 记 combat 战斗 + -ive
- 考 同义 combative = bellicose; combative = argumentative

List | **21** words ★ 复习一下学过的单词！

☐ agile	☐ claw	☐ fecund	☐ quarry
☐ arable	☐ default	☐ foolhardy	☐ relinquish
☐ boulder	☐ deplete	☐ keen	☐ reluctant
☐ canvas	☐ ecstatic	☐ perspire	☐ salutary
☐ circumspect	☐ expropriate	☐ phlegmatic	☐ score

SSAT词汇 List 23

★★★
reminisce [ˌremɪˈnɪs] *v.* 回忆，追忆

- 变 reminiscence *n.* 回忆，怀旧
- 记 re- 再次 + mini- 小 + -sce：重新（re）回忆（reminisce）起自己的小车（mini cooper）
- 考 同义 reminisce = recollect；reminiscence = recollection
  类比 reminisce/回忆 to past/过去（动宾）

★★
succumb [səˈkʌm] *v.* 屈服，死

- 记 suc-（suck）吮吸 + cumb-（thumb）大拇指：犯了错的孩子不愿屈服（succumb），只能低头吮吸（suck）大拇指（thumb）以示反抗
- 考 同义 succumb = surrender；succumb = yield
  类比 survivor/幸存者 to succumb/死 ⇒ bachelor/单身 to marry/结婚（缺乏）

★★★
discern [dɪˈsɜːn] *v.* 识别，辨别

- 变 discerning *a.* 有辨别力的
- 记 因为关心（concern）这个领域，所以能轻易识别（discern）好坏
- 考 类比 discern/识别 to perceptive/感知 ⇒ see/看见 to witness/目击（同义）
  perceptive/感知的 to discern/辨别 ⇒ persistent/坚持的 to persevere/坚持（同义）
  drowsy/昏昏欲睡的 to sleepy/困的 ⇒ insightful/有洞察力的 to discerning/敏锐的（同义）

★
plethora [ˈpleθərə] *n.* 大量

- 记 这个单词来自 16 世纪希腊语中的 fullness，原意指的是"流血过多"，可以把 pleth 看成 plenty，记住其"大量的"意思
- 考 同义 plethora = excess

★
igneous [ˈɪɡnɪəs] *a.* 火成岩的

- 记 igneous 打乱顺序可以构成 O genius：哦，在火成岩（igneous）这个领域你可真是个天才（genius）啊

☆ reminisce　　☆ succumb　　☆ discern　　☆ plethora　　☆ igneous

考 类比：igneous (火成岩的) to rock (石头) ⇒ watercolor (水彩的) to painting (画)（修饰）

★★★ impetus

['ɪmpɪtəs] *n.* 势头，冲力

变 impetuous *a.* 冲动的，鲁莽的
记 一个人过于冲动（impetuous），说明其没有耐心（impatience）
考 同义 momentum = impetus；impetus = motivation；impetuous = rash

★★ molecule

['mɒlɪkjuːl] *n.* 分子

记 谐音：茉莉 + -cule (cute)：茉莉花的分子（molecule）很可爱（cute）
考 类比：atom (原子) to molecule (分子) ⇒ word (单词) to sentence (句子)（组成）
molecule (分子) to atoms (原子) ⇒ tissue (组织) to cells (细胞)（组成）

★★★ tournament

['tɔːnəmənt] *n.* 锦标赛

记 队员们参加锦标赛（tournament），就好像报上名字（name）之后到处去旅游（tour）似的
考 类比：series (系列) to episode (电视剧的一集) ⇒ tournament (锦标赛) to game (比赛)（组成）
spectator (观众) to tournament (锦标赛) ⇒ bystander (路人) to event (事件)（人物及其对象）
spectator (观众) to tournament (锦标赛) ⇒ witness (目击者) to crime (犯罪)（人物及其对象）

★★★ diligent

['dɪlɪdʒənt] *a.* 勤奋的

变 diligence *n.* 勤奋
记 Diligence is the mother of success.
考 同义 diligent = assiduous；diligent = hardworking；diligent = industrious
industry = diligence
类比 gentle (文雅的) to praise (表扬) ⇒ diligent (勤奋的) to success (成功)（因果）
heat (热的) to vapor (蒸汽) ⇒ diligent (勤奋的) to success (成功)（因果）
owl (猫头鹰) to wisdom (智慧) ⇒ ant (蚂蚁) to diligence (勤奋)（动物）

★ mow

[maʊ] *v.* 割

变 mower *n.* 割草机
记 草本来是呈（m）状的，割（mow）完之后倒着放就变成了 w 状
考 类比：mow (割) to lawn (草) ⇒ prune (修剪) to tree (树)（动宾）
mower (割草机) to grass (草) ⇒ clock (表) to time (时间)（事物及其对象）

irate ★★
[aɪˈreɪt] *a.* 生气的，发怒的

记 花钱买到盗版（pirate）唱片，她很生气（irate）
考 同义 irate = enraged

类比 irate 发怒的 to angry 生气的 → dazzling 耀眼的 to bright 明亮的 （＞程度）
lukewarm 微温的 to boiling 煮沸的 → annoyed 烦人的 to irate 发怒的 （＜程度）

fitness ★★
[ˈfɪtnəs] *n.* 健康

考 类比 treaty 协议 to peace 和平 → exercise 锻炼 to fitness 健康 （事物及其对象）
doctor 医生 to health 健康 → personal trainer 私人教练 to fitness 健康 （人物及其对象）

caress ★
[kəˈres] *v.* 爱抚

记 因为关心（care）所以爱抚（caress）
考 同义 caress = stroke

dexterous ★★★
[ˈdekstrəs] *a.* 灵巧的，敏捷的

变 dexterity *n.* 灵巧，敏捷
记 词根（dexter）在拉丁语中是"右"的意思，古人认为善用右手的人会比较敏捷
考 同义 dexterous = nimble；dexterous = adroit；dexterity = nimbleness

类比 sage 圣人 to wisdom 智慧 → mechanic 机修工 to dexterity 灵巧 （人物及其特点）
timeless 永恒的 to ephemeral 短暂的 → ungainly 笨拙的 to dexterous 敏捷的 （反义）

doze ★
[dəʊz] *v.* 打瞌睡

记 因为吃了感冒药（dose），所以开始打瞌睡（doze）
考 同义 sleep = doze

类比 sleep 睡觉 to doze 打瞌睡 → wail 哀号 to sob 啜泣 （同义）

coerce ★
[kəʊˈɜːs] *v.* 强制，迫使

记 当然（course）啦，同学们，虽然我出了这本书，但是我也不能强迫（coerce）你们记单词
考 同义 coerce = force；coerce = compel

preamble ★★
[priˈæmbl] *n.* 序文

记 pre- 之前 + -amble（ample）大量的：在真正阅读本小说之前（pre），还有大量的（ample）文字作为序文（preamble）
考 同义 preamble = formal introduction

类比

prologue 序言	to	novel 小说	⇒	preamble 序文	to	statute 法律	（事物及其部分）
foreword 序言	to	novel 小说	⇒	preamble 序文	to	statute 法律	（事物及其部分）
overture 序曲	to	opera 歌剧	⇒	preamble 序文	to	statute 法规	（事物及其部分）

★★ cacophony [kæˈkɒfəni] n. 不和谐的音

记 caco- 不好的 + -phony 声音：不和谐的声音
考 同义 cacophony = dissonance

类比

| cacophony 不和谐的音 | to | noise 噪音 | ⇒ | music 音乐 | to | sound 声音 | （种属） |
| lullaby 摇篮曲 | to | calm 平静 | ⇒ | cacophony 不和谐的音 | to | noise 噪音 | （事物及其目的） |

★★★ mercy [ˈmɜːsi] n. 仁慈

变 merciful a. 仁慈的；merciless a. 残忍的
记 谐音：摩西：圣经中的摩西是个很仁慈（mercy）的人
考 同义 beneficent = merciful；merciless = ruthless

类比

thank 感激	to	gratitude 感谢	⇒	pardon 宽恕	to	mercy 仁慈	（同义）
ruthless 残忍的	to	mercy 仁慈	⇒	naïve 幼稚的	to	worldliness 世俗	（缺乏）
condescending 屈尊的	to	respect 尊敬	⇒	merciless 残忍的	to	compassion 同情	（反义）

★★ reprimand [ˈreprɪmɑːnd] v. 谴责，训斥

记 因为老师对学生要求（demand）太高，所以被领导训斥（reprimand）
考 同义 censure = reprimand；chide = reprimand

类比

| reprimand 训斥 | to | commend 表扬 | ⇒ | loathe 厌恶 | to | adore 羡慕 | （反义） |
| reprimand 斥责 | to | disapproval 不赞成 | ⇒ | compliment 赞扬 | to | approval 批准 | （＞程度） |

注 关于"谴责"的单词在 SSAT 的习题中有很多，如：berate, reproach, scold, disparage。

List | 22 words

★ 复习一下学过的单词！

□ altimeter	□ exaggeration	□ quill	□ stool
□ autobiography	□ jovial	□ recollect	□ terse
□ avocation	□ lens	□ salvage	□ veto
□ badger	□ ornery	□ satiate	□ whim
□ combative	□ paltry	□ sojourn	□ witness

☆ cacophony   ☆ mercy   ☆ reprimand

SSAT词汇 List 24

★★ prescription
[prɪˈskrɪpʃn] *n.* 药方

记 pre- 提前 + scrip 写 + -tion；处方药的药方（prescription）需要医生提前（pre）写（script）好

考 类比：
- score 乐谱 **to** composer 作曲家 → prescription 药方 **to** doctor 医生（人物及其对象）
- teacher 老师 **to** assignment 作业 → doctor 医生 **to** prescription 药方（人物及其对象）

★★ vital
[ˈvaɪtl] *a.* 重要的，有活力的

考 同义：dynamic = vital；indispensable = vital；vital = energetic；vital = crucial

★ triplets
[ˈtrɪpləts] *n.* 三胞胎

记 tri- 这个词缀在英文中就是"三"的意思

考 类比：twins 双胞胎 **to** triplets 三胞胎 → duets 二重奏 **to** trios 三重奏（纵向）

★★★ daunt
[dɔːnt] *v.* 恐吓，使气馁

变 undaunted *a.* 勇敢的；dauntless *a.* 无畏的

记 凶悍的姑姑（aunt）让人害怕（daunt）

考 同义：undaunted = gallant

类比：
- intimidate 恐吓 **to** daunt 恐吓 → dismay 使惊慌 **to** horrify 使恐惧（同义）
- dauntless 无畏的 **to** fear 恐惧 → eager 渴望的 **to** reluctance 勉强（反义）
- dauntless 无畏的 **to** timid 胆小的 → remorseful 后悔的 **to** unrepentant 不悔的（反义）

★ convert
[kənˈvɜːt] *v.* 转变，转换

记 con- + -vert 转

☆ prescription　☆ vital　☆ triplets　☆ daunt　☆ convert

考 同义　transform = convert

pause　[pɔːz] n. 暂停

记　保罗（Paul）按下录音机上的暂停（pause）键
考 同义　pause = respite; pause = hesitation; pause = truce; falter = pause
　　类比　flag/旗子 to country/国家 ⇒ comma/逗号 to pause/暂停（事物及其用途）

foundation　[faʊnˈdeɪʃn] n. 基础，地基

考 同义　pedestal = foundation
　　类比　building/建筑物 to foundation/地基 ⇒ plant/植物 to root/根（事物及其部分）
　　　　　building/建筑物 to foundation/地基 ⇒ tree/树 to root/根（事物及其部分）
　　　　　foundation/地基 to building/建筑物 ⇒ pedestal/基座 to statue/小雕像（事物及其部分）

skitter　[ˈskɪtə] v. 快走

记　走快点（skitter）一起去看滑稽剧（skit）
考 类比　jabber/快而含糊地说 to talk/说话 ⇒ skitter/快走 to walk/走路（种属）
　　　　　jabber/快而含糊地说 to talk/说话 ⇒ skitter/快走 to move/移动（种属）

cello　[ˈtʃeləʊ] n. 大提琴

记　你好（hello）大提琴（cello）
考 类比　ax/大斧头 to hatchet/小斧头 ⇒ cello/大提琴 to violin/小提琴（>程度）
　　　　　cello/大提琴 to viola/中提琴 ⇒ tuba/大号 to trumpet/小号（>程度）
　　　　　cello/大提琴 to viola/中提琴 ⇒ tuba/大号 to oboe/双簧管（>程度）

velocity　[vəˈlɒsɪti] n. 速度

记　我们在小学学的：位移（s）= 速度（v）× 时间（t），其中的 v 即为 velocity
考 类比　speedometer/测速仪 to velocity/速度 ⇒ scales/天平 to weigh/称重（事物及其用途）
　　　　　altimeter/测高仪 to height/高度 ⇒ speedometer/测速仪 to velocity/速度（事物及其用途）
　　　　　speedometer/测速仪 to velocity/速度 ⇒ barometer/气压计 to pressure/压力（事物及其用途）

incentive ★
[ɪnˈsentɪv] *n.* 动机

记 上课认真的（attentive）动机（incentive）是为了获得好成绩
考 同义 incentive = inspiration；incentive = motivator

facile ★★
[ˈfæsaɪl] *a.* 容易的，轻率的

记 通过面部（facial）来判断一个人，未免过于轻率（facile）
考 同义 facile = easy
类比 facile 轻易的 to effort 努力 ⇒ inconsiderate 轻率的 to thoughtful 体贴的 （缺乏）

precaution ★
[prɪˈkɔːʃn] *n.* 预防，警惕

记 pre- 提前 + caution 谨慎：提前（pre）谨慎（caution）即为预防（precaution）
考 同义 precaution = safeguard

brusque ★★★
[bruːsk] *a.* 唐突的，无礼的

记 谐音：布鲁斯克：布鲁克斯是一个很无礼的（brusque）人
考 同义 brusque = abrupt
类比 brusque 唐突的 to abrupt 唐突的 ⇒ servile 奴性的 to obsequious 奉承的 （同义）
brusque 唐突的 to uncremoniousness 随意，无礼 ⇒ obstinate 顽固的 to intractability 难驾驭 （同义）

succinct ★
[səkˈsɪŋkt] *a.* 简洁的

记 suc-（sub）朝下 + cinc-（sink）+ t：船开始下沉（sink）了，有什么遗言请简明扼要（succinct）地说
考 同义 succinct = concise
注 关于"简洁的"单词在 SSAT 的习题中有很多，如：brief, terse, laconic。

conductor ★★★
[kənˈdʌktə] *n.* 指挥

考 类比 tractor 拖拉机 to farmer 农民 ⇒ baton 指挥棒 to conductor 指挥 （人物及其工具）
baton 指挥棒 to conductor 指挥 ⇒ brush 刷子 to painter 粉刷匠 （人物及其工具）
conductor 指挥 to orchestra 管弦乐队 ⇒ director 导演 to cast 全体演员 （人物及其对象）
director 导演 to script 脚本 ⇒ conductor 指挥家 to score 乐谱 （人物及其对象）
director 导演 to actor 演员 ⇒ conductor 指挥 to musicians 音乐家 （人物及其对象）

☆ incentive ☆ facile ☆ precaution ☆ brusque ☆ succinct
☆ conductor

★ devise
[dɪˈvaɪz] v. 设计

- 变 device n. 装置
- 记 设计（devise）一条里维斯（Levi's）牛仔裤
- 考 同义 apparatus = device

类比 devise 设计出 to formulate 构想出 ⇒ exclaim 大声说出 to blurt 脱口而出 （同义）

★ premonition
[ˌpriːməˈnɪʃn] n. 预告，征兆

- 记 警告（admonition）其实已经是一个不好的征兆（premonition）
- 考 同义 premonition = forewarning

类比 premonition 预告 to prophesy 预言 ⇒ preface 前言 to prologue 序言 （同义）

★★ elegy
[ˈelədʒi] n. 挽歌，哀歌

- 记 Thomas Gray 的著名墓园挽诗 Elegy Written in a Country Churchyard
- 考 类比 ode 颂 to praise 赞扬 ⇒ elegy 挽歌 to grief 悲痛 （事物及其用途）

obituary 讣告 to article 文章 ⇒ elegy 挽歌 to poem 诗歌 （种属）

- 注 elegy 这个单词的英文释义为：a sad poem or song, especially about someone who has died。

★★ radiant
[ˈreɪdiənt] a. 光芒四射的，容光焕发的

- 记 听到喜欢的广播（radio）节目，很开心（radiant）
- 考 同义 radiant = luminous；radiant = glowing

类比 livid 非常生气的 to anger 生气 ⇒ radiant 容光焕发的 to happiness 快乐 （＞程度）

List | **23** words   ★ 复习一下学过的单词！

☐ cacophony	☐ discern	☐ irate	☐ preamble
☐ caress	☐ doze	☐ mercy	☐ reminisce
☐ coerce	☐ fitness	☐ molecule	☐ reprimand
☐ dexterous	☐ igneous	☐ mow	☐ succumb
☐ diligent	☐ impetus	☐ plethora	☐ tournament

☆ devise   ☆ premonition   ☆ elegy   ☆ radiant

SSAT词汇 List 25

onslaught
['ɒnslɔːt] *n.* 猛攻，突击

记 父亲教女儿（daughter）遇到状况时如何攻击（onslaught）敌人
考 同义 attack = onslaught
类比 onslaught/攻击 to assault/攻击 ⇒ assail/攻击 to attack/攻击 （同义）

demolish
[dɪ'mɒlɪʃ] *v.* 拆除，破坏

记 魔鬼（demon）拆除（demolish）了你家房子
考 同义 destroy = demolish
类比 writing/写作 to erase/擦除 ⇒ building/建筑 to demolish/破坏 （动宾）
　　 amend/改变 to change/改变 ⇒ destroy/破坏 to demolish/破坏 （同义）

desecrate
['desɪkreɪt] *v.* 亵渎

记 de- 否定 + secr-（sacred）神圣的 + -ate
考 同义 desecrate = profane
类比 desecrate/亵渎 to sanctity/神圣 ⇒ blemish/玷污 to reputation/名声 （动宾）

hedonist
['hiːdənɪst] *n.* 享乐主义者

变 hedonistic *a.* 享乐主义的
记 享乐主义（Hedonism）又叫伊壁鸠鲁主义（Epicureanism），是一种哲学思想，认为享乐是人类最重要的追求
考 类比 hedonistic/享乐主义的 to pleasure/快乐 ⇒ vindictive/复仇的 to vengeance/复仇 （同义）
　　　 hedonist/享乐主义者 to pleasure/快乐 ⇒ miser/守财奴 to money/钱 （人物及其对象）
　　　 beauty/美丽 to aesthete/审美家 ⇒ pleasure/快乐 to hedonist/享乐主义者 （人物及其对象）

☆ onslaught　　☆ demolish　　☆ desecrate　　☆ hedonist

bigoted ★★
['bɪɡətɪd] *a.* 顽固的，心胸狭窄的

记 偏执的人更接近上帝。传说第一位诺曼底公爵罗洛拒绝亲吻法国皇帝查理三世的脚时，说了"bi got"，相当于今天的 by God（老天作证）。所以 bigot 是法国人对诺曼底人的蔑称，但是无宗教色彩

考 类比 bigoted 狭隘的 to fair 公平的 ⇒ guileful 狡猾的 to ingenuous 朴实的 （反义）

abdicate ★★★
['æbdɪkeɪt] *v.* 退位，放弃

记 他的言语间暗示（indicate）了主席要退位（abdicate）
考 同义 abdicate = resign；abdicate = renounce
类比 abdicate 退位 to king 国王 ⇒ resign 辞职 to president 总统 （人物及其动作）
resign 辞职 to occupation 工作 ⇒ abdicate 退位 to authority 权威 （缺乏）

philanthropist ★★
[fɪ'lænθrəpɪst] *n.* 慈善家

变 philanthropic *a.* 慈善的，仁慈的
记 phil- 喜欢 + anthrop- 人类 + -ist
考 类比 philanthropic 仁慈的 to benevolence 仁慈 ⇒ miserly 吝啬的 to stinginess 吝啬 （同义）
generous 大方的 to frugal 节俭的 ⇒ philanthropist 慈善家 to miser 小气鬼 （反义）
generous 大方的 to philanthropist 慈善家 ⇒ stingy 小气的 to miser 守财奴 （人物及其特点）

reputable ★
['repjʊtəbl] *a.* 声誉好的

记 repute 名声 + -able
考 同义 reputable = star
注 这个题的思路有些复杂，star 这个英文单词的释义为：of outstanding excellence。

required ★
[rɪ'kwaɪəd] *a.* 必需的

记 同义 obligatory = required
类比 possible 可能的 to required 要求的 ⇒ can 能 to must 必须 （＜程度）

chasm ★
['kæzəm] *n.* 裂口

记 这幅画虽然中间有个裂口（chasm），但是依旧很吸引（charm）人
考 同义 chasm = cavern
类比 chasm 裂口 to gap 缺口 （＞程度）

canyon 峡谷 to gully 冲沟 → chasm 裂口 to groove 凹槽 （同义）

gully 水沟 to canyon 峡谷 → crack 裂缝 to chasm 裂口 （同义）

myth ★★★ [mɪθ] n. 神话

变 mythical a. 神话的，虚幻的
记 成龙 2005 年的电影 Myth《神话》
考 同义 mythical = imaginary；myth = legend

类比
dragon fly 蜻蜓 to insect 昆虫 → dragon 龙 to myth 神话 （种属）

refute 反驳 to argument 言论 → debunk 拆穿 to myth 神话 （动宾）

myth 神话 to classical 古典的 → custom 习俗 to traditional 传统的 （修饰）

myth 神话 to history 历史 → unicorn 独角兽 to horse 马 （纵向）

marvel 奇迹 to myth 神话 → fact 事实 to history 历史 （同类）

surreptitious ★★ [ˌsʌrəpˈtɪʃəs] a. 秘密的

记 sur- + reptit- (repeat) + -ous：他上台前一直默默 (surreptitious) 重复 (repeat) 着自己的台词
考 同义 surreptitious = sneak；surreptitious = clandestine

类比
disingenuous 虚伪的 to craftiness 狡猾 → surreptitious 秘密的 to stealth 秘密 （同义）

注 关于"秘密的"单词在 SSAT 的习题中有很多，如：covert, secretive, stealthy, furtive。

nourish ★★ [ˈnʌrɪʃ] v. 滋养

变 nourishment n. 食物，营养品；undernourishment n. 营养不良
记 nour- (our) + rish- (rich)：我们的 (our) 富有 (rich) 全靠金钱滋养 (nourish)
考 同义 malnutrition = undernourishment

类比
drought 干旱 to rain 下雨 → famine 饥荒 to nourishment 营养 （缺乏）

feed 喂 to nourish 滋养 → water 浇水 to hydrate 水化 （同义）

jubilee ★ [ˈdʒuːbɪliː] n. 周年纪念

记 谐音：朱比利：朱比利迎来了和老婆的 50 周年结婚纪念日 (jubilee)
考 同义 jubilee = anniversary

ruddy
['rʌdi] *a.* 面色红润的

记 一个面色红润的（ruddy）泰迪熊（teddy）摆在商店中
考 同义 florid = ruddy

quantity
['kwɒntɪti] *n.* 数量

考 同义 quantity = magnitude
类比 innumerable / 不计其数的 **to** quantity / 数量 ⇒ invaluable / 无价的 **to** worth / 价值 （修饰）

limpid
['lɪmpɪd] *a.* 透明的，平静的

记 这里的水清澈透明（limpid），自己的腿（limb）在水中看得一清二楚
考 同义 limpid = clear

officious
[əˈfɪʃəs] *a.* 好管闲事的

记 办公室（office）里某些人非常好管闲事（officious）
考 同义 officious = meddling
类比 interloper / 闯入者 **to** officious / 好管闲事的 ⇒ braggart / 自吹自擂者 **to** conceited / 自负的 （人物及其特点）

squander
['skwɒndə] *v.* 浪费

记 女生在商场里边漫步（wander）边浪费（squander）钱买东西
考 同义 splurge = squander

gallop
['gæləp] *n.* 疾驰，飞奔

记 马在飞奔（gallop）后，需要一加仑（gallon）的水来补充体力
考 类比 jog / 慢跑 **to** sprint / 快跑 ⇒ trot / 慢跑 **to** gallop / 飞奔 （＜程度）
canter / 慢跑 **to** gallop / 飞奔 ⇒ jog / 慢跑 **to** sprint / 快跑 （＜程度）

List | 24 words   ★ 复习一下学过的单词！

☐ brusque	☐ devise	☐ pause	☐ skitter
☐ cello	☐ elegy	☐ precaution	☐ succinct
☐ conductor	☐ facile	☐ premonition	☐ triplets
☐ convert	☐ foundation	☐ prescription	☐ velocity
☐ daunt	☐ incentive	☐ radiant	☐ vital

SSAT词汇 List 26

★ curve
[kɜːv] n. 曲线

记 把这个小破木头雕刻（carve）成曲线（curve）形状

考 类比 spiral 螺旋 to curve 曲线 ⇒ screw 螺丝 to arc 弧 （纵向）

★★ flute
[fluːt] n. 笛子

记 用笛子（flute）流利地（fluent）吹出一首情歌

考 类比 piccolo 短笛 to flute 笛子 ⇒ pony 小马 to horse 马 （种属）
cooper 制桶工人 to barrel 桶 ⇒ flutist 笛手 to flute 笛子 （人物及其工具）

注 这个题的思路有些复杂：cooper 是通过制作 barrel 来赚钱，而 flutist 是通过演奏 flute 来赚钱。

★ arena
[əˈriːnə] n. 竞技场，活动场所

记 在竞技场（arena）这个区域（area），不是你死就是我亡

考 类比 audience 观众 to theater 剧院 ⇒ spectators 观众 to arena 竞技场 （空间）
arena 竞技场 to conflict 战斗 ⇒ forum 论坛 to discussion 讨论 （空间）

★★★ approve
[əˈpruːv] v. 批准

变 approval n. 批准；disapprove v. 不赞成；disapproval n. 不赞成

考 同义 approve = judge favorably；approve = ratify；approve = endorse；approve = assent
approval = sanction；frown = disapproval；disapprove = refute

类比 approve 批准 to deny 否认 ⇒ acknowledge 承认 to refute 反驳 （反义）
applaud 鼓掌 to approval 赞成 ⇒ beckon 召唤 to invitation 邀请 （同义）
reprimand 斥责 to disapproval 不赞成 ⇒ compliment 赞扬 to approval 批准 （＞程度）

☆ curve　　☆ flute　　☆ arena　　☆ approve

boast [bəʊst] v. 自夸，吹牛

变 boastful a. 夸耀的
记 她坐在船（boat）上自吹自擂（boast）
考 类比 mendicant 乞丐 to beg 乞求 ⇒ braggart 吹牛者 to boast 吹牛 （人物及其动作）
pomposity 自大 to boastful 夸耀的 ⇒ conceit 自负 to arrogant 自大的 （同义）

vine [vaɪn] n. 藤

记 葡萄藤（vine）上的葡萄可以酿酒（wine）
考 类比 grape 葡萄 to vine 葡萄藤 ⇒ plum 李子 to tree 树 （空间）

oboe [ˈəʊbəʊ] n. 双簧管

记 可以把单词中的两个 o 看作双簧管（oboe）上的两个孔
考 类比 drum 鼓 to tympani 定音鼓 ⇒ woodwind 木管乐器 to oboe 双簧管 （种属）
cello 大提琴 to viola 中提琴 ⇒ tuba 大号 to oboe 双簧管 （>程度）

dissociate [dɪˈsəʊʃieɪt] v. 分离，分裂

记 dis- 否定 + -sociate (associate) 结合
考 同义 dissociate = split off；dissociate = separate

taunt [tɔːnt] v. 嘲笑，讥讽

记 我嘲笑（tease）自己的姑姑（aunt）一把年纪还不结婚
考 同义 taunt = tease

plead [pliːd] v. 恳求

记 恳求（plead）领导（leader）
考 同义 plead = beg；beseech = plead
类比 recommend 推荐 to urge 敦促 ⇒ request 请求 to plead 恳求 （<程度）

replete [rɪˈpliːt] a. 充满的

记 中国有的地方资源耗尽（deplete），有的地方却资源充盈（replete）
考 同义 replete = full

integrity [ɪnˈtegrɪti] n. 正直，诚实

变 integrate v. 使……完整

记 我的人生目标就是希望别人在夸我的时候，说我是 a man of integrity
考 同义 integrate = combine；integrity = honesty
类比 integrity (to) honesty ⇒ resolution (to) determination （同义）
正直　　　诚实　　　决心　　　决定

submissive [səbˈmɪsɪv] *a.* 顺从的

变 submissiveness *n.* 顺从
记 submit 除了"提交"之外，本身就有"服从"之意，其形容词即为 submissive
考 同义 meek = submissive；submissive = compliant；submissive = passive
类比 obedience (to) submissiveness ⇒ outset (to) commencement （同义）
听话　　　顺从　　　开始　　　开始
ecstatic (to) happy ⇒ servile (to) submissive （＞程度）
狂喜的　　开心的　　奴性的　　顺从的
submissive (to) recalcitrant ⇒ refined (to) vulgar （反义）
顺从的　　叛逆的　　精炼的　　粗俗的

condense [kənˈdens] *v.* 压缩；凝结

记 由于材料遭到压缩（condense），所以食物很稠密（dense）
考 类比 condense (to) compact ⇒ refine (to) pure （同义）
压缩　　　紧凑的　　精炼　　　纯的
condense (to) expand ⇒ desire (to) reject （反义）
压缩　　　扩张　　　欲望　　　拒绝
evaporate (to) condense ⇒ thaw (to) freeze （反义）
蒸发　　　压缩　　　融化　　　冷冻
注 evaporate 这个单词的英文释义为：a liquid changes into a gas or steam，而 condense 这个单词的英文释义为：a gas or vapour changes into a liquid。

furnace [ˈfɜːnɪs] *n.* 炉子

记 房东给每个房间提供（furnish）一个炉子（furnace）用来取暖
考 类比 humidifier (to) moisture ⇒ furnace (to) heat （事物及其用途）
加湿器　　湿度　　　炉子　　　热度
refrigerator (to) cool ⇒ furnace (to) heat （事物及其用途）
冰箱　　　凉爽　　　炉子　　　热度

quell [kwel] *v.* 平息，镇压，安慰

记 经过短暂镇压（quell）之后，社会上显得一片平静（quiet）
考 同义 quell = stifle
类比 crush (to) riot ⇒ quell (to) uprising （动宾）
镇压　　　暴乱　　　平息　　　起义
extinguish (to) fire ⇒ quell (to) uprising （动宾）
灭　　　　火　　　　平息　　　起义
注 关于"安慰"的单词在 SSAT 的习题中有很多，如：soothe, calm, pacify, mollify, lull, appease, conciliate。

reiterate ★
[riˈɪtəreɪt] *v.* 重申

记 re- + -iterate (literate) 受过教育的：重复告诉 (reiterate) 别人自己是受到过教育的 (literate)

考 类比 rehash 重讲 to discuss 讨论 → reiterate 重申 to state 陈述 （同类）

reimbursement ★
[ˌriːɪmˈbɜːsmənt] *n.* 赔偿

记 re- + im- (in-) + burse- (purse) + ment：重新 (re) 进入 (in) 你的钱包 (purse) 即为赔偿 (reimbursement)

考 类比 insurance 保险 to accident 事故 → reimbursement 赔偿 to loss 损失 （事物及其对象）

blade ★★★
[bleɪd] *n.* 刀片

记 不要乱玩刀片 (blade)，否则妈妈会骂 (blame) 的

考 类比
drill 钻子 to bore 钻孔 → blade 刀片 to cut 切 （事物及其用途）
shovel 铁铲 to dig 挖 → blade 刀片 to cut 切 （事物及其用途）
needle 针 to stitch 缝 → blade 刀片 to cut 切 （事物及其用途）
blade 刀片 to ice-skate 滑冰鞋 → runner 转轮 to sled 雪橇 （事物及其部分）

redundant ★★
[rɪˈdʌndənt] *a.* 多余的，过剩的

记 太多 (abundant) 了，多得有点过多 (redundant) 了

考 同义 redundant = superfluous；redundant = unnecessary
类比 redundant 多余的 to necessary 必需的 → vague 模糊的 to explicit 清楚的 （缺乏）
redundant 多余的 to repetitive 重复的 → heated 激动的 to excited 兴奋的 （同义）

List | 25 words   ★ 复习一下学过的单词！

□ abdicate	□ gallop	□ nourish	□ reputable
□ bigoted	□ hedonist	□ officious	□ required
□ chasm	□ jubilee	□ onslaught	□ ruddy
□ demolish	□ limpid	□ philanthropist	□ squander
□ desecrate	□ myth	□ quantity	□ surreptitious

SSAT词汇 List 27

chauffeur
[ˈʃəʊfə] n. 专车司机

记 谐音：舒服；乘坐专车司机（chauffeur）开的车当然要比出租车舒服多了

考 类比 sentinel 哨兵 to guard 护卫队 → chauffeur 专车司机 to driver 司机 （种属）

scale
[skeɪl] n. 天平；鱼鳞；音调范围

考 类比
- note 音符 to chord 和弦 → tone 音调 to scale 音阶 （组成）
- step 横档 to ladder 梯子 → tone 音调 to scale 音阶 （组成）
- odometer 里程表 to distance 距离 → scale 天平 to weight 重量 （事物及其用途）
- scissors 剪刀 to trim 修剪 → scales 天平 to weigh 称重 （事物及其用途）
- weight 重量 to scale 天平 → altitude 高度 to altimeter 测高仪 （事物及其对象）
- scale 天平 to weight 重量 → thermometer 温度计 to temperature 温度 （事物及其对象）
- speedometer 测速仪 to velocity 速度 → scales 天平 to weigh 称重 （事物及其用途）
- hour 小时 to watch 表 → pound 磅 to scale 天平 （事物及其用途）
- scale 鱼鳞 to fish 鱼 → hide 兽皮 to horse 马 （事物及其部分）

deliberate
[dɪˈlɪbəreɪt] v. 深思熟虑，仔细考虑

记 接受过教育的（literate）人在面对这个问题的时候也会深思熟虑（deliberate）

考 同义 contemplate = deliberate

注 关于"考虑"的单词在SSAT的习题中有很多，如：plan, intend, consider。

affectation
[ˌæfekˈteɪʃn] *n.* 装模作样

- affect 有一个意思是 to put on a false show of；stimulate
- 同义 affected = artificial

类比 affectation（装模作样）to behavior（行为）→ buffoonery（滑稽行为）to action（行为） （种属）

deplore
[dɪˈplɔː] *v.* 谴责，悲哀

- 他去南极探索（explore）出事，同事表示悲哀（deplore）
- 同义 lament = deplore

quench
[kwentʃ] *v.* 熄灭，解渴

- 夏天坐在板凳（bench）上非常热，所以需要喝汽水解渴（quench）
- 同义 quench = satisfy（quench 这个单词的英文释义为：to relieve or satisfy with liquid）

enhance
[ɪnˈhɑːns] *v.* 提高，增加

- 同义 enhance = improve

propose
[prəˈpəʊz] *v.* 建议

- pro- 朝前 + pose 摆姿势：提建议（propose）即为朝前（pro）摆出自己的立场和姿态（pose）
- 同义 propose = suggest

incumbent
[ɪnˈkʌmbənt] *n.* 现任者

- 员工遭到现任（incumbent）领导对其工作的重重阻碍（encumber）
- 类比 incumbent（在职者）to office（办公室）→ tenant（租户）to dwelling（住处）（人物及其对象）
  incumbent（在职者）to office（办公室）→ champion（冠军）to title（头衔）（人物及其对象）

leather
[ˈleðə] *n.* 皮革，皮革制品

- 天气（weather）变化严重影响皮革（feather）的质量
- 类比 leather（皮革）to belt（皮带）→ canvas（帆布）to jeans（牛仔裤）（事物及其用途）
  linen（亚麻布）to flax（亚麻）→ leather（皮革）to fur（皮毛）（事物及其用途）

注 这个题的思路有些复杂：linen 的原材料是 flax，而 leather 的原材料是 fur。

sanguine ★★ ['sæŋgwɪn] *a.* 乐观的

- 记 乐观的（sanguine）企鹅（penguin）
  sangu-来自拉丁语"血"，彼时医生相信人体内的血液越多人就越乐观
- 考 同义 sanguine = cheerful
  类比 dejected 沮丧的 to sanguine 乐观的 ⇒ ignorant 无知的 to ingenious 机灵的 （反义）

frank ★★ [fræŋk] *a.* 坦诚的

- 变 frankness *n.* 坦诚
- 记 弗兰克（Frank）是个诚实的（frank）小伙子
- 考 同义 frank = candid；frank = guileless
  类比 explicit 明确的 to distortion 扭曲 ⇒ frank 直率的 to circumlocution 累赘陈述 （反义）
- 注 关于"坦诚"的单词在 SSAT 的习题中有很多，如：candor，honesty，integrity。

animate ★★ ['ænɪmət] *a.* 有生命的，有生气的

- 记 小动物（animal）给人一种生机勃勃的（animate）感觉
- 考 同义 animate = vivacious
  类比 animate 有生气的 to living 活泼的 ⇒ ephemeral 短暂的 to unendurable 无法持久的 （同义）

observe ★★★ [əb'zɜːv] *v.* 观察

- 变 observer *n.* 观察者；observant *a.* 机警的
- 记 观察（observe）数月，获得成就，值得（deserve）赞美
- 考 同义 vigilant = observant；behold = observe
  类比 gaze 凝视 to observer 观察者 ⇒ hear 听 to listener 听众 （人物及其动作）

aspire ★ [ə'spaɪə] *v.* 渴望，立志

- 记 别人越鼓励（inspire）你，你越渴望（aspire）成功
- 考 同义 aspire = aim；aspire = pursue

intellect ★ ['ɪntəlekt] *n.* 智力

- 变 intellectual *a.* 聪明的，博学的
- 记 聪明的（intelligent）人智力（intellect）都高
- 考 同义 acumen = intellect；intellectual = scholarly

vessel ★★

['vesəl] *n.* 容器，船

记 谐音：外送：负责外送东西的人需要一个容器（vessel）来装载外卖
考 同义 vessel = container

类比 vessel/船 to ferry/渡船 ⇒ attire/衣物 to dress/衣服 （同义）

biology ★★★

[baɪ'ɒlədʒi] *n.* 生物

变 biologist *n.* 生物学家
记 bio- 生命 + -logy 学科：研究生命的学科即为生物（biology）
考 类比
astronomer/天文学家 to stars/星星 ⇒ biologist/生物学家 to life/生命 （人物及其对象）
psychologist/心理学家 to biologist/生物学家 ⇒ mind/思想 to life/生命 （纵向）
biologist/生物学家 to scientist/科学家 ⇒ surgeon/外科医生 to doctor/医生 （种属）
organism/有机体 to biology/生物学 ⇒ money/钱 to economics/经济学 （事物及其对象）
math/数学 to statistics/统计学 ⇒ biology/生物学 to zoology/动物学 （种属）

psychology ★★

[saɪ'kɒlədʒi] *n.* 心理学

变 psychologist *n.* 心理学家
考 类比
pathology/病理学 to disease/疾病 ⇒ psychology/心理学 to mind/精神 （事物及其对象）
paleontologist/古生物学者 to dinosaurs/恐龙 ⇒ psychologist/心理学家 to mental/精神病 （事物及其对象）

veil ★

[veɪl] *n.* 面纱

记 雾霾天出门戴面纱（veil），能让你活得（live）更长久
考 同义 shroud = veil

List | 26 words   ★ 复习一下学过的单词！

□ approve	□ curve	□ oboe	□ reiterate
□ arena	□ dissociate	□ plead	□ replete
□ blade	□ flute	□ quell	□ submissive
□ boast	□ furnace	□ redundant	□ taunt
□ condense	□ integrity	□ reimbursement	□ vine

110   ☆ vessel   ☆ biology   ☆ psychology   ☆ veil

SSAT词汇 List 28

★ remiss [rɪˈmɪs] *a.* 怠慢的，疏忽的
记 re- 相反 + miss：因为我不再（re）想念（miss）他，所以对他很怠慢（remiss）
考 类比 remiss / 疏忽的 — to — dutifulness / 责任 ⇒ intemperate / 放纵的 — to — moderation / 适度（反义）

★ deduce [dɪˈdjuːs] *v.* 推论，推断
记 de- 向下 + duc- 引导 + e：向下（de）引导（duc）即为推断（deduce）
考 同义 deduce = infer

★★ brawl [brɔːl] *n.* 争吵
记 因为一个碗（bowl）而导致的争吵（brawl）
考 类比 brawl / 争吵 — to — war / 战争 ⇒ shoplifting / 偷窃 — to — murder / 谋杀（＜程度）
      spat / 口角 — to — brawl / 争吵 ⇒ admonish / 警告 — to — condemn / 定罪（＜程度）

★★★ surly [ˈsɜːli] *a.* 乖戾的，无力的
记 因为对自己过于确信（sure），所以脾气乖戾（surly）
考 同义 surly = unfriendly；grumpy = surly；surly = bad-tempered
  类比 amiable / 和蔼的 — to — grumpy / 脾气坏的 ⇒ friendly / 友好的 — to — surly / 乖戾的（反义）

★★ impasse [ˈɪmpɑːs] *n.* 僵局
记 im- 否定 + -passe（pass）：无法通过，陷入僵局（impasse）
考 同义 plight = impasse；deadlock = impasse
  类比 bottleneck / 瓶颈 — to — traffic / 交通 ⇒ impasse / 僵局 — to — negotiation / 谈判（修饰）

☆ remiss ☆ deduce ☆ brawl ☆ surly ☆ impasse

utilize
[ˈjuːtɪlaɪz] v. 使用

[记] utilize 的名词形式 utility 即为我们口语中常说的 SUV（Sports Utility Vehicle）中的 U
[考] 同义　utilize = make use of；utilize = exploit

vie
[vaɪ] v. 竞争

[记] 通过（via）比武（vie）的方式来给女儿招亲
[考] 同义　compete = vie

assure
[əˈʃɔː] v. 保证，担保

[变] assurance n. 保证，确保
[记] 因为很确信（sure），所以敢保证（assure）
[考] 同义　guarantee = assure；assurance = confidence

类比　diversion (消遣) to boredom (无聊) ⇒ assurance (保证) to uncertainty (不确定) （缺乏）

indifferent
[ɪnˈdɪfrənt] a. 冷漠的

[变] indifference n. 冷漠
[记] 注意这个单词是"冷漠的"意思，不是"相同的"意思
[考] 同义　apathy = indifference；indifferent = nonchalant；distant = indifferent
　　　aloof = indifferent

类比　inattentive (疏忽的) to distracted (走神的) ⇒ uncommitted (不受约束的) to indifferent (冷漠的) （因果）

clay
[kleɪ] n. 泥土，黏土

[记] 谐音：可累：玩黏土（clay）可累人了
[考] 类比
spatula (抹刀) to clay (黏土) ⇒ chisel (凿子) to marble (大理石) （事物及其对象）
clay (黏土) to potter (制陶工人) ⇒ marble (大理石) to sculptor (雕塑家) （人物及其对象）
stone (石头) to sculpture (雕刻) ⇒ clay (黏土) to pottery (陶器) （事物及其对象）
papyrus (莎草纸) to scroll (卷轴) ⇒ tablet (写字板) to clay (泥土) （事物及其用途）

[注] papyrus 这个单词的英文释义为：a written scroll made of papyrus；tablet 这个单词的英文释义为：the flat piece of clay or stone which people used to write on before paper was invented。

poultry
[ˈpəʊltri] n. 家禽

[记] poul-（poor）+ try：穷人（poor）吃家禽（poultry），富人吃海鲜

112　　☆ utilize　　☆ vie　　☆ assure　　☆ indifferent　　☆ clay
　　　☆ poultry

考 同义 poultry = fowl

类比 $\frac{\text{coop}}{\text{鸡笼}}$ to $\frac{\text{poultry}}{\text{家禽}}$ ⇒ $\frac{\text{aquarium}}{\text{水族馆}}$ to $\frac{\text{fish}}{\text{鱼}}$ （空间）

$\frac{\text{shellfish}}{\text{甲壳类动物}}$ to $\frac{\text{lobster}}{\text{虾}}$ ⇒ $\frac{\text{poultry}}{\text{禽类}}$ to $\frac{\text{chicken}}{\text{小鸡}}$ （种属）

advent ☆
['ædvent] *n.* 到来，出现

记 对于电灯的到来（advent），我们需要感谢爱迪生的发明（invent）
考 同义 advent = arrival

consensus ☆
[kən'sensəs] *n.* 一致

记 con- + sens- (sense) + us：大家（con）感受（sense）一致（consensus）
考 同义 harmony = consensus

adorn ☆
[ə'dɔːn] *v.* 装饰

记 家里面装饰（adorn）得很好，让其他人羡慕（adore）
考 同义 adorn = decorate

类比 $\frac{\text{artificial}}{\text{人工的}}$ to $\frac{\text{synthetic}}{\text{合成的}}$ ⇒ $\frac{\text{adorn}}{\text{装饰}}$ to $\frac{\text{decorate}}{\text{装饰}}$ （同义）

$\frac{\text{cosmetics}}{\text{化妆品}}$ to $\frac{\text{embellish}}{\text{装饰}}$ ⇒ $\frac{\text{ornament}}{\text{装饰物}}$ to $\frac{\text{adorn}}{\text{装饰}}$ （事物及其用途）

invisible ☆
[ɪn'vɪzəbl] *a.* 隐身的，看不到的

记 in- 否定 + vis- 看 + -ible
考 同义 invisible = unseen

类比 $\frac{\text{illegible}}{\text{难以辨认的}}$ to $\frac{\text{read}}{\text{读}}$ ⇒ $\frac{\text{invisible}}{\text{不可视的}}$ to $\frac{\text{see}}{\text{看}}$ （缺乏）

conscientious ☆
[ˌkɒnʃɪ'enʃəs] *a.* 认真的

记 认真的 conscientious = 道德心 conscience + 有意识的 conscious
考 类比 $\frac{\text{conscientious}}{\text{认真的}}$ to $\frac{\text{ethical}}{\text{有道德的}}$ ⇒ $\frac{\text{immoral}}{\text{不道德的}}$ to $\frac{\text{unscrupulous}}{\text{肆无忌惮的}}$ （同义）

scoundrel ☆☆
['skaʊndrəl] *n.* 恶棍，无赖

记 一个恶棍（scoundrel）趴在商场柜台（counter）上调戏售货员
考 同义 rogue = scoundrel

类比 $\frac{\text{glutton}}{\text{贪吃者}}$ to $\frac{\text{moderation}}{\text{节制}}$ ⇒ $\frac{\text{scoundrel}}{\text{恶棍}}$ to $\frac{\text{virtue}}{\text{道德}}$ （缺乏）

☆ advent　　☆ consensus　　☆ adorn　　☆ invisible　　☆ conscientious
☆ scoundrel

wrist
[rɪst] *n.* 手腕

记 用手腕（wrist）拿笔去写字（write）

考 类比
cuff 袖口 to wrist 手腕 ⇒ collar 领子 to neck 脖子 （空间）
ring 戒指 to finger 手指 ⇒ cuff 袖口 to wrist 手腕 （空间）

assignment
[ə'saɪnmənt] *n.* 任务，作业

考 类比
teacher 老师 to assignment 作业 ⇒ barber 理发师 to haircut 理发 （人物及其对象）
teacher 老师 to assignment 作业 ⇒ doctor 医生 to prescription 药方 （人物及其对象）

obstruct
[əb'strʌkt] *v.* 妨碍，阻碍

变 obstruction *n.* 障碍，阻碍
记 建造（construct）房子过程中总有人来阻碍（obstruct）和捣乱
考 类比
snag 障碍 to blockade 阻塞 ⇒ barrier 障碍 to obstruction 障碍 （同义）
barrier 障碍 to obstruct 阻碍 ⇒ camouflage 伪装 to conceal 隐藏 （事物及其用途）
obstruct 妨碍 to impede 阻碍 ⇒ impenetrable 不能通过的 to impervious 无法入侵的 （同义）

List | 27 words

★ 复习一下学过的单词！

- affectation
- animate
- aspire
- biology
- chauffeur
- deliberate
- deplore
- enhance
- frank
- incumbent
- intellect
- leather
- observe
- propose
- psychology
- quench
- sanguine
- scale
- veil
- vessel

SSAT词汇 List 29

★★ douse
[daʊs] v. 浸湿，浸泡

记 把衣服（blouse）泡（douse）入水中
洪水使得房子（house）浸泡（douse）在水中
考 同义 douse = soak
类比 douse/浸湿 —to→ flame/火焰 ⇒ quash/镇压 —to→ rebellion/叛逆（动宾）
douse/浸泡 —to→ liquid/液体 ⇒ kindle/点燃 —to→ flame/火焰（事物及其用途）

★ odious
[ˈəʊdɪəs] a. 可憎的，可恶的

记 这个乐队的音乐还算悦耳（melodious），但是乐手的为人太可恶（odious）了
考 同义 odious = unpleasant

★★★ precede
[prɪˈsiːd] v. 领先，在……之前

变 precedent a. 先前的；unprecedented a. 前所未有的
记 pre- 在前 + ced- 走路
考 同义 precede = come before；unprecedented = exceptional
类比 antecedent/先前的 —to→ precedent/先例的 ⇒ succedent/随后的 —to→ subsequent/后来的（同义）

★★ feint
[feɪnt] v. 佯攻，伪装

记 用水假装（feint）油漆（paint）
考 同义 feint = mock attack
类比 equivocation/含糊 —to→ meaning/意义 ⇒ feint/伪装 —to→ intention/意图（缺乏）

★ stratify
[ˈstrætɪfaɪ] v. 分层

记 strat-（stretch）伸展 + -ify：一层层伸展开来（stretch）即为分层（stratify）

☆ douse   ☆ odious   ☆ precede   ☆ feint   ☆ stratify

haunt [hɔːnt] v. 萦绕

- 记 姑姑（aunt）虽然已经过世，但是她的身影经常萦绕（haunt）在我心头
- 考 类比 ghost 鬼怪 — to — haunt 萦绕 ⇒ guru 大师 — to — teach 教 （人物及其动作）

episode ['epɪsəʊd] n. 插曲

- 变 episodic a. 间歇性的
- 记 大家在网上下载的美剧，经常有这样的标示 S01E01，其中的 E 指的就是 episode
- 考 同义 episodic = intermittent

类比 series 系列 — to — episode 电视剧的一集 ⇒ tournament 锦标赛 — to — game 比赛 （组成）

cringe [krɪndʒ] v. 畏缩

- 记 妈妈很害怕（cringe）冰箱（fridge）里的食物坏掉
- 考 同义 cringe = cower

类比 sneer 嘲笑 — to — disdain 鄙视 ⇒ cringe 畏缩 — to — fear 害怕 （同义）

注 cringe 这个单词的英文释义为：to shrink back, as in fear; cower.

interloper ['ɪntələʊpə] n. 闯入者

- 记 inter- 两者之间 + lop(e) 大步慢跑 + -er：闯入者（interloper）即为大步跑到别人之间的人
- 考 类比 interloper 闯入者 — to — guest 客人 ⇒ division 分割 — to — whole 整体 （反义）

interloper 闯入者 — to — welcome 欢迎 ⇒ invader 入侵者 — to — greet 欢迎 （纵向）

interloper 闯入者 — to — officious 好管闲事的 ⇒ braggart 自吹自擂者 — to — conceited 自负的 （人物及其特点）

puck [pʌk] n. 冰球

- 记 运气（luck）不好，被冰球（puck）击中
- 考 类比 stick 棍子 — to — puck 冰球 ⇒ bat 球棒 — to — ball 球 （事物及其对象）

puck 冰球 — to — hockey 冰球运动 ⇒ ball 球 — to — soccer 足球 （事物及其部分）

同义 stratify = layer

circumlocution

[ˌsɜ:kəmləˈkju:ʃn] *n.* 累赘的陈述

记 circum- 环绕 + locu- 说话 + tion

考 类比 explicit 明确的 to distortion 扭曲 ⇒ frank 直率的 to circumlocution 累赘陈述 （反义）

embellishment 装饰 to decorative 装饰性的 ⇒ circumlocution 累赘陈述 to indirect 不直接的 （同义）

bungle

[ˈbʌŋ.gl] *v.* 笨拙的做，弄糟

记 生物学家在丛林（jungle）里笨拙（bungle）地收集草木

考 同义 bungle = handle clumsily; bungle = fumble

类比 bungle 弄糟 to blunder 犯错 ⇒ commiserate 同情 to condole 慰问 （同义）

wary

[ˈweəri] *a.* 谨慎的

记 小心（wary）战争（war）

考 类比 circumspect 慎重的 to wary 谨慎的 ⇒ reckless 鲁莽的 to foolhardy 有勇无谋的 （同义）

注 关于"谨慎的，留意的"单词在 SSAT 的习题中有很多，如：vigilant，attentive，cautious。

panorama

[ˌpænəˈrɑ:mə] *n.* 全景

记 pan- 全 + -orama (Roma)：罗马的全部景色就在这张全景（panorama）图里了

考 同义 panorama = comprehensive view

类比 panorama 全景 to view 景色 ⇒ pepper 胡椒 to spice 香料 （种属）

negligible

[ˈneglɪdʒəbl] *a.* 不重要的，可忽略的

记 neglig- (neglect) 忽略 + -ible

考 同义 trifling = negligible

注 关于"不重要的"单词在 SSAT 的习题中有很多，如：trivial，unimportant。

pluck

[plʌk] *n.* 勇气；*v.* 拔，弹

记 这个人勇气（pluck）可嘉，但是欠缺运气（luck）

考 同义 pluck = courage

类比 horn 喇叭 to blow 吹 ⇒ harp 竖琴 to pluck 弹 （动宾）

etch

[etʃ] v. 蚀刻

记 去取（fetch）硫酸来进行蚀刻（etch）
考 同义 etch = engrave

citadel

[ˈsɪtədəl] n. 要塞，城堡

记 这个城市（city）里有很多堡垒（citadel）
考 同义 citadel = fort；citadel = fortress；citadel = stronghold

terrier

[ˈterɪə] n. 小猎犬

记 谐音：泰瑞尔：一只名叫泰瑞尔的小猎犬（terrier）
考 类比 snake/蛇 to python/蟒蛇 ⇒ dog/狗 to terrier/小猎犬 （种属）

kiln

[kɪln] n. 窑

记 一只兔子被困在密闭的窑（kiln）中，结果窒息而死（kill）
考 同义 kiln = oven
类比 oven/炉子 to kiln/窑 ⇒ baker/面包师 to potter/制陶工人 （纵向）
注 kiln 这个单词的英文释义为：an oven, furnace, or heated enclosure used for processing a substance by burning, firing, or drying。

List | 28 words ★ 复习一下学过的单词！

☐ adorn	☐ clay	☐ indifferent	☐ scoundrel
☐ advent	☐ conscientious	☐ invisible	☐ surly
☐ assignment	☐ consensus	☐ obstruct	☐ utilize
☐ assure	☐ deduce	☐ poultry	☐ vie
☐ brawl	☐ impasse	☐ remiss	☐ wrist

SSAT词汇 List 30

announce [əˈnaʊns] v. 宣布

变 announcer n. 宣布者
考 同义 announcer = herald；announce = proclaim
类比 announce (宣布) to inform (通知) → wrap (包装) to conceal (隐藏) （动作及其目的）

anarchy [ˈænəki] n. 无政府主义

变 anarchist n. 无政府主义者
记 an- 否定 + -archy 统治
1976年英国著名的PUNK乐队推出了首单 Anarchy in the U. K.，在英国引起轩然大波
考 类比 anarchy (无政府主义) to law (法律) → discord (不和谐) to agreement (一致) （缺乏）
recluse (隐士) to publicity (公开) → anarchist (无政府主义者) to order (规则) （人物及其对象）
iconoclast (偶像破坏者) to convention (传统) → anarchist (无政府主义者) to government (政府) （人物及其对象）

breeze [briːz] n. 微风

记 即使是微风（breeze），也能把身体差的人给吹冻（freeze）住了
考 类比 hurricane (飓风) to breeze (微风) → tidal (浪潮) to wave ripple (涟漪) （>程度）
breeze (微风) to wind (风) → drizzle (毛毛雨) to downpour (暴雨) （<程度）
blizzard (暴风雪) to snowflake (雪片) → hurricane (飓风) to breeze (微风) （>程度）
heat (热) to radiator (暖气) → breeze (微风) to fan (电扇) （事物及其用途）

portray [pɔːˈtreɪ] v. 描绘

变 portrait n. 肖像

记 port + ray：这幅画描绘（portray）了清晨港口（port）的第一道光线（ray）

考 类比
paper 纸 to novel 小说 ⇒ canvas 画布 to portrait 肖像画 （空间）
caricature 漫画 to portrait 画 ⇒ hyperbole 夸张言辞 to statement 言论 （＞程度）
object 物体 to still life 静物 ⇒ person 人物 to portrait 肖像画 （种属）
portrait 肖像画 to painting 画画 ⇒ ballet 芭蕾舞音乐 to music 音乐 （种属）
jazz 爵士乐 to music 音乐 ⇒ portrait 肖像画 to painting 绘画 （种属）
diary 日记 to record 记录 ⇒ silhouette 剪影 to portrait 肖像 （同义）
autobiography 自传 to author 作者 ⇒ self-portrait 自画像 to artist 画家 （人物及其目的）
recede 撤退 to retreat 撤退 ⇒ depict 描绘 to portray 描绘 （同义）

★★ choreography [ˌkɒrɪˈɒɡrəfi] n. 编舞

变 choreographer n. 编舞者

记 chore- 唱歌跳舞 + graph- 写 + y：编舞（choreography）工作就好像用舞蹈在舞台上写字一样

考 类比
playwright 剧作家 to script 剧本 ⇒ choreographer 舞编 to dance 舞蹈 （人物及其对象）
choreographer 舞编 to dancers 舞蹈家 ⇒ director 导演 to actors 演员 （人物及其对象）

★ transplant [ˈtrænsplɑːnt] v. 移植，转移

记 trans- 转 + plant 植物：转换（trans）植物（plant）的位置，即为移植（transplant）

考 同义 transplant = move to other places

类比 ordeal 折磨 to calamity 灾难 ⇒ transplant 迁移 to reorient 再调整 （同义）

★★ strenuous [ˈstrenjʊəs] a. 费力的

记 要花费力气（strength）的东西都是很费力的（strenuous）

考 同义 trying = strenuous；strenuous = arduous

★ aversion [əˈvɜːʃn] n. 厌恶

记 我极其厌恶（aversion）中文（version）配音的美国电影

考 同义 aversion = dislike

类比 reject 拒绝 to aversion 厌恶 ⇒ choose 选择 to preference 偏好 （＜程度）

antipathy (反感) to sympathy (同情) ⇒ aversion (厌恶) to love (热爱) （反义）

progeny ★
['prɒdʒəni] *n.* 子孙后代

- 记 progeny 可以看作 provide gene（提供基因），由此联想到"产生子孙后代"
- 考 同义 progeny = descendant

wrath ★★
[rɒθ] *n.* 愤怒

- 记 对这种人渣愤怒（wrath）不值得（worth）
- 考 同义 wrath = ire; fury = wrath; wrath = frenzy

helix ★
['hi:lɪks] *n.* 螺旋

- 记 菲利克斯（Felix）拿着一个螺旋（helix）
- 考 类比 helix (螺旋) to spring (弹簧) ⇒ sphere (球形) to baseball (棒球) （事物及其特点）

authorize ★
['ɔ:θəraɪz] *v.* 批准，认可

- 考 同义 authorize = permit

throng ★★
[θrɒŋ] *n.* 人群

- 记 *Game of Thrones* 里出现了众多人物（throng）
- 考 类比 horde (一群) to throng (一群) ⇒ hurl (投掷) to throw (扔) （同义）
  throng (人群) to people (人) ⇒ swarm (一群虫子) to insects (昆虫) （同义）

static ★
['stætɪk] *a.* 静态的

- 记 因为 stay，所以 static
- 考 同义 static = inactive

knot ★★
[nɒt] *n.* 打结

- 变 knotty *a.* 打结的，棘手的
- 记 我们平时常见的"中国结"的英文即为 Chinese Knot
- 考 同义 knotty = difficult
  类比 connected (连接的) to net (网) ⇒ tied (系住的) to knot (结) （修饰）
  knotty (棘手的) to difficult (困难的) ⇒ prickly (易怒的) to irritating (易怒的) （同义）

☆ progeny   ☆ wrath   ☆ helix   ☆ authorize   ☆ throng
☆ static   ☆ knot

edible
['edɪbl] *a.* 可食用的

记 生的牛肉可以直接食用（edible）这事还真难以置信（incredible）

考 类比 potable 可饮用的 **to** water 水 ⇒ edible 可食用的 **to** vegetable 蔬菜 （修饰）
　　　potable 可饮用的 **to** water 水 ⇒ edible 可食用的 **to** food 食物 （修饰）

fabricate
['fæbrɪkeɪt] *v.* 制造，伪造

变 fabrication *n.* 捏造
记 用劣质布料（fabric）来伪造（fabricate）丝绸
考 同义 fabrication = lie；fabricate = falsify
　 类比 make 制作 **to** fabricate 伪造 ⇒ take apart 拆开 **to** disassemble 拆卸 （同义）
注 fabricate 这个单词的英文释义既有 to make or to create 的意思，也有 to make up for the purpose of deception 的意思。

muster
['mʌstə] *v.* 集合，召集

记 大师（master）要求所有人立即集合（muster）
考 同义 muster = congregate；muster = assemble；muster = convene

prey
[preɪ] *n.* 猎物，被捕食的动物

变 predatory *a.* 掠夺的，捕食的
记 猎人祈祷（pray）自己能找到猎物（prey）
考 同义 prey = target；predatory = carnivorous

urbane
[ɜːˈbeɪn] *a.* 彬彬有礼的，有礼貌的

记 城里人（urban）往往都很有礼貌（urbane）
考 同义 urbane = polite

List | **29** words　　　　　　　　　　　　★ 复习一下学过的单词！

□ bungle	□ episode	□ kiln	□ precede
□ circumlocution	□ etch	□ negligible	□ puck
□ citadel	□ feint	□ odious	□ stratify
□ cringe	□ haunt	□ panorama	□ terrier
□ douse	□ interloper	□ pluck	□ wary

SSAT词汇 List 31

★★★ sympathy ['sɪmpəθi] n. 同情心

- 变 sympathetic a. 有同情心的；sympathize v. 同情
- 记 sym-（same）+ path- 情感 + y：拥有相同情感即为有同情心
- 考 同义 sympathy = compassion

类比
revert 恢复 to reversion 恢复	⇒	sympathize 同情 to sympathy 同情	（同义）
improvisation 即兴 to preparation 准备	⇒	hostility 敌意 to sympathy 同情心	（反义）
antipathy 反感 to sympathy 同情	⇒	aversion 厌恶 to love 热爱	（反义）
adversary 敌人 to enmity 敌意	⇒	underdog 弱者 to sympathy 同情	（人物及其特点）

★★★ refine [rɪ'faɪn] v. 精炼，提纯

- 变 refined a. 有教养的；unrefined a. 不纯的；refinement n. 精致，文雅
- 记 re- + fine 好
- 考 同义 unrefined = crude；refined = genteel；refined = sophisticated

类比
condense 压缩 to compact 紧凑的	⇒	refine 精炼 to pure 纯的	（同义）
refined 有教养的 to vulgar 粗俗的	⇒	submissive 顺从的 to recalcitrant 叛逆的	（反义）
refined 有教养的 to courteous 有礼貌的	⇒	initial 开始的 to primary 初级的	（同义）
crass 粗鲁的 to refinement 文雅	⇒	pretentious 自命不凡的 to modesty 谦虚	（反义）
feral 野生的 to domestication 驯养	⇒	crude 粗鲁的 to refinement 文雅	（反义）
crude 粗糙的 to refinement 文雅	⇒	bland 乏味的 to flavor 味道	（缺乏）
simplify 简化 to complexity 复杂	⇒	refine 精炼 to impurity 杂质	（缺乏）

☆ sympathy　　☆ refine

★ psychiatrist

[saɪˈkaɪətrɪst] n. 精神病医生

记 psych- 精神 + -iatrist 人

考 类比

cardiologist 心脏学家 to heart 心 ⇒ psychiatrist 精神病专家 to mind 大脑 （人物及其对象）

pianist 钢琴家 to musicians 音乐家 ⇒ psychiatrist 精神病医生 to physician 内科医生 （种属）

★★ content

[kənˈtent] a. 满意的

变 malcontent a. 不满的；discontent n. 不满

考 同义 content = satisfied malcontent = dissatisfied

类比

discontent 不满 to rebellion 叛逆 ⇒ friction 摩擦 to spark 火花 （因果）

grumpy 脾气坏的 to malcontent 不满的 ⇒ prudent 谨慎的 to sage 明智的 （因果）

★ wreak

[riːk] v. 发泄，报仇

记 内心脆弱（weak），只敢找家人发泄（wreak）

考 同义 wreak = inflict

★ putrid

[ˈpjuːtrɪd] a. 恶臭的

记 充满恶臭的（putrid）礼物（tribute）

考 类比

putrid 恶臭的 to garbage 垃圾 ⇒ aromatic 有香味的 to spice 香料 （事物及其特点）

注 关于"恶臭的"单词在 SSAT 的习题中有很多，如：malodorous, stinking, fetid, noisome, rancid。

★★★ commencement

[kəˈmensmənt] n. 开始，毕业典礼

变 commence v. 开始

记 注意这个单词的两个中文翻译是很有趣的，一个"开始"，一个"结束"（毕业典礼）

考 同义 commence = institute；commencement = beginning

类比

obedience 听话 to submissiveness 顺从 ⇒ outset 开始 to commencement 开始 （同义）

valediction 告别演说 to commencement 毕业典礼 ⇒ dedication 题词 to opening 开业 （空间）

★ token

[ˈtəʊkən] n. 代表，象征

记 拿着（taken）皇帝钦赐的宝剑，象征（token）权利

考 同义 token = symbol

★ ransack

['rænsæk] *v.* 洗劫，搜查

记 ran + sack：拿个麻袋（sack）洗劫（ransack）之后就跑（ran）了
考 同义 ransack = search thoroughly

★ rendezvous

['rɒndɪvuːz] *n.* 约会

记 这个单词本身是个法语词，所以发音有些奇怪，大家一定要注意
考 同义 rendezvous = meeting

rendezvous

★ kennel

['kenl] *n.* 狗窝

记 在狗窝（kennel）里给狗修建了一条小的隧道（channel）
考 类比 stable/马厩 to horse/马 ⇒ kennel/狗窝 to dog/狗 （空间）

★ trial

['traɪəl] *n.* 审判，审讯

记 法官尝试（try）着去审判（trial）
考 类比 judgment/判决 to trial/审讯 ⇒ election/选举 to campaign/竞选活动 （事物及其部分）
    triumph/胜利 to competition/比赛 ⇒ verdict/裁定 to trial/审讯 （事物及其部分）

★★★ peel

[piːl] *n.* 皮

记 谐音"皮"
考 类比 bark/树皮 to tree/树 ⇒ peel/皮 to banana/香蕉 （事物及其部分）
    banana/香蕉 to peel/皮 ⇒ corn/玉米 to husk/外壳 （事物及其部分）
    egg/鸡蛋 to shell/蛋壳 ⇒ banana/香蕉 to peel/香蕉皮 （事物及其部分）
    banana/香蕉 to peel/皮 ⇒ peach/桃子 to skin/皮 （事物及其部分）

★★★ spicy

['spaɪsi] *a.* 辛辣的

变 spice *n.* 香料
记 我们常说的"辣的食物"英文即为 spicy food

考 同义　savory = spicy；spicy = aromatic

类比　panorama 全景 —to→ view 景色　⇒　pepper 胡椒 —to→ spice 香料　（种属）

safe 安全的 —to→ dangerous 危险的　⇒　bland 平淡的 —to→ spicy 辛辣的　（反义）

putrid 臭的 —to→ garbage 垃圾　⇒　aromatic 芳香的 —to→ spice 香料　（事物及其特点）

注　spicy 这个单词的英文释义为：having the flavor, aroma, or quality of spice。

puerile　['pjʊərɪl] *a.* 幼稚的，孩子气的

记　这个人，说好听了叫单纯（pure），说难听了就是幼稚（puerile）
考　同义　puerile = foolish

altar　['ɔːltə] *n.* 祭坛，圣坛

记　不要乱改变（alter）圣坛（altar）上东西的摆放位置

考　类比　table 桌子 —to→ altar 圣坛　⇒　song 歌曲 —to→ hymn 圣歌　（种属）

altar 祭坛 —to→ table 桌子　⇒　goblet 高脚杯 —to→ cup 杯子　（种属）

table 桌子 —to→ altar 祭坛　⇒　recess 凹处 —to→ alcove 凹室　（种属）

（alcove 这个单词的英文释义为：a small recessed section of a room）

注　altar 这个单词的英文释义为：a holy table in the church。

pride　[praɪd] *n.* 狮群

记　骄傲的（pride）狮群（pride）

考　类比　pride 狮群 —to→ lion 狮子　⇒　school 鱼群 —to→ fish 鱼　（组成）

注　pride 这个单词"骄傲的"意思我们很熟悉，此处是熟词僻义。

ghastly　['gɑːstli] *a.* 可怕的，恐怖的

记　见到鬼（ghost）觉得很可怕（ghastly）
考　同义　ghastly = horrible

nudge　[nʌdʒ] *v.* 轻推

记　Richard Thaler 于 2008 年推出的一本好书叫 *Nugde*
考　同义　nudge = shove

nudge

severe

[sɪˈvɪə] *a.* 严峻的，严厉的

变 severity *n.* 严厉

记 老师制定了七（seven）条严厉的（severe）规定，学生们再也不敢（never）破坏纪律

考 同义 austere = severe；extreme = severe；solemn = severe；harsh = severe
severity = harshness

List | **30** words ★ 复习一下学过的单词！

□ anarchy	□ choreography	□ muster	□ strenuous
□ announce	□ edible	□ portray	□ throng
□ authorize	□ fabricate	□ prey	□ transplant
□ aversion	□ helix	□ progeny	□ urbane
□ breeze	□ knot	□ static	□ wrath

☆ severe

SSAT词汇 List 32

★ conflate　　[kənˈfleɪt] v. 合并

- 记　把通货膨胀（inflate）和通货紧缩（deflate）合并在一起（conflate）就没有经济问题了
- 考　同义　conflate = mix up

★★★ illusion　　[ɪˈluːʒn] n. 错觉，幻觉

- 变　illusory a. 虚幻的，虚假的
- 记　因为生病（ill）很严重，所以常产生幻觉（illusion）
- 考　同义　illusion = mirage；illusory = fantasy

★★ suffocate　　[ˈsʌfəkeɪt] v. 压制，使窒息

- 变　suffocation n. 窒息
- 记　鼻子不通气，遭受（suffer）到窒息（suffocate）的处罚
- 考　同义　suffocate = deprive of air

　　类比　starvation 挨饿　to　food 食物　→　suffocation 窒息　to　air 空气　（缺乏）

★★ purloin　　[pɜːˈlɔɪn] v. 偷窃

- 记　pur-（pure）+ -loin（lion）：去动物园偷（purloin）了一只纯种的（pure）的狮子（lion）
- 考　同义　steal = purloin

★★ crust　　[krʌst] n. 地壳；面包壳

- 记　偶遇地震，地壳（crust）开始爆发（burst）
- 考　类比　bread 面包　to　crust 面包壳　→　orange 橘子　to　rind 橘子皮　（事物及其部分）

　　　　　canopy 华盖　to　forest 森林　→　crust 地壳　to　earth 地球　（事物及其部分）

　　（canopy 这个单词的英文释义为：the uppermost spreading branchy layer of a forest）

spectrum ★

['spektrəm] *n.* 光谱，范围

记 spect- 看 + rum：人能看（spect）到的范围（spectrum）
考 同义 spectrum = range

crawl ★★

[krɔːl] *v.* 爬

记 一只狗慢慢地爬（crawl）向一块生（raw）肉
考 类比 sow/播种 to reap/收获 ⇒ crawl/爬 to walk/走 （时间先后）
baby/小孩子 to crawl/爬 ⇒ frog/青蛙 to jump/跳 （人物及其特点）

taciturn ★★★

['tæsɪtɜːn] *a.* 不爱说话的

变 tacit *a.* 默认的，默许的
记 tacit-（tact）+ turn：徐庶无计（tact）可献，只好转向（turn）沉默（taciturn）
考 同义 taciturn = silent
类比 taciturn/沉默的 to words/言语 ⇒ thrifty/节约的 to money/钱 （缺乏）
reclusive/隐居的 to sociable/社交的 ⇒ taciturn/沉默的 to chatty/话多的 （反义）
taciturn/不太说话的 to quiet/安静的 ⇒ trusting/信任的 to gullible/易受骗的 （<程度）

flippant ★

['flɪpənt] *a.* 轻浮的，无礼的

变 flippancy *n.* 轻浮，轻率
记 轻浮的（flippant）人觉得《怦然心动》（Flipped）这个电影不好看
考 同义 flippant = impudent
类比 flippancy/轻浮 to jollity/快乐 ⇒ insolence/傲慢 to pride/自豪 （同义：正反向）
注 关于"轻浮的"单词在 SSAT 的习题中有很多，如：disrespectful, insolent。

flippant

dell ★

[del] *n.* 小山谷

记 戴尔（DELL）公司的诞生地就是美国的一个小山谷（dell）
考 同义 dell = valley

balk ★

['bɔːk] *v.* 阻止，阻碍

记 狗叫（bark）阻碍（balk）了你前进的步伐
考 同义 balk = prevent

distinct [dɪˈstɪŋkt] a. 明显的，独特的

- 变 indistinct a. 模糊的，不清楚的
- 记 站在人群中很容易被辨认（distinguish），所以是独特的（distinct）
- 考 同义 distinct = unique；indistinct = hazy

vow [vaʊ] v. 发誓

- 考 同义 oath = vow；pledge = vow

  类比 vow/发誓 to promise/许诺 ⇒ epiphany/顿悟 to realization/领悟 （＞程度）

olfactory [ɒlˈfæktəri] a. 嗅觉的

- 记 在这个酒厂（factory）工作的办公室女性（ol）有很好的嗅觉（olfactory）
- 考 类比
  - olfactory/嗅觉的 to smell/闻 ⇒ tactile/触觉的 to touch/接触 （同义）
  - taste/品尝 to gustatory/味觉的 ⇒ smell/闻 to olfactory/嗅觉的 （同义）
  - nose/鼻子 to olfactory/嗅觉的 ⇒ finger/手指 to tactile/触觉的 （事物及其特点）
  - nose/鼻子 to olfactory/嗅觉的 ⇒ ear/耳朵 to auditory/听觉的 （事物及其特点）

ponder [ˈpɒn.də] v. 沉思

- 记 谐音：胖的：好好思考（ponder）一下自己为什么如此胖
- 考 同义 contemplate = ponder；consider = ponder；ponder = ruminate

foster [ˈfɒstə] v. 培养，养育；鼓励

- 记 妈妈在森林（forest）里养育（foster）自己的孩子
- 考 同义 foster = promote；encourage = forster
- 注 foster 这个单词的英文释义为：to promote the growth or development。

unrealistic [ˌʌnriəˈlɪstɪk] a. 不切实际的

- 变 realistic a. 现实的
- 记 un- 否定 + realistic 现实的
- 考 同义 quixotic = unrealistic

  类比 unicorn/独角兽 to mythological/神话的 ⇒ horse/马 to realistic/现实的 （事物及其特点）

blight
[blaɪt] *n.* 枯萎病

记 b 不 + light 灯光：没有灯光就枯萎（blight）
考 同义 blight = disease

appendix
[əˈpendɪks] *n.* 附录

记 appendix 这个单词本来指人的"阑尾"，因为阑尾对人是可有可无的，所以引申出"附录"的意思，一般加在书的最后

考 类比 thesis / 论文 — to — appendix / 附录 （事物及其部分）
        dissertation / 论文 — to — appendix / 附录 （事物及其部分）

wily
[ˈwaɪli] *a.* 狡猾的

记 莉莉（Lily）是个很狡猾的（wily）姑娘
考 同义 crafty = wily；wily = cunning
注 wily = crafty = cunning 虽然翻译为"狡猾的"，但是多用于正向，强调当事人的聪明。

List | **31** words ★复习一下学过的单词！

- □ altar
- □ commencement
- □ content
- □ ghastly
- □ kennel
- □ nudge
- □ peel
- □ pride
- □ psychiatrist
- □ puerile
- □ putrid
- □ ransack
- □ refine
- □ rendezvous
- □ severe
- □ spicy
- □ sympathy
- □ token
- □ trial
- □ wreak

SSAT词汇 List 33

★★★ reckless ['rekləs] a. 鲁莽的，不顾后果的

- 变 recklessly ad. 鲁莽地
- 记 reck- (neck) + less：因为鲁莽（reckless）上路，导致开车追尾弄伤了自己的脖子（neck）
- 考 同义 recklessly = rashly；reckless = heedless

类比
foolhardy 蛮干的	to	recklessness 鲁莽	⇒	serene 安静的	to	tranquility 安静	（同义）
aimless 漫无目的的	to	direction 方向	⇒	reckless 鲁莽的	to	caution 谨慎	（缺乏）
circumspect 慎重的	to	wary 谨慎的	⇒	reckless 鲁莽的	to	foolhardy 有勇无谋的	（同义）
impromptu 即兴的	to	preparation 准备	⇒	reckless 鲁莽的	to	caution 谨慎	（缺乏）
intangible 无形的	to	palpable 可感知的	⇒	prudent 谨慎的	to	reckless 鲁莽的	（反义）

★ incensed [ɪn'senst] a. 愤怒的

- 记 incense 这个单词本是"焚香"之意，引申为"激怒"
- 考 同义 incensed = angry
- 注 关于"愤怒的"单词在SSAT的习题中有很多，如：infuriated, irritated。

★★★ harmonious [hɑː'məʊnɪəs] a. 和谐的

- 变 harmony n. 和谐；harmonize v. 使和谐，使协调
- 记 我们常说的"和谐社会"就是 harmonious society
- 考 同义 harmonize = conform；harmony = consensus

类比
| harmonious 悦耳的 | to | music 音乐 | | | | | （修饰） |
| symmetry 对称 | to | eye 眼睛 | ⇒ | harmony 和谐 | to | ear 耳朵 | （事物及其特点） |

intrude

[ɪnˈtruːd] *v.* 闯入，侵扰

记 in + trud-（true）+ e：闯入（intrude）真理（true）的大门

考 类比 $\dfrac{\text{interrupt}}{\text{打断}}$ to $\dfrac{\text{speak}}{\text{说话}}$ ⇒ $\dfrac{\text{intrude}}{\text{闯入}}$ to $\dfrac{\text{enter}}{\text{进入}}$ （种属）

注 关于"闯入，侵扰"的单词在 SSAT 的习题中有很多，如：pry，meddle，inquire。

joggle

[ˈdʒɒɡl] *v.* 轻轻摇动

记 慢跑（jog）的时候身体在轻轻摇动（joggle）

考 同义 joggle = shake

stench

[stentʃ] *n.* 恶臭

记 因为恶臭（stink），所以恶臭（stench）

考 类比 $\dfrac{\text{odor}}{\text{臭味}}$ to $\dfrac{\text{stench}}{\text{恶臭}}$ ⇒ $\dfrac{\text{sad}}{\text{伤心的}}$ to $\dfrac{\text{tragic}}{\text{悲剧的}}$ （＜程度）

hackneyed

[ˈhæknɪd] *a.* 陈腐的，平庸的

记 hackney 这个单词的意思众多，可以是地名"哈克尼区"，也可以是"陈腐的"，也可以是"出租马车"和"做苦工的人"，而且这些单词从辞源上来说都是有联系的，想进一步了解的话，可以自己去翻翻词典

考 同义 hackneyed = boring

类比 $\dfrac{\text{hackneyed}}{\text{陈腐的}}$ to $\dfrac{\text{expression}}{\text{表达}}$ ⇒ $\dfrac{\text{threadbare}}{\text{磨损的}}$ to $\dfrac{\text{attire}}{\text{衣物}}$ （修饰）

whip

[wɪp] *n.* 鞭子

记 第 87 届奥斯卡获奖影片《爆裂鼓手》（*Whiplash*）

考 类比 $\dfrac{\text{whip}}{\text{鞭子}}$ to $\dfrac{\text{lash}}{\text{鞭笞}}$ ⇒ $\dfrac{\text{club}}{\text{棍棒}}$ to $\dfrac{\text{beat}}{\text{击打}}$ （动宾）

composure

[kəmˈpəʊʒə] *n.* 沉着，冷静

记 compose 除了有"组成"之意外，本身也有"平静"的意思

考 同义 composure = self-control

autonomous

[ɔːˈtɒnəməs] *a.* 自治的，自主的

记 中国的五个自治区英文即为 autonomous regions

考 类比 $\dfrac{\text{follow}}{\text{跟随}}$ to $\dfrac{\text{lead}}{\text{引导}}$ ⇒ $\dfrac{\text{dependent}}{\text{依靠的}}$ to $\dfrac{\text{autonomous}}{\text{自治的}}$ （反义）

ostentation ★★★
[ˌɒstenˈteɪʃn] n. 卖弄

- 变 ostentatious a. 招摇的，引人注意的
- 记 我当老师的目的（intention）可不是为了卖弄（ostentation）
- 考 同义 ostentatious = flashy；ostentatious = showy；ostentatious = pretentious
- 类比 ostentation 卖弄 [to] simplicity 朴素 ⇒ hypocrisy 虚伪 [to] sincerity 真诚 （反义）

aria ★★★
[ˈɑːriə] n. 咏叹调，独唱曲

aria

- 记 谐音：啊一啊：感觉一个歌手在唱咏叹调
- 考 类比 soliloquy 独白 [to] play 戏剧 ⇒ aria 咏叹调 [to] opera 歌剧 （种属）
  aria 咏叹调 [to] opera 歌剧 ⇒ monologue 独白 [to] play 戏剧 （种属）

transmit ★
[trænzˈmɪt] v. 发射，传播

- 考 同义 transmit = send symbol

cyclical ★
[ˈsaɪklɪkl] a. 循环的，往复的

- 记 cycli-（cycle）+ -cal
- 考 同义 cyclical = recurrent；cyclical = repetitive

burgeon
[ˈbɜːdʒən] v. 发芽，迅速成长

- 记 医生（surgeon）给病人做完手术之后，病人身体好转，迅速成长（burgeon）
- 考 同义 burgeon = flourish

recoil ★★
[rɪˈkɔɪl] v. 退缩，畏缩

- 记 re- + -coil (oil)：地沟油就是反复（re）使用过的油（oil），老百姓都对此望而却步（recoil）
- 考 同义 recoil = withdraw
- 类比 grisly 可怕的 [to] recoil 退缩 ⇒ heartrending 悲惨的 [to] weep 哭泣 （因果）

labyrinth ★★
[ˈlæbərɪnθ] n. 迷宫

- 变 labyrinthine a. 迷宫的，复杂的
- 记 可以通过一部电影来记住这个表示"迷宫"的词：《潘神的迷宫》（Pan's Labyrinth）
- 考 同义 maze = labyrinth

| 类比 | labyrinth 迷宫 | to | network 网状 | ⇒ | maze 迷宫 | to | passages 通道 | （纵向） |
| | palatial 壮丽的 | to | space 地方 | ⇒ | labyrinthine 复杂的 | to | corridor 走廊 | （修饰） |

★ droll [drəʊl] *a.* 滑稽的，搞笑的

记 这个演员边说话边流口水（drool），显得很搞笑（droll）

考 类比 cross 生气的 — to — angry 生气的 ⇒ droll 滑稽的 — to — funny 搞笑的 （同义）

★★★ resolution [ˌrezəˈluːʃn] *n.* 决议

变 resolve *v.* 决定，下决心
记 我们每年元旦的时候都会给自己制定一个 New Year's Resolution
考 同义 resolve = decide

类比
gibber 胡言乱语	to	sense 意义	⇒	vacillate 犹豫	to	resolution 决心	（缺乏）
lax 放松的	to	resolution 决心	⇒	deceitful 欺骗的	to	sincerity 真诚	（缺乏）
integrity 正直	to	honesty 诚实	⇒	resolution 决心	to	determination 决定	（同义）
congress 国会	to	statute 法规	⇒	meeting 会议	to	resolution 决议	（空间）

★★ collaboration [kəˌlæbəˈreɪʃn] *n.* 合作

变 collaborative *a.* 合作的
记 col- + labor 劳动 + -ation：大家在一起合作（collaboration）劳动
考 同义 collaboration = work together

类比
| collaboration 合作 | to | cooperation 合作 | ⇒ | collation 校对 | to | correction 改正 | （同义） |
| varied 多变的 | to | identical 一样的 | ⇒ | collaborative 合作的 | to | unilateral 单边的 | （反义） |

List | 32 words ★复习一下学过的单词！

☐ appendix	☐ crust	☐ illusion	☐ suffocate
☐ balk	☐ dell	☐ olfactory	☐ taciturn
☐ blight	☐ distinct	☐ ponder	☐ unrealistic
☐ conflate	☐ flippant	☐ purloin	☐ vow
☐ crawl	☐ foster	☐ spectrum	☐ wily

☆ droll   ☆ resolution   ☆ collaboration

SSAT词汇 List 34

★★★ surrender
[sə'rendə] *v.* 投降

记 被敌人包围（surround）只能投降（surrender）

考 同义 relinquish = surrender; capitulate = surrender; yield = surrender
succumb = surrender; sacrifice = surrender
（sacrifice 这个单词的英文释义为：destruction or surrender of something for the sake of something else。）

类比 capitulate (to) surrender ⇒ remonstrate (to) protest （同义）
投降　　　认输　　　　　抗议　　　　抗议

intransigent (to) compromise ⇒ dogged (to) surrender （反义）
不妥协的　　妥协　　　　　顽强的　　投降

★★ noble
['nəubl] *a.* 高尚的，贵族的

变 ignoble *a.* 卑鄙的，不光彩的；nobility *n.* 贵族，高尚

考 同义 noble = gallant; base = ignoble

类比 confidant (to) enemy ⇒ nobility (to) dishonor （反义）
知己　　　敌人　　　　高尚　　　丢脸

★★ obstinate
['ɒbstɪnət] *a.* 顽固的，倔强的

记 我的直觉（instinct）告诉我要坚持（obstinate）下去

考 同义 obstinate = stubborn

类比 persistent (to) obstinate ⇒ valiant (to) brave （同义）
固执的　　　固执的　　　　勇敢的　　勇敢的

brusque (to) unceremoniousness ⇒ obstinate (to) intractability （同义）
唐突的　　　随意，无礼　　　　　顽固的　　难驾驭

★★ chaotic
[keɪ'ɒtɪk] *a.* 混沌的，混乱的

记 这个单词的名词形式 chaos 即为我们从小开玩笑说的"吵死"

考 同义 chaotic = disorderly

☆ surrender　　☆ noble　　☆ obstinate　　☆ chaotic

类比　obsolete/过时 to disuse/停止使用 ⇒ chaotic/混乱 to confusion/困惑　（同义）

注　chaotic 这个单词的英文释义为：a state of utter confusion。

collide　[kəˈlaɪd] *v.* 碰撞，冲突

考　同义　collide = jostle
　　类比　alter/更改 to distort/扭曲 ⇒ bump/碰撞 to collide/冲突　（同义）

disconcert　[ˌdɪskənˈsɜːt] *v.* 使惊慌失措

变　disconcerting *a.* 仓皇失措的
记　明星演唱会（concert）混乱一片，让粉丝们惊慌失措（disconcert）
考　同义　disconcerting = unsettling

malice　[ˈmælɪs] *n.* 恶意，恶毒

变　malicious *a.* 恶意的，恶毒的
记　爱丽丝（Alice）心怀恶意（malice）
考　同义　malicious = spiteful；malice = spite；malice = hatred；hostile = malicious
　　类比　malicious/恶毒的 to harm/伤害 ⇒ destructive/破坏的 to damage/破坏　（同义）
　　　　　careless/粗心的 to neglect/忽略 ⇒ malicious/恶毒的 to sabotage/破坏　（动作及其情感）

注　关于"恶毒"的单词在 SSAT 的习题中有很多，如：hatred, resentment, rancor, enmity。

tracery　[ˈtreɪsəri] *n.* 窗饰

记　按照窗饰（tracery）所提供的线索来追踪（trace）罪犯
考　同义　tracery = design

paragon　[ˈpærəɡən] *n.* 模范

记　五角大楼（Pentagon）是全世界建筑的典范（paragon）
考　类比　paragon/模范 to epitome/典型 ⇒ vacuum/真空 to void/真空　（同义）

inscribe　[ɪnˈskraɪb] *v.* 题写，题词

变　inscription *n.* 题字，题词
记　订阅（subscribe）杂志，需要签字（inscribe）
考　同义　inscribe = chisel　inscription = endorsement

warn [wɔːn] v. 警告

变 warning n. 警告

考 类比 consume 消耗 [to] devour 吞食 ⇒ warn 警告 [to] alert 警告 （同义）
　　　　 siren 警报 [to] warning 警告 ⇒ light 光 [to] illumination 照亮 （事物及其目的）

contrite [kənˈtraɪt] a. 后悔的

记 他谋划（contrive）去害别人，结果自己也受到连累，所以很后悔（contrite）

考 同义 contrite = regretful

　　 类比 penitent 忏悔者 [to] contrite 后悔的 ⇒ zealot 狂热者 [to] fanatical 狂热的 （人物及其特点）
　　　　　 merciful 仁慈的 [to] clemency 仁慈 ⇒ contrite 后悔的 [to] remorse 懊悔 （同义）

注 关于"后悔的"单词在 SSAT 的习题中有很多，如：rueful, repented, remorseful。

applause [əˈplɔːz] n. 欢呼，喝彩

记 ap- + -plause（pause）暂停：在演出中，演员必须暂停（pause）演出来接受观众的喝彩（applause）

考 同义 ovation = applause

celestial [sɪˈlestɪəl] a. 天上的

记 古时中国被称为"天朝大国"，对应的英文即为 celestial empire

考 类比 terrestrial 陆地的 [to] earth 陆地 ⇒ celestial 天上的 [to] heaven 天堂 （同义）
　　　　　 earth 地球 [to] terrestrial 地球的 ⇒ planet 行星 [to] celestial 天上的 （空间）

mendicant [ˈmendɪkənt] n. 乞丐

记 谐音：Mandy can't：Mandy can't 去做一个乞丐（mendicant）

考 同义 beggar = mendicant

　　 类比 mendicant 乞丐 [to] beg 乞求 ⇒ braggart 吹牛者 [to] boast 吹牛 （人物及其动作）

revoke [rɪˈvəʊk] v. 撤销，撤回

变 irrevocable a. 无法撤销的

记 re- 收回 + vok-（voice）+ e：收回（re）自己说过的话（voice）即为撤销（revoke）

考 同义 revoke = rescind；irrevocable = irreversible

★★ tropical

[ˈtrɒpɪkl] *a.* 热带的

记 我们常说的"热带鱼"即为 tropical fish

考 类比 mountain 山 to valley 峡谷 ⇒ temperate 温和的 to tropical 热带的 （反义）

frigid 严寒的 to tropical 热带的 ⇒ raw 生的 to cooked 加工过的 （反义）

★ apron

[ˈeɪprən] *n.* 围裙

记 这个人只有在四月（April）做饭的时候才穿围裙（apron）

考 类比 apron 围裙 to protect 保护 ⇒ lamp 灯 to illuminate 照亮 （事物及其用途）

apron 围裙 to cook 厨师 ⇒ coverall 工作服 to scientist 科学家 （人物及其特点）

★ hapless

[ˈhæplɪs] *a.* 不幸的

记 hap-（happy）快乐的 + -less 否定

考 同义 hapless = unlucky

类比 spiritual 精神的 to divine 神圣的 ⇒ wretched 可怜的 to hapless 倒霉的 （同义）

★ abate

[əˈbeɪt] *v.* 减轻，减少

记 因为被打（beat），所以攻击力减少（abate）

考 同义 abate = placate

注 关于"减轻，节制"的单词在 SSAT 的习题中有很多，如：alleviate, assuage, curtail, dampen, mitigate, moderate.

List | **33** words ★ 复习一下学过的单词！

□ aria	□ cyclical	□ intrude	□ recoil
□ autonomous	□ droll	□ joggle	□ resolution
□ burgeon	□ hackneyed	□ labyrinth	□ stench
□ collaboration	□ harmonious	□ ostentation	□ transmit
□ composure	□ incensed	□ reckless	□ whip

☆ tropical ☆ apron ☆ hapless ☆ abate

SSAT词汇 List 35

★
automatic ［ˌɔːtəˈmætɪk] *a.* 自动的

考 同义　automatic = involuntary

★★★
botany ［ˈbɒtəni] *n.* 植物学

变　botanist *n.* 植物学家

考 类比
botany 植物学 — to — plants 植物 → meteorology 气象学 — to — weather 天气　（事物及其对象）
neuroscience 神经科学 — to — brain 大脑 → botany 植物学 — to — plants 植物　（事物及其对象）
botanist 植物学家 — to — plants 植物 → geologist 地质学家 — to — minerals 矿物　（人物及其对象）
weather 天气 — to — meteorologists 气象学家 → vegetation 植被 — to — botanist 植物学家　（人物及其对象）

★★★
domestic ［dəˈmestɪk] *a.* 国内的，驯养的

变　domestication *n.* 驯养；domesticated *a.* 家养的，驯服的

考 类比
domestic 家养的 — to — dog 狗 → wild 野生的 — to — coyote 豺狼　（修饰）
domestic 家养的 — to — dog 狗 → wild 野生的 — to — wolf 狼　（修饰）
human 人 — to — civilized 文明的 → dog 狗 — to — domesticated 驯养的　（修饰）
feral 野生的 — to — domestication 驯养 → crude 粗鲁的 — to — refinement 文雅　（反义）
foreign 外国的 — to — domestic 国内的 → liberated 解放的 — to — incarcerated 监禁的　（反义）

★
vibrate ［vaɪˈbreɪt] *v.* 振动

记　手机调成英文版，然后设置里面调成"振动"，所对应的英文单词即为 vibrate

考 类比
blossom 开花 — to — bloom 开花 → quiver 震颤 — to — vibrate 震动　（同义）

coop ★
[kuːp] *n.* 鸡笼

- 记 这个鸡笼（coop）好酷（cool）
- 考 类比 coop[鸡笼] to poultry[家禽] ⇒ aquarium[水族馆] to fish[鱼] （空间）

ambience ★
[ˈæmbiəns] *n.* 氛围，气氛

- 记 现场观众（audience）气氛（ambience）热烈
- 考 同义 mood = ambience
- 注 ambience 这个单词的英文释义为：a feeling or mood associated with a particular place, person, or thing。

gregarious ★★
[grɪˈɡeəriəs] *a.* 社交的，群居的

- 记 格雷格（Greg）是个喜欢社交的（gregarious）孩子
- 考 同义 gregarious = sociable
  类比 introspective[内省的] to withdrawn[沉默的] ⇒ gregarious[社交的] to social[社会的] （同义）
  satiate[使满足] to satisfy[满足] ⇒ gregarious[社交的] to social[社交的] （同义）

criminal ★★
[ˈkrɪmɪnl] *n.* 罪犯

- 考 同义 criminal = felon；criminal = desperado

provoke ★★★
[prəˈvəʊk] *v.* 激怒，煽动

- 变 provocateur *n.* 煽动者
- 记 pro- 朝前 + vok-（voice）+ e：被激怒（provoke）的时候，就想朝前（pro）说出自己心声（voice）
- 考 同义 incite = provoke；instigate = provoke
  类比 swipe[偷窃] to pilfer[偷窃] ⇒ provoke[激怒] to vex[使烦恼] （同义）
  provocateur[煽动者] to trouble[麻烦] ⇒ mediator[调停者] to agreement[一致] （人物及其特点）
- 注 关于"煽动"的单词在 SSAT 的习题中有很多，如：agitate，foment。

petition ★
[pɪˈtɪʃn] *n.* 请愿

- 记 我再次重申（repetition），对于这次比赛（competition）中我队受到的不公正待遇，我会继续请愿（petition）上级来处理的
- 考 类比 petition[请愿] to ask[要求] ⇒ narrate[叙述] to tell[告诉] （同义）

sauce ★
[sɔːs] *n.* 酱料

- 记 我们常说的快餐店的番茄酱都叫 ketchup，也可以称为 tomato sauce

考 类比 pasta 意大利面 to sauce 酱料 ⇒ toast 吐司 to jam 果酱 （事物及其部分）

congenital [kən'dʒenɪtl] a. 先天的，天生的

记 这俩兄弟天生（congenital）意气相投（congenial）
考 同义 congenital = inborn
类比 nature 自然 to nurture 培养 ⇒ congenital 先天的 to acquired 后天习得的 （纵向）
注 关于"天生的"单词在 SSAT 的习题中有很多，如：natal, innate, inherent。

marvel ['mɑːvl] n. 奇迹

记 美国漫威公司（也译作惊奇公司）英文即为 marvel
考 同义 marvel = wonder
类比 marvel 奇迹 to myth 神话 ⇒ fact 事实 to history 历史 （同类）

annoy [ə'nɔɪ] v. 骚扰，惹恼

变 annoying a. 恼人的；annoyed a. 恼人的
考 同义 annoy = torment
类比 pest 害虫 to annoying 烦人的 ⇒ plateau 高原 to level 平坦的 （事物及其特点）
abash 使困窘 to embarrassment 尴尬 ⇒ annoy 惹恼 to irritation 激怒 （同义）
insult 侮辱 to compliment 夸奖 ⇒ please 取悦 to annoy 激怒 （反义）
gadfly 讨人厌者 to annoying 恼人的 ⇒ churl 粗鄙之人 to rude 粗鲁的 （事物及其特点）
annoying 烦人的 to insufferable 难以容忍的 ⇒ chatty 爱讲话的 to long-winded 冗长的 （<程度）
annoyed 恼人的 to distraught 心烦意乱的 ⇒ moody 情绪化的 to depressed 非常沮丧的 （<程度）
注 关于"激怒"的单词在 SSAT 的习题中有很多，如：provoke, stir, irritate, ire。

calendar ['kælɪndə] n. 日历

考 类比 calendar 日历 to day 日子 ⇒ clock 表 to hour 小时 （事物及其用途）
calendar 日历 to days 日子 ⇒ chronometer 计时器 to time 时间 （事物及其用途）
calendar 日历 to date 日子 ⇒ clock 表 to hour 小时 （事物及其用途）

captivate ['kæptɪveɪt] v. 迷住，迷惑

记 警察本来是去抓（capture）坏人，结果却被坏人迷住（captivate）了

☆ congenital　　☆ marvel　　☆ annoy　　☆ calendar　　☆ captivate

考 同义　enthrall = captivate；captivate = charm

★★ versatile　[ˈvɜːsətaɪl] *a.* 多才多艺的

记　vers- (versus) 对抗 + -atile (elite) 精英：经过多轮对抗 (versus)，发现双方均是精英 (versatile)，都很多才多艺 (versatile)

考 同义　versatile = adaptable；versatile = changing

类比　versatile 多才多艺的 to adapt 适应 ⇒ buoyant 有浮力的 to float 漂浮　（动作及其情感）

★★ commission　[kəˈmɪʃn] *n.* 佣金；委托，委任

记　为了佣金 (commission)，大家在一起做任务 (mission)

考 类比
commission 委任 to appointment 任命 ⇒ intermission 休息 to break 休息 （同义）
salesperson 销售 to commission 佣金 ⇒ author 作者 to royalty 版税 （人物及其对象）
broker 经纪人 to commission 佣金 ⇒ worker 工人 to remuneration 报酬 （人物及其对象）

★★★ collage　[ˈkɒlɑːʒ] *n.* 剪贴画

记　这幅剪贴画 (collage) 是由很多大学 (college) 校门组成的

考 类比
palette 调色盘 to colors 颜色 ⇒ collage 剪贴画 to images 图像 （组成）
song 歌曲 to medley 混合曲 ⇒ picture 图画 to collage 剪贴画 （组成）
collage 剪贴画 to painting 绘画 ⇒ mosaic 马赛克 to tile 瓷砖 （组成）

★ extricate　[ˈekstrɪkeɪt] *v.* 使解脱，使解放

记　ex- 朝外 + tric- 拉 + -ate

考 类比　exculpate 开脱 to blame 责备 ⇒ extricate 解脱 to difficulty 困难 （缺乏）

List | **34** words　★ 复习一下学过的单词！

□ abate	□ collide	□ malice	□ revoke
□ applause	□ contrite	□ mendicant	□ surrender
□ apron	□ disconcert	□ noble	□ tracery
□ celestial	□ hapless	□ obstinate	□ tropical
□ chaotic	□ inscribe	□ paragon	□ warn

☆ versatile　☆ commission　☆ collage　☆ extricate

SSAT词汇 List 36

★★★ temperate
['tempərət] a. 温和的，适度的

变 intemperate a. 酗酒的，放纵的；temperance n. 温和，适度
记 温度（temperature）适中（temperate）
考 同义 moderate = temperate；restraint = temperance（temperance 这个单词的英文释义为 moderation and self-restraint, as in behavior or expression）

类比
mountain 山 to valley 峡谷 ⇒ temperate 温和的 to tropical 热带的 （反义）
impecunious 贫穷的 to affluent 富裕的 ⇒ sober 清醒的 to intemperate 酗酒的 （反义）
remiss 疏忽的 to dutifulness 责任 ⇒ intemperate 放纵的 to moderation 适度 （反义）
dispassionate 平心静气的 to partisanship 党派偏见 ⇒ intemperate 放纵的 to moderation 节制 （反义）

★★ parch
[pɑ:tʃ] v. 烤，烧焦

变 parchment n. 羊皮纸；parched a. 烧焦的，非常口渴的
记 公园（park）里的小树被烧焦（parch）了
考 同义 parch = burn

类比
pallid 苍白的 to color 颜色 ⇒ parched 烧焦的 to moisture 湿度 （缺乏）
scroll 卷轴 to parchment 羊皮纸 ⇒ book 书 to paper 纸 （组成）
sated 满足的 to ravenous 贪婪的 ⇒ quenched 熄灭的 to parched 烧焦的 （反义）
ravenous 贪婪的 to hunger 饥饿 ⇒ parched 非常口渴的 to thirsty 口渴的 （>程度）
humorous 幽默的 to hilarious 极其搞笑的 ⇒ warm 温暖的 to parched 烧焦的 （<程度）

★ gala
['gɑ:lə] a. 节日的

记 国内因演唱《追梦赤子心》而走红的 GALA 乐队
有了三星（galaxy）手机，感觉跟过年似的（gala）
考 同义 gala = festive

abortive ★
[əˈbɔːtɪv] *a.* 失败的，流产的

- 记 大约（about）是早上十点传来了她流产的（abortive）消息
- 考 同义 abortive = unsuccessful

spoil ★★★
[spɔɪl] *v.* 破坏

- 考 同义 mar = spoil；spoil = deface
- 类比 cheese 奶酪 — to — mold 发霉 ⇒ milk 牛奶 — to — spoil 洒 （事物及其动作）

comprise ★
[kəmˈpraɪz] *v.* 组成

- 考 同义 comprise = be made up of；contain = comprise

petrify ★
[ˈpetrɪfaɪ] *v.* 石化

- 变 petrified *a.* 石化的
- 记 生物沉积石化（petrify），继而变成汽油（petrol）
- 考 类比 fossil 化石 — to — petrified 石化的 ⇒ solution 溶液 — to — dissolved 溶解的 （修饰）

erudite ★★★
[ˈeruːdaɪt] *a.* 博学的

- 记 e- 朝外 + rudi-（rude）+ te：走出粗鲁（rude）状态，引申为博学的（erudite）
- 考 同义 erudite = knowledgable
- 类比 erudite 博学的 — to — pedantic 迂腐的 ⇒ pious 虔诚的 — to — sanctimonious 假装虔诚的 （同义：正反向）

exorbitant ★★
[ɪɡˈzɔːbɪtənt] *a.* 过高的，过分的

- 记 ex- 朝外 + orbit + -ant：超过轨道（orbit），显得过高（exorbitant）
- 考 同义 exorbitant = excessive
- 类比 erratic 不稳定的 — to — predictable 可预测的 ⇒ exorbitant 过分的 — to — reasonable 合理的 （反义）

caricature ★
[ˈkærɪkətʃʊə] *n.* 夸张的讽刺漫画

- 记 这个单词里面包含 car 和 cat：猫在开车，说明这是一幅讽刺漫画（caricature）
- 考 类比 caricature 漫画 — to — drawing 画 ⇒ hyperbole 夸张言辞 — to — statement 言论 （＞程度）
  caricature 漫画 — to — portrait 画 ⇒ hyperbole 夸张言辞 — to — statement 言论 （＞程度）

★★★ lucid ['luːsɪd] a. 清晰的

谐音：Lucy 的：Lucy 的眼睛清澈透明（lucid）

同义：lucid = understandable

类比：
- lucid 清晰的 to clear 清楚的 → sullen 愠怒的 to gloomy 沮丧的（同义）
- lucid 明晰的 to pellucid 明晰的 → lofty 崇高的 to elevated 高尚的（同义）
- cogent 令人信服的 to persuasiveness 说服力 → lucid 清晰的 to clarity 澄清（同义）

★ puncture ['pʌŋktʃə] v. 刺穿

记：某次在一个饭店看到把"三文鱼刺身"翻译成 the salmon punctures the body

同义：stab = puncture；puncture = perforate

类比：puncture 刺穿 to perforate 穿孔 → preview 预习 to peruse 精读（同类）

the salmon punctures the body …… 26 $

puncture

★ parry ['pæri] v. 回避，挡开

记：水果姐（Katty Parry）尝试着回避（parry）狗仔

同义：parry = deflect

parry

★ derogatory [dɪ'rɒgətri] a. 贬损的

记：他因为过于傲慢（arrogant），所以被大家贬损（derogatory）

类比：impressive 使人钦佩的 to inspiring 激励的 → derogatory 贬低的 to critical 批评的（同义）

★★ stomp [stɒmp] v. 跺脚

记：他非常生气，暴风雨（storm）般地开始跺脚（stomp）

类比：
- clap 鼓掌 to stomp 跺脚 → hand 手 to foot 脚（纵向）
- stomp 跺脚 to step 踩 → shove 猛推 to push 推（＞程度）
- stomp 跺脚 to walk 走路 → shout 大叫 to speak 说话（＞程度）

★★★ chapter ['tʃæptə] n. 章节

记：翻开大部分英文书的目录部分就可以看到这个词

类比：movement 乐章 to symphony 交响乐 → chapter 章节 to book 书（组成）

146　☆ lucid　☆ puncture　☆ parry　☆ derogatory　☆ stomp
　　☆ chapter

paragraph 段落 to sentence 句子 ⇒ book 书 to chapter 章节 （组成）
chapter 章节 to book 书 ⇒ scene 场景 to play 戏剧 （组成）
novel 小说 to chapter 章节 ⇒ ballad 歌谣 to stanza 诗节 （组成）

insult

[ɪnˈsʌlt] v. 侮辱

考 类比　flame 火焰 to burn 点燃 ⇒ insult 侮辱 to anger 生气 （因果）
　　　　insult 侮辱 to compliment 夸奖 ⇒ please 取悦 to annoy 激怒 （反义）

impair

[ɪmˈpeə] v. 损害，危害

记　im- 否定 + pair：不让（im）一对（pair）夫妻在一起，这样就损害（impair）他们的关系
考　同义　impair = damage

constant

[ˈkɒnstənt] a. 经常的

考　同义　constant = steadfast；incessant = constant
　　类比　occasional 偶然的 to constant 经常的 ⇒ intermittent 间歇的 to incessant 连续的 （＜程度）

wreath

[riːθ] n. 花冠，花环

记　趁着天气（weather）好，出去采花做花环（wreath）
考　同义　wreath = nosegay

List | **35** words　　　★ 复习一下学过的单词！

□ ambience　□ captivate　□ criminal　□ petition
□ annoy　□ collage　□ domestic　□ provoke
□ automatic　□ commission　□ extricate　□ sauce
□ botany　□ congenital　□ gregarious　□ versatile
□ calendar　□ coop　□ marvel　□ vibrate

☆ insult　　☆ impair　　☆ constant　　☆ wreath

SSAT词汇 List 37

shove [ʃʌv] v. 猛推
记 推（shove）车的时候不小心把别人的车给刮（shave）了
考 同义 nudge = shove

类比
- snack 吃零食 to devour 吞食 ⇒ push 推 to shove 强推 （<程度）
- stomp 跺脚 to step 踩 ⇒ shove 猛推 to push 推 （>程度）

retaliation [rɪˌtæliˈeɪʃn] n. 复仇
记 好莱坞电影《特种部队Ⅱ——全面反击》(Retaliation)
考 同义 retaliation = reprisal

epilogue [ˈepɪlɒg] n. 结语，尾声
记 一场戏剧有它的开场白（prologue）和收尾（epilogue）

类比
- epilogue 结语 to book 书 ⇒ finale 终曲 to symphony 交响乐 （事物及其部分）
- epilogue 结语 to novel 小说 ⇒ finale 终曲 to symphony 交响乐 （事物及其部分）
- postscript 附言 to letter 信 ⇒ epilogue 结语 to play 戏剧 （事物及其部分）
- finale 终曲 to opera 歌剧 ⇒ epilogue 尾声 to play 戏剧 （事物及其部分）

divulge [daɪˈvʌldʒ] v. 泄露，暴露
记 诺亚不小心泄露（divulge）了洪水（deluge）的消息
考 同义 divulge = tell; disclose = divulge; reveal = divulge

类比
- divulge 泄露 to disclose 揭露 ⇒ appraise 评估 to estimate 估计 （同义）
- divulge 泄露 to public 公开的 ⇒ rectify 改正 to right 正确的 （同义）

inventory

[ˈɪnvəntri] *n.* 存货清单

记 到底是谁发明（invent）了存货清单（inventory）这个东西呢

考 类比 inventory/存货清单 to goods/货品 ⇒ roll/名单 to members/成员 （空间）

arboreal

[ɑːˈbɔːriəl] *a.* 树木的

记 谐音：阿伯：阿伯身体像树木（arboreal）一样健壮

考 类比 arboreal/树木的 to tree/树 ⇒ aquatic/水生的 to water/水 （同义）

muffle

[ˈmʌfl] *v.* 裹住，抑制

变 muffler *n.* 消音器

记 很多封建社会的女人，稀里糊涂（muddle）地就被裹（muffle）了小脚

考 类比
muffle/消音 to sound/声音 ⇒ dim/暗淡 to light/光 （动宾）
muffle/消音 to sound/声音 ⇒ restrain/约束 to motion/移动 （动宾）
lubricate/润滑 to smoothly/光滑地 ⇒ muffle/蒙住 to quietly/安静地 （动作及其目的）
muffle/抑制 to noise/噪音 ⇒ dam/大坝 to flood/洪水 （事物及其对象）
anesthetic/麻醉剂 to pain/疼痛 ⇒ muffler/消音器 to noise/噪音 （事物及其对象）

muffle

previous

[ˈpriːviəs] *a.* 之前的

记 美剧开头都会说一句 Previously on…

考 同义 foregone ＝ previous

discreet

[dɪˈskriːt] *a.* 谨慎的

记 注意区分 "谨慎的" discreet 和 "分散的" discrete

考 同义 cautious ＝ discreet；discreet ＝ guarded；discreet ＝ prudent

类比 discreet/谨慎的 to brash/仓促的 ⇒ grave/严肃的 to frivolous/轻佻的 （反义）

babble

[ˈbæbl] *v.* 含糊不清地说；*n.* 小溪潺潺流水声

记 这个单词的发音就好像是小孩子在 bla～bla～bla～bla

考 类比
babble/乱说 to talk/说话 ⇒ scribble/乱涂 to write/写 （同义：正反向）
floundering/挣扎 to movement/行动 ⇒ babble/乱说 to speech/演讲 （同义：正反向）

☆ inventory   ☆ arboreal   ☆ muffle   ☆ previous   ☆ discreet
☆ babble

muddle 使困惑	to	reasoning 说理	⇒	babble 乱说	to	speech 演讲	（同义 正反向）
meander 蜿蜒前进	to	direction 方向	⇒	babble 乱说	to	meaning 意义	（缺乏）
wind 风	to	whistle 呼啸声	⇒	brook 小溪	to	babble 潺潺流水声	（事物及其特点）

★ plumage   ['plu:mɪdʒ] *n.* 羽毛

记 放时间久了（age）的李子（plum）身上长满了毛，从远处看上去跟羽毛（plumage）似的
考 同义　plumage = feathers

★★★ fastidious   [fæ'stɪdɪəs] *a.* 挑剔的，苛求的

记 fast 绝食 + -tidious（tedious）单调的：因食物单调（tedious）而绝食（fast），说明这个人真的很挑剔（fastidious）
考 同义　fastidious = critical

类比
fastidious 挑剔的	to	meticulous 一丝不苟的	（＞程度）
careful 认真的	to	fastidious 挑剔的	⇒	concerned 关心的	to	obsessed 迷恋的	（＜程度）
fastidious 挑剔的	to	fussy 小题大做的	⇒	uncouth 粗野的	to	barbarian 野蛮的	（同义）

★ pounce   [paʊns] *v.* 猛扑

记 看到路上一盎司（ounce）金子，猛扑（pounce）过去抓住它
考 类比
| shun 躲避 | to | embrace 接受 | ⇒ | shrink 退缩 | to | pounce 猛扑 | （反义） |

★★★ track   [træk] *n.* 轨道，足迹

记 火车（train）在轨道（track）上跑
考 类比
canoe 独木舟	to	river 河流	⇒	train 火车	to	track 轨道	（空间）
bus 公车	to	road 道路	⇒	locomotive 火车头	to	track 轨道	（空间）
track 轨道	to	horse racing 赛马	⇒	court 球场	to	tennis 网球	（空间）

★ garnish   ['gɑ:nɪʃ] *v.* 装饰

记 gar-（car）+ nish（谐音：内饰）：车（car）内的装饰品（garnish）用来装饰（garnish）
考 类比
| garnish 装饰 | to | salad 沙拉 | ⇒ | decorate 装饰 | to | cake 蛋糕 | （动宾） |

注 关于"装饰"的单词在 SSAT 的习题中有很多，如：embellish, decorate, ornament。

patronize

['pætrənaɪz] v. 赞助，光顾

记 patron- (parent) + -ize：父母亲 (parent) 就是我们最大的赞助 (patronize) 人
考 同义 patronize = sponsor

类比 extortionist / 勒索者 — to — threaten / 威胁 ⇒ zealot / 热心者 — to — patronize / 资助 （人物及其动作）

butcher

['bʊtʃə] n. 屠夫

考 类比
hammer / 锤子 — to — carpenter / 木匠 ⇒ knife / 刀 — to — butcher / 屠夫 （人物及其工具）
scalpel / 手术刀 — to — cleaver / 切肉刀 ⇒ surgeon / 医生 — to — butcher / 屠夫 （纵向）
drug / 药 — to — pharmacist / 药剂师 ⇒ meat / 肉 — to — butcher / 屠夫 （人物及其对象）

pallid

['pælɪd] a. 苍白的，暗淡的

记 可以把 pallid 和 pale 放在一起记
记 同义 pale = pallid

类比 pallid / 苍白的 — to — color / 颜色 ⇒ parched / 烧焦的 — to — moisture / 湿度 （缺乏）

barren

['bærən] a. 贫瘠的

记 谐音：拜仁：德甲劲旅拜仁队去年颗粒无收，显得很贫瘠 (barren)
考 同义 barren = desolate
注 关于"贫瘠的"单词在 SSAT 的习题中有很多，如：deserted, lifeless。

rectangle

['rektæŋgl] n. 长方形

考 类比
circle / 圆 — to — bottle / 瓶子 ⇒ rectangle / 长方形 — to — monitor / 监视器 （事物及其特点）
circle / 圆形 — to — octagon / 八边形 ⇒ rectangle / 长方形 — to — pentagon / 五边形 （同类）

List | **36** words ★ 复习一下学过的单词！

- abortive
- caricature
- chapter
- comprise
- constant
- derogatory
- erudite
- exorbitant
- gala
- impair
- insult
- lucid
- parch
- parry
- petrify
- puncture
- spoil
- stomp
- temperate
- wreath

SSAT词汇 List 38

★ sandal
['sændl] *n.* 凉鞋

记 这位明星公开场合脱凉鞋（sandal）抠脚，让自己陷入丑闻（scandal）

考 类比 sandal 凉鞋 to footwear 鞋类 ⇒ watch 表 to timepiece 计时器 （种属）

★★ decibel
['desɪbel] *n.* 分贝

记 decibel 这个单词在 SSAT 中出现一定都和 sound 或 volume 声音类的单词搭配

考 类比
pound 磅 to weight 重量 ⇒ decibel 分贝 to sound 声音 （事物及其用途）
decibel 分贝 to sound 声音 ⇒ degree 度数 to temperature 温度 （事物及其用途）
lumen 流明 to brightness 亮度 ⇒ decibel 分贝 to volume 音量 （事物及其用途）

★★★ compliment
['kɒmplɪmənt] *n.* 赞扬，恭维；免费

变 complimentary *a.* 赞美的；*a.* 免费的

记 注意区分"称赞"（compliment）和"补充"（complement）

考 同义 complimentary = free；compliment = acclaim

类比
exalt 赞扬 to criticize 批评 ⇒ compliment 赞美 to offend 冒犯 （反义）
insult 侮辱 to compliment 赞美 ⇒ please 使喜欢 to annoy 打扰 （反义）
complement 补充 to compliment 赞美 ⇒ style 风格 to stile 阶梯 （同音形似）
reprimand 斥责 to disapproval 不赞成 ⇒ compliment 赞扬 to approval 批准 （＞程度）

注 关于"赞扬"的单词在 SSAT 的习题中有很多，如：acclamation, eulogy, commend。

★★★ movement
['muːvmənt] *n.* 运动；乐章

考 类比 floundering 挣扎 to movement 行动 ⇒ babble 乱说 to speech 演讲 （同义：正反向）

floundering 乱动	to	movement 移动	⇒ muddle 乱弄	to	reasoning 讲理	（同义：正反向）
muscle 肌肉	to	movement 运动	⇒ battery 电池	to	watch 表	（事物及其用途）
stilted 呆板的	to	speech 演讲	⇒ wooden 僵硬的	to	movement 动作	（修饰）
articulate 口齿清晰的	to	speech 演讲	⇒ graceful 优雅的	to	movement 动作	（修饰）
austere 简朴的	to	style 造型	⇒ controlled 受约束的	to	movement 行为	（修饰）
barricade 路障	to	access 通道	⇒ bind 捆绑	to	movement 运动	（缺乏）
movement 乐章	to	symphony 交响乐	⇒ act 幕	to	play 演出	（组成）
movement 乐章	to	symphony 交响乐	⇒ chapter 章节	to	book 书	（组成）

★★ account ['əkaʊnt] n. 账户；描述

考 同义 account = report

类比
| image 图像 | to | distort 扭曲 | ⇒ account 言论 | to | slant 故意歪曲 | （动宾）
| password 密码 | to | account 账户 | ⇒ key 钥匙 | to | house 房间 | （事物及其对象）

★★ glove [glʌv] n. 手套

记 一副象征爱（love）的手套（glove）

考 类比
| glove 手套 | to | hand 手 | ⇒ hose 长筒袜 | to | foot 脚 | （空间）
| gauntlet 金属手套 | to | glove 手套 | ⇒ helmet 头盔 | to | hat 帽子 | （种属）
| sword 剑 | to | fence 击剑 | ⇒ glove 手套 | to | box 拳击 | （事物及其用途）
| knitter 编织工 | to | needles 针 | ⇒ boxer 拳击手 | to | gloves 手套 | （人物及其工具）

★ ewe [juː] n. 母羊

记 一只敬畏（awe）母羊（ewe）的公羊

考 类比
| ram 公羊 | to | ewe 母羊 | ⇒ stallion 公马 | to | mare 母马 | （相对）
| gander 公鹅 | to | goose 母鹅 | ⇒ ram 公羊 | to | ewe 母羊 | （相对）

★ tobacco [təˈbækəʊ] n. 烟草

考 类比
| tobacco 烟草 | to | cigarette 香烟 | ⇒ wheat 小麦 | to | bread 面包 | （组成）

malinger

[məˈlɪŋgə] v. 装病以逃避工作

记 ma 妈 + linger 徘徊：妈妈（ma）来回徘徊（linger），在考虑是否要装病以逃避工作（malinger）

考 类比 malinger / 装病以逃避工作 to work / 工作 ⇒ hide / 躲藏 to discovery / 发现 （缺乏）

hexagonal

[heksˈægənl] a. 六边形的

记 hex-（six）+ agon-（angle）+ al

考 类比 sphere / 球体 to round / 圆形 ⇒ honeycomb / 蜂巢 to hexagonal / 六边形 （事物及其特点）

yacht

[jɒt] n. 游艇

记 谐音：腰疼：常年坐游艇（yacht）在海上吹海风，导致自己腰疼

考 类比 taxi / 出租车 to bus / 公车 ⇒ yacht / 游艇 to liner / 班轮 （<程度）

yacht / 游艇 to boat / 船 ⇒ banquet / 宴会 to meal / 饭 （>程度）

thrifty ★★★

[ˈθrɪfti] a. 节约的，节俭的

变 thrift n. 节俭

记 妈妈过了三十（thirty）年节约的（thrifty）日子

考 类比 taciturn / 沉默的 to words / 言语 ⇒ thrifty / 节约的 to money / 钱 （缺乏）

ravenous / 贪婪的 to hungry / 饥饿的 ⇒ stingy / 小气的 to thrifty / 节约的 （>程度）

注 关于"节俭的"单词在 SSAT 的习题中有很多，如：frugal, sparing, stingy, abstemious, economical

stern

[stɜːn] a. 严厉的

记 谐音：死瞪：严厉的（stern）老师拿眼睛死瞪着你

考 同义 stern = strict

capture

[ˈkæptʃə] v. 捕捉，捕获

记 美国队长（captain）被捕获（capture）

考 同义 capture = seize；capture = secure（secure 这个单词的英文释义为：to capture or confine）

painstaking

[ˈpeɪnzteɪkɪŋ] a. 勤勉的，小心的

记 努力（painstaking）付出爱情，却除了痛苦（pain）一无所获（take）

考 类比 painstaking / 小心的 to careful / 谨慎的 ⇒ dependable / 可靠的 to reliable / 可依赖的 （同义）

castle
['kɑ:sl] *n.* 城堡

考 类比 moat/护城河 to castle/城堡 ⇒ lock/锁 to house/房间 （事物及其对象）
dungeon/地牢 to castle/城堡 ⇒ brig/船上禁闭室 to ship/船 （事物及其部分）

fleet
[fli:t] *n.* 舰队；*v.* 飞逝

变 fleeting *a.* 飞逝的，转瞬间的
记 时间好像长了脚（feet）似的，转瞬即逝（fleet）
考 同义 ephemeral = fleeting；fleet = armada
类比 ship/船 to fleet/船队 ⇒ puppy/小狗 to litter/一窝狗 （组成）

motif
[məʊ'ti:f] *n.* 主题

记 可以和 motive 一起记
考 同义 motif = theme
注 关于"主题"的单词在 SSAT 的习题中有很多，如：subject，thesis。

clarity
['klærɪti] *n.* 清楚，明晰

变 clarify *v.* 澄清；clarification *n.* 澄清
记 clar-（clear）+ -ity
考 同义 clarify = explain；clarity = clearness；clarity = lucidity；clarification = explanation
类比 obscure/朦胧的 to clarity/清楚 ⇒ grave/严肃 to comedy/喜剧 （缺乏）
cogent/令人信服的 to persuasiveness/说服力 ⇒ lucid/清晰的 to clarity/澄清 （同义）
correction/纠正 to erroneous/错误的 ⇒ clarification/澄清 to ambiguous/模糊的 （缺乏）

candid
['kændɪd] *a.* 公正的，坦白的

变 candor *n.* 坦白
记 公正的（candid）候选人（candidate）
考 同义 candid = frank；candid = honest；candid = forthright；candor = honesty
candor = integrity

List | **37** words　　　　　　　　　　　　　★ 复习一下学过的单词！

□ arboreal	□ divulge	□ muffle	□ previous
□ babble	□ epilogue	□ pallid	□ rectangle
□ barren	□ fastidious	□ patronize	□ retaliation
□ butcher	□ garnish	□ plumage	□ shove
□ discreet	□ inventory	□ pounce	□ track

SSAT词汇 List 39

★
congeal
[kənˈdʒiːl] v. 凝结，凝固

记 con- + -geal (jelly) 胶状物：用胶状物 (jelly) 把东西凝结 (congeal) 在一起
考 同义 congeal = coagulate
类比 congeal 凝结 to solid 固体 ⇒ melt 融化 to liquid 液体 （事物及其特点）

★
royalty
[ˈrɔɪəlti] n. 版税

记 皇室 (royal) 成员出书可以多拿版税 (royalty)
考 类比 royalty 版税 to author 作者 ⇒ stipend 薪金 to intern 实习生 （人物及其对象）
salesperson 销售 to commission 佣金 ⇒ author 作者 to royalty 版税 （人物及其对象）
注 royalty 这个单词"皇室"的意思我们很熟悉，这里是熟词僻义。

★★
prejudice
[ˈpredʒʊdɪs] n. 偏见

变 prejudiced a. 有偏见的；unprejudiced a. 无偏见的
记 Jane Austin 的著名小说《傲慢与偏见》(Pride and Prejudice)
考 同义 prejudiced = biased；nonpartisan = unprejudiced
类比 prejudiced 有偏见的 to unbiased 无偏见的 ⇒ worry 担忧 to blithe 愉快的 （反义）

★★
satire
[ˈsætaɪə] n. 讽刺文学

记 SAT 考试阅读部分多出些讽刺文学 (satire) 的东西
考 同义 lampoon = satire
类比 limerick 五行打油诗 to poem 诗 ⇒ lampoon 讽刺文 to satire 讽刺文学 （种属）

★★★
hasten
[ˈheɪsn] v. 加速

变 hastily ad. 匆忙的

记 英语谚语 more haste less speed 中文翻译为"欲速则不达"
考 同义 hastily = quickly；expedite = hasten；hasten = accelerate
类比 pace 步伐 → hasten 加快 ⇒ course 过程 → facilitate 促进 （动宾）

rectify ['rektɪfaɪ] *v.* 改正

记 rect- 正，直 + -ify
因为认可（ratify）你，所以给你一个改正（rectify）的机会
考 同义 rectify = fix；rectify = modify；rectify = amend
类比 divulge 泄露 → public 公开的 ⇒ rectify 改正 → right 正确的 （同义）

mania ['meɪnɪə] *n.* 狂热

变 kleptomania *n.* 盗窃癖
记 男人（man）对足球都很狂热（mania）
考 类比 enthusiastic 热情的 → mania 狂热 ⇒ commendatory 赞赏的 → eulogy 颂扬 （＜程度）
extortionist 勒索者 → blackmail 敲诈 ⇒ kleptomaniac 偷窃癖 → steal 偷 （人物及其动作）
注 这个单词在英文中大多以合成词形式出现，除了上面提到的"盗窃癖"kleptomania 之外，英语中还有"纵火狂"pyromania、"藏书癖"bibliomania 和"偏执狂"monomania 等。

stare [steə] *v.* 凝视，盯着看

记 凝视（stare）星星（star）
考 类比 whisper 低语 → scream 尖叫 ⇒ glance 扫视 → stare 凝视 （＜程度）
period 句号 → exclamation point 感叹号 ⇒ glance 扫视 → stare 凝视 （＜程度）
stare 凝视 → glimpse 一瞥 ⇒ dime 一角 → cent 一分 （＞程度）

sculpture ['skʌlptʃə] *n.* 雕塑，雕刻

变 sculptor *n.* 雕刻家
记 著名的咖啡馆"雕刻时光"的英文即为 sculpting in time
考 类比 stone 石头 → sculpture 雕刻 ⇒ clay 黏土 → pottery 陶器 （事物及其用途）
baker 烘焙师 → bread 面包 ⇒ sculptor 雕刻家 → statue 雕塑 （人物及其对象）
sculptor 雕刻家 → statue 雕塑 ⇒ composer 作曲家 → music 音乐 （人物及其对象）

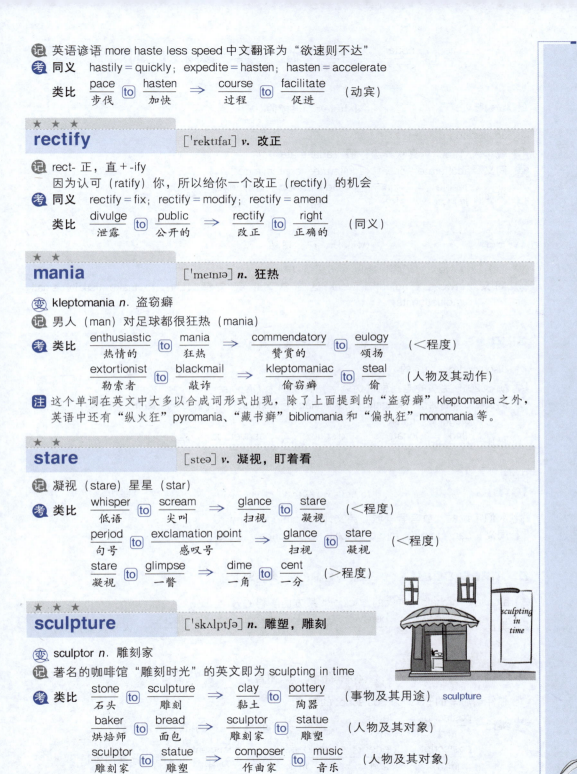
sculpture

clay / 黏土 `to` potter / 陶艺家 ⇒ marble / 大理石 `to` sculptor / 雕刻家 （人物及其工具）

adulterate ★★
[əˈdʌltəreɪt] v. 掺假

- 变 adulterated a. 掺假的
- 记 成年人（adult）喜欢弄虚作假（adulterate）
- 考 同义 adulterate＝cheat；adulterate＝contaminate
  类比 feeble / 虚弱的 `to` vigor / 精力 ⇒ adulterated / 掺杂的 `to` purity / 纯洁 （缺乏）

tweak ★
[twiːk] v. 拧，扭动

- 记 因为扭（tweak）了腰，所以受伤变弱（weak）
- 考 同义 tweak＝adjust（tweak 这个单词的英文释义为：to make usually small adjustments）

disguise ★★★
[dɪsˈɡaɪz] v. 伪装；n. 伪装

- 变 disguised a. 伪装的
- 记 胡歌 2015 主演的电视剧《伪装者》英文即为 Disguiser
- 考 同义 disguised＝incognito；camouflage＝disguise；disguise＝false front
  disguise＝mask
  类比 find / 寻找 `to` locate / 定位 ⇒ disguise / 伪装 `to` masquerade / 伪装 （同义）

forbid ★★
[fəˈbɪd] v. 禁止

- 记 我们常说的"故宫紫禁城"英文即为 Forbidden City
- 考 同义 ban＝forbid；forbid＝prohibit；proscribe＝forbid

archaeologist ★
[ˌɑːkiˈɒlədʒɪst] n. 考古学家

- 记 archae-（archaic）古代的 + -ologist 某方面学科的人
- 考 类比 sociologist / 社会学家 `to` behavior / 行为 ⇒ archaeologist / 考古学家 `to` artifact / 手工艺品 （人物及其对象）

postscript ★★
[ˈpəʊstˌskrɪpt] n. 附言

- 记 邮件最后写的 PS 即为 postscript 的缩写
- 考 类比 postscript / 附言 `to` letter / 信 ⇒ epilogue / 收场白 `to` play / 戏剧 （事物及其部分）
  postscript / 附言 `to` letter / 信件 ⇒ addendum / 附录 `to` document / 文件 （事物及其部分）

★★ pith

[pɪθ] *n.* 植物茎秆中的白色条纹，精髓

- 记 道路（path）上有斑马线，斑马线呈白色条纹（pith）状
- 考 类比 pencil 铅笔 to lead 铅 ⇒ stem 茎 to pith 白丝 （从属）
- 注 pith 的英文释义为：a soft white substance that fills the stems of some plants.

★ contagious

[kənˈteɪdʒəs] *a.* 传染的

- 记 注意区分"传染的" contagious 和"邻近的，接壤的" contiguous
- 考 同义 contagious = infectious

★★ solar

[ˈsəʊlə] *a.* 太阳的

- 考 类比
  - lunar 月亮的 to moon 月亮 ⇒ solar 太阳的 to sun 太阳 （同义）
  - sun 太阳 to solar 太阳的 ⇒ earth 陆地 to terrestrial 陆地的 （同义）
  - heart 心 to body 身体 ⇒ sun 太阳 to solar system 太阳系 （空间）

★★ uniform

[ˈjuːnɪfɔːm] *a.* 一致的

- 考 同义 homogeneous = uniform；uniform = even
- 注 uniform 这个单词"制服"的意思我们很熟悉

★★★ vanity

[ˈvænɪti] *n.* 虚荣心

- 变 vain *a.* 自负的
- 记 著名小说《名利场》的英文是 *Vanity Fair*
- 考 同义 conceited = vain；pride = vanity
- 类比
  - vain 自负的 to humble 谦虚的 ⇒ extroverted 外向的 to shy 内向的 （反义）
  - modest 谦虚的 to vanity 虚荣心 ⇒ innocent 单纯的 to guilt 罪行 （缺乏）

List | 38 words ★复习一下学过的单词！

☐ account	☐ compliment	☐ hexagonal	☐ sandal
☐ candid	☐ decibel	☐ malinger	☐ stern
☐ capture	☐ ewe	☐ motif	☐ thrifty
☐ castle	☐ fleet	☐ movement	☐ tobacco
☐ clarity	☐ glove	☐ painstaking	☐ yacht

SSAT词汇 List 40

perplexed
[pə'plekst] *a.* 困惑的

变 perplexity *n.* 困惑
考 同义 perplexity = confusion; bewildered = perplexed
类比 conundrum to perplexed ⇒ entertainment to diverting （同义）
谜　　　　困惑的　　　娱乐　　　娱乐的

conceited
[kən'siːtɪd] *a.* 自负的

记 自负的（conceited）即为自欺（deceitful）欺人的
考 同义 conceited = vain; conceited = arrogant; conceited = proud
类比 lummox to clumsy ⇒ egotist to conceited （人物及其特点）
笨拙的人　笨拙的　　自高自大者　自负的
interloper to officious ⇒ braggart to conceited （人物及其特点）
闯入者　　好管闲事的　自吹自擂者　自负的

plummet
['plʌmɪt] *v.* 垂直落下

记 一个李子（plum）落下来（plummet）了
考 同义 plummet = fall

shovel
['ʃʌvl] *n.* 铁铲

记 工人用铁铲（shovel）把垃圾猛推（shove）进垃圾场
考 类比 shovel to dig ⇒ blade to cut （事物及其用途）
铁铲　　挖　　　刀片　　切
scissors to cut ⇒ shovel to excavate （事物及其用途）
剪刀　　切　　　铁铲　　挖掘
scissors to cut ⇒ shovel to scoop （事物及其用途）
剪刀　　切　　　铁铲　　舀
mix to blender ⇒ dig to shovel （事物及其用途）
混合　　搅拌器　　挖　　铁铲

symmetry ['sɪmətri] n. 对称

- 变 symmetrical a. 对称的
- 记 sym- (same) + metr- (measure)
- 考 类比
  - symmetry 对称 to eye 眼睛 ⇒ harmony 和谐 to ear 耳朵 （事物及其特点）
  - lopsided 倾向一方的 to symmetrical 对称的 ⇒ fractured 破碎的 to whole 完整的 （反义）
  - symmetrical 对称的 to amorphous 无形的 ⇒ balanced 平衡的 to unshaped 无形的 （纵向）

exhaust [ɪɡ'zɔːst] n. 废气；v. 使筋疲力尽

- 变 exhausted a. 筋疲力尽的；exhaustion n. 精疲力竭
- 考 类比
  - careful 仔细的 to picky 挑剔的 ⇒ tired 累的 to exhausted 精疲力竭的 （<程度）
  - rest 休息 to exhaustion 精疲力竭 ⇒ water 水 to thirst 口渴的 （缺少）
  - smoke 烟 to fire 火 ⇒ exhaust 废气 to car 汽车 （事物及其部分）
  - exuberant 繁茂的 to enthusiastic 热情的 ⇒ exhausted 疲倦的 to weary 疲倦的 （同义）

imbibe [ɪm'baɪb] v. 吸收，喝

- 记 用一根管子（pipe）去吸水（imbibe）
- 考 同义 imbibe = drink

reduce [rɪ'djuːs] v. 减少

- 变 reduction n. 减少
- 考 同义 delete = reduce; diminish = reduce; descent = reduction; reduction = cutback; diminution = reduction

blueprint ['bluːprɪnt] n. 蓝图

- 考 类比
  - map 地图 to navigate 航行 ⇒ blueprint 蓝图 to build 建造 （事物及其用途）
  - architect 建筑师 to blueprint 蓝图 ⇒ composer 作曲家 to score 乐谱 （人物及其对象）
  - blueprint 蓝图 to house 房子 ⇒ recipe 菜单 to cake 蛋糕 （事物及其用途）
  - syntax 句法 to sentence 句子 ⇒ blueprint 蓝图 to building 建筑 （事物及其用途）
  - budget 预算 to cost 花费 ⇒ blueprint 蓝图 to design 设计 （事物及其部分）

tailor (to) pattern ⇒ builder (to) blueprint （人物及其对象）
裁缝　　图案　　　建造者　　蓝图

agenda (to) meeting ⇒ blueprint (to) building （事物及其用途）
议程表　　会议　　　蓝图　　　建筑

cartographer (to) maps ⇒ architect (to) blueprints （人物及其对象）
地图编纂者　　　地图　　建筑师　　　蓝图

★ alien

alien [ˈeɪliən] *a.* 外国的，怪异的

- 变　alienate *v*. 疏远，离间；inalienable *a*. 不可分割的，不可疏远的
- 记　公司迎来了一个外国（alien）客户（client）
- 考　同义　alien = strange；alienate = estrange；inalienable = unchangeable

★ portentous

portentous [pɔːˈtentəs] *a.* 不祥的，恶兆的

- 记　过于自命不凡的（pretentious）人都前途不详（portentous）
- 考　同义　portentous = ominous

★ dim

dim [dɪm] *v.* 使暗淡，使昏暗；*a.* 暗淡的，昏暗的

- 记　情侣看电影的真实目的（aim）是图电影院里暗淡的（dim）光
- 考　类比　
  muffle (to) sound ⇒ dim (to) light （动宾）
  消音　　声音　　　暗淡　　光

  dark (to) dim ⇒ tiny (to) small （同义）
  暗的　　暗的　　　小的　　小的

★★ legitimate

legitimate [lɪˈdʒɪtɪmət] *a.* 合法的

- 变　illegitimate *a*. 违法的
- 记　leg- 法律 + itimate
- 考　同义　legitimate = legal；illegitimate = delinquent

★★ rust

rust [rʌst] *v.* 生锈

- 变　rusty *a*. 生锈的
- 记　我们都相信（trust）这种铁是不会生锈的（rust）
- 考　类比　
  wood (to) decay ⇒ iron (to) rust （事物及其动作）
  木材　　腐烂　　　铁　　　生锈

  apple (to) rotten ⇒ metal (to) rusty （修饰）
  苹果　　腐烂的　　铁　　　生锈的

  bread (to) moldy ⇒ steel (to) rusty （修饰）
  面包　　发霉的　　钢铁　　生锈的

★ stark

stark [stɑːk] *a.* 荒凉的，光秃秃的

- 记　盯着（stare）别人光秃秃的（stark）头看

考 同义   stark = vacant

grand ［grænd］ a. 宏伟的，豪华的

考 类比   least/最少的 —to→ most/最多的 ⇒ grand/宏伟的 —to→ unimpressive/不引人注意的 （反义）

sophisticated ［səˈfɪstɪkeɪtɪd］ a. 复杂的

变 unsophisticated a. 不懂世故的；sophistication n. 复杂
考 同义   callow = unsophisticated；naïve = unsophisticated
类比   ruthless/残忍的 —to→ compassion/同情 ⇒ naïve/幼稚的 —to→ sophistication/复杂 （缺乏）

cagey [ˈkeɪdʒi] a. 精明的，谨慎的

记 小鸟要谨慎（cagey），否则会被关进笼子（cage）里
考 同义   cagey = shrewd

presumptive ［prɪˈzʌmptɪv］ a. 假定的

变 presumptuous a. 专横的，放肆的
记 这个单词的动词就是我们熟悉的 presume
考 同义   presumptive = plausible；presumptive = feasible；impertinent = presumptuous

buffer [ˈbʌfə] n. 缓冲

记 为了安全，我提供（offer）给你一个缓冲（buffer）区
考 类比   buffer/缓冲区 —to→ impact/冲击力 ⇒ armor/盔甲 —to→ hit/击打 （事物及其用途）
        buffer side/缓冲面 —to→ impact/撞击 ⇒ antiseptic/防腐剂 —to→ infection/感染 （事物及其用途）

List | 39 words   ★ 复习一下学过的单词！

- adulterate
- archaeologist
- congeal
- contagious
- disguise
- forbid
- hasten
- mania
- pith
- postscript
- prejudice
- rectify
- royalty
- satire
- sculpture
- solar
- stare
- tweak
- uniform
- vanity

☆ grand   ☆ sophisticated   ☆ cagey   ☆ presumptive   ☆ buffer

SSAT词汇 List 41

★★ guarantee [ˌɡærənˈtiː] v. 保证
变 guaranteed a. 保证的
考 同义 vouch = guarantee；guarantee = assure
类比 guaranteed/保证的 to certain/确定的 ⇒ rapid/快速的 to quick/快速的 （同义）

★ ambivalent [æmˈbɪvələnt] a. 矛盾的
记 ambi- 二 + valent：因为两边都可行，所以处于矛盾的（ambivalent）状况
考 类比 ambivalent/矛盾的 to certainly/确定地 ⇒ grotesque/丑陋的 to beautify/美化 （反义）

★★ blossom [ˈblɒsəm] n. 开花
记 《生活大爆炸》中的 Amy 其实是个小童星，她在 1991 年就主演了一部长达五季的美剧，而且《生活大爆炸》中的 Leonard 也在这部剧中客串，这部剧的名字就叫 Blossom
考 类比 blossom/开花 to bloom/开花 ⇒ quiver/震颤 to vibrate/震动 （同义）
butterfly/蝴蝶 to caterpillar/毛毛虫 ⇒ blossom/开花 to bud/花蕾 （发展阶段）

★★ abstruse [əbˈstruːs] a. 深奥的，难懂的
记 abs- 离开 + -truse（truth）：远离真理，它实在太深奥难懂（abstruse）
考 同义 abstruse = obscure；abstruse = difficult to understand

★★ abridge [əˈbrɪdʒ] v. 删减，缩短
记 建一座桥（bridge）的目的就是为了缩短（abridge）路程
考 同义 abridge = shorten；abridge = curtail

★★ amnesia [æmˈniːziə] n. 健忘症
记 a- 否定 + mnes- 记忆 + ia：来自希腊神话记忆女神莫涅莫辛涅（Mnemosyne）

amnesia

☆ guarantee ☆ ambivalent ☆ blossom ☆ abstruse ☆ abridge
☆ amnesia

考 类比　insomnia/失眠 to sleep/睡觉 ⇒ amnesia/健忘 to memory/记忆　（缺乏）

penury ★
['penjʊəri] n. 贫困，贫穷

记 penu- (penny) 便士 + ry：花钱的时候每一便士（penny）都要考虑，说明很贫困（penury）
考 同义　penury = poverty

contend ★★
[kən'tend] v. 主张，斗争

变 contentious a. 好争论的
记 我主张（contend）小学生在学校的内容（content）就应该是玩耍
考 同义　contend = assert; contentious = combative

nullify ★
['nʌlɪfaɪ] v. 使无效，作废

记 nul 在拉丁语中是"无效，零"的意思
考 类比　cancel/取消 to subscription/订阅 ⇒ nullify/作废 to contract/合同　（动宾）

hoe ★
[həʊ] n. 锄头

记 这个农民很粗心，锄头（hoe）锄到脚趾（toe）
考 类比　hoe/锄头 to weed/草 ⇒ insecticide/杀虫剂 to pest/害虫　（事物及其对象）

injustice ★
[ɪn'dʒʌstɪs] n. 不公正

记 in- 否定 + just 公正的 + -ice
考 类比　compensation/补偿 to injustice/不正义 ⇒ eraser/橡皮 to pencil/铅笔　（事物及其用途）

peculiar ★★★
[pɪ'kjuːlɪə] a. 特殊的，奇怪的

记 美国密苏里州的"卡斯县"Cass County 有一个小镇就叫作 Peculiar，在开车前往这个镇的时候，即可在路上看到标语：Where the "odds" are with you，你能看出其中的双关吗？
考 同义　peculiar = unusual; peculiar = bizarre; strange = peculiar

Peculiar

peculiar

curtail ★★★
[kɜː'teɪl] v. 缩减

记 由于缩水，所有洗后的窗帘（curtain）都缩短（curtail）了
考 同义　curtail = shorten; curtail = abate; curtail = limit; abridge = curtail

☆ penury　☆ contend　☆ nullify　☆ hoe　☆ injustice
☆ peculiar　☆ curtail

excursion ★★
[ɪkˈskɜːʃn] n. 远足

记 ex- 朝外 + cur- 跑 + sion
考 同义 excursion = jaunt；excursion = outing

ignite ★★★
[ɪgˈnaɪt] v. 点燃，点火

变 ignition n. 点火
记 在漆黑的夜晚（night）要点燃（ignite）火把，才能照亮前方的路
考 同义 kindle = ignite

类比 ignite 点燃 to blaze 火焰 ⇒ trim 修剪 to decrease 减少 （因果）

ignite 点燃 to abrasion 摩擦 ⇒ fail 失败 to mistake 错误 （因果）

ignition 点火 to start 开始 ⇒ brake 车闸 to stop 停止 （动作及其目的）

注 这个题的思路有些复杂：车点火（ignition）了就是车启动（start）了，车刹住（brake）就是车停止（stop）了。

cactus ★
[ˈkæktəs] n. 仙人掌

记 仙人掌（cactus）扎手，导致（cause）感染
考 类比 camel 骆驼 to animal 动物 ⇒ cactus 仙人掌 to plant 植物 （种属）

porcupine 箭猪 to animal 动物 ⇒ cactus 仙人掌 to plant 植物 （种属）

restraint ★★
[rɪˈstreɪnt] v. 抑制，克制

记 rest + rain + t：一到下雨（rain）天，就要克制（restraint）自己想休息（rest）的欲望
考 同义 restraint = reserve（reserve 这个单词的英文释义为：restraint, closeness, or caution in one's words and actions restraint, closeness, or caution in one's words and actions）
restraint = temperance（temperance 这个单词的英文释义为 moderation and self-restraint, as in behavior or expression）

plant ★
[plɑːnt] n. 工厂

考 类比 plant 工厂 to charter 执照 ⇒ factory 工厂 to license 执照 （纵向）
注 plant 这个单词"植物"的意思我们很熟悉，此处为熟词僻义。

allude ★★
[əˈluːd] v. 暗指，间接提到

变 allusion n. 暗示，提及

记 老板暗示（allude），这份合同要包含（include）以下条款
考 同义　allusion = reference；imply = allude
　 类比　$\dfrac{\text{allude}}{\text{暗指}}$ to $\dfrac{\text{refer}}{\text{提及}}$ ⇒ $\dfrac{\text{imply}}{\text{暗示}}$ to $\dfrac{\text{state}}{\text{说明}}$　（＜程度）
注 关于"间接提到"的单词在 SSAT 的习题中有很多，如：insinuate，innuendo。

★ siren　　　　　　　['saɪərən] *n.* 警报

记 希腊神话中半人半鸟的女海妖 Siren 常以美妙歌声迷住海员，使船只触礁沉没。后来船员装上了汽笛，因为也发生在海里，故命名为 siren
考 类比　$\dfrac{\text{siren}}{\text{警报}}$ to $\dfrac{\text{warning}}{\text{警告}}$ ⇒ $\dfrac{\text{light}}{\text{光}}$ to $\dfrac{\text{illumination}}{\text{照亮}}$　（事物及其目的）

List | **40** words　　　　　　　　　　　　　　　★ 复习一下学过的单词！

☐ alien	☐ dim	☐ perplexed	☐ rust
☐ blueprint	☐ exhaust	☐ plummet	☐ shovel
☐ buffer	☐ grand	☐ portentous	☐ sophisticated
☐ cagey	☐ imbibe	☐ presumptive	☐ stark
☐ conceited	☐ legitimate	☐ reduce	☐ symmetry

SSAT词汇 List 42

★ imperative
[ɪmˈperətɪv] *a.* 必要的，命令的

记 一个帝国（imperial）君主的命令（imperative）是不能抗拒的
老婆下命令（imperative）：无需比较（comparative）价格，看到这个包立马付钱

考 同义 imperative = compulsory；imperative = required

★★★ destroy
[dɪˈstrɔɪ] *v.* 破坏

考 同义 corrupt = destroy；obliterate = destroy；raze = destroy；destroy = subvert；decimate = destroy

类比
surprise / 吃惊 **to** startle / 吃惊 ⇒ destroy / 破坏 **to** ruin / 破坏 （同义）
amend / 修改 **to** change / 修改 ⇒ destroy / 破坏 **to** demolish / 破坏 （同义）

★★★ overture
[ˈəʊvətjʊə] *n.* 前奏曲，序幕

记 over + -ture（tune）曲调：在有些概念唱片中，第一首歌曲（tune）的结束（over）其实为第二首歌曲（tune）的序幕（overture）

考 类比
overture / 序曲 **to** opera / 歌剧 ⇒ preface / 序 **to** book / 书 （事物及其部分）
overture / 序曲 **to** opera / 歌剧 ⇒ preamble / 序文 **to** statute / 法规 （事物及其部分）
introduction / 序 **to** book / 书 ⇒ overture / 前奏曲 **to** play / 戏剧 （事物及其部分）

★ yawn
[jɔːn] *v.* 打哈欠

记 虽然天已破晓（dawn），该起床了，但自己却仍然哈欠（yawn）连连

考 类比
depressed / 沮丧的 **to** mope / 闷闷不乐 ⇒ tired / 劳累的 **to** yawn / 打哈欠 （动作及其情感）

★★ copious
[ˈkəʊpɪəs] *a.* 大量的，丰富的

记 copi-（copy）+ -ous

考 类比　copious/大量的 to ample/大量的 ⇒ tactful/机智的 to diplomatic/圆滑的 （同义）
　　　　copious/大量的 to abundant/大量的 ⇒ docile/温顺的 to meek/温顺的 （同义）
注 关于"大量的"单词在 SSAT 的习题中有很多，如：abundant，plentiful，abounding。

★★ fragile ['frædʒaɪl] *a.* 脆弱的

记 frail 和 fragile 两个单词不但形似，意思也相同
考 同义　wispy = fragile；fragile = delicate
　 类比　fragile/脆弱的 to break/打碎 ⇒ flammable/易燃的 to burn/燃烧 （事物及其特点）

★ posthumous ['pɒstjʊməs] *a.* 死后的

记 生前无人问津，死后（posthumous）才出名，真是荒谬（humorous）
考 同义　posthumous = after death

★★ goad [ɡəʊd] *v.* 刺激，激励

记 老山羊（goat）激励（goad）小山羊（goat）要好好学习
考 同义　goad = prod
　 类比　berate/批评 to criticize/批评 ⇒ goad/刺激 to urge/督促 （同义）

★★★ tactile ['tæktaɪl] *a.* 有触觉的

记 机智的（tactful）人对危险都提前有一定的觉察（tactile）
考 类比　olfactory/嗅觉的 to smell/闻 ⇒ tactile/触觉的 to touch/接触 （同义）
　　　　tactile/触觉的 to touch/接触 ⇒ auditory/听觉的 to sound/听 （同义）
　　　　nose/鼻子 to olfactory/嗅觉的 ⇒ finger/手指 to tactile/触觉的 （事物及其特点）

★ mogul ['məʊɡl] *n.* 显要人物

记 谐音：蒙古：此人是蒙古国的重要人物（mogul）
考 同义　mogul = magnate
　 类比　warmonger/好战者 to pacifist/和平主义者 ⇒ nobody/小人物 to mogul/大亨 （反义）

★★★ compassion [kəm'pæʃn] *n.* 同情，怜悯

记 com- + passion 热情：大家一起（com）热情（passion）地去帮助那些怜悯（compassion）的人

☆ fragile　　☆ posthumous　　☆ goad　　☆ tactile　　☆ mogul
☆ compassion

- 考 同义 　compassion = sympathy；compassion = sympathetic response
- 类比 　$\dfrac{\text{condescending}}{\text{屈尊的}}$ to $\dfrac{\text{respect}}{\text{尊敬}}$ ⇒ $\dfrac{\text{merciless}}{\text{无情的}}$ to $\dfrac{\text{compassion}}{\text{同情}}$ （反义）
- 　　　　$\dfrac{\text{ruthless}}{\text{无情的}}$ to $\dfrac{\text{compassion}}{\text{同情}}$ ⇒ $\dfrac{\text{naïve}}{\text{幼稚的}}$ to $\dfrac{\text{sophistication}}{\text{世故}}$ （反义）
- 注 关于"同情"的单词在 SSAT 的习题中有很多，如：condolence，forgiveness。

★ confront　　　　['kən'frʌnt] *v.* 面对，遭遇

- 记 在坏人面前（front）要勇于面对（confront）
- 考 同义　confront = oppose；accost = confront

★★ legislate　　　　['ledʒɪsleɪt] *v.* 立法

- 变 legislation *n.* 立法
- 记 leg- 法律 + -islate
- 考 同义　legislate = make into law
- 类比　$\dfrac{\text{retract}}{\text{撤销}}$ to $\dfrac{\text{statement}}{\text{言论}}$ ⇒ $\dfrac{\text{repeal}}{\text{废除}}$ to $\dfrac{\text{legislation}}{\text{立法}}$ （动宾）

★ culpable　　　　['kʌlpəbl] *a.* 有罪的

- 记 中国政府在环境保护方面谴责特朗普的一句话：Yet Trump also failed to mention other important points: that Western nations are historically much more culpable than developing nations for global carbon emissions, and on a per capita basis continues to be by far the worst offender.
- 考 同义　culpable = worth of blame

★★★ tepid　　　　['tepɪd] *a.* 微温的

- 记 他胆子太小（trepid），只敢喝温（tepid）水
- 考 同义　tepid = lukewarm
- 类比　$\dfrac{\text{scalding}}{\text{滚烫的}}$ to $\dfrac{\text{tepid}}{\text{微温的}}$ ⇒ $\dfrac{\text{ecstatic}}{\text{狂喜的}}$ to $\dfrac{\text{satisfied}}{\text{满意的}}$ （＞程度）
- 　　　$\dfrac{\text{hot}}{\text{热的}}$ to $\dfrac{\text{warm}}{\text{暖和的}}$ ⇒ $\dfrac{\text{spicy}}{\text{辣的}}$ to $\dfrac{\text{tepid}}{\text{微温的}}$ （＞程度）

★ stag　　　　[stæg] *n.* 雄鹿

- 记 这个舞台（stage）上突然爬上来了一只鹿（stag）
- 考 类比　$\dfrac{\text{stag}}{\text{雄鹿}}$ to $\dfrac{\text{doe}}{\text{母鹿}}$ ⇒ $\dfrac{\text{gander}}{\text{雄鹅}}$ to $\dfrac{\text{goose}}{\text{雌鹅}}$ （相对）

★ galvanize　　　　['gælvənaɪz] *v.* 通电，刺激，激起

- 记 这个单词来自于意大利生理学家 Luigi Galvani 的名字，他最有名的实验是解剖青蛙后，

把青蛙的脊柱用铜钩钩住，再和铁栅栏相接触，造成青蛙肌肉持续性收缩，因此后人用他的名字来表示"刺激"

考 同义　galvanize = arouse

rescind
[rɪˈsɪnd] *v.* 撤销

记 这个公司撤销（rescind）了必须工作满 3 年才能辞职（resign）的条件

考 同义　revoke = rescind

类比　break（打破）to promise（诺言）⇒ rescind（撤销）to offer（录取通知）（动宾）

taint
[teɪnt] *v.* 污染，弄脏

记 白墙上被一个油漆（paint）点给弄脏（taint）了

考 同义　taint = infect；contaminate = taint

fallacy
[ˈfæləsi] *n.* 谬论，谬误

变 fallacious *a.* 谬误的，骗人的

记 不小心掉入（fall）传销组织，发现里面的人说话基本都是谬论（fallacy）

考 同义　fallacy = error；fallacious = illogical

List | **41** words　　　　　　　　　　　　★复习一下学过的单词！

□ abridge	□ blossom	□ guarantee	□ peculiar
□ abstruse	□ cactus	□ hoe	□ penury
□ allude	□ contend	□ ignite	□ plant
□ ambivalent	□ curtail	□ injustice	□ restraint
□ amnesia	□ excursion	□ nullify	□ siren

SSAT词汇 List 43

juvenile ['dʒuːvənaɪl] *a.* 青少年的，幼稚的

记 Hebe 是希腊神话中的青春女神（The Goddess of Youth），对应罗马神话中的 Juventas，表示年轻的词根 juven 正是来源于此
考 同义 juvenile = green；juvenile = young

recurrent [rɪ'kʌrənt] *a.* 复发的，周期性的

变 recurrence *n.* 再发生，循环
记 正在发生的（occurrent）这种现象会在你之后的生活中反复发生（recurrent）
考 同义 cyclical = recurrent

类比 recurrent（周期性的） to dream（梦） → chronic（慢性的） to illness（疾病） （修饰）
recurrence（循环） to periodic（周期的） → determination（决心） to persevering（坚定的） （修饰）

mire ['maɪə] *n.* 泥潭，沼泽

记 一匹马（mare）陷足于污泥（mire）内，老畜生怎能出蹄
考 同义 mire = mud

embrace [ɪm'breɪs] *v.* 接受，拥抱

记 em- + brace 架子：brace 本意是指挂在墙上的起支撑作用的架子，所以 embrace 引申有"拥抱"之意
考 类比 shun（躲避） to embrace（接受） → shrink（退缩） to pounce（猛扑） （反义）

varnish ['vɑːnɪʃ] *v.* 上清漆

记 衣柜上原有的清漆消失（vanish）了，需要重新上清漆（varnish）
考 类比 paint（涂） to wall（墙） → varnish（上清漆） to floor（地板） （动宾）

★ incendiary

[ɪnˈsendɪəri] *a.* 燃烧的，煽动的

【记】in- + cendi- （candle）蜡烛 + -ary：蜡烛（candle）里面（in）的火正在燃烧（incendiary）
【考】同义 incendiary = inflammatory

★★ pedagogue

[ˈpedəɡɒɡ] *n.* 教师

【记】ped- 儿童 + agog- 引导 + ue：引导儿童的人：这个词本来指的是那些富有人家的奴隶，每天的任务就是接送有钱人家的孩子上下学，以及监督他们的学习
【考】同义 teacher = pedagogue

类比 pedagogue 教师 to teaching 教学 ⇒ preacher 传教士 to sermon 布道 （人物及其动作）

★★★ brush

[brʌʃ] *n.* 刷子

【考】类比
baton 指挥棒 to conductor 指挥 ⇒ brush 刷子 to painter 粉刷匠 （人物及其工具）
painter 画家 to brush 刷子 ⇒ calligrapher 书法家 to pen 笔 （人物及其工具）
brush 刷子 to painter 油漆匠 ⇒ bow 弓 to violinist 小提琴家 （人物及其工具）
brush 刷子 to painter 油漆匠 ⇒ keyboard 键盘 to typist 打字员 （人物及其工具）

★★★ monarch

[ˈmɒnək] *n.* 君主，帝王

【变】monarchy *n.* 君主政体，君主国
【记】mon- （mono）一个 + arch 拱形门：一个人（mono）在拱形门（arch）里称王（monarch）
【考】类比
throne 王座 to monarch 君主 ⇒ bench 法官座椅 to judge 法官 （人物及其特点）
quack 庸医 to doctor 医生 ⇒ pretender 冒充者 to monarch 君主 （同义：正反向）
sovereign 君主 to monarchy 君主国 ⇒ principal 校长 to school 学校 （空间）
democracy 民主 to parliament 议会 ⇒ monarch 君主 to autocracy 独裁制 （事物及其特点）
（这个题的思路有些复杂：有 parliament 即可说明这个国家 democracy 的特点，而 autocracy 的特点就是 monarch）

★★ laud

[lɔːd] *v.* 赞美，称赞

【变】laudable *a.* 值得赞赏的；laudatory *a.* 赞美的
【记】赞美（laud）上帝（Lord）
【考】同义 laud = praise；laudable = praiseworthy；laudatory = complimentary
类比 minatory 威胁的 to threaten 威胁 ⇒ laudatory 赞美的 to praise 表扬 （同义）

pardon ★

['pɑːdn] v. 原谅

考 类比 select 选择 to choose 选择 ⇒ pardon 原谅 to excuse 原谅 （同义）
       record 记录 to document 档案 ⇒ excuse 原谅 to pardon 原谅 （同义）

oppress ★★

[ə'pres] v. 压迫，压抑

记 op- 加强 + press 压
考 同义 persecute = oppress; surpress = oppress; quash = oppress

ornament ★★★

['ɔːnəmənt] n. 装饰

变 ornate a. 华丽的，装饰的
记 or + name + -ent：很明显，很多明星换（or）名字（name）是为了装饰（ornament）自己的形象，比如：刘德华的原名是刘福荣，梁咏琪的原名是梁碧芝，成龙的原名是陈港生
考 同义 florid = ornate
  类比 florid 绚丽的 to prose 散文 ⇒ ornate 华丽的 to building 楼 （修饰）
       hyperbole 夸张 to exaggeration 夸张 ⇒ ornament 装饰 to decoration 装饰 （同义）
       cosmetics 化妆品 to embellish 装饰 ⇒ ornament 装饰物 to adorn 装饰 （事物及其用途）
注 关于"装饰"的单词在 SSAT 的习题中有很多，如：decorate, embellish, garnish。

murky ★

['mɜːki] a. 黑暗的

记 mur-墨 + ky-（sky）：沾了墨的天空显得很黑暗（murky）
考 同义 murky = gloomy

gangly ★★

['gæŋli] a. 身材瘦长的

记 谐音：竿：我们经常说人身材瘦得跟个竿似的
考 同义 gangly = slender; gangly = skinny; wispy = gangly

poacher ★

['pəutʃə] n. 偷猎者

记 因为他曾经当过偷猎者（poacher），所以新的球队不能找他来当教练（coach）
考 类比 poacher 偷猎者 to game 猎物 ⇒ rustler 偷牛贼 to cattle 牛 （人物及其对象）
（game 这个单词在此处的英文释义为：wild animals or birds that people hunt for sport or food）

broach ★

[brəutʃ] v. 提出，开始讨论

记 她提出（broach）的这个解决方法，违背（breach）了自己一向做事情的原则

考 类比 introduction 介绍 to person 人 ⇒ broach 提出 to topic 话题 （动宾）

★★★ prune

[pruːn] v. 修剪，删除；n. 李子干

记 高处的树枝够不到，园丁只好跳（sprung）起来去修剪（prune）
考 同义 prune = trim

类比
mow 割草 to lawn 草 ⇒ prune 修剪 to tree 树 （动宾）
prune 修剪 to plant 植物 ⇒ sow 播种 to earth 土地 （动宾）
plum 李子 to prune 李子干 ⇒ grape 葡萄 to raisin 葡萄干 （同义）
prune 修剪 to eradicate 根除 ⇒ abbreviate 缩短 to delete 删除 （＜程度）

★★★ guile

[gaɪl] n. 狡猾，诡计

变 guileless a. 诚实的
记 注意区别"狡猾"（guile）和"犯罪"（guilt）
考 同义 guileless = naïve；cunning = guile

类比
innocent 天真的 to guile 狡猾 （缺乏）
guile 狡猾 to deceive 欺骗 （同义）
bigoted 顽固的 to fair 公平 ⇒ ingenuous 天真的 to guile 狡猾 （缺乏）

★ devastate

['devəsteɪt] v. 毁灭，毁坏

变 devastated a. 毁坏的
记 谐音：devil state：恶魔（devil）说（state）去摧毁（devastate）你
考 类比 devastated 毁坏的 to upset 扰乱 ⇒ ferocious 凶狠的 to hurtful 有害的 （＞程度）

List | 42 words

★ 复习一下学过的单词！

- compassion
- confront
- copious
- culpable
- destroy
- fallacy
- fragile
- galvanize
- goad
- imperative
- legislate
- mogul
- overture
- posthumous
- rescind
- stag
- tactile
- taint
- tepid
- yawn

☆ prune　　☆ guile　　☆ devastate

SSAT词汇 List 44

★★ screw [skruː] n. 螺丝

- 变 screwdriver n. 螺丝刀
- 记 screw 这个单词有很多俚语的意思，比如"You're screwed."中文意思就是"你死定了"。
- 考 类比 spiral 螺旋 to curve 曲线 ⇒ screw 螺丝 to arc 弧（纵向）
  hammer 锤子 to nail 钉子 ⇒ screwdriver 螺丝刀 to screw 螺丝钉（事物及其对象）

★ prophesy [ˈprɒfɪsaɪ] v. 预言，预告

- 记 教授（professor）开始对股票走向做出预言（prophesy）
- 考 同义 prophesy = foretell
  类比 premonition 预告 to prophesy 预言 ⇒ preface 前言 to prologue 序言（同义）

★ atypical [eɪˈtɪpɪkl] a. 非典型的，不合规则的

- 记 a- 反义 + typical 典型的
- 考 同义 atypical = unusual

★★★ cobble [ˈkɒbl] v. 修补

- 变 cobbler n. 补鞋匠
- 记 柯布（Cobb）是个不错的补鞋（cobble）人
- 考 同义 cobbler = repair shoes
  类比 cobbler 补鞋匠 to shoes 鞋子 ⇒ tailor 裁缝 to clothing 服装（人物及其对象）
  golfer 高尔夫球手 to club 球棒 ⇒ cobbler 补鞋匠 to awl 锥子（人物及其工具）
  hammer 锤子 to carpenter 木匠 ⇒ awl 锥子 to cobbler 补鞋匠（人物及其工具）

★ frenetic

[frəˈnetɪk] *a.* 狂热的，发狂的

- 变 frantic *a.* 发狂的，狂热的
- 记 法国人（French）看球的时候都比较容易发狂（frenetic）
- 考 同义 frantic = desperate；energetic = frenetic

★★★ volume

[ˈvɒljuːm] *n.* 容积，体积

- 记 我们平时喝水的杯子外边或者电视机的摇控器上都会有 VOL 的字样，前者表示"容积"，后者表示"音量"，都是 volume 的缩写
- 考 类比
  - potency 力量 to weaken 减弱 ⇒ volume 体积 to collapse 倒塌 （事物及其动作）
  - magnitude 震级 to earthquake 地震 ⇒ decibel 分贝 to sound 声音 （事物及其用途）
  - lumens 流明 to brightness 亮度 ⇒ decibel 分贝 to volume 音量 （事物及其对象）
  - mile 英里 to length 长度 ⇒ quart 夸脱 to volume 容积 （事物及其对象）
  - mile 英里 to distance 距离 ⇒ quart 夸脱 to volume 容积 （事物及其对象）
  - distance 距离 to yard 码 ⇒ volume 容积 to pint 品脱 （事物及其对象）
  - liter 升 to volume 容积 ⇒ gram 克 to mass 质量 （事物及其对象）
  - liter 升 to volume 容积 ⇒ foot 英寸 to distance 距离 （事物及其对象）
  - liter 升 to volume 容积 ⇒ pound 磅 to weight 重量 （事物及其对象）
  - area 面积 to volume 体积 ⇒ triangle 三角形 to pyramid 金字塔 （纵向）

★ crest

[krest] *n.* 浪尖

- 记 我们常用的"佳洁士牙膏"的英文即为 crest
- 考 类比 mountain 山 to peak 顶峰 ⇒ wave 波涛 to crest 浪尖 （事物及其部分）
- 注 关于"顶点"的单词在 SSAT 的习题中有很多，如：pinnacle, zenith, acme。

crest

★ abjure

[əbˈdʒʊə] *v.* 发誓放弃

- 记 玩蹦极的时候伤（injure）到自己，发誓放弃（abjure）这个爱好
- 考 同义 abjure = renounce

★★★ prominent
['prɒmɪnənt] *a.* 突出的，显著的

- 变 prominence *n.* 卓越，显著
- 记 因为贡献杰出（eminent），所以行为突出（prominent）
- 考 同义 prominent = conspicuous；prominent = outstanding；prominence = standout

★★★ cartographer
[kɑːˈtɒɡrəfə] *n.* 地图编辑者

- 变 cartography *n.* 地图制作
- 记 cart-（card）+ graph 写：在卡上写字，然后将卡片做成地图的人就是地图编辑者 cartographer
- 考 类比

verbal 口头的 to oral 口头的	⇒	cartography 地图制造 to map 地图 （同义）
map 地图 to cartographer 地图编辑者	⇒	cake 蛋糕 to baker 烘焙师 （人物及其对象）
cartographer 地图编辑者 to map 地图	⇒	chef 主厨 to meal 饭 （人物及其对象）
coopers 桶匠 to barrel 桶	⇒	cartographer 地图编辑者 to map 地图 （人物及其对象）
pugilist 拳击手 to boxing 拳击	⇒	cartographer 地图编辑者 to map 地图 （人物及其对象）
cartographer 地图编辑者 to maps 地图	⇒	architect 建筑师 to blueprints 蓝图 （人物及其对象）

★★ remuneration
[rɪˌmjuːnəˈreɪʃn] *n.* 报酬，酬劳

- 记 有专家说这个单词其实最初是写成 renumeration 的，其中的 numeration 表示"数字的算法"，之后才引申出了现在的 remuneration 这个单词
- 考 同义 reparation = remuneration

类比

remuneration 报酬 to labor 劳动	⇒	trophy 奖品 to victory 胜利 （事物及其对象）
broker 经纪人 to commission 佣金	⇒	worker 工人 to remuneration 报酬 （人物及其对象）

★★★ counsel
[ˈkaʊnsl] *v.* 建议，劝告；*n.* 忠告

- 变 counselor *n.* 顾问
- 记 我们常说的心理咨询师就叫 psychological counselor
- 考 同义 advise = counsel；advice = counsel

类比 mentor 指导者 to professor 教授 ⇒ advisor 给予建议者 to counselor 顾问 （同义）

★ correspond

[ˌkɒrɪˈspɒnd] *v.* 符合，一致

- 变 correspondence *n.* 通讯

考 同义　correspond = agree；correspondence = letters

★ curator　[kjʊəˈreɪtə] *n.* 馆长

记　新馆长（curator）很好奇（curious）自己接下来的仕途走向
考　类比　librarian/图书管理员 to library/图书馆 ⇒ curator/馆长 to museum/博物馆　（空间）

★★ innate　[ɪˈneɪt] *a.* 天生的

记　in- + nat- 拉丁词根 + e，表示"to be born"的意思
考　类比　habit/习惯 to innate/天生 ⇒ practice/惯例 to natural/自然的　（纵向）
注　关于"天生的"单词在 SSAT 的习题中有很多，如：natal, inherent, congenital。

★★★ boisterous　[ˈbɔɪstərəs] *a.* 喧闹的，狂暴的

记　谐音：boys：男孩子多了当然就很喧闹（boisterous）
考　同义　boisterous = uproarious
　　类比　loudmouth/高声讲话的人 to boisterous/喧闹的 ⇒ nomad/流浪者 to wandering/流浪的　（人物及其特点）
注　关于"喧闹的"单词在 SSAT 的习题中有很多，如：noisy, chaotic, clamorous, tumultuous。

★★ triangle　[ˈtraɪæŋgl] *n.* 三角形

考　类比　area/面积 to volume/体积 ⇒ triangle/三角形 to pyramid/金字塔　（纵向）
　　　　　wheel/车轮 to circle/圆形 ⇒ wedge/楔子 to triangle/三角形　（事物及其特点）
　　　　　centipede/蜈蚣 to spider/蜘蛛 ⇒ pentagon/五角形 to triangle/三角形　（同类）

★ manifest　[ˈmænɪfest] *a.* 显然的，明显的

记　manifest 的变体是 manifesto（宣言），我们常说的《共产党宣言》为 the Communist Manifesto
考　同义　manifest = obvious

manifest

★ feign　[feɪn] *v.* 假装，做作

记　有些老外（foreign）总装作（feign）很厉害的样子
考　同义　feign = simulate
　　类比　feign/假装 to deceive/欺骗 ⇒ flee/逃跑 to elude/躲避　（同义）

☆ curator　　☆ innate　　☆ boisterous　　☆ triangle　　☆ manifest
☆ feign

withdraw [wɪðˈdrɔː] v. 撤退，收回

- **变** withdrawn a. 沉默寡言的
- **记** 在很多银行取款机上都会有（withdraw）这个单词，是"取钱"的意思
- **考** 同义　recoil = withdraw；retract = withdraw

类比　abbreviate (缩短) to shorten (缩短) ⇒ retract (撤退) to withdraw (回撤)　（同义）

introspective (内省的) to withdrawn (沉默的) ⇒ gregarious (社交的) to social (社会的)　（同义）

bestow (授予) to withdraw (收回) ⇒ arrive (到达) to depart (出发)　（反义）

List | 43 words　　　★ 复习一下学过的单词！

□ broach	□ guile	□ monarch	□ pedagogue
□ brush	□ incendiary	□ murky	□ poacher
□ devastate	□ juvenile	□ oppress	□ prune
□ embrace	□ laud	□ ornament	□ recurrent
□ gangly	□ mire	□ pardon	□ varnish

SSAT词汇 List 45

★ egress
['iːgres] n. 外出，出口

记 e- 朝外 + -gress 走路：朝外走的地方即为出口（egress）
考 同义 egress = exit
类比 windward 迎风面 to leeward 背风面 ⇒ ingress 入口 to egress 出口 （反义）

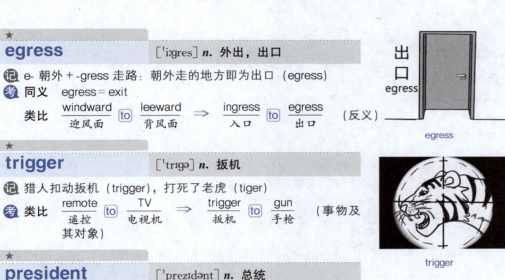

egress

★ trigger
['trɪgə] n. 扳机

记 猎人扣动扳机（trigger），打死了老虎（tiger）
考 类比 remote 遥控 to TV 电视机 ⇒ trigger 扳机 to gun 手枪 （事物及其对象）

trigger

★ president
['prezɪdənt] n. 总统

记 总统（president）犯法与庶民（resident）同罪
考 类比 abdicate 退位 to king 国王 ⇒ resign 辞职 to president 总统 （人物及其动作）
team 队伍 to captain 队长 ⇒ republic 共和国 to president 总统 （人物及其对象）

★★ amend
[ə'mend] v. 修改，改善

记 mend 本身就是"修理"的意思
美国宪法的《修正案》即为 Amendment
考 同义 amend = improve
类比 amend 改变 to change 改变 ⇒ destroy 破坏 to demolish 破坏 （同义）
注 关于"改善"的单词在 SSAT 的习题中有很多，如：optimize, perfect, ameliorate, modify, rectify。

★★ tongue
[tʌŋ] n. 舌头

考 同义 inarticulate = tongue-tied

☆ egress　　☆ trigger　　☆ president　　☆ amend　　☆ tongue

类比　taste　to　tongue　⇒　touch　to　skin　（事物及其用途）
　　　品尝　　　舌头　　　　触摸　　　皮肤

　　　gills　to　breathe　⇒　tongue　to　taste　（事物及其用途）
　　　鱼鳃　　　呼吸　　　　舌头　　　品尝

★ predicament　[prɪˈdɪkəmənt] n. 困境

- 记　预测（prediction）到自己会在 SSAT 的学习上遇到困境（predicament）
- 考　同义　plight＝predicament
- 注　关于"困境"的单词在 SSAT 的习题中有很多，如：quandary，dilemma，uncertainty，perplexity。

★ absolve　[əbˈzɒlv] v. 免除，赦免

- 记　他戴罪立功，解决（solve）问题，所以得到赦免（absolve）
- 考　同义　absolve＝clear；absolve＝forgive

★★ narrate　[nəˈreɪt] v. 叙述

- 变　narrator n. 叙述者
- 记　你只需叙述（narrate）即可，无需点评（rate）
- 考　同义　narrate＝tell

　　类比　petition　to　ask　⇒　narrate　to　tell　（同义）
　　　　　请愿　　　　要求　　　叙述　　　告诉

　　　　　scribe　to　copy　⇒　narrator　to　tell　（人物及其动作）
　　　　　抄写员　　　抄写　　　叙述者　　　阐述

★ stream　[striːm] n. 小溪

考　类比　stream　to　river　⇒　cottage　to　house　（种属）
　　　　　小溪　　　河　　　　小屋　　　房子

　　　　　stream　to　drop　⇒　boulder　to　pebble　（＞程度）
　　　　　小溪　　　水滴　　　大石头　　　鹅卵石

　　　　　stagnant　to　pond　⇒　flowing　to　stream　（事物及其特点）
　　　　　静止的　　　池塘　　　流动的　　　小溪

★ induce　[ɪnˈdjuːs] v. 引导，引起

- 记　in-＋duc- 引导＋e
- 考　同义　induce＝bring about

★★ obsequious　[əbˈsiːkwɪəs] a. 谄媚的，顺从的

- 记　ob-（after）＋sequ- 跟随＋-ious：紧跟其后，显得谄媚（obsequious）
- 考　同义　servile＝obsequious

182　　☆ predicament　　☆ absolve　　☆ narrate　　☆ stream　　☆ induce
　　　☆ obsequious

concede ★★★
[kənˈsiːd] *v.* 承认；让步

- 记 con- + ced- 走 + e：大家一起朝后走，撤退，即为让步（concede）
- 考 同义 concede = grant；concede = yield；relinquish = concede

disseminate ★★
[dɪˈsemɪneɪt] *v.* 传播，散播

- 记 dis- + semin 种子 + -ate：朝外（dis）散播（disseminate）种子（semin）
- 考 同义 disseminate = separate；disseminate = broadcast；disseminate = spread
- 类比 disseminate 散播 to information 消息 ⇒ exclude 驱逐 to outcast 流浪者 （动宾）

dawn ★
[dɔːn] *n.* 黎明

- 考 类比 dawn 黎明 to dusk 黄昏 ⇒ start 开始 to finish 结束 （反义）

locomotion ★
[ˌləʊkəˈməʊʃn] *n.* 运动，移动

- 记 locomotion 这个单词中的 motion 本来就是"运动"的意思
- 考 类比 speak 说话 to communication 交流 ⇒ walk 走路 to locomotion 移动 （种属）

precipice ★
[ˈpresɪpɪs] *n.* 悬崖

- 变 precipitous *a.* 险峻的，陡峭的
- 记 总统（president）参加攀爬悬崖（precipice）的比赛
- 考 同义 precipice = side of cliff
- 类比 precipitous 陡峭的 to cliff 悬崖 ⇒ breathtaking 惊人的 to vista 风景 （修饰）

reverence ★★
[ˈrevərəns] *n.* 尊敬

- 记 这本参考书（reference）因其严谨性而受到大家的喜爱，作者也受到尊敬（reverence）
- 考 类比 conviction 信念 to opinion 观点 ⇒ reverence 尊敬 to admiration 羡慕 （＞程度）
- 类比 impious 不虔诚的 to reverence 尊敬 ⇒ superficial 肤浅的 to depth 深度 （缺乏）

foment ★
[fəʊˈment] *v.* 煽动，激起

- 记 有人煽动（foment）引起骚动（ferment）
- 考 同义 foment = instigate
- 注 关于"煽动，激起"的单词在 SSAT 的习题中有很多，如：provoke，agitate。

wire ['waɪə] n. 电线

变 wired a. 极其兴奋的
考 同义 wired = excited

类比
electricity/电 —to→ wire/电线 ⇒ water/水 —to→ aqueduct/导水管 （空间）
electricity/电 —to→ wire/电线 ⇒ water/水 —to→ pipe/水管 （空间）
wire/电线 —to→ cable/电缆 ⇒ singer/歌手 —to→ choir/合唱队 （组成）

fragment [fræg'ment] n. 碎片

记 这个杯子因为很脆弱（fragile），所以被拍成碎片（fragment）
考 同义 fragment = portion

List | 44 words　　　　　　　　　　★ 复习一下学过的单词！

□ abjure	□ correspond	□ frenetic	□ remuneration
□ atypical	□ counsel	□ innate	□ screw
□ boisterous	□ crest	□ manifest	□ triangle
□ cartographer	□ curator	□ prominent	□ volume
□ cobble	□ feign	□ prophesy	□ withdraw

☆ wire　　☆ fragment

SSAT词汇 List 46

★ tenuous
['tenjʊəs] *a.* 稀薄的，纤细的

记 劣质原材料导致这个网球（tennis）非常纤细（tenuous），毫不圆润
考 同义 tenuous = flimsy

类比 tenuous (脆弱的) to friendship (友谊) ⇒ unstable (不稳定的) to government (政府) （修饰）

★ calorie
['kæləri] *n.* 卡路里

记 谐音：卡路里
考 类比 carat (克拉) to diamond (钻石) ⇒ calories (卡路里) to heat (热度) （修饰）

★★ hibernate
['haɪbəneɪt] *v.* 冬眠

记 hi + ber-（bear）+ nate："嗨（hi），小熊（bear）你吃（ate）饱了干什么？""我吃饱了就冬眠（hibernate）啊！"
考 同义 hibernate = sleep

类比 sleep (睡觉) to hibernation (冬眠) ⇒ race (比赛) to marathon (马拉松) （<程度）
hibernate (冬眠) to nap (午休) ⇒ gorge (狼吞虎咽) to nibble (轻咬) （>程度）
bird (鸟) to migration (迁徙) ⇒ bear (熊) to hibernation (冬眠) （事物及其特点）
migrate (迁徙) to swallow (燕子) ⇒ hibernate (冬眠) to ground hog (土拨鼠) （事物及其特点）

★ arbitrator
['ɑːbɪtreɪtə] *n.* 仲裁人

变 arbitrate *v.* 仲裁，公断
记 谐音：2B：仲裁人（arbitrator）手里拿着一支2B铅笔进行仲裁（arbitrate）
考 同义 arbitrator = judge

☆ tenuous　　☆ calorie　　☆ hibernate　　☆ arbitrator

类比　arbitrate／仲裁　to　dispute／争论　⇒　solve／解决　to　mystery／迷　（动宾）

falter　['fɔːltə] v. 踌躇，支支吾吾

记　因为他犯错（fault）了，所以他在犹豫（falter）要不要去主动道歉
考　同义　falter ＝ hesitate

omniscient　[ɒmˈnɪsɪənt] a. 全知的，无所不知的

记　omni- 全 ＋ sci- 知道 ＋ ent
考　同义　omniscient ＝ knowledgeable

torrent　['tɒrənt] n. 奔流

记　天气酷热（torrid），汗如雨下（torrent）
考　同义　torrent ＝ current；deluge ＝ torrent

bankrupt　['bæŋkrʌpt] a. 破产的

记　bank ＋ -rupt 破裂：银行破裂，即为破产（bankrupt）
考　同义　insolvent ＝ bankrupt
　　类比　bankrupt／破产的　to　fund／资金　⇒　arid／干旱的　to　rain／雨　（缺乏）

nail　[neɪl] n. 钉子

考　类比　affix／粘贴　to　stamp／邮票　⇒　hammer／锤打　to　nail／钉子　（动宾）
　　　　 tape／胶带　to　stick／粘　⇒　nail／钉子　to　puncture／刺穿　（事物及其用途）
　　　　 hammer／锤子　to　nail／钉子　⇒　screwdriver／螺丝刀　to　screw／螺丝钉　（事物及其对象）

acknowledge　[əkˈnɒlɪdʒ] v. 承认；感谢

考　类比　include／包括　to　omit／忽略　⇒　acknowledge／承认　to　ignore／忽视　（反义）
　　　　 approve／批准　to　deny／否认　⇒　acknowledge／承认　to　refute／反驳　（反义）
　　　　 repudiate／否定　to　deny／否认　⇒　acknowledge／承认　to　accept／接受　（同义）
　　　　 negate／否定　to　deny／否认　⇒　acknowledge／承认　to　accept／接受　（同义）

☆ falter　☆ omniscient　☆ torrent　☆ bankrupt　☆ nail
☆ acknowledge

homage → to acknowledge ⇒ admission → to accept （同义）
敬意　　答谢　　　　准许进入　　接受

★★★
amorphous
[əˈmɔːfəs] *a.* 无定形的

- 记 a- 否定 + morph- (form) + -ous
- 考 同义 amorphous = shapeless; amorphous = rambling
- 类比
  - amorphous → to shape ⇒ anonymous → to name （缺乏）
    无形的　　形状　　　匿名的　　姓名
  - amorphous → to shape ⇒ stoic → to emotion （缺乏）
    无形的　　形状　　　禁欲的　　情感
  - amorphous → to shape ⇒ odorless → to scent （缺乏）
    无形的　　形状　　　无气味的　　气味
  - symmetrical → to amorphous ⇒ balanced → to unshaped （纵向）
    对称的　　无形的　　　平衡的　　无形的

★
breach
[briːtʃ] *n.* 违背，违反

- 记 最终还是没有达到 (reach) 自己的目标，违背 (breach) 了当初的承诺
- 考 同义 breach = violation

★★★
caution
[ˈkɔːʃn] *n.* 谨慎

- 变 cautious *a.* 谨慎的
- 记 大街上常见到的路标：小心路滑 (Caution! Wet Floor!)
- 考 同义 cautious = discreet
- 类比
  - young → to escapade ⇒ age → to caution （人物及其特点）
    青年　　恶作剧　　　老年　　谨慎
  - aimless → to direction ⇒ reckless → to caution （缺乏）
    漫无目的的　　方向　　　鲁莽的　　谨慎
  - zealous → to enthusiastic ⇒ cautious → to prudent （同义）
    热心的　　热情的　　　谨慎的　　谨慎的
  - cautious → to impulsive ⇒ secretive → to proverbial （反义）
    谨慎的　　冲动的　　　秘密的　　众所周知的
- 注 关于"谨慎的"单词在 SSAT 的习题中有很多，如：vigilant, attentive, wary, meticulous, exacting。

★
mingle
[ˈmɪŋgl] *v.* 混合

- 记 单身 (single) 男女相亲，然后结婚 (mingle)
- 考 同义 mingle = mix

★★★
famine
[ˈfæmɪn] *n.* 饥荒

- 记 农民 (farmer) 不种地，人们闹饥荒 (famine)

☆ amorphous　　☆ breach　　☆ caution　　☆ mingle　　☆ famine

考 类比　famine to food ⇒ drought to water （缺乏）
　　　饥荒　　食物　　干旱　　水
　　　drought to rain ⇒ famine to nourishment （缺乏）
　　　干旱　　下雨　　饥荒　　营养
　　　famine to abundance ⇒ poverty to wealth （反义）
　　　饥荒　　大量　　　贫穷　　财富

★★★ spectator ［spekˈteɪtə］ n. 观众

记　spect- 看 + -ator

考 类比　audience to theater ⇒ spectator to arena （空间）
　　　观众　　剧院　　　观众　　竞技场
　　　spectator to game ⇒ bystander to event （人物及其对象）
　　　观众　　比赛　　　路人　　事件
　　　spectator to tournament ⇒ witness to crime （人物及其对象）
　　　观众　　锦标赛　　　目击者　　犯罪
　　　spectator to tournament ⇒ bystander to event （人物及其对象）
　　　观众　　锦标赛　　　路人　　事件

★★★ marble [ˈmɑːbl] n. 大理石

记　宝贵的大理石（marble）被破坏（mar）了

考 类比　marble to quarry ⇒ ore to mine （空间）
　　　大理石　采石场　　矿石　矿藏
　　　spatula to clay ⇒ chisel to marble （事物及其对象）
　　　抹刀　　黏土　　凿子　　大理石
　　　clay to potter ⇒ marble to sculptor （人物及其对象）
　　　黏土　　制陶工人　大理石　雕刻家

★★ antidote [ˈæntidəʊt] n. 解药

记　anti- 反 + -dote（dose）一剂药；解药（antidote）就是跟毒药（dose）反着来（anti）的一种药

考 同义　antidote = remedy；antidote = antitoxin
　类比　antibiotic to infection ⇒ antidote to poisoning （事物及其用途）
　　　抗生素　　感染　　　解药　　中毒

★ hinder [ˈhɪndə] v. 阻碍

记　有人在背后（behind）给你来阴的，阻碍（hinder）你的发挥

考 同义　hinder = delay；deter = hinder

注　关于"阻碍"的单词在 SSAT 的习题中有很多，如：thwart, foil, prevent, impede, frustrate。

trot ★★★

[trɒt] *v.* 慢跑

记 tro- 三 + t：一步三（tro）颠跑得很慢（trot）

考 类比 jog 慢跑 to sprint 快跑 ⇒ trot 慢跑 to gallop 飞奔 （＜程度）
　　　sprint 快跑 to trot 慢跑 ⇒ shout 叫喊 to call 呼叫 （＞程度）

List | 45 words　　　　　　　　　　　　　　　　★复习一下学过的单词！

□ absolve	□ egress	□ narrate	□ reverence
□ amend	□ foment	□ obsequious	□ stream
□ concede	□ fragment	□ precipice	□ tongue
□ dawn	□ induce	□ predicament	□ trigger
□ disseminate	□ locomotion	□ president	□ wire

SSAT词汇 List 47

★ recital
[rɪˈsaɪtl] *n.* 独奏会

考 类比　recital/独奏会 to pianist/钢琴家 ⇒ exhibit/展览 to artist/艺术家（人物及其对象）
　　　　recital/独奏会 to pianist/钢琴家 ⇒ banquet/宴会 to king/国王（人物及其对象）

★ cardiologist
[ˌkɑːdiˈɒlədʒɪst] *n.* 心脏学家

记 曾经听过一个故事：女人和男人离婚后，嫁给了一位心脏学家。在某个场合女人和男人再次见面，女人说："当时分手的时候，My heart was broken。"男人幽默地回答："So that's why you married a cardiologist?"

考 类比　cardiologist/心脏学家 to heart/心 ⇒ psychiatrist/精神病专家 to mind/大脑（人物及其对象）

★★ trite
[traɪt] *a.* 陈腐的

记 一个老土的（trite）部落（tribe）

考 同义　cliché = trite；trite = common

注 关于"陈腐的"单词在 SSAT 的习题中有很多，如：banal, commonplace, prosaic。

★★★ meander
[miˈændə] *v.* 漫步，蜿蜒前进

变 meandering *a.* 曲折的，蜿蜒前进的

记 meander 来自于米安德河，位于今土耳其的一条河流，因其弯曲的样貌而著称

考 同义　meander = wander；meander = wind
　类比　meandering/曲折的 to river/河流 ⇒ winding/弯曲的 to road/道路（修饰）
　　　　meander/蜿蜒前进 to direction/方向 ⇒ babble/乱说 to meaning/意义（缺乏）

meander

★ enumerate

[ɪˈnjuːməreɪt] *v.* 列举，枚举

- 记 e- 朝外 + numer-（number）+ -ate：按照数字（number）朝外一个一个列举（enumerate）出来
- 考 同义　itemize = enumerate

★★ insurgent

[ɪnˈsɜːdʒənt] *a.* 反叛的

- 变 insurgency *n.* 叛乱，暴动
- 记 in + surg(e) 汹涌，大浪 + -ent：反叛（insurgent）即为组织内部（in）起了大波浪（surge）；好莱坞大片《分歧者》的第二部《绝地反击》，英文即为 *Insurgent*
- 考 同义　insurgent = rebellious；insurgency = revulsion

★★★ refute

[rɪˈfjuːt] *v.* 反驳

- 变 refutation *n.* 反驳
- 记 我说什么就是什么，拒绝（refuse）接受反驳（refute）
- 考 同义　disprove = refute；disproof = refutation；refutation = denial

  类比　$\dfrac{\text{approve}}{\text{批准}}$ to $\dfrac{\text{deny}}{\text{否认}}$ ⇒ $\dfrac{\text{acknowledge}}{\text{承认}}$ to $\dfrac{\text{refute}}{\text{反驳}}$ （反义）

★ related

[rɪˈleɪtɪd] *a.* 相关的

- 变 unrelated *a.* 无关的
- 考 同义　akin = related；unrelated = irrelevant

★ accord

[əˈkɔːd] *n.* 一致

- 考 同义　accord = settlement
- 注 accord 这个单词的英文释义为：a settlement or compromise of conflicting opinions。

★ mask

[mɑːsk] *n.* 面具

- 记 孩子问（ask）妈妈："你把我的面具（mask）放哪儿了？"
- 考 类比　$\dfrac{\text{mask}}{\text{面具}}$ to $\dfrac{\text{face}}{\text{脸}}$ ⇒ $\dfrac{\text{shoe}}{\text{鞋子}}$ to $\dfrac{\text{foot}}{\text{脚}}$ （空间）

★★ partisanship

[ˌpɑːtɪˈzænʃɪp] *n.* 党派行，党派偏见

- 变 nonpartisan *a.* 无党派的
- 记 partisan-（party）党派 + -ship
- 考 同义　nonpartisan = unprejudiced

类比 dispassionate 平心静气的 to partisanship 党派偏见 ⇒ intemperate 放纵的 to moderation 节制 （反义）

inhospitable [ˌɪnhɒˈspɪtəbl] a. 不热情的

考 类比 inhospitable 不热情的 to welcoming 欢迎的 ⇒ unbearable 无法容忍的 to enjoyable 快乐的 （反义）

tranquil [ˈtræŋkwɪl] a. 安静的，平静的

变 tranquility n. 宁静，平静；tranquilize v. 使安静

记 英语词汇里面有很多读起来就给人很美好、很恬静、很飘逸的单词，比如这里的 tranquil

考 同义 serene = tranquil；tranquil = peace；tranquility = serenity；quiescence = tranquility

类比 foolhardy 蛮干的 to recklessness 鲁莽 ⇒ serene 安静的 to tranquility 安静 （同义）

adjacent 邻近的 to neighboring 邻近的 ⇒ tranquil 安静的 to quiet 安静的 （同义）

common 常见的 to prevalent 普遍的 ⇒ peaceful 平和的 to tranquil 安静的 （同义）

incessant [ɪnˈsesnt] a. 不断的，不停的

记 in- 否定 + cess- (cease) 停止 + -ant

考 同义 incessant = constant

类比 occasional 偶然的 to constant 经常的 ⇒ intermittent 间歇的 to incessant 连续的 （<程度）

desert [ˈdezət] n. 沙漠；[dɪˈzɜːt] v. 抛弃

变 deserted a. 被抛弃了的

考 同义 desert = abandon；deserted = forlorn

类比 moist 潮湿的 to arid 干旱的 ⇒ sublime 崇高的 to deserted 抛弃的 （反义）

assent 同意 to dissent 异议 ⇒ assert 坚持 to desert 抛弃 （反义）

desert 沙漠 to arid 干旱的 ⇒ rainforest 雨林 to humid 潮湿的 （修饰）

oasis 绿洲 to desert 沙漠 ⇒ lantern 灯 to darkness 黑暗 （缺乏）

Hawaii 夏威夷 to island 岛 ⇒ Sahara 撒哈拉 to desert 沙漠 （修饰）

★★★ vigor

['vɪgə] *n.* 活力，精力

变 vigorous *a.* 精力充沛的；vigorousness *n.* 朝气蓬勃；invigorated *a.* 精力充沛的
记 谐音：维哥：维吾尔族小哥充满活力（vigor）
考 同义 vigor = strength；vigorous = energetic

类比
- frail 脆弱的 to emaciated 憔悴的 ⇒ robust 强健的 to invigorated 精力充沛的 （同义）
- boredom 无聊 to variety 多样性 ⇒ fatigue 疲惫 to vigorousness 朝气蓬勃 （缺乏）
- feeble 虚弱的 to vigor 精力 ⇒ adulterated 掺杂的 to purity 纯洁 （缺乏）

★★★ mammal

['mæml] *n.* 哺乳动物

记 每个国家的语言可能不同，但是几乎全世界小孩子在叫妈妈的时候发的音都是 mamma，这可能和印欧语词根 mater- 有关，而今天英语 mother 的词根即为 mater 也是同样道理

考 类比
- gill 鳃 to fish 鱼 ⇒ lung 肺 to mammal 哺乳动物 （事物及其部分）
- bone 骨头 to mammal 哺乳动物 ⇒ girder 大梁 to skyscraper 摩天大楼 （事物及其部分）
- bat 蝙蝠 to mammal 哺乳动物 ⇒ butterfly 蝴蝶 to insect 昆虫 （种属）
- frog 青蛙 to amphibian 两栖动物 ⇒ whale 鲸鱼 to mammal 哺乳动物 （种属）
- larva 幼虫 to insect 昆虫 ⇒ embryo 胚胎 to mammal 哺乳动物 （动物的不同阶段）
- dolphin 海豚 to mammal 哺乳动物 ⇒ penguin 企鹅 to bird 鸟类 （种属）
- chicken 鸡 to bird 鸟 ⇒ tiger 老虎 to mammal 哺乳动物 （种属）

★★ shuttle

['ʃʌtl] *n.* 航天飞船；班车

记 请大家抓紧时间，因为班车（shuttle）即将关门（shut）
考 类比
- sedan 轿车 to car 汽车 ⇒ space shuttle 航天飞机 to spaceship 宇宙飞船 （同义）
- anthem 圣歌 to inspire 激励 ⇒ shuttle 班车 to transport 运输 （事物及其用途）

★★ consequence

['kɒnsɪkwəns] *n.* 后果，结果

变 consequential *a.* 结果的，重要的
考 同义 consequence = result；consequential = ultimate

类比 trivial 琐碎的 to consequential 重要的 ⇒ robust 强健的 to lethargic 无生气的 （反义）

★★★ orchestra ['ɔːkɪstrə] n. 管弦乐队

记 我最喜欢英国切斯特郡（Chester）的管弦乐队（orchestra）

考 类比 tile 瓷砖 to mosaic 马赛克 ⇒ musician 音乐家 to orchestra 管弦乐队 （组成）

orchestra 管弦乐队 to musician 音乐家 ⇒ regiment 军团 to soldier 士兵 （组成）

conductor 指挥 to orchestra 管弦乐队 ⇒ director 导演 to cast 全体演员 （人物及其对象）

List | 46 words ★ 复习一下学过的单词！

☐ acknowledge	☐ breach	☐ hibernate	☐ omniscient
☐ amorphous	☐ calorie	☐ hinder	☐ spectator
☐ antidote	☐ caution	☐ marble	☐ tenuous
☐ arbitrator	☐ falter	☐ mingle	☐ torrent
☐ bankrupt	☐ famine	☐ nail	☐ trot

SSAT词汇 List 48

levee
['levi] *n.* 堤坝，码头

记 次日清晨，离开（leave）码头（levee）

考 类比 levee/堤坝 to river/河流 ⇒ shoulder/路肩 to road/道路 （事物及其用途）

注 这个题的思路有些复杂：levee 的英文解释为：a place on a river where boats can let passengers on or off，而 shoulder 的英文解释为：the edge or border running on either side of a roadway。

abduct
[æb'dʌkt] *v.* 绑架

记 两名货（product）商被恐怖分子绑架（abduct）了

考 同义 abduct = kidnap

stipend
['staɪpend] *n.* 薪金

记 把 stipend 看作 spend 和 tip 的结合：他的薪金（stipend）全花（spend）在给小费（tip）上了

考 类比 royalty/版税 to author/作者 ⇒ stipend/薪金 to intern/实习生 （人物及其对象）

craven
['kreɪvn] *a.* 懦弱的，胆小的

记 不够勇敢（brave），很胆小（craven）

考 类比 courage/勇气 to craven/胆小的 ⇒ valor/勇猛 to timid/胆小的 （缺乏）

tawdry
['tɔːdri] *a.* 廉价而俗丽的

记 中世纪的一个小国家 Northumbria，有一位忧国忧民而死的皇后 St. Audrey，人们为了纪念她就在每年她的周年日时摆摊出售一些货物，其中最有名的就是一种叫作 St. Audrey's lace 的项链，这个词终于在 17 世纪的时候演变成今天的 tawdry

考 同义 tawdry = cheap

☆ levee   ☆ abduct   ☆ stipend   ☆ craven   ☆ tawdry

tear ★★
['ter] v. 撕破；[tɪə] n. 眼泪

考 类比
- tear 撕破 : to : pull 拉 ⇒ burst 爆炸 : to : inflate 膨胀 （＞程度）
- cut 切 : to : wound 伤口 ⇒ cry 哭 : to : tears 眼泪 （动作及其目的）
- weep 哭泣 : to : tears 眼泪 ⇒ breathe 呼吸 : to : carbon dioxide 二氧化碳 （动作及其对象）

cuff ★★
[kʌf] n. 袖口

记 可以把 cuff 看作 cut off：袖口（cuff）看上去好像把胳膊和手给切开（cut off）了似的

考 类比
- cuff 袖口 : to : wrist 手腕 ⇒ collar 领子 : to : neck 脖子 （空间）
- lapel 西服翻领 : to : chest 胸 ⇒ cuff 袖口 : to : arm 胳膊 （空间）
- ring 戒指 : to : finger 手指 ⇒ cuff 袖口 : to : wrist 手腕 （空间）

meticulous ★★★
[mɪˈtɪkjʊləs] a. 一丝不苟的

记 me＋ticu-（ticket）＋l＋-ous：我（me）一丝不苟（meticulous）地查票（ticket）

考 同义 meticulous＝finicky；exacting＝meticulous

类比
- aggravate 激怒 : to : infuriate 激怒 ⇒ meticulous 一丝不苟的 : to : precise 精准的 （同义）
- vigilant 警觉的 : to : careful 仔细的 ⇒ meticulous 一丝不苟的 : to : thorough 周密的 （＞程度）
- careful 认真的 : to : meticulous 一丝不苟的 ⇒ unreliable 不可靠的 : to : treacherous 奸诈的 （＜程度）

renowned ★★
[rɪˈnaʊnd] a. 著名的

记 re-＋nown-（know）＋ed：重复让大家知道你是谁，这样才会很有名（renowned）

考 同义 eminent＝renowned；renowned＝illustrious

border ★
[ˈbɔːdə] n. 边界

考 类比
- border 边界 : to : country 国家 ⇒ shoreline 海岸线 : to : ocean 海洋 （事物及其部分）
- border 边界 : to : country 国家 ⇒ perimeter 周长 : to : object 物体 （事物及其部分）

mendacity ★
[menˈdæsɪti] n. 谎言，虚伪

记 menda-（Amanda）＋city：阿曼达（Amanda）居住的城市（city）充满了谎言（mendacity）

考 类比 mendacity/谎言 to honesty/真实 → avarice/贪婪 to generosity/大方 （反义）

writhe ★

['raɪð] *v.* 扭曲，扭动

记 字写（write）得歪歪扭扭（writhe）
考 同义 writhe = twist；writhe = squirm

contort ★★

[kən'tɔːt] *v.* 扭曲

记 con- + -tort 扭曲
考 同义 contort = deform；contort = twist
类比 contort/扭曲 to straighten/使变直 → entangle/纠缠 to streamline/使成流线型 （反义）

choir ★★

['kwaɪə] *n.* 合唱队

记 choir 和 chorus 都表示"合唱团"的意思
考 类比 choir/合唱队 to singer/歌手 → cast/全体演员 to actor/演员 （组成）
wire/电线 to cable/电缆 → singer/歌手 to choir/合唱队 （组成）

wing ★★

[wɪŋ] *n.* 翅膀

考 类比 toe/脚趾 to foot/脚 → feather/羽毛 to wing/翅膀 （事物及其部分）
cherub/天使 to wings/翅膀 → imp/小恶魔 to horns/角 （人物及其特点）
flap/振动 to wing/翅膀 → wave/挥手 to hand/手 （动宾）
fish/鱼 to fin/鱼鳍 → bird/鸟 to wing/翅膀 （事物及其部分）

fussy ★★

['fʌsi] *a.* 好挑剔的

记 谐音 法西斯：当年的法西斯是很挑剔的（fussy）
考 类比 fastidious/挑剔的 to fussy/小题大做 → uncouth/粗野的 to barbarian/野蛮的 （同义）
glutton/贪吃者 to voracious/贪婪的 → stickler/坚持细节者 to fussy/挑剔的 （人物及其特点）

disarray ★

[ˌdɪsə'reɪ] *n.* 无序，混乱

记 dis- + array 排列
考 同义 disarray = havoc；disarray = catastrophe

talkative

★★

talkative ['tɔːkətɪv] *a.* 话多的

考 同义　loquacious = talkative；garrulous = talkative

★★

snack [snæk] *n.* 零食；*a.* 吃零食

考 类比

snack 吃零食 → devour 吞食 ⇒ push 推 → shove 强推　（＜程度）

nap 小憩 → sleep 睡觉 ⇒ snack 零食 → meal 饭　（＜程度）

catnap 小憩 → sleep 睡觉 ⇒ snack 零食 → meal 饭　（＜程度）

★★★

zeal [ziːl] *n.* 热情，热心

变　zealot *n.* 狂热者；zealous *a.* 热心的

记　海洋馆的人都对海豹（seal）很是热心（zeal）

考 同义　zealous = fervent

类比

apathy 冷漠 → phlegmatic 迟钝的 ⇒ zeal 热情 → enthusiastic 热心的　（同义）

zealous 热心的 → enthusiastic 热情的 ⇒ cautious 谨慎的 → prudent 谨慎的　（同义）

penitent 忏悔者 → contrite 后悔的 ⇒ zealot 狂热者 → fanatical 狂热的　（人物及其特点）

extortionist 勒索者 → threaten 威胁 ⇒ zealot 热心者 → patronize 资助　（人物及其动作）

professional 专业人员 → experience 经验 ⇒ fanatic 狂热者 → zeal 热情　（人物及其特点）

注　关于"热情的"单词在 SSAT 的习题中有很多，如：ardent，avid，dedicated，passionate。

★

thorn [θɔːn] *n.* 刺

记　国王的王座（throne）上长了刺（thorn）

考 类比　thorn 刺 → rose 玫瑰 ⇒ quill 刚毛 → porcupine 豪猪　（事物及其部分）

List | **47** words　　　　　　　　★ 复习一下学过的单词！

□ accord	□ incessant	□ meander	□ related
□ cardiologist	□ inhospitable	□ orchestra	□ shuttle
□ consequence	□ insurgent	□ partisanship	□ tranquil
□ desert	□ mammal	□ recital	□ trite
□ enumerate	□ mask	□ refute	□ vigor

SSAT词汇 List 49

★★ ditty
['dɪti] *n.* 小曲，小调

记 民间流传很多儿童不宜的小曲（dirty）、小调（ditty）

考 类比
- ditty 小曲 to oratorio 清唱剧 ⇒ anecdote 轶事 to novel 小说 （<程度）
- epic 史诗 to haiku 俳句 ⇒ symphony 交响乐 to ditty 小曲 （>程度）
- limerick 五行打油诗 to epic 史诗 ⇒ ditty 小曲 to opera 歌剧 （<程度）

★★★ plausible
['plɔːzəbl] *a.* 貌似可行的

考 同义 presumptive = plausible；creditable = plausible；plausible = reasonable

类比
- plausible 可行的 to believe 相信 ⇒ conspicuous 明显的 to notice 注意 （同义）
- probable 可能的 to certain 确定的 ⇒ plausible 貌似可行的 to definite 确定的 （<程度）

★ introspection
[ˌɪntrəˈspekʃn] *n.* 内省，反省

变 introspective *a.* 内省的，反省的

记 intro- 朝内 + spect- 看 + -tion：经常朝内（intro）看（spect）来反省（introspection）自己

考 同义 introspection = examination

类比
- introspective 内省的 to withdrawn 沉默的 ⇒ gregarious 社交的 to social 社会的 （同义）

★ champion
['tʃæmpɪən] *v.* 支持

考 同义 champion = side with

注 champion 这个单词"冠军"的意思我们是很熟悉的，此处是熟词僻义。

maudlin ['mɔːdlɪn] a. 易流泪的

记 这个单词源自 Mary Mardalene，她因替人类赎罪，所以她的画像一般都呈现流泪状

考 同义 maudlin = sentimental

类比 humorous 幽默的 to hilarious 非常滑稽的 ⇒ sad 悲伤的 to maudlin 易流泪的 （＜程度） maudlin

bewilder [bɪ'wɪldə] v. 使迷惑，使困惑

变 bewildered a. 困惑的

记 即使带了指南针，也依然在野外（wild）迷了路，让人觉得困惑（bewilder）

考 同义 bewilder = baffle; bewilder = confuse; bewilder = perplex; bewildered = confused

rummage ['rʌmɪdʒ] v. 搜索，翻找

记 在自己的行李（luggage）里到处翻找（rummage）

考 同义 rummage = search

recompense ['rekəmpens] n. 赔偿

记 re- + compense (compensate) 赔偿

考 同义 recompense = restitution

incipient [ɪn'sɪpɪənt] a. 初期的，起始的

记 这种蔬菜刚开始（incipient）咀嚼的时候会比较清淡无味（insipid）

考 同义 incipient = emerging

cooperation [kəʊˌɒpə'reɪʃn] n. 合作

考 类比 collaboration 合作 to cooperation 合作 ⇒ collation 校对 to correction 纠正 （同义）

cooperation 合作 to collusion 勾结 ⇒ imitation 模仿 to forgery 伪造 （同义 正反向）

disinterested 公正的 to favoritism 偏袒 ⇒ adversarial 对抗的 to cooperation 合作 （反义）

pediatrics [ˌpiːdɪ'ætrɪks] n. 小儿科

记 ped 古希腊含义为"儿童"，研究儿童病症的学科即为小儿科

考 类比 geriatrics 老年病学 to aged 年老的 ⇒ pediatrics 儿科 to children 儿童 （人物及其对象）

☆ maudlin　　☆ bewilder　　☆ rummage　　☆ recompense　　☆ incipient
☆ cooperation　　☆ pediatrics

senior → citizens geriatrics ⇒ children → pediatrics （人物及其对象）
老人   老年病学   儿童   儿科

★ durable

durable [ˈdjʊərəbl] *a.* 耐用的，持久的

记 因为持久（during），所以耐用（durable）
考 同义 durable = long-lasting

★★ invade

invade [ɪnˈveɪd] *v.* 侵略，侵袭

变 invader *n.* 侵略者；invasion *n.* 入侵
记 in + vade 韦德：韦德（vade）带球侵袭（invade）对方禁区
考 类比
invade → enter ⇒ dislodge → remove （同义）
入侵   进入   驱逐   移动

interloper → welcome ⇒ invader → greet （纵向）
闯入者   欢迎   入侵者   欢迎

trespasser → property ⇒ invader → nation （人物及其对象）
侵入者   财产   入侵者   国家

注 关于"侵略"的单词在 SSAT 的习题中有很多，如：encroach, trespass, transgress, violate, infringe。

★★ ingenuity

ingenuity [ˌɪndʒɪˈnjuːɪti] *n.* 心灵手巧，独创力

变 ingenious *a.* 机灵的，有独创性的
记 西门子公司的品牌宣言为"博大精深，同心致远"（Ingenuity for Life）
考 同义 ingenious = inventive；ingenuity = inventiveness

SIEMENS
Ingenuity for life
博大精深，同心致远

ingenuity

★ cylinder

cylinder [ˈsɪlɪndə] *n.* 圆筒，气缸

记 《麦田里的守望者》的作者塞林格（Salinger）很胖，看上去像一个圆筒（cylinder）
考 类比
cylinder → can ⇒ cube → dice （种属）
圆筒   罐   立方体   骰子

cylinder → circle ⇒ pyramid → point （事物及其部分）
圆筒   圆   金字塔   点

注 这个题的思路有些复杂：cylinder 的上面是 circle，而 pyramid 上面是个尖顶；pyramid 一般周边是 triangle，底座是 rectangle。

★★ tutor

tutor [ˈtjuːtə] *n.* 导师

考 类比
tutor → lecturer ⇒ mentor → guider （同义）
老师   讲师   指导师   指导者

tutor → pupil ⇒ coach → athlete （人物及其对象）
老师   学生   教练   运动员

vague [veɪg] a. 模糊的

- 记 时尚（vogue）的定义是很模糊的（vague）
- 考 同义 vague = nebulous；vague = obscure；vague = unclear
- 类比 redundant（多余的） to necessary（必需的） ⇒ vague（模糊的） to explicit（明确的） （反义）

jaunt [dʒɔːnt] n. 短途旅游

- 记 姑姑（aunt）去参加短途旅游（jaunt）
- 考 同义 excursion = jaunt；jaunt = outing
- 类比 jaunt（短途旅游） to jovial（快乐的） ⇒ odyssey（长途跋涉） to suffering（苦难） （纵向）

weep [wiːp] v. 哭泣

- 记 标榜自己为文艺青年的金句为：永远年轻、永远热泪盈眶（forever youthful, forever weeping）
- 考 类比 grisly（可怕的） to recoil（退缩） ⇒ heartrending（悲惨的） to weep（哭泣） （因果）
  weep（哭泣） to tears（眼泪） ⇒ breathe（呼吸） to carbon dioxide（二氧化碳） （动作及其对象）

List | 48 words   ★ 复习一下学过的单词！

☐ abduct	☐ cuff	☐ mendacity	☐ stipend	☐ thorn
☐ border	☐ disarray	☐ meticulous	☐ talkative	☐ wing
☐ choir	☐ fussy	☐ renowned	☐ tawdry	☐ writhe
☐ contort	☐ levee	☐ snack	☐ tear	☐ zeal
☐ craven				

SSAT词汇 List 50

jail
[dʒeɪl] *n.* 监狱

记 jailed *a.* 监禁的
考 类比 cage 笼子 to zoo 动物园 ⇒ cell 牢房 to jail 监狱 （空间）
　　　　sick 生病的 to healthy 健康的 ⇒ jailed 监禁的 to free 自由的 （反义）

deficient
[dɪˈfɪʃnt] *a.* 不足的，有缺陷的

记 有的人工作高效（efficient），有的人则缺陷重重（deficient）
考 同义 deficient = lacking；deficient = inadequate

jeopardize
[ˈdʒepədaɪz] *v.* 危害

记 死后去天堂（paradise）就不会受到任何危害（jeopardize）吗？
　 哥伦比亚公司推出的益智类游戏节目《危险边缘》英文即为 JEOPARDY
考 同义 jeopardize = endanger

federal
[ˈfedərəl] *a.* 联邦的

记 federal 经常出现在缩写词中，比如：联邦调查局 FBI 的全称就是 Federal Bureau of Investigation，联邦特快 FedEx 的全称就是 Federal Express
考 类比 federal 联邦的 to nation 国家 ⇒ municipal 市政府的 to city 城市 （同义）

federal

hide
[haɪd] *n.* 兽皮

考 类比 scale 鱼鳞 to fish 鱼 ⇒ hide 兽皮 to horse 马 （事物及其部分）
　　　　husk 外壳 to corn 玉米 ⇒ hide 兽皮 to horse 马 （事物及其部分）
注 hide 这个单词"隐藏"的意思我们是很熟悉的，此处是熟词僻义。

★★★ savory

['seɪvəri] *a.* 可口的，味美的

- 变 savor *v.* 尽情享受
- 记 因为可口（savory），所以喜欢（favorite）
- 考 同义 savory = aromatic；savory = spicy；savory = tasty

类比 $\dfrac{\text{sweet}}{\text{甜的}}$ to $\dfrac{\text{savory}}{\text{味咸的}}$ ⇒ $\dfrac{\text{sugar}}{\text{糖}}$ to $\dfrac{\text{salt}}{\text{盐}}$ （纵向）

- 注 savory 这个单词的英文释义为：piquant, pungent, or salty to the taste; not sweet。

★★★ chill

[tʃɪl] *v.* 使寒冷

- 变 chilly *a.* 寒冷的
- 记 站在山（hill）顶，感到高处不胜寒（chill）
- 考 同义 chilly = cold

类比 $\dfrac{\text{chilly}}{\text{寒冷的}}$ to $\dfrac{\text{wind}}{\text{风}}$ ⇒ $\dfrac{\text{warm}}{\text{暖和的}}$ to $\dfrac{\text{fire}}{\text{火}}$ （因果）

$\dfrac{\text{shadow}}{\text{阴影}}$ to $\dfrac{\text{glim}}{\text{灯火}}$ ⇒ $\dfrac{\text{chilly}}{\text{寒冷的}}$ to $\dfrac{\text{warm}}{\text{暖和的}}$ （反义）

$\dfrac{\text{chill}}{\text{使寒冷}}$ to $\dfrac{\text{freeze}}{\text{冷冻}}$ ⇒ $\dfrac{\text{giggle}}{\text{咯咯笑}}$ to $\dfrac{\text{guffaw}}{\text{大笑}}$ （＜程度）

★★ acumen

['ækjʊmən] *n.* 聪明，敏锐

- 记 谐音：IQ man：一个有 IQ 的 man，说明他很聪明（acumen）
- 考 同义 acumen = keenness；acumen = intellect

类比 $\dfrac{\text{acumen}}{\text{聪明}}$ to $\dfrac{\text{intelligence}}{\text{智力}}$ ⇒ $\dfrac{\text{confusion}}{\text{混乱}}$ to $\dfrac{\text{commotion}}{\text{骚乱}}$ （同义）

★ vault

[vɔːlt] *v.* 撑竿跳

- 记 微博加 V 的姑姑（aunt）开始玩撑竿跳（vault）了
- 考 同义 vault = jump

★★ preface

['prefɪs] *n.* 前言；*v.* 以……为开始

- 记 pre- 提前 + face：一本书的前言（preface）就好比先让你看到这本书的脸（face）
- 考 同义 preface = introduce

类比 $\dfrac{\text{overture}}{\text{序曲}}$ to $\dfrac{\text{opera}}{\text{歌剧}}$ ⇒ $\dfrac{\text{preface}}{\text{序}}$ to $\dfrac{\text{book}}{\text{书}}$ （事物及其部分）

$\dfrac{\text{appetizer}}{\text{开胃菜}}$ to $\dfrac{\text{meal}}{\text{饭}}$ ⇒ $\dfrac{\text{preface}}{\text{序}}$ to $\dfrac{\text{book}}{\text{书}}$ （事物及其部分）

$\dfrac{\text{prelude}}{\text{前奏}}$ to $\dfrac{\text{suite}}{\text{组曲}}$ ⇒ $\dfrac{\text{preface}}{\text{序言}}$ to $\dfrac{\text{novel}}{\text{小说}}$ （事物及其部分）

$\dfrac{\text{premonition}}{\text{预告}}$ to $\dfrac{\text{prophesy}}{\text{预言}}$ ⇒ $\dfrac{\text{preface}}{\text{前言}}$ to $\dfrac{\text{prologue}}{\text{序言}}$ （同义）

discipline ★★
['dɪsɪplɪn] *n.* 纪律

变 disciplinarian *n.* 纪律严明的人；self-discipline *n.* 自律
考 同义 martinet = disciplinarian；austerity = self-discipline；decree = discipline
类比 commander (司令官) to decree (法令) ⇒ principal (校长) to discipline (纪律) （人物及其动作）

dismantle ★
[dɪsˈmæntl] *v.* 拆卸，拆除

记 dis- + mantle 这个单词在古拉丁语中是"斗篷"cloak 的意思，现在有"地幔"的意思，所以 dismantle 有"拆卸，拆除"之意
考 同义 dismantle = break down；dismantle = separate；dismantle = take apart
类比 evolve (进化) to dismantle (拆除) ⇒ predict (预测) to withhold (保留) （反义）
注 dismantle 这个单词的英文释义为：to put an end to in a gradual systematic way.

squall ★
[skwɔːl] *n.* 暴风

记 暴风（squall）太猛了，吹得广场（square）都不见了
考 同义 squall = storm

petal ★
[ˈpetl] *n.* 花瓣

记 用金属（metal）做的花瓣（petal）
考 类比 petal (花瓣) to flower (花) ⇒ tooth (梳子上的齿) to comb (梳子) （组成）

eulogy ★★
[ˈjuːlədʒi] *n.* 颂扬，颂词

记 eu- 优 + log- 说话 + -y：说好听的话即为赞扬（eulogy）
考 同义 eulogy = tribute；eulogy = commendation
类比 exhortation (训词) to urge (敦促) ⇒ eulogy (颂扬) to praise (表扬) （事物及其目的）
enthusiastic (热情的) to mania (狂热) ⇒ commendatory (赞赏的) to eulogy (颂扬) （＜程度）

haiku ★
[ˈhaɪkuː] *n.* 俳句

记 谐音 害苦：俳句（haiku）太难懂，害苦了阅读的学生
考 类比 epic (史诗) to haiku (俳句) ⇒ symphony (交响乐) to ditty (小调) （种属）
epic (史诗) to haiku (俳句) ⇒ symphony (交响乐) to song (歌曲) （种属）
注 haiku 这个单词的英文释义为：a Japanese poem with three lines and usually 17 syllables.

★ mash

[mæʃ] v. 捣碎

记 把大蒜捣（mash）成灰（ash）
考 类比 egg / 鸡蛋 —to— scramble / 打鸡蛋 ⇒ potato / 土豆 —to— mash / 捣碎 （动宾）

★ physician

[fɪˈzɪʃn] n. 内科医生

记 这个人既是内科医生（physician），也是物理学家（physicist）
考 类比 pianist / 钢琴手 —to— musicians / 音乐家 ⇒ psychiatrist / 精神病医生 —to— physician / 内科医生 （种属）

★ incorrigible

[ɪnˈkɒrɪdʒəbl] a. 不可救药的，积习难改的

记 in- 否定 + -corrigible（correct）：不能改正确的（correct），是不可救药的（incorrigible）
考 同义 incorrigible = unmanageable；incorrigible = unrightable

★★★ tangible

[ˈtændʒəbl] a. 有形的，可触知的

变 intangible a. 无法触之的，无形的
记 tang-（touch）接触 + -ible
考 同义 tangible = touchable

类比 potable / 可饮用的 —to— drink / 喝 ⇒ tangible / 可触知的 —to— touch / 接触 （同义）
intangible / 无法接触的 —to— touching / 接触的 ⇒ inaudible / 听不见的 —to— hearing / 听力的 （反义）
secret / 秘密 —to— exposure / 暴露 ⇒ intangible / 无法接触的 —to— tangible / 接触的 （反义）
intangible / 无形的 —to— palpable / 可感知的 ⇒ prudent / 谨慎的 —to— reckless / 鲁莽的 （反义）

List | **49** words　　　　　　　　　　★ 复习一下学过的单词！

□ bewilder	□ durable	□ jaunt	□ rummage
□ champion	□ incipient	□ maudlin	□ tutor
□ cooperation	□ ingenuity	□ pediatrics	□ vague
□ cylinder	□ introspection	□ plausible	□ weep
□ ditty	□ invade	□ recompense	

☆ mash　　☆ physician　　☆ incorrigible　　☆ tangible

SSAT词汇 List 51

★ alcove
[ˈælkəʊv] *n.* 凹室

记 al + -cove（cave）洞穴：一个洞穴（cave）即为一个凹进去的凹室（alcove）
考 类比 table桌子 to altar祭坛 ⇒ recess凹处 to alcove凹室 （种属）
（altar 这个单词的英文释义为：a holy table）
注 alcove 这个单词的英文释义为：a small recessed section of a room。

★ immunity
[ɪˈmjuːnɪti] *n.* 免疫力

记 谐音：疫苗：有了疫苗，才有了免疫力（immunity）
考 同义 immunity = protection

★ tremendous
[trɪˈmendəs] *a.* 巨大的

记 tre- 三 + mend + -ous：修理（mend）之后是之前的三（tre）倍大，显得巨大（tremendous）无比
考 同义 tremendous = enormous

★ turmoil
[ˈtɜːmɔɪl] *n.* 混乱

记 2008 年我学会了两个短语：一个是彼时的俄罗斯格鲁吉亚战争，每天报纸上都可以看到 Political Turmoil；另一个是那一年的经济危机，彼时到处可见 Economic Turmoil
考 同义 tumult = turmoil

★ ★ reserved
[rɪˈzɜːvd] *a.* 沉默的，矜持的

考 同义 aloof = reserved；reticent = reserved
类比 hidden隐藏的 to obvious公开的 ⇒ reserved矜持的 to rambunctious喧闹的 （反义）
注 reserve 这个单词"储备"的意思我们是很熟悉的，此处是熟词僻义。

★ transcribe
[trænˈskraɪb] *v.* 抄写

记 trans- 转 + scribe 写：把文本从一种介质上转到另外一种介质上，需要抄写（transcribe）

☆ alcove　　☆ immunity　　☆ tremendous　　☆ turmoil　　☆ reserved
☆ transcribe

考 同义 transcribe = copy

filament ['fɪləmənt] n. 灯丝

记 注意区分"天空"(firmament) 和"灯丝"(filament)
考 同义 filament = thread
类比 wick/灯芯 to candle/蜡烛 ⇒ filament/灯丝 to bulb/灯泡 (空间)

renounce [rɪ'naʊns] v. 放弃

变 renunciation n. 放弃
记 我宣布 (announce) 放弃 (renounce) 对孩子的抚养权
考 同义 abjure = renounce; repudiate = renounce; abdicate = renounce
renunciation = forgoing

adhere [əd'hɪə] v. 黏附,依附

变 adherent n. 追随者
考 同义 adhere = stick; adherent = follower
类比 lubricant/润滑油 to slide/滑 ⇒ glue/胶水 to adhere/粘 (事物及其用途)
adherent/追随者 to follower/跟随者 ⇒ boss/老板 to demagogue/蛊惑民心者 (同义)
(demagogue 这个单词的英文释义可以理解为:bad leader)

prompt [prɒmpt] a. 敏捷的,立即的

记 小费 (tips) 的全称即为 to insure prompt service
考 同义 immediate = prompt

avarice ['ævərɪs] n. 贪婪,贪财

记 谐音:爱我 rice:这个人很贪婪 (avarice),连我家大米 (rice) 都爱
考 同义 avarice = greed; cupidity = avarice
类比 avarice/贪婪 to greed/贪婪 ⇒ insight/洞察力 to epiphany/顿悟 (同义)
avarice/贪婪 to money/钱 ⇒ gluttony/贪食 to food/事物 (动作及其对象)
mendacity/谎言 to honesty/诚实 ⇒ avarice/贪婪 to generosity/大方 (反义)

obscene [əb'si:n] a. 下流的

记 这个场景 (scene) 有些下流 (obscene)
考 同义 bawdy = obscene

★★★ convention
[kənˈvenʃn] *n.* 大会，习俗

- 变 convene *v.* 召集；conventional *a.* 传统的
- 记 抛弃旧习俗（convention），研究新发明（invention）
- 考 同义　convene = assemble；conventional = customary
- 类比　iconoclast/偶像破坏者 to convention/传统 ⇒ anarchist/无政府主义者 to government/政府 （人物及其对象）

★★★ belligerent
[bəˈlɪdʒrənt] *a.* 好战的

- 变 belligerence *n.* 斗争性，好战
- 记 词根"bell"来自战争女神 Bellona，她的丈夫是战神（Mars）
- 考 同义　belligerent = pugnacious；belligerent = warlike；belligerent = hostile
　　belligerent = bellicose；belligerent = offensive
- 类比　belligerent/好战的 to fight/斗争 ⇒ extravagant/奢侈的 to spend/花费 （修饰）
　　invaluable/贵重的 to worthless/无价值的 ⇒ belligerent/好战的 to peaceful/和平的 （反义）
　　belligerent/好战的 to assertive/独断的 ⇒ despairing/绝望的 to discouraged/气馁的 （＞程度）
　　（assertive 这个单词的英文释义为：aggressively self-assured）
- 注 belligerent 的英文释义为：inclined to or exhibiting assertiveness, hostility, or combativeness。

★★★ pragmatic
[præɡˈmætɪk] *a.* 实际的，实用主义的

- 记 经过反复练习（practice）确定了这个东西很实用（pragmatic）
- 考 同义　pragmatic = practical
- 类比　pragmatic/实际的 to realist/现实主义者 ⇒ fanciful/想象的 to idealist/理想主义者 （人物及其特点）

★★★ flounder
[ˈflaʊndə] *n.* 比目鱼；*v.* 错乱地挣扎或说话

- 记 谁是比目鱼（flounder）王朝的建立者（founder）？
- 考 同义　flounder = stumble
- 类比　flounder/比目鱼 to shark/鲨鱼 ⇒ tick/虱扁 to flea/虱子 （同类）
　　flounder/乱动 to move/移动 ⇒ stutter/结巴 to pronounce/发音 （同义：正反向）
　　floundering/乱动 to movement/移动 ⇒ muddle/乱弄 to reasoning/讲理 （同义：正反向）
　　floundering/乱动 to movement/移动 ⇒ babble/乱说 to speech/演讲 （同义：正反向）

★★★ bulb
[bʌlb] *n.* 灯泡；球茎

- 记 光头鲍勃（Bob）手握灯泡（bulb）
- 考 类比　wick/灯芯 to candle/蜡烛 ⇒ filament/灯丝 to bulb/灯泡 （空间）

bulb

| bean 豆子 | to | sprout 发芽 | ⇒ | bulb 球茎 | to | shoot 发芽 | （事物及其动作） |
| light bulb 灯泡 | to | electricity 电 | ⇒ | yo-yo 溜溜球 | to | string 线 | （事物及其部分） |

★★★ extravagant   [ɪkˈstrævəgənt] *a.* 奢侈的，浪费的

记 ex- 朝外 + trava-（travel）+ gant：经常外出（ex）旅游（travel），说明很奢侈（extravagant）

考 同义 lavish = extravagant；extravagant = prodigal

类比 | extravagant 奢侈的 | to | spend 花费 | ⇒ | belligerent 好战的 | to | fight 战斗 | （修饰）

★★★ peak   [piːk] *n.* 山峰

记 站在山峰（peak）上大声说（speak）自己的丰功伟绩

考 同义 peak = pinnacle；summit = peak

类比 | mountain 山 | to | peak 顶峰 | ⇒ | wave 波涛 | to | crest 浪尖 | （事物及其部分）
| roof 房顶 | to | building 建筑物 | ⇒ | peak 山峰 | to | mountain 山 | （事物及其部分）

★ pauper   [ˈpɔːpə] *n.* 乞丐

记 马克·吐温的代表作《王子与贫儿》英文为 The Prince and the Pauper

考 类比 | pauper 乞丐 | to | poor 穷的 | ⇒ | tycoon 大亨 | to | wealthy 富有的 | （修饰）

The Prince and the Pauper
pauper

List | **50** words　　　　　　　　　　　★ 复习一下学过的单词！

□ acumen	□ eulogy	□ jail	□ preface
□ chill	□ federal	□ jeopardize	□ savory
□ deficient	□ haiku	□ mash	□ squall
□ discipline	□ hide	□ petal	□ tangible
□ dismantle	□ incorrigible	□ physician	□ vault

SSAT词汇 List 52

★★ stipulate
['stɪpjʊleɪt] v. 规定，保证

- 变 stipulation n. 规定
- 记 这个词起源于拉丁语，在古罗马的法律中，只要借贷双方遵循一定的问答协议，那么口头协定也是算数的，而 stipulate 正是运用在这种协定中来保护双方利益的
- 考 同义 regulate = stipulate

类比 volume 卷 to encyclopedia 百科全书 ⇒ clause 条款 to stipulation 规定 （组成）

★ fodder
['fɒdə] n. 饲料

- 记 fodder 这个单词在古英语中其实指的就是 food
- 考 类比 fodder 饲料 to cattle 牛 ⇒ fuel 燃料 to engine 发动机 （事物及其对象）

★★★ valor
['vælə] n. 勇猛

- 变 valiant a. 勇敢的
- 记 爱情虽可贵，勇气 (valor) 值 (value) 千金
- 考 同义 valor = courage; valiant = brave

类比
courage 勇气 to craven 胆小的 ⇒ valor 勇猛 to timid 胆小的 （缺乏）
modesty 谦虚 to humble 谦虚的 ⇒ courage 勇气 to valiant 勇敢的 （同义）
persistent 固执的 to obstinate 固执的 ⇒ valiant 勇敢的 to brave 勇敢的 （同义）

★ kindle
['kɪndl] v. 点燃，照亮

- 记 用 Kindle 阅读器来点亮 (kindle) 你的生活
- 考 同义 kindle = ignite

类比
douse 浸泡 to liquid 液体 ⇒ kindle 点燃 to flame 火焰 （事物及其用途）
drizzle 毛毛雨 to downpour 暴雨 ⇒ kindle 点燃 to blaze 火焰 （<程度）

☆ stipulate　　☆ fodder　　☆ valor　　☆ kindle

blanket
['blæŋkɪt] n. 毯子

记 把毯子（blanket）放在篮子（basket）里

考 类比 butter/黄油 to bread/面包 → blanket/毯子 to bed/床 （空间）
　　　fold/折叠 to blanket/毯子 → coil/把……绕成圈 to rope/绳子 （动宾）

saddle
['sædl] n. 马鞍

记 因为她个子太矮，只能爬梯子（ladder）上马鞍（saddle）

考 类比 saddle/马鞍 to horse/马 → cushion/垫子 to chair/椅子 （事物及其部分）

bliss
[blɪs] n. 极乐

记 因为有上帝保佑（bless），所以我很快乐（bliss）

考 类比 mirth/欢乐 to misery/痛苦 → bliss/极乐 to agony/痛苦 （反义）
　　　catastrophe/灾难 to problem/问题 → bliss/极乐 to pleasure/快乐 （＞程度）

注 bliss 这个单词的英文释义为：extreme happiness；ecstasy。

discord
['dɪskɔːd] n. 不一致，不和

记 因为这和标准不一致（discord），所以遭到了抛弃（discard）

考 类比 anarchy/无政府 to law/法律 → discord/不一致 to agreement/统一 （缺乏）

subtle
['sʌtl] a. 微妙的

考 同义 understated = subtle
　 类比 subtle/微妙的 to obvious/明显的 → quiet/安静的 to loud/吵闹的 （反义）
　　　 nuance/细微差别 to subtle/微妙的 → hint/暗示 to indirect/不直接的 （事物及其特点）

embezzle
[ɪm'bezl] v. 盗用，挪用

记 em- + bezz- (buzz) 嗡嗡叫 + le：贪官每次在挪用（embezzle）公款的时候脑子中都有警钟在嗡嗡叫（buzz）

考 同义 embezzle = steal；embezzle = defraud；embezzle = appropriate
　　　（appropriate 这个单词的英文释义为：to take or make use of without authority or right）

process
['prəʊses] n. 过程，步骤

考 类比 production/生产 to process/步骤 → play/戏 to scene/场景 （组成）

expedite / 加快 → to → process / 过程 ⇒ accelerate / 加速 → to → pace / 步伐　（动宾）

collusion
[kəˈluːʒn] *n.* 合谋，共谋

记　这个共谋（collusion）案件涉及（inclusion）两个人
考　类比　cooperation / 合作 → to → collusion / 共谋 ⇒ imitation / 模仿 → to → forgery / 伪造　（同义：正反向）

diplomat
[ˈdɪpləmæt] *n.* 外交官，圆滑的人

变　diplomatic *a.* 外交的；diplomacy *n.* 外交手腕
记　外交官（diplomat）都必须有一定的学历证书（diploma）
考　同义　diplomatic = tactful；diplomat = representative
　　类比　diplomat / 外交官 → to → tact / 机智 ⇒ jester / 小丑 → to → clowning / 小丑般的　（人物及其特点）
　　　　　tact / 老练 → to → diplomat / 外交官 ⇒ agility / 敏捷 → to → gymnast / 体操运动员　（人物及其特点）
　　　　　ambassador / 大使 → to → diplomacy / 外交手腕 ⇒ spy / 间谍 → to → espionage / 间谍活动　（人物及其特点）

skunk
[skʌŋk] *n.* 臭鼬

记　臭鼬（skunk）的皮肤（skin）发出气味
考　类比　scent / 味道 → to → skunk / 臭鼬 ⇒ quills / 刚毛 → to → porcupine / 豪猪　（事物及其特点）
　　　　　porcupine / 豪猪 → to → quill / 刚毛 ⇒ skunk / 臭鼬 → to → odor / 气味　（事物及其特点）
　　　　　butterfly / 蝴蝶 → to → camouflage / 伪装 ⇒ skunk / 臭鼬 → to → odor / 气味　（事物及其特点）
　　　　　zebra / 斑马 → to → skunk / 臭鼬 ⇒ leopard / 美洲豹 → to → Dalmatian / 斑点狗　（同类）

ambulatory
[ˌæmbjuˈleɪtəri] *a.* 流动的，走动的

记　救护车（ambulance）在马拉松现场来回走动（ambulatory），以防万一
考　同义　ambulatory = walking

imagination
[ɪˌmædʒɪˈneɪʃn] *n.* 想象力

变　imaginary *a.* 虚构的，假想的
考　同义　mythical = imaginary
　　类比　imagination / 想象力 → to → thought / 想法 ⇒ music / 音乐 → to → sound / 声音　（种属）

213

pellucid
[pe'lu:sɪd] *a.* 透明的，清晰的

记 pel- (per) + lucid 清晰的，透明的：从头到尾始终清晰

考 类比 lucid 清晰的 to pellucid 清晰的 ⇒ lofty 崇高的 to elevated 高尚的 （同义）

servile
['sɜ:vaɪl] *a.* 奴性的

记 一个充满奴性的（servile）的仆人（servant）

考 同义 servile = obsequious

类比
brusque 唐突的 to abrupt 唐突的 ⇒ servile 奴性的 to obsequious 奉承的 （同义）
ecstatic 狂喜的 to happy 快乐的 ⇒ servile 奴性的 to submissive 顺从的 （>程度）
compliant 顺从的 to servile 奴性的 ⇒ trusting 信任的 to gullible 易受骗的 （<程度）

apt
[æpt] *a.* 恰当的，适合的

记 这个软件（app）很适合（apt）我

考 同义 apt = agreeable

schedule
['ʃedju:l] *n.* 计划表

变 scheduled *a.* 已安排好的

考 同义 agenda = schedule

类比
order 顺序 to sequence 序列 ⇒ schedule 时间表 to plan 计划 （同义）
odd 奇怪的 to agenda 议程表 ⇒ quirky 奇怪的 to schedule 时间表 （纵向）
spontaneous 即兴的 to calculated 有计划的 ⇒ impromptu 即兴的 to scheduled 已安排好的 （反义）

List | **51** words ★ 复习一下学过的单词！

- adhere
- alcove
- avarice
- belligerent
- bulb
- convention
- extravagant
- filament
- flounder
- immunity
- obscene
- pauper
- peak
- pragmatic
- prompt
- renounce
- reserved
- transcribe
- tremendous
- turmoil

SSAT词汇 List 53

★ scold
[skəʊld] v. 责骂

- 记　冷酷无情（cold）地责骂（scold）敌人
- 考　同义　scold = berate；chide = scold
- 注　关于"责骂"的单词在 SSAT 的习题中有很多，如：reprimand，censure，reproach，disparage。

★★ bond
[bɒnd] v. 结合，团结，绑

- 变　bonding a. 结合
- 记　我们要紧密团结（bond）在 James Bond 周围
- 考　同义　alliance = bonding
- 类比　bond 绑 to unite 结合 ⇒ match 火柴 to light 亮光 （因果）

★ enclose
[ɪnˈkləʊz] v. 围绕，装入

- 考　同义　enclose = envelop

★★★ compete
[kəmˈpiːt] v. 竞争，竞赛

- 变　competent a. 有能力的；competition n. 比赛
- 考　同义　compete = vie；competent = able；competent = capable
- 类比　triumph 胜利 to competition 比赛 ⇒ verdict 裁定 to trial 审判 （事物及其部分）
- competition 竞赛 to contestant 竞争者 ⇒ election 选举 to candidate 候选人 （人物及其目的）

★ enervate
[ˈenəveɪt] v. 使衰弱，使失去活力

- 记　e- 朝外 + nerv-（nerve）神经 + -ate：朝外（e）宣称自己神经（nerve）衰弱（enervate）
- 考　类比　extinguish 熄灭 to fire 火 ⇒ enervate 使衰弱 to strength 力量 （动宾）

cache
★

[kæʃ] *n.* 隐藏处

记 新婚夫妇晚上不睡觉，找个隐藏处（cache）数份子钱（cash）
考 同义　cache = hiding place

prosper
★★★

[ˈprɒspə] *v.* 繁荣，成功

变 prosperous *a.* 繁荣的
记 找个合适的（proper）地方开饭店，一定会成功（prosper）的
考 同义　flourish = prosper；flourish = thrive；prosper = advance

类比　impecunious 贫穷的 —to→ hovel 小屋 ⇒ prosperous 繁荣的 —to→ mansion 大厦　（修饰）

sink
★★

[sɪŋk] *v.* 下沉；*n.* 水槽

记 陷入（sink）深深的沉思（think）中
考 同义　sink = go down；basin = sink

类比　bathroom 洗手间 —to→ toilet bowl 抽水马桶 ⇒ kitchen 厨房 —to→ sink 水槽　（空间）

cleft
★

[kleft] *v.* 劈开，分开

记 这块木头因为被劈开（cleft），所以只剩下（left）一半了
考 同义　cleft = split

lexicon
★★★

[ˈleksɪkən] *n.* 词典，字典

记 这本字典（lexicon）起源于美国莱克星顿（Lexington）
考 同义　lexicon = dictionary

类比　anthology 选集 —to→ lexicon 字典 ⇒ works 作品 —to→ words 单词　（纵向）

lexicon 字典 —to→ words 单词 ⇒ anthology 选集 —to→ works 作品　（组成）

lexicon 字典 —to→ dictionary 字典 ⇒ officer 警官 —to→ policeman 警察　（同义）

lexicon 字典 —to→ words 单词 ⇒ movie 电影 —to→ pictures 画面　（组成）

litigant
★★

[ˈlɪtɪɡənt] *n.* 诉讼当事人

记 诉讼当事人（litigant）是个很聪明的（intelligent）家伙
考 同义　litigant = suer

continent
★★

[ˈkɒntɪnənt] *n.* 大陆

记 我们常见的国外酒店里的吃的，由面包、果酱和咖啡等组成的早餐就叫"大陆性早餐"，

英文即为 continental breakfast

考 类比　state/州 → to → country/国家　⇒　country/国家 → to → continent/大陆　（＜组成）

town/城镇 → to → city/城市　⇒　country/国家 → to → continent/大陆　（＜组成）

cape/海角 → to → continent/大陆　⇒　gulf/海湾 → to → ocean/海洋　（空间）

（这道题的思路有些复杂：对于 cape 我们可以这样理解：a large piece of land surrounded by water，对于 gulf 我们可以这样理解：a large area of sea enclosed by land）

★★★
gratuitous
[grəˈtjuːɪtəs] *a.* 无端的，免费的

记 对于香港电影，美国电影评论家 David Bordwell 曾说到其"尽皆过火，尽是癫狂"（All too extravagant, too gratuitously wild）

考 同义　gratuitous = free；gratuitous = unnecessary

★
gyrate
[ɪdʒaɪˈreɪt] *v.* 旋转

记 杰瑞（Jerry）在原地旋转（gyrate）

考 同义　gyrate = spin

类比　bulwark/堡垒 → to → protect/保护　⇒　coil/线圈 → to → gyrate/旋转　（事物及其特点）

★
dispute
[dɪˈspjuːt] *v.* 辩论，争吵

记 兄弟俩因为电脑（computer）的使用权而开始争吵（dispute）

考 类比　arbitrate/仲裁 → to → dispute/辩论　⇒　solve/解决 → to → mystery/谜　（动宾）

★★
camouflage
[ˈkæməflɑːʒ] *n.* 伪装，演示

记 女孩子喜欢用美颜相机（camera）来伪装（camouflage）自己

考 同义　camouflage = disguise

类比　butterfly/蝴蝶 → to → camouflage/伪装　⇒　skunk/臭鼬 → to → odor/气味　（动物及其特点）

barrier/障碍 → to → obstruct/阻碍　⇒　camouflage/伪装 → to → conceal/隐藏　（事物及其用途）

★
nadir
[ˈneɪdɪə] *n.* 最低点

记 纳粹（Nazi）最终走向最低点（nadir）

考 类比　acme/顶点 → to → nadir/低点　⇒　attic/阁楼 → to → basement/地下室　（反义）

descent/下降 → to → nadir/低点　⇒　ascent/上升 → to → pinnacle/顶点　（纵向）

☆ gratuitous　　☆ gyrate　　☆ dispute　　☆ camouflage　　☆ nadir

navigate ★★

[ˈnævɪgeɪt] *v.* 驾驶，操纵

- **变** navigator *n.* 领航员
- **记** 这名海军（navy）负责驾驶（navigate）轮船
- **考** 类比：
  - map 地图 —to→ navigate 操纵 ⇒ blueprint 蓝图 —to→ build 建造 （事物及其用途）
  - watchman 看守人 —to→ protect 保护 ⇒ navigator 领航员 —to→ guide 引导 （人物及其动作）

arrogant ★★★

[ˈærəgənt] *a.* 自大的，傲慢的

- **变** arrogance *n.* 自大
- **记** 谐音：爱若过：爱若过头，会让对方慢慢变得自大（arrogant）
- **考** 同义：arrogant = haughty; hubris = arrogance; conceited = arrogant

  类比：
  - pomposity 自大 —to→ boastful 自大 ⇒ conceit 自负 —to→ arrogant 傲慢的 （同义）
  - meek 温顺的 —to→ arrogant 傲慢的 ⇒ mean 吝啬的 —to→ prodigal 挥霍的 （反义）
  - modesty 谦虚 —to→ arrogance 自大 ⇒ debility 衰弱 —to→ strength 力量 （反义）
  - arrogant 傲慢的 —to→ humble 谦虚的 ⇒ forget 忘记 —to→ remember 记得 （反义）
  - dignity 尊严 —to→ arrogance 自大 ⇒ deference 顺从 —to→ idolization 盲目崇拜 （＜程度）
  - frugal 节俭的 —to→ miserly 吝啬的 ⇒ confident 自信的 —to→ arrogant 傲慢的 （同义：正反向）

cogent ★

[ˈkəʊdʒənt] *a.* 令人信服的

- **记** 她是一个令人信服的（cogent）代理商（agent）
- **考** 类比：
  - cogent 令人信服的 —to→ persuasiveness 说服 ⇒ lucid 清晰的 —to→ clarity 清晰 （同义）

List | 52 words　　　　★ 复习一下学过的单词！

- ☐ ambulatory
- ☐ apt
- ☐ blanket
- ☐ bliss
- ☐ collusion
- ☐ diplomat
- ☐ discord
- ☐ embezzle
- ☐ fodder
- ☐ imagination
- ☐ kindle
- ☐ pellucid
- ☐ process
- ☐ saddle
- ☐ schedule
- ☐ servile
- ☐ skunk
- ☐ stipulate
- ☐ subtle
- ☐ valor

SSAT词汇 List 54

★ fission
['fɪʃn] *n.* 裂变，分裂

- 记 先融合（fusion）后裂变（fission）
- 考 类比 fission 裂变 to energy 能量 ⇒ combustion 燃烧 to heat 热量 （事物及其用途）

★★★ listless
['lɪstlɪs] *a.* 无精打采的

- 记 list 列表，榜单 + -less：名落孙山，没上榜单（list），所以显得无精打采（listless）
- 考 同义 listless = without energy; lethargic = listless; listless = sluggish

★★ permanent
['pɜːmənənt] *a.* 永久的，永恒的

- 变 impermanence *n.* 短暂
- 考 同义 permanent = indelible
  类比 permanent 永恒的 to everlasting 持久的 ⇒ urgent 紧急的 to crucial 至关重要的 （同义）
  perpetuity 永恒 to impermanence 短暂 ⇒ interminable 无休止的 to occasional 偶然的 （反义）

★ rickety
['rɪkəti] *a.* 摇晃的，虚弱的

- 记 这个火箭（rocket）摇摇晃晃（rickety）地就上天了
- 考 同义 feeble = rickety

★ profane
[prə'feɪn] *v.* 亵渎

- 记 我们常说的"脏话"，最正式的表达方式应该是 profane language
  美国某网站曾将美国某著名说唱歌手的某首歌评价为 the most profanity-laced rap song，因为其歌词里一共有 392 处脏话
- 考 同义 desecrate = profane

★★★ jog

[dʒɒg] *v.* 慢跑

记 小狗（dog）在慢跑（jog）

考 类比
- walk 走路 → scurry 快走 ⇒ jog 慢跑 → sprint 快跑 （<程度）
- jog 慢跑 → sprint 快跑 ⇒ hold 拿住 → grip 紧握 （<程度）
- jog 慢跑 → exercise 锻炼 ⇒ barter 以物易物 → trade 贸易 （种属）
- canter 慢跑 → gallop 快跑 ⇒ jog 慢跑 → sprint 快跑 （<程度）
- jog 慢跑 → sprint 快跑 ⇒ trot 慢跑 → gallop 飞奔 （<程度）

★ stab

[stæb] *v.* 刺，戳

记 一刀刺（stab）向马厩（stable）里的马

考 同义 stab = puncture

★★★ composer

[kəm'pəʊzə] *n.* 作曲家

变 decomposition *n.* 分解，变质

记 打开自己的iTunes，每首歌曲后面都会有这首歌作曲家（composer）的名字

考 同义 disintegration = decomposition

类比
- composer 作曲家 → score 乐谱 ⇒ author 作者 → book 书 （人物及其对象）
- score 乐谱 → composer 作曲家 ⇒ prescription 药方 → doctor 医生 （人物及其对象）
- sculptor 雕刻家 → statue 雕塑 ⇒ composer 作曲家 → music 音乐 （人物及其对象）
- architect 建筑师 → blueprint 蓝图 ⇒ composer 作曲家 → score 乐谱 （人物及其对象）
- composer 作曲家 → arranger 重新编曲者 ⇒ writer 作家 → dramatist 剧作家 （种属）

★ extend

[ɪk'stend] *v.* 延伸，延展

变 extension *n.* 延伸，延期；extensive *a.* 广泛的，大量的

考 同义 extend = jut；extension = delay；vast = extensive

★★★ prologue

['prəʊlɒg] *n.* 开场白，序言

记 可以把场白（prologue）和尾声（epilogue）一起记忆

考 同义	prologue = introduction

类比: entrance 入口 — to — house 房子 ⇒ prologue 序文 — to — story 故事 （空间）

premonition 预告 — to — prophesy 预言 ⇒ preface 前言 — to — prologue 序言 （同义）

prologue 序言 — to — novel 小说 ⇒ preamble 序文 — to — statute 法律 （事物及其部分）

play 戏剧 — to — prologue 序言 ⇒ constitution 宪法 — to — Bill of Right 权利法案 （事物及其部分）

★★ restrict　[rɪˈstrɪkt] v. 限制，约束

记　我们经常说的"限制级"的字母 R 即为英文 restricted
考　同义　confine = restrict
类比　allow 允许 — to — restrict 限制 ⇒ encourage 鼓励 — to — prevent 阻止 （反义）

restrict

★ domicile　[ˈdɒmɪsaɪl] n. 住宅，居住地

记　可以把 domi 看作 home，所以 domicile 有"居住地"的意思
考　同义　domicile = abode

★★★ initiate　[ɪˈnɪʃɪeɪt] v. 开始

变　initial a. 最初的；initiation n. 开始
考　同义　initial = first；initiate = start；initiate = commence；initiate = originate
类比　initiate 开始 — to — conclude 结束 ⇒ relish 喜爱 — to — detest 憎恶 （反义）

transition 转变 — to — alteration 改变 ⇒ start 开始 — to — initiation 开始 （同义）

refined 有教养的 — to — courteous 有礼貌的 ⇒ initial 开始的 — to — primary 初级的 （同义）

★★★ fanatic　[fəˈnætɪk] n. 狂热入迷者

记　因为这个电视节目很棒（fantastic），所以我变成了它的狂热粉（fanatic）
考　类比　professional 专业人员 — to — experience 经验 ⇒ fanatic 狂热者 — to — zeal 热情 （人物及其特点）

fanatic 狂热者 — to — devoted 忠诚的 ⇒ gourmet 美食家 — to — ravenous 贪吃的 （人物及其特点）

braggart 吹牛者 — to — boastful 好吹牛的 ⇒ fanatic 狂热入迷者 — to — ardent 狂热的 （人物及其特点）

flour ★★
['flaʊə] n. 面粉

考 类比
- sugar 糖 to gum 口香糖 ⇒ flour 面粉 to cake 蛋糕 （组成）
- wheat 小麦 to flour 面粉 ⇒ grape 葡萄 to wine 葡萄酒 （组成）
- flour 面粉 to bread 面包 ⇒ lemon 柠檬 to lemonade 柠檬汁 （组成）

grace ★★★
[greɪs] a. 优雅

变 gracious a. 优雅的；graceful a. 优雅的
记 格蕾丝（Grace）是个优雅的（grace）姑娘
考 同义 gracious = kind

类比
- specialist 专家 to skill 技巧 ⇒ dancer 舞蹈家 to grace 优雅 （人物及其特点）
- grace 优雅的 to queen 皇后 ⇒ wizened 干瘦的 to old lady 老女人 （人物及其特点）
- articulate 口齿清晰的 to speech 演讲 ⇒ graceful 优雅的 to movement 动作 （修饰）
- somnolent 催眠的 to wakeful 醒着的 ⇒ graceful 优雅的 to clumsy 笨拙的 （反义）
- idle 闲置的 to employed 被雇用的 ⇒ graceful 优雅的 to clumsy 笨拙的 （反义）

gaunt ★
[gɔːnt] a. 枯瘦的

记 枯瘦的（gaunt）姑姑（aunt）
考 同义 gaunt = thin

类比
- atrocious 凶残的 to bad 坏的 ⇒ gaunt 枯瘦的 to thin 瘦弱的 （同义）

whisper ★★
['wɪspə] v. 低声说话

记 新中国成立以来，第一支来华举办演唱会的乐队叫 Wham，他们开创了外国乐队来华演出的先例。他们有一首非常有名的歌曲就叫 Careless Whisper
考 类比
- tiptoe 踮着脚尖走路 to walk 走路 ⇒ whisper 低声说话 to speech 演讲 （种属）
- whisper 私语 to bellow 吼叫 ⇒ suggest 建议 to command 命令 （＜程度）
- whisper 低语 to scream 尖叫 ⇒ glance 扫视 to stare 凝视 （＜程度）

palatable

[ˈpælətəbl] *a.* 美味的

- 记 palat- (plate) 盘子 + -able：盘子 (plate) 里的东西很好吃 (palatable)
- 考 同义 palatable = delicious

类比 $\underset{\text{好吃的}}{\text{palatable}}$ to $\underset{\text{好吃的}}{\text{delicious}}$ ⇒ $\underset{\text{芳香的}}{\text{aromatic}}$ to $\underset{\text{芳香的}}{\text{fragrant}}$ （同义）

impart

[ɪmˈpɑːt] *v.* 给予，传授

- 记 拆成 I'm part：把我的一部分 (part) 给你就是"给予" (impart)
- 考 同义 impart = teach；impart = convey

List | 53 words　　　　　　　　　　　　　　★ 复习一下学过的单词！

☐ arrogant	☐ cogent	☐ enervate	☐ nadir
☐ bond	☐ compete	☐ gratuitous	☐ navigate
☐ cache	☐ continent	☐ gyrate	☐ prosper
☐ camouflage	☐ dispute	☐ lexicon	☐ scold
☐ cleft	☐ enclose	☐ litigant	☐ sink

☆ palatable　　　☆ impart

SSAT词汇 List 55

★★ theme
[θi:m] *n.* 主题

记 我们常说的"主题公园"的英文即为 Theme Park
考 同义 motif = theme
类比
topic (to) discourse ⇒ theme (to) essay （事物及其部分）
主题　　论述　　　　主题　　论文
point (to) argument ⇒ theme (to) thesis （事物及其部分）
观点　　论证　　　　主题　　论文

★★★ stingy
['stɪndʒi] *a.* 吝啬的，小气的

变 stinginess *n.* 吝啬
记 英国著名歌手斯汀（Sting）（曾演唱过电影《这个杀手不太冷》的主题曲）非常吝啬（stingy）
考 类比
ravenous (to) hungry ⇒ stingy (to) thrifty （>程度）
贪婪的　　饥饿的　　小气的　　节约的
parsimonious (to) stingy ⇒ meager (to) small
吝啬的　　　小气的　　瘦的　　　小的
（同义）
sage (to) judicious ⇒ miser (to) stingy （人物及其特点）
圣人　　明智的　　小气鬼　　吝啬的
frugality (to) stingy ⇒ pride (to) haughty （同义：正反向）
朴素　　小气的　　自豪　　傲慢的
philanthropic (to) benevolence ⇒ miserly (to) stinginess （同义）
仁慈的　　　仁慈　　　　吝啬的　　吝啬
miser (to) generous ⇒ benefactor (to) stingy （人物及其特点）
小气鬼　　大方的　　捐赠者　　吝啬的
generous (to) philanthropist ⇒ stingy (to) miser （人物及其特点）
大方的　　慈善家　　　小气的　　守财奴

注 关于"吝啬的"单词在 SSAT 的习题中有很多，如：thrifty, sparing, abstemious, economical。

★ auditory
['ɔ:dɪtəri] *a.* 听觉的

记 audi- 听 + -tory

考 类比 tactile 触觉的 to touch 接触 ⇒ auditory 听觉的 to sound 听 （同义）

nose 鼻子 to olfactory 嗅觉的 ⇒ ear 耳朵 to auditory 听觉的 （事物及其特点）

★★★ adept

['ædept] *a.* 熟练的，擅长的

记 改编（adapt）文章是他的强项（adept）
考 同义 adept = proficient；adept = expert；adept = agile
类比 adept 熟练的 to unskilled 不熟练的 ⇒ mischievous 淘气的 to obedient 顺从的 （反义）

★ proof

[pru:f] *n.* 证据

变 disproof *n.* 反驳
考 同义 disproof = refutation
类比 testimony 证词 to witness 目击者 ⇒ proof 证据 to theorist 理论家 （人物及其动作）

hypothesis 假设 to scientist 科学家 ⇒ proof 证据 to mathematician 数学家 （人物及其对象）

★ libel

['laɪbl] *v.* 诽谤，中伤

记 给别人乱贴标签（label）其实就是为了诽谤（libel）别人
考 同义 libel = slander；libel = defame

★ hinge

[hɪndʒ] *n.* 铰链，折页

记 铰链（hinge）挂（hang）在门之间
考 类比 shoe 鞋子 to lace 鞋带 ⇒ door 门 to hinge 铰链 （事物及其部分）
注 hinge 这个单词的英文释义为：a piece of metal, wood, or plastic that is used to join a door to its frame or to join two things together so that one of them can swing freely.

hinge

★★ sufficient

[sə'fɪʃnt] *a.* 充足的

考 类比 sufficient 足够的 to plentiful 大量的 ⇒ adequate 足够的 to lavish 丰富的 （同义）

sufficient 充足的 to plentiful 足够的 ⇒ inactive 不活跃的 to idle 懒惰的 （同义）

mope
[məʊp] n. 闷闷不乐

记 妈妈让孩子拖地（mop），所以孩子闷闷不乐（mope）
考 同义 mope = pout
类比 depressed（沮丧的） to mope（闷闷不乐） ⇒ tired（疲倦的） to yawn（打哈欠） （同义）

abolish
[əˈbɒlɪʃ] v. 废除

记 废除（abolish）旧的东西，打磨（polish）新的东西
考 类比 end（结束） to abolish（废除） ⇒ begin（开始） to establish（建立） （同义）
注 关于"废除，废弃"的单词在 SSAT 的习题中有很多，如：repeal, invalidate, negate, nullify, revoke。

alias
[ˈeɪliəs] n. 别名，化名

记 新拳击手用阿里（Ali）当作（as）自己的化名（alias）
考 同义 alias = pseudonym；alias = assumed name

partial
[ˈpɑːʃl] a. 局部的，偏爱的

变 impartial a. 公平公正的，不偏不倚的
记 im- 否定 + part + -ial：不会（im）只喜欢某一个部分（part）即为公正的（impartial）
考 同义 partial = incomplete；impartial = disinterested；impartial = objective
类比 flammable（易燃的） to inflammable（易燃的） ⇒ impartial（公正的） to disinterested（公正的） （同义）

sprinkle
[ˈsprɪŋkl] v. 喷洒

记 春天（spring）的早晨，草地上有个喷头在喷（sprinkle）水
考 类比 funny（好笑的） to hilarious（滑稽的） ⇒ sprinkle（喷洒） to drop（水滴） （<程度）
sprinkle（喷洒） to deluge（洪水） ⇒ flurry（小旋风） to blizzard（暴风雪） （<程度）

crass
[kræs] a. 愚钝的，粗鲁的

记 笨手笨脚的（crass）我被草（grass）划破了脚
考 同义 crass = crude；crass = stupid
类比 bombastic（夸大的） to quiet（安静的） ⇒ demure（端庄娴静的） to crass（粗鲁的） （反义）

crass 粗鲁的 to refinement 文雅 ⇒ pretentious 自命不凡的 to modesty 谦虚 （反义）

quart

[kwɔːt] *n.* 夸脱

记 我需要四分之一（quarter）夸脱（quart）的啤酒

考 类比
liter 升 to quart 夸脱 ⇒ meter 米 to yard 码 （同类）
pint 品脱 to quart 夸脱 ⇒ week 周 to year 年 （同类）
cup 杯 to quart 夸脱 ⇒ minute 分钟 to hour 小时 （同类）
mile 英里 to length 长度 ⇒ quart 夸脱 to volume 容积 （事物及其对象）
quart 夸脱 to volume 体积 ⇒ mile 英里 to distance 距离 （事物及其对象）

注 在英国，1 夸脱相当于 1.14 升，而在美国，1 夸脱相当于 0.95 升。

corpulent

[ˈkɔːpjʊlənt] *a.* 肥胖的

记 注意区分"肥胖的" corpulent 和"富裕的" opulent
考 同义 corpulent = fat；corpulent = overweight

arachnid

[əˈræknɪd] *n.* 蛛形纲动物

记 ara + -chnid（child）：小孩子（child）见到蛛形纲动物（arachnid）觉得害怕
考 类比
clam 蛤 to mollusk 软体动物 ⇒ spider 蜘蛛 to arachnid 蛛形纲动物 （种属）
kangaroo 袋鼠 to marsupial 袋类动物 ⇒ spider 蜘蛛 to arachnid 蛛形纲动物 （种属）

somnolent

[ˈsɒmnələnt] *a.* 困的

记 来自罗马神话睡神索蒙纳斯（Somnus）
考 同义 somnolent = sleepy
类比 somnolent 困的 to wakeful 醒着的 ⇒ graceful 优雅的 to clumsy 笨拙的 （反义）

somnolent

antiseptic

[ˌæntɪˈseptɪk] *n.* 防腐剂

记 anti- 反 + septic 细菌的（这是个古希腊词根，来源已无从考究，同学们可以联想，把 septic 联想成 September，九月是个暖和的月份，容易滋生细菌）

考 类比
pesticide 杀虫剂 to insects 昆虫 ⇒ antiseptic 防腐剂 to germs 细菌 （事物及其对象）
antiseptic 防腐剂 to infection 感染 ⇒ antibiotic 抗生素 to bacteria 细菌 （事物及其对象）
buffer side 缓冲面 to impact 撞击 ⇒ antiseptic 防腐剂 to infection 感染 （事物及其对象）

husk ★★

[hʌsk] *n.* 外皮

记 绿巨人浩克（HULK）的皮肤（husk）不是很好

考 类比
husk 外壳 to corn 玉米 ⇒ hide 兽皮 to horse 马 （事物及其部分）
banana 香蕉 to peel 皮 ⇒ corn 玉米 to husk 外壳 （事物及其部分）
husk 外壳 to corn 玉米 ⇒ shell 坚果壳 to nut 坚果 （事物及其部分）

husk

List | 54 words

★ 复习一下学过的单词！

☐ composer	☐ flour	☐ jog	☐ prologue
☐ domicile	☐ gaunt	☐ listless	☐ restrict
☐ extend	☐ grace	☐ palatable	☐ rickety
☐ fanatic	☐ impart	☐ permanent	☐ stab
☐ fission	☐ initiate	☐ profane	☐ whisper

SSAT词汇 List 56

★★★
tumult
['tjuːmʌlt] *n.* 骚乱，骚动

记 tu 土 + mu 木 + lt：城市里大兴土木，显得非常混乱（tumult）
考 同义 tumult = commotion；tumult = disorder；tumult = turmoil；tumult = bedlam

★★★
surgeon
['sɜːdʒən] *n.* 外科医生

记 外科医生（surgeon）的数量迅速飙升（surge on）
考 类比
- surgeon 医生 to hospital 医院 ⇒ coroner 验尸官 to morgue 停尸房 （空间）
- scalpel 手术刀 to razor 剃刀 ⇒ surgeon 外科医生 to barber 理发师 （纵向）
- scalpel 手术刀 to cleaver 切肉刀 ⇒ surgeon 医生 to butcher 屠夫 （纵向）
- mechanic 机械师 to surgeon 医生 ⇒ drill 钻子 to scalpel 手术刀 （纵向）
- biologist 生物学家 to scientist 科学家 ⇒ surgeon 外科医生 to doctor 医生 （种属）
- dentist 牙医 to drill 钻子 ⇒ surgeon 医生 to scalpel 手术刀 （人物及其工具）
- tailor 裁缝 to scissor 剪刀 ⇒ surgeon 医生 to scalpel 手术刀 （人物及其工具）

★★
vaccination
[ˌvæksɪ'neɪʃn] *n.* 接种疫苗

记 家长犹豫（vacillate）是否该给孩子接种疫苗（vaccination）
考 类比
- vaccination 接种疫苗 to flu 流感 ⇒ medicine 药 to disease 疾病 （事物及其对象）
- medication 药物 to cure 治疗 ⇒ vaccination 疫苗 to prevention 预防 （事物及其用途）

★
bleak
[bliːk] *a.* 荒凉的

记 查尔斯·狄更斯的作品《荒凉山庄》英文为 Bleak House
考 同义 bleak = cheerless；bleak = unwelcoming

bleak

dough ★★
[dəʊ] *n.* 生面团

记 包饺子需要提前买（bought）生面团（dough）

考 类比 knead 捏 to dough 面团 → soak 浸泡 to beans 豆子 （动宾）
knead 捏 to dough 面团 → strum 弹奏 to guitar 吉他 （动宾）
dough 生面团 to bread 面包 → butter 黄油 to cake 蛋糕 （不同阶段）

squalid ★
[ˈskwɒlɪd] *a.* 肮脏的

记 肮脏的（squalid）广场（square）
考 同义 squalid = dirty

ample ★★★
[ˈæmpl] *a.* 丰富的，大量的

考 同义 ample = a lot；generous = ample
类比 copious 大量的 to ample 大量的 → tactful 机智的 to diplomatic 圆滑的 （同义）
注 关于"大量的"单词在 SSAT 的习题中有很多，如：abundant, plentiful。

amplify ★
[ˈæmplɪfaɪ] *v.* 放大

记 大量（ample）产品的功能被广告无限放大（amplify）
考 类比 amplify 放大 to sound 声音 → bolster 支持 to courage 勇气 （动宾）
exacerbate 使恶化 to worse 糟糕的 → amplify 放大 to loud 大声的 （因果）

imminent ★
[ˈɪmɪnənt] *a.* 即将来临的

记 新一拨移民（immigration）浪潮即将到来（imminent）
考 同义 imminent = forthcoming；imminent = impending

lapse ★
[læps] *n.* 小过错

记 上课睡觉（sleep）是个错误（lapse）
考 类比 lapse 过失 to error 错误 → inkling 暗示 to indication 指示 （＜程度）
注 关于"错误"单词在 SSAT 的习题中有很多，如：blunder, error, fault。

pigment ★★
[ˈpɪɡmənt] *n.* 颜色，色素

记 猪（pig）的身上都有一个带颜色（pigment）的戳

考 同义　pigment = color

类比　pigment 颜色 to albino 白化病 ⇒ hair 头发 to bald 光头 （缺乏）

neutron 中子 to atom 原子 ⇒ yellow 黄色 to pigment 颜色 （种属）

innocuous
[ɪˈnɒkjʊəs] *a.* 无害的

记 因为单纯（innocent），所以无害（innocuous）
考 同义　innocuous = harmless

condone
[kənˈdəʊn] *v.* 宽恕，赦免

记 他给仇人的家属送去慰问（condole），因此得到了仇人的宽恕（condone）
考 同义　condone = approve

类比　condone 宽恕 to pardon 原谅 ⇒ glorify 赞美 to praise 表扬 （同义）

expedite
[ˈekspɪdaɪt] *v.* 加速，加快

变 expedition *n.* 远征，加速
记 ex- 朝外 + ped- 脚 + -ite：脚朝外放，即为加速（expedite）
考 同义　expedite = hasten；expedite = hurry；precipitate = expedite

类比　expedite 加快 to process 过程 ⇒ accelerate 加速 to pace 步伐 （动宾）

exploit 英勇行为 to adventure 冒险 ⇒ safari 旅行 to expedition 远征 （同义）

decree
[dɪˈkriː] *n.* 法令，判决

记 医院下判决（decree）：开水导致病人八度（degree）伤残
考 同义　order = decree；decree = discipline；decree = ordinance

类比　commander 司令官 to decree 法令 ⇒ principal 校长 to discipline 纪律 （人物及其对象）

cocoon
[kəˈkuːn] *n.* 茧

记 《寻梦环游记》（*Coco*）这部电影在 2017 年破茧（cocoon）而出
考 类比　chick 小鸡 to egg 鸡蛋 ⇒ moth 蛾 to cocoon 茧 （发展过程）

cocoon

231

altercation [ɔːltəˈkeɪʃn] n. 争论

- 记 注意区分"改变"alteration、"轮流"alternation 和"争论"altercation
- 考 同义 altercation = dispute

  类比 altercation/争论 to argument/争论 ⇒ analysis/分析 to break down/分解 （同义）

- 注 关于"争论"的单词在 SSAT 的习题中有很多，如：quarrel, argument, spat。

rehearse [rɪˈhɜːs] v. 彩排

- 记 re- + hear + -se (see)：彩排 (rehearse) 即为重复 (re) 地听 (hear) 和看 (see)，以便找出问题来
- 考 类比 test/测试 to study/学习 ⇒ play/演出 to rehearse/彩排 （动作及其目的）

coward [ˈkaʊəd] n. 胆小鬼

- 变 cowardly a. 胆小的
- 记 我当年第一次认识这个单词是在钱钟书老先生的《围城》中，书中描写到：柔嘉不愿意姑母来把事闹大，但瞧丈夫这样退却，鄙薄得不复伤心，嘶声说："你是个 Coward! Coward! Coward! 我再不要看见你这个 Coward!"每个字像鞭子一样打一下，要鞭出她丈夫的胆气来，她还嫌不够狠，顺手抓起桌上一把象牙梳子用力朝他扔去。
- 考 类比 lurid/可怕的 to horror/惊愕 ⇒ cowardly/胆小的 to fear/恐惧 （因果）

stifle [ˈstaɪfl] v. 扼杀，窒息

- 变 stifling a. 沉闷的，令人窒息的
- 记 斯蒂芬妮 Stephanie 被生活压迫到窒息 (stifle)
- 考 同义 quell = stifle; stifle = withhold

  类比 stifling/沉闷的 to temperate/适度的 ⇒ dazzling/耀眼的 to light/明亮的 （>程度）

List | **55** words ★复习一下学过的单词！

□ abolish	□ auditory	□ libel	□ somnolent
□ adept	□ corpulent	□ mope	□ sprinkle
□ alias	□ crass	□ partial	□ stingy
□ antiseptic	□ hinge	□ proof	□ sufficient
□ arachnid	□ husk	□ quart	□ theme

☆ altercation   ☆ rehearse   ☆ coward   ☆ stifle

SSAT词汇 List 57

★★★ sensitive
['sensətɪv] a. 敏感的

变 insensitive a. 不敏感的；sensitivity n. 敏感
考 同义 delicacy = sensitivity；callous = insensitive
类比 altruistic 利他的 to selfish 自私的 → sensitive 敏感的 to ignorant 无感的 （反义）

★★★ elongate
['iːlɒŋgeɪt] v. 拉伸，延长

记 e- 朝外 + long + -ate
考 类比 elongate 拉伸 to tension 张力 → rotate 扭转 to torsion 转矩 （因果）
torque 扭矩 to twist 扭转 → tension 张力 to elongate 拉伸 （因果）
torsion 转矩 to rotate 扭转 → gravity 重力 to pull 拉 （事物及其动作）

★ adage
['ædɪdʒ] n. 格言，谚语

记 经得住时间（age）考验的句子即为格言（adage）
考 同义 adage = proverb；adage = maxim

★★★ reveal
[rɪ'viːl] v. 揭示，显露

记 学生在复习（review）的时候，暴露（reveal）出自己的问题所在
考 同义 reveal = disclose；reveal = divulge
类比 sequester 隔绝 to reveal 显露 → grant 同意 to deny 否认 （反义）
conceal 隐藏 to reveal 显现 → ascend 上升 to descend 下降 （反义）

★ disparage
[dɪ'spærɪdʒ] v. 蔑视，毁谤

记 因为被蔑视（disparage），所以很绝望（desperate）
考 同义 criticize = disparage；disparage = disdain

★
vacuous
[ˈvækjʊəs] a. 空洞的，缺乏意义的

记 vac- 空 + -uous
考 同义 vacuous = lacking

★★★
assist
[əˈsɪst] v. 帮助

变 assistance n. 帮助
考 同义 assist = support；assist = help；benefit = assist；assistance = service
类比 single-handed 单枪匹马的 to assistance 帮助 ⇒ anonymous 匿名的 to authorship 作者身份 （缺乏）

★
worm
[wɜːm] n. 虫子

变 silkworm n. 蚕
记 虫子（worm）喜欢待在暖和（warm）的地方
考 类比 mouse 老鼠 to cat 猫 ⇒ worm 虫子 to bird 鸟 （相对）
silk 丝绸 to silkworm 蚕 ⇒ wool 羊毛 to sheep 羊 （事物及其特点）
silk 丝绸 to silkworm 蚕 ⇒ honey 蜂蜜 to bee 蜜蜂 （事物及其特点）

★★
ameliorate
[əˈmiːliəreɪt] v. 改善，改进

记 天使爱美丽（Amelie）致力于改善（ameliorate）大家的生活
考 同义 ameliorate = improve
类比 improve 提升 to ameliorate 改善 ⇒ farce 闹剧 to humor 幽默 （同义）

ameliorate

★★★
flaw
[flɔː] n. 瑕疵，缺陷

变 flawless a. 完美无瑕的
记 甚至法律（law）本身也是有瑕疵的（flaw）
考 同义 immaculate = flawless；impeccable = flawless
类比 newspaper 报纸 to typo 错误 ⇒ personality 性格 to flaw 缺陷 （事物及其部分）

★
sour
[ˈsaʊə] a. 酸的

记 我们（our）山西的醋好酸（sour）啊
考 类比 milk 牛奶 to sour 酸的 ⇒ bread 面包 to stale 馊的 （修饰）
acrid 辛辣的 to smell 闻 ⇒ sour 酸的 to taste 尝 （动作及其情感）

frown

[fraʊn] v. 皱眉，不开心

- 记 布朗（Brown）先生不开心（frown）
- 考 同义 frown = disapproval

类比
- grin (露齿笑) to delight (高兴) → frown (皱眉) to dismay (沮丧) （动作及其情感）
- frown (皱眉) to disgust (恶心) → grin (露齿笑) to delight (高兴) （动作及其情感）
- contempt (鄙视) to sneer (嘲笑) → displeasure (不愉快) to frown (皱眉) （同义）
- smile (微笑) to laugh (大笑) → frown (不开心) to cry (哭泣) （<程度）
- smile (微笑) to frown (皱眉) → cheer (欢呼) to wince (畏缩) （反义）

（wince 这个单词的英文释义为：to shrink back involuntarily as from pain）

imply

[ɪmˈplaɪ] v. 暗示，隐含

- 变 implicate v. 牵连，暗指；implied a. 含蓄的，暗指的
- 记 员工招聘（employ）的时候，面试者暗示（imply）员工要给点钱才能上岗
- 考 同义 tacit = implied；implicate = involve；imply = suggest；imply = implicate

类比
- allude (暗示) to refer (提及) → imply (暗示) to state (陈述) （<程度）
- refer (提及) to imply (暗示) → touch (接触) to guess (猜测) （>程度）

注 关于"暗示"的单词在 SSAT 的习题中有很多，如：insinuate, innuendo, allude。

surmount

[səˈmaʊnt] v. 超过，克服

- 记 sur- 超 + -mount (mountain)：超过（surmount）一座又一座山
- 考 同义 surmount = overcome

subsequent

[ˈsʌbsɪkwənt] a. 随后的

- 记 sub- 在……后面 + -sequent (sequence) 序列：按照序列（sequence）排在后面的（sub）即为随后的（subsequent）
- 考 同义 subsequent = later；subsequent = following

类比
- antecedent (先前的) to precedent (先例的) → succedent (随后的) to subsequent (后来的) （同义）

commotion

[kəˈməʊʃn] n. 骚动，暴乱

- 记 com- + motion 移动：大家一起移动，容易产生暴动（commotion）
- 考 同义 commotion = disturbance；agitation = commotion；tumult = commotion；commotion = loud cry；commotion = upheaval

类比
- awe (敬畏) to disregard (忽略) → commotion (骚乱) to quietude (安静) （反义）

acumen 聪明 **to** intelligence 智力 → confusion 混乱 **to** commotion 骚乱 （同义）

★★★ brief　　　[bri:f] *a.* 简短的

变 brevity *n.* 简短
记 《时间简史》的英文为 *A Brief History of Time*
考 同义　brevity = shortness；concise = brief
　　类比　brief 简短的 **to** time 时间 → short 短的 **to** distance 距离 （修饰）
注 关于"简短的，简洁的"单词在 SSAT 的习题中有很多，如：terse，laconic，succinct。

★ discourse　　　['dɪskɔ:s] *v.* 论述，演讲

记 我的演讲（discourse）当然（of course）还是有很多缺陷的
考 类比　topic 主题 **to** discourse 论述 → theme 主题 **to** essay 论文 （事物及其部分）
　　　　prattle 咿呀学语 **to** baby 小孩 → discourse 论述 **to** scholar 学者 （人物及其动作）

★ proclivity　　　[prə'klɪvɪtɪ] *n.* 倾向

记 今天午饭，我倾向于（proclivity）吃西兰花（broccoli）
考 同义　propensity = proclivity；proclivity = inclination

★ mumble　　　['mʌmbl] *v.* 含糊说话

记 小孩子嘴里含糊（mumble）地叫着妈妈（mum）
考 类比　mumble 含糊说 **to** talk 说话 → scribble 乱涂 **to** write 写 （种属）
　　　　mumble 含糊说 **to** speak 说话 → chuckle 窃笑 **to** laugh 笑 （种属）

List | 56 words　　　　　　　　　　★ 复习一下学过的单词！

□ altercation	□ condone	□ imminent	□ squalid
□ ample	□ coward	□ innocuous	□ stifle
□ amplify	□ decree	□ lapse	□ surgeon
□ bleak	□ dough	□ pigment	□ tumult
□ cocoon	□ expedite	□ rehearse	□ vaccination

SSAT词汇 List 58

fiasco
[fɪ'æskəʊ] *n.* 惨败

记 给大家推荐一个歌手，他的名字叫 Lupe Fiasco。其实他的歌很好听，但是一直默默无闻，红不起来，有算命的说是因为他名字起得不好

考 同义 fiasco = total failure；catastrophe = fiasco

fiasco

overwhelm
[ˌəʊvə'welm] *v.* 淹没，压倒

记 因为担子过重（overweight），所以导致挑担子的人被压倒（overwhelm）

考 同义 deluge = overwhelm；overwhelm = overpower；inundate = overwhelm

procure
[prə'kjʊə] *v.* 取得，获得

记 病人得到（procure）安全的（secure）药物

考 同义 obtain = procure；acquire = procure

acrid
['ækrɪd] *a.* 辛辣的，刻薄的

记 这个东西的味道又酸（acid）又辣（acrid）

考 同义 acrid = bitter；harsh = acrid

类比 acrid 辛辣的 to smell 闻 ⇒ sour 酸的 to taste 尝 （动作及其情感）

brave
[breɪv] *a.* 勇敢的

变 bravery *n.* 勇敢

考 同义 valiant = brave

类比 honor 荣誉 to bravery 勇敢 ⇒ guilt 内疚感 to crime 犯罪 （因果）

guts 勇气 to bravery 勇敢 ⇒ brains 智力 to intelligence 智力 （同义）

☆ fiasco ☆ overwhelm ☆ procure ☆ acrid ☆ brave

237

persistent 固执的 — to — obstinate 固执的 ⇒ valiant 勇敢的 — to — brave 勇敢的 （同义）

recruit ★

[rɪˈkruːt] v. 招募

记 re- + -cruit (crew) 员工：招募 (recruit) 就需要不断来新员工 (crew)

考 类比 customer 消费者 — to — advertise 广告 ⇒ soldier 士兵 — to — recruit 招募 （人物及其对象）

beam ★

[biːm] n. 横梁

记 姥姥家的横梁 (beam) 上挂着一篮子豆豆 (bean)

考 类比 bone 骨头 — to — body 身体 ⇒ beam 横梁 — to — building 建筑 （事物及其部分）

nocturnal ★

[nɒkˈtɜːnl] a. 夜晚的

记 nocturnal "夜晚的" 和 night 的开头字母都是 n，而相对的 diurnal "白天的" 和 day 的开头字母都是 d

考 同义 nocturnal = by night

stroll ★

[strəʊl] n. 漫步，散步

记 因为常走路 (stroll)，所以身体强壮 (strong)

考 类比 walk 走路 — to — stroll 漫步 ⇒ converse 说话 — to — chat 聊天 （同义）

querulous ★

[ˈkwerʊləs] a. 爱抱怨的，暴躁的

记 因为脾气暴躁 (querulous)，所以爱跟别人吵架 (quarrel)

考 类比 querulous 爱抱怨的 — to — complain 抱怨 ⇒ dangerous 危险的 — to — risk 冒险 （同义）

opera ★★★

[ˈɒprə] n. 歌剧

记 我负责这出歌剧 (opera) 的全国运转 (operate)

考 类比
stanza 诗节 — to — poem 诗 ⇒ act 幕 — to — opera 歌剧 （组成）
soliloquy 独白 — to — play 戏剧 ⇒ aria 咏叹调 — to — opera 歌剧 （种属）
aria 咏叹调 — to — opera 歌剧 ⇒ monologue 独白 — to — play 戏剧 （种属）
limerick 五行打油诗 — to — epic 史诗 ⇒ ditty 小曲 — to — opera 歌剧 （<程度）

overture 序曲 to opera 歌剧 ⇒ preface 序 to book 书 （事物及其部分）

finale 终曲 to opera 歌剧 ⇒ epilogue 尾声 to play 戏剧 （事物及其部分）

overture 序曲 to opera 歌剧 ⇒ preamble 序文 to statute 法规 （事物及其部分）

★ postpone

[pəˈspəʊn] v. 推迟

记 post- 朝后 + pon- 放 + e
考 同义 waive = postpone

类比 procrastinate 拖延 to action 行动 ⇒ postpone 推迟 to event 事件 （动宾）

★★★ torque

[tɔːk] n. 转矩，扭矩

记 谐音：逃课：逃课去玩扭矩（torque）
考 类比 torque 扭矩 to twist 扭转 ⇒ tension 张力 to elongate 拉伸 （因果）

torsion 转矩 to rotate 扭转 ⇒ torque 转矩 to twist 扭转 （因果）

elongate 拉伸 to tension 张力 ⇒ rotate 旋转 to torque 扭矩 （因果）

★ foe

[fəʊ] n. 敌人

记 乔（Joe）是我的敌人（foe）
考 同义 foe = enemy

★★ wisdom

[ˈwɪzdəm] n. 智慧

考 同义 sagacity = wisdom

类比 owl 猫头鹰 to wisdom 智慧 ⇒ pig 猪 to indolence 懒惰 （动物及其特点）

owl 猫头鹰 to wisdom 智慧 ⇒ ant 蚂蚁 to diligence 勤奋 （动物及其特点）

seer 预言家 to prophecy 预言 ⇒ sage 圣人 to wisdom 智慧 （人物及其特点）

sage 圣人 to wisdom 智慧 ⇒ mechanic 机修工 to dexterity 灵巧 （人物及其特点）

★ coax

[kəʊks] v. 哄骗

记 coax 和 hoax 都是"欺骗"的意思

考 同义 coax = wheeddle
注 关于"哄骗"的单词在 SSAT 的习题中有很多，如：hoax, cajole。

ingenuous ★★ [ɪnˈdʒenjʊəs] *a.* 天真的，朴实的

变 ingenuousness *n.* 率直，真诚；disingenuous *a.* 虚伪的，狡猾的
记 注意区分 "机灵的"（ingenious）和 "天真的"（ingenuous）
考 同义 ingenuous = innocent；disingenuous = dishonest

类比
bigoted 顽固的 to fair 公平的 ⇒ guile 狡猾 to ingenuous 天真朴实的 （缺乏）
earnestness 认真 to ingenuousness 率直 ⇒ contradiction 矛盾 to opposition 反对 （同义）
disingenuous 狡猾的 to craftiness 狡猾 ⇒ surreptitious 秘密的 to stealth 秘密 （同义）

myriad ★ [ˈmɪrɪəd] *a.* 大量的，无数的

记 注意区分 "大量的" myriad 和 "海市蜃楼" mirage
考 同义 myriad = innumerable

generous ★★★ [ˈdʒenərəs] *a.* 大方的

变 generosity *n.* 大方，慷慨
考 同义 altruism = generosity；generous = benevolent；generous = ample
bounty = generous gift

类比
profligate 放荡的 to moral 道德 ⇒ miser 小气鬼 to generous 大方的 （反义）
mendacity 谎言 to honesty 诚实 ⇒ avarice 贪婪 to generosity 大方 （反义）
generous 大方的 to frugal 节俭的 ⇒ philanthropist 慈善家 to miser 小气鬼 （反义）
miser 小气鬼 to generous 大方的 ⇒ benefactor 捐赠者 to stingy 吝啬的 （反义）
generous 大方的 to philanthropist 慈善家 ⇒ stingy 小气的 to miser 守财奴 （人物及其特点）

calculate ★★★ [ˈkælkjʊleɪt] *v.* 计算

变 calculator *n.* 计算器；calculated *a.* 有计划的，蓄意的；calculation *n.* 计算
考 类比
sundial 日晷 to clock 钟表 ⇒ abacus 算盘 to calculator 计算器 （同义：新旧之称）
typewriter 打字机 to write 写 ⇒ calculator 计算器 to compute 计算 （事物及其用途）

☆ ingenuous ☆ myriad ☆ generous ☆ calculate

clamp → grip ⇒ calculator → compute （事物及其用途）
夹钳　　紧抓　　　计算器　　　计算

calculation → math ⇒ grammar → writing （事物及其部分）
计算　　　　数学　　　语法　　　写作

impulsive → calculated ⇒ concrete → subjective （反义）
冲动的　　　蓄意的　　　具体的　　　主观的

spontaneous → calculated ⇒ impromptu → scheduled （反义）
即兴的　　　　有计划的　　即兴的　　　已安排好的

List | 57 words　　　★ 复习一下学过的单词！

- adage
- ameliorate
- assist
- brief
- commotion
- discourse
- disparage
- elongate
- flaw
- frown
- imply
- mumble
- proclivity
- reveal
- sensitive
- sour
- subsequent
- surmount
- vacuous
- worm

SSAT词汇 List 59

★★★ hostile ['hɒstaɪl] *a.* 有敌意的

变 hostility *n.* 敌意
记 医闹的人都对医院（hospital）充满敌意（hostile）
考 同义 hostile = unfriendly; hostile = antagonistic; malicious = hostile
hostile = aggressive; hostility = animosity

类比 $\dfrac{\text{hostile}}{\text{敌意的}}$ to $\dfrac{\text{nemesis}}{\text{复仇}}$ ⇒ $\dfrac{\text{fortified}}{\text{加强的}}$ to $\dfrac{\text{stronghold}}{\text{要塞}}$ （修饰）

注 关于"有敌意的"单词在 SSAT 的习题中有很多，如：bellicose, belligerent。

★ hutch [hʌtʃ] *n.* 笼子

记 我需要一个像这样（such）的笼子（hutch）
考 类比 $\dfrac{\text{rabbit}}{\text{兔子}}$ to $\dfrac{\text{hutch}}{\text{兔笼}}$ ⇒ $\dfrac{\text{pig}}{\text{猪}}$ to $\dfrac{\text{sty}}{\text{猪圈}}$ （空间）

★★ torpid ['tɔːpɪd] *a.* 迟钝的，不活泼的

记 谐音：调皮的：调皮过后没精神，显得不活泼（torpid）
考 同义 lethargic = torpid

类比 $\dfrac{\text{torpid}}{\text{不活泼的}}$ to $\dfrac{\text{sluggish}}{\text{懒惰的}}$ ⇒ $\dfrac{\text{comic}}{\text{好笑的}}$ to $\dfrac{\text{funny}}{\text{搞笑的}}$ （同义）

★★ limb [lɪm] *n.* 四肢，枝干

记 小羊羔（lamb）的四肢（limb）很柔弱
考 类比 $\dfrac{\text{leg}}{\text{腿}}$ to $\dfrac{\text{limb}}{\text{四肢}}$ ⇒ $\dfrac{\text{finger}}{\text{手指}}$ to $\dfrac{\text{digit}}{\text{手指，脚趾}}$ （组成）
(digit 这个单词的英文释义为：any of the divisions in which the limbs of most vertebrates)

$\dfrac{\text{limb}}{\text{四肢}}$ to $\dfrac{\text{body}}{\text{身体}}$ ⇒ $\dfrac{\text{clasp}}{\text{钩子}}$ to $\dfrac{\text{necklace}}{\text{项链}}$ （种属）
(clasp 这个单词的英文释义为：a device that fastens a piece of jewellery)

wretched ★

['retʃɪd] *a.* 可怜的，悲伤地

- 记 可怜的（wretched）老巫婆（witch）
- 考 同义 woeful = wretched
  - 类比 spiritual (精神的) to divine (神圣的) ⇒ wretched (可怜的) to hapless (倒霉的) （同义）

circumference ★★

[sə'kʌmfərəns] *n.* 圆周，周长

- 记 物体的周长（circumference）会根据环境（circumstance）的改变而改变
- 考 同义 circumference = round measurement
  - 类比 girth (周长) to circumference (圆周) ⇒ thickness (浓度) to density (密度) （同义）

spring ★★★

[sprɪŋ] *n.* 弹簧；春天；泉水；*v.* 弹起

- 考 类比
  - salary (薪水) to income (收入) ⇒ spring (泉水) to water (水) （种属）
  - helix (螺旋) to spring (弹簧) ⇒ sphere (球体) to baseball (棒球) （事物及其特点）
  - eruption (爆发) to volcano (火山) ⇒ spring (泉水) to well (水井) （事物及其特点）
  - seven colors (七色) to rainbow (彩虹) ⇒ flower (花) to spring (春天) （事物及其特点）
  - water (水) to spring (泉水) ⇒ lava (岩浆) to volcano (火山) （事物及其部分）

fortuitous ★

[fɔː'tjuːɪtəs] *a.* 幸运的，偶然的

- 记 因为运气（fortune）好，所以很幸运（fortuitous）
- 考 同义 fortuitous = accidental
  - 类比 fortuitous (幸运的) to luck (运气) ⇒ chivalrous (有风度的) to manners (礼貌) （同义）

intrepid ★★

[ɪn'trepɪd] *a.* 无畏的，胆大的

- 变 trepidation *n.* 恐惧
- 记 in- + trepid 胆小的
- 考 同义 trepidation = fear；intrepid = fearless

headway ★

['hedweɪ] *n.* 前进，进步

- 考 同义 headway = progression

rustle ★★
['rʌsl] v. 沙沙作响；偷牛

- 变 rustler n. 偷牛贼
- 记 树叶相互推搡（hustle）发出沙沙作响（rustle）声
- 考 类比 rustle 沙沙作响 to roar 咆哮 ⇒ walk 走路 to run 跑步 （＜程度）
  poacher 偷猎者 to game 猎物 ⇒ rustler 偷牛贼 to cattle 牛 （人物及其对象）

respite ★★
['respaɪt] n. 暂缓，暂时休息

- 记 尽管（despite）暂时休息（respite）了一下，但是依旧觉得很累
- 考 同义 pause = respite；respite = rest

commiserate ★★
[kə'mɪzəreɪt] v. 同情，怜悯

- 记 com- + miser 吝啬鬼 + -ate：大家都很同情（commiserate）的穷人后来证明是个吝啬鬼（miser）
- 考 类比 bungle 弄糟 to blunder 犯错 ⇒ commiserate 同情 to condole 慰问 （同义）

ensemble ★★
[ɒn'sɒmbl] n. 全体演员

- 记 全体演员（ensemble）集合（assemble）
- 考 类比 actor 演员 to ensemble 全体演员 ⇒ player 队员 to team 球队 （组成）
  ensemble 全体演员 to dancer 舞者 ⇒ band 乐队 to musician 音乐家 （组成）

browse ★
[braʊz] v. 浏览

- 记 在美国应付店员的一句话就是"I'm just browsing."（我就随便看看。）
- 考 类比 chat 聊天 to converse 交谈 ⇒ browse 浏览 to look 看看 （同义）

fierce ★
[fɪəs] a. 凶猛的，猛烈的

- 记 猛烈的（fierce）大火（fire）
- 考 同义 furious = fierce

chassis ★
['ʃæsi] n. 底架，底盘

- 记 这个班级（class）的某位同学开了一辆底盘（chassis）很低的车来上学
- 考 同义 chassis = frame

注 chassis 这个单词的英文释义为：the supporting frame of a structure as an automobile or television。

asylum

[əˈsaɪləm] *n.* 收容所

记 美国有一家非常著名的专门翻拍热门大牌电影的公司就叫 The Asylum。旗下作品有 *The Da Vinci Treasure*，*I Am Omega*，*Atlantic Rim*，*Starving Games*，这些片子可能大家都没听说过，但是可以去搜搜看，会让你大吃一惊。

考 同义 asylum = sanctuary

类比 student 学生 —to→ school 学校 ⇒ refugee 避难者 —to→ asylum 收容所 （空间）

dwell

[dwel] *v.* 居住

变 dwelling *n.* 住处
记 有住（dwell）的地方就很好（well）
考 同义 dwell = inhabit

类比 club 棍棒 —to→ weapon 武器 ⇒ cave 洞穴 —to→ dwelling 居住地 （种属）

incumbent 在职者 —to→ office 办公室 ⇒ tenant 租户 —to→ dwelling 住处 （人物及其空间）

refrigerator

[rɪˈfrɪdʒəreɪtə] *n.* 冰箱

考 类比 refrigerator 冰箱 —to→ meat 肉 ⇒ bank 银行 —to→ money 钱 （空间）

refrigerator 冰箱 —to→ milk 牛奶 ⇒ library 图书馆 —to→ book 书 （空间）

refrigerator 冰箱 —to→ cool 凉爽 ⇒ furnace 炉子 —to→ heat 热度 （事物及其特点）

List | 58 words   ★ 复习一下学过的单词！

- acrid
- beam
- brave
- calculate
- coax
- fiasco
- foe
- generous
- ingenuous
- myriad
- nocturnal
- opera
- overwhelm
- postpone
- procure
- querulous
- recruit
- stroll
- torque
- wisdom

☆ asylum   ☆ dwell   ☆ refrigerator

SSAT词汇 List 60

zany ['zeɪnɪ] *a.* 古怪滑稽的
记 任何（any）人都没有他古怪搞笑（zany）
考 同义 zany = funny

agog [ə'gɒg] *a.* 有强烈兴趣的，热切的
记 ago + -g (gg)：很久以前（ago），我渴望（agog）邻家哥哥（gg）做我男朋友
考 同义 agog = eager

fabric ['fæbrɪk] *n.* 织物，布料
记 用劣质布料（fabric）来伪造（fabricate）丝绸
考 类比
weave 编织 to fabric 布料 ⇒ write 写 to text 文本 （动宾）
apple 苹果 to fruit 水果 ⇒ wool 羊毛 to fabric 织物 （种属）
glass 玻璃 to window 窗户 ⇒ fabric 布料 to clothing 衣服 （组成）
bruise 瘀青 to skin 皮肤 ⇒ stain 瑕疵 to fabric 织物 （事物及其特点）

amnesty ['æmnəstɪ] *n.* 大赦
记 谐音 I'm nasty：虽然我是个卑鄙的人（I'm nasty），但是依然得到了父母的宽恕（amnesty）
考 同义 amnesty = absolution；amnesty = grand pardon

exalt [ɪg'zɔːlt] *v.* 赞扬，提升
变 exalted *a.* 高尚的
记 表扬（exalt）小孩子要精确（exact），而不能总说"你真棒"之类模糊的话
考 同义 exalt = elevate

类比　exalt to criticize → compliment to offend （反义）
　　　赞扬　　批评　　　　赞美　　　冒犯

　　　glorious to exalted → trivial to unimportant （同义）
　　　荣耀的　　高尚的　　琐碎的　　不重要的

★★ nuance
[ˈnjuːɑːns] *n.* 细微差别

记 两块金子的重量只有一盎司（ounce）的区别（nuance）

考 同义　nuance = difference

　　类比　distinction to nuance → castigation to admonishment （＞程度）
　　　　　区别　　　　小差别　　惩罚　　　　警告

　　　　　nuance to distinction → hint to suggestion （＜程度）
　　　　　细微差别　区别　　　　暗示　　建议

　　　　　nuance to subtle → hint to indirect （事物及其特点）
　　　　　细微差别　微妙的　　暗示　　不直接的

★ archaic
[ɑːˈkeɪɪk] *a.* 古代的，古老的

记 老的（archaic）东西请放到档案馆（archive）里

考 类比　massive to size → archaic to age （修饰）
　　　　大的　　型号　　古代的　　年纪

　　　　ancient to modern → archaic to new age （反义）
　　　　古代的　　现代的　　古老的　　新时代

★ index
[ˈɪndeks] *n.* 索引

记 食指的英文即为 index finger

考 类比　index to topics → roster to names （组成）
　　　　索引　　话题　　　花名册　　名字

★ throne
[θrəʊn] *n.* 王座

记 《权力的游戏》的英文为：*Game of Thrones*

考 类比　throne to monarch → bench to judge
　　　　王座　　君主　　　法官座椅　法官
　　　　（人物及其特点）

　　　　bench to judge → throne to king （人物及其特点）
　　　　法官座椅　法官　王座　　君王

Game of Thrones
throne

★ salutation
[ˌsæljuːˈteɪʃn] *n.* 称呼，问候

记 我当年第一次见这个单词，是在美国小朋友必看故事书之一的 *Charlotte' Web* 里，小蜘蛛第一次见到小猪打招呼说的就是 salutation

考 类比　salutation to letter → introduction to book （空间）
　　　　问候　　　　信　　　介绍　　　　书

注 这个题的思路有些复杂，salutation 这个单词的英文释义为：a word or phrase of greeting used to begin a letter or message；而 introduction 的英文释义则为：the first part of a book or speech that gives a general idea of what is to follow。

★★★ violate
['vaɪəleɪt] v. 违反，侵犯

变 violation n. 违反
记 暴力（violent）被视为违反（violate）游戏规则
考 同义 breach = violation；transgress = violate

类比 transgress 违反 to law 法律 ⇒ violate 违反 to agreement 协议 （动宾）

注 关于"侵略，违反"的单词在 SSAT 的习题中有很多，如：encroach，trespass，invade，infringe。

★ curd
[kɜːd] n. 凝乳

记 我们常说的豆腐即为 beancurd
考 类比 clot 血块 to blood 血液 ⇒ curd 凝乳 to milk 牛奶 （同义）

★ sneak
[sniːk] v. 潜伏；a. 暗中进行的

记 小偷穿着运动鞋（sneaker）鬼鬼祟祟地（sneak）走
考 同义 prowl = sneak；sneak = skulk；surreptitious = sneak

★★★ malfunction
[ˌmælˈfʌŋkʃn] n. 不起作用，出故障

记 mal- 否定 + function 功能，作用
考 同义 malfunction = failure

类比 injury 受伤 to heal 治疗 ⇒ malfunction 出故障 to repair 修理 （动宾）
wound 受伤 to heal 治疗 ⇒ malfunction 出故障 to repair 修理 （动宾）
evict 驱逐 to admit 允许进入 ⇒ malfunction 出故障 to operate 启动 （反义）

★★ inadvertently
[ˌɪnədˈvɜːtəntli] ad. 非故意地

记 in- 否定 + advertent 留意的 + -ly
考 同义 inadvertently = accidentally；inadvertently = unintentionally

★★★ serene
[sɪˈriːn] a. 平静的，安详的

变 serenity n. 平静

- 记 一阵警报（siren）打破了宁静（serene）
- 考 同义　serene = tranquil；tranquility = serenity；serenity = peace；serenity = quietude
  类比　foolhardy 蛮干的 to recklessness 鲁莽 ⇒ serene 安静的 to tranquility 安静 （同义）

enmity
['enmɪti] *n.* 敌意，憎恨

- 记 对于敌人（enemy）充满敌意（enmity）
- 考 同义　enmity = hatred
  类比　adversary 敌人 to enmity 敌意 ⇒ underdog 失败者 to sympathy 同情 （人物及其特点）

delectable
[dɪˈlektəbl] *a.* 令人愉快的

- 记 能让孩子选择（select）的课外活动，才是令孩子们愉快的（delectable）课程
- 考 同义　delectable = enjoyable

sedentary
[ˈsedntri] *a.* 久坐的，安静的

- 记 sed- 坐 + entary
- 考 类比　active 活泼的 to mobile 可移动的 ⇒ sedentary 久坐的 to immobile 不可移动的 （同义）

repress
[rɪˈpres] *v.* 压制，镇压

- 记 re- + press 压
- 考 同义　repress = prevent

List | 59 words　　★复习一下学过的单词！

□ asylum	□ dwell	□ hostile	□ respite
□ browse	□ ensemble	□ hutch	□ rustle
□ chassis	□ fierce	□ intrepid	□ spring
□ circumference	□ fortuitous	□ limb	□ torpid
□ commiserate	□ headway	□ refrigerator	□ wretched

SSAT词汇 List 61

★ hover
['hɒvə] v. 盘旋，翱翔

记 飞机始终在空中盘旋（hover），不愿结束（over）行程
考 同义 hover = soar
类比 hover 盘旋 to airborne 空中的 → totter 蹒跚 to unstable 不稳定的 （同义）

★★★ sentry
['sentri] n. 哨兵；v. 放哨

记 这个人当了一个世纪（century）的哨兵（sentry）
考 同义 sentry = watch
类比 goalie 门将 to net 网 → sentry 哨兵 to fort 堡垒 （人物及其对象）
herald 报信者 to proclaim 宣布 → sentry 哨兵 to guard 守卫 （人物及其动作）

★★★ novel
['nɒvl] n. 小说；a. 新颖的

变 novelist n. 小说家；novelty n. 新奇
记 小说（novel）是我的真爱（love）
考 同义 innovation = novelty
类比 newspaper 报纸 to inform 通知 → novel 小说 to entertain 娱乐 （事物及其用途）
clip 电影一部分 to movie 电影 → excerpt 摘录 to novel 小说 （事物及其部分）
letter 字母 to novel 小说 → note 音符 to symphony 交响乐 （组成）
ditty 小曲 to oratorio 清唱剧 → anecdote 轶事 to novel 小说 （<程度）
novel 小说 to chapter 章节 → ballad 歌谣 to stanza 诗节 （组成）
paper 纸 to novel 小说 → canvas 画布 to portrait 肖像画 （空间）
oration 演说 to heard 听 → novel 小说 to read 读 （动宾）

☆ hover　　☆ sentry　　☆ novel

epilogue 结语	to	novel 小说	→ finale 终曲	to	symphony 交响乐	（事物及其部分）
prologue 序言	to	novel 小说	→ preamble 序文	to	statute 法律	（事物及其部分）
foreword 序言	to	novel 小说	→ preamble 序文	to	statute 法律	（事物及其部分）
prelude 前奏	to	suite 组曲	→ preface 序言	to	novel 小说	（事物及其部分）
poem 诗	to	rhyme 节奏	→ novel 小说	to	plot 情节	（事物及其特点）
fiction 小说	to	novelist 小说家	→ fact 事实	to	historian 历史学家	（人物及其对象）

★★★

sprint ［sprɪnt］ v. 快跑

记 在春天（spring）要常进行快跑（sprint）训练

考 类比

canter 慢跑	to	gallop 快跑	→ jog 慢跑	to	sprint 快跑	（＜程度）
saunter 漫步	to	sprint 快跑	→ drizzle 毛毛雨	to	pour 骤雨	（＜程度）
sprint 快跑	to	trot 慢跑	→ shout 叫喊	to	call 呼叫	（＞程度）
jog 慢跑	to	sprint 快跑	→ trot 慢跑	to	gallop 飞奔	（＜程度）
walk 走路	to	scurry 快走	→ jog 慢跑	to	sprint 快跑	（＜程度）
jog 慢跑	to	sprint 快跑	→ hold 拿住	to	grip 紧握	（＜程度）
synopsis 大纲	to	summary 概要	→ sprint 疾跑	to	race 赛跑	（同义）
sprint 快跑	to	speed 忍耐力	→ marathon 马拉松	to	endurance 忍耐力	（事物及其特点）

★

facsimile ［fækˈsɪməli］ n. 复制

记 fac-（face）＋-simile（similar）：复制（facsimile）彼此即为相似的（similar）外表（face）

考 同义　facsimile = exact copy；facsimile = duplicate

★★★

wood ［wʊd］ n. 木头

变 wooden a. 僵硬的

记 像木头（wood）一样僵硬（wooden）

考 类比

sand 沙子	to	glass 玻璃	→ wood 木头	to	paper 纸张	（组成）
wood 木材	to	decay 腐烂	→ iron 铁	to	rust 生锈	（事物及其特点）

wood 木头	to	ebony 乌木	⇒	flower 花 to chrysanthemum 菊花	（种属）
ebony 乌木	to	wood 木头	⇒	raven 大乌鸦 to bird 鸟	（种属）
wood 木头	to	rotten 腐烂的	⇒	bread 面包 to moldy 发霉的	（修饰）
crumb 面包屑		bread 面包	⇒	splinter 碎木 to wood 木头	（事物及其部分）
gas 汽油	to	vehicle 车辆	⇒	wood 木头 to stove 炉子	（事物及其用途）
stilted 呆板的	to	speech 演讲	⇒	wooden 僵硬的 to movement 动作	（修饰）

★ corrupt

[kəˈrʌpt] v. 破坏

考 同义 corrupt = destroy
注 corrupt 这个单词的英文释义为：to destroy or subvert the honesty or integrity of; corrupt 这个单词"贪污的"意思我们是很熟悉的，此处为熟词僻义。

★★★ prudent

[ˈpruːdnt] a. 谨慎的

变 prudence n. 审慎；imprudent a. 轻率的；jurisprudence n. 法理学
记 这个单词来自 prude，原指那些"谈性色变的"人，后引申成为"谨慎的"；普鲁登斯（Prudence）是个很谨慎的（prudent）小姑娘
考 同义 imprudent = foolish；discreet = prudent

类比
prudent 谨慎的	to	indiscretion 轻率	⇒	frugal 节俭的 to wastefulness 浪费	（反义）
intangible 无形的	to	palpable 可感知的	⇒	prudent 谨慎的 to reckless 鲁莽的	（反义）
zealous 热情的	to	enthusiastic 热心的	⇒	cautious 小心的 to prudent 谨慎的	（同义）
grumpy 脾气坏的	to	malcontent 不满的	⇒	prudent 谨慎的 to sage 明智的	（因果）

★ sprout

[spraʊt] v. 发芽

记 春天（spring）种子发芽（sprout）
考 类比
bean 豆子	to	sprout 发芽	⇒	bulb 球茎 to shoot 发芽	（事物及其动作）
sprout 发芽	to	seed 种子	⇒	hatch 孵化 to egg 鸡蛋	（事物及其动作）

★★★ robust

[rəʊˈbʌst] a. 健康的

记 早年有一个和"娃哈哈"齐名的矿泉水牌子，就叫"乐百氏"，其英文即为 Robust

robust

252　　☆ corrupt　　☆ prudent　　☆ sprout　　☆ robust

考 类比
bald 光秃的 to hirsute 多毛的 ⇒ anemic 贫血的 to robust 健康的 （反义）
meager 缺乏的 to abundant 大量的 ⇒ decrepit 衰老破旧的 to robust 强健的 （反义）
frail 脆弱的 to emaciated 瘦弱的 ⇒ robust 强健的 to invigorated 精力充沛的 （同义）
trivial 琐碎的 to consequential 重要的 ⇒ robust 强健的 to lethargic 无生气的 （反义）

heap [hi:p] n. 堆

记 一堆堆（heap）便宜货（cheap）
考 同义 heap = pile

churlish [ˈtʃɜːlɪʃ] a. 没礼貌的

记 谐音：车厘子：吃车厘子把核吐得到处都是，真没礼貌（churlish）
考 同义 churlish = impolite
注 关于"没礼貌的"单词在 SSAT 的习题中有很多，如：impertinent，impudent。

tractable [ˈtræktəbl] a. 易驾驭的，易管理的

记 tract- 拉 + -able
考 同义 tractable = easily controlled

chain [tʃeɪn] n. 链条

记 我们常说的便利店英文即为 chain store
记 类比
bouquet 花束 to flower 花 ⇒ chain 链条 to link 一个链条 （组成）
link 一个链条 to chain 链条 ⇒ word 单词 to sentence 句子 （组成）
link 一个链条 to chain 链条 ⇒ island 岛 to archipelago 群岛 （组成）
patter 滴答声 to rain 雨 ⇒ clank 叮当声 to chain 链子 （事物及其特点）

flurry [ˈflʌri] n. 阵风

记 我们常吃的"麦旋风"英文即为 McFlurry
考 类比
flurry 阵风 to blizzard 暴风雪 ⇒ drizzle 毛毛雨 to downpour 大雨 （<程度）
sprinkle 喷洒 to deluge 洪水 ⇒ flurry 小旋风 to blizzard 暴风雪 （<程度）

flurry

advocate ★★
['ædvəkeɪt] *v.* 提倡，主张；*n.* 提倡者

记 ad- 加强 + voc-（voice）+ -ate：明星用自己的声音（voice）来提倡（advocate）民众要环保

考 同义 advocate = promote；advocate = proponent

meager ★★★
['miːgə] *a.* 瘦的，贫乏的

记 渴望（eager）自己能迅速变瘦（meager）

考 同义 meager = paltry；meager = sparse；scant = meager；meager = inadequate

类比
parsimonious 吝啬的 to stingy 小气的 → meager 瘦的 to small 小的 （同义）

meager 贫乏的 to abundant 大量的 → decrepit 衰老的 to robust 健硕的 （反义）

hoist ★
[hɔɪst] *v.* 举起

记 主人（host）举起（hoist）酒杯提议干一个

考 同义 hoist = lift

disburse ★
[dɪs'bɜːs] *v.* 支付，支出

记 dis- + -burse（purse）：支付（disburse）即为钱包（burse）里的钱朝外走

考 同义 disburse = pay out

exemplify ★
[ɪg'zemplɪfaɪ] *v.* 例证，示例

变 exemplary *a.* 例证的

记 exempl-（example）+ -ify

考 同义 exemplify = illustrate；exemplary = model

注 关于"例证，示例"的单词在 SSAT 的习题中有很多，如：epitomize，symbolize。

List | 60 words ★ 复习一下学过的单词！

☐ agog	☐ enmity	☐ malfunction	☐ serene
☐ amnesty	☐ exalt	☐ nuance	☐ sneak
☐ archaic	☐ fabric	☐ repress	☐ throne
☐ curd	☐ inadvertently	☐ salutation	☐ violate
☐ delectable	☐ index	☐ sedentary	☐ zany

SSAT词汇 List 62

★★★ pecuniary [pɪˈkjuːnɪəri] a. 金钱的

变 impecunious a. 贫穷的

记 pecu 这个词根本身是"牛"的意思，在以农业为主导的社会里，牛是非常珍贵的资源，所以就有了"财富"的意思

考 类比
- pecuniary 金钱的 to money 钱 ⇒ sartorial 裁缝的 to sew 缝 （同义）
- pecuniary 金钱的 to money 钱 ⇒ culinary 烹饪的 to cookery 烹饪术 （同义）
- impecunious 贫穷的 to hovel 小屋 ⇒ prosperous 繁荣的 to mansion 大厦 （修饰）
- sober 未醉的 to intemperate 酗酒的 ⇒ impecunious 贫穷的 to affluent 有钱的 （反义）

★ murder [ˈmɜːdə] n. 谋杀

考 类比
- brawl 争吵 to war 战争 ⇒ shoplifting 偷窃 to murder 谋杀 （<程度）
- murder 谋杀 to genocide 种族屠杀 ⇒ gun 枪 to tank 坦克 （<程度）

★ forlorn [fəˈlɔːn] a. 孤独的，凄凉的

记 for + -lorn (long)：因为孤独 (forlorn)，所以希望能和你多待一会儿 (long)

考 同义 deserted = forlorn；forlorn = lonely

★★ abrupt [əˈbrʌpt] a. 唐突的；陡峭的

记 ab- + -rupt 破裂

考 同义 abrupt = brusque

类比 brusque 唐突的 to abrupt 唐突的 ⇒ servile 奴性的 to obsequious 奉承的 （同义）

注 关于"陡峭的"单词在 SSAT 的习题中有很多，如：precipitous，steep。

★★★ diagnose

['daɪəgnəʊz] v. 诊断

变 diagnosis n. 诊断
记 谐音：带个 nose：古时医生水平很高，诊断（diagnose）的时候带个（nose）即可
考 同义 analysis = diagnosis

类比 appraise 评价 — to — worth 价值 ⇒ diagnose 诊断 — to — problem 问题 （动宾）

diagnose 诊断 — to — doctor 医生 ⇒ verdict 判决 — to — jury 陪审团 （人物及其动作）

★★★ descend

[dɪ'send] v. 下降

变 descent n. 下降；descendant n. 后裔，子孙
记 "上升" ascend 和 "下降" descend 是一对反义词
考 同义 descent = reduction；progeny = descendant

类比 conceal 隐藏 — to — reveal 显现 ⇒ ascend 上升 — to — descend 下降 （反义）

deceleration 减速 — to — speed 速度 ⇒ descent 下降 — to — altitude 高度 （事物及其对象）

★★ sustenance

['sʌstɪnəns] n. 食物，生计

记 sustenance 的动词即为我们熟知的 sustain
考 同义 sustenance = food；sustenance = nutrition

★★ terminate

['tɜːmɪneɪt] v. 终结，结束

记 阿诺·施瓦辛格 1984 年的电影《终结者》的英文即为 *Terminator*
考 同义 terminate = end；terminate = discontinue

terminate

★ exacerbate

[ɪɡ'zæsəbeɪt] v. 恶化，加剧

记 ex- 朝外 + acer 宏基 + bate：宏基（acer）公司推出（ex）的新电脑越来越差（exacerbate）
考 同义 exacerbate = worsen

类比 exacerbate 使恶化 — to — worse 糟糕的 ⇒ amplify 放大 — to — loud 大声的 （因果）

★ crouch

[kraʊtʃ] v. 蹲下，畏缩

记 首部获奥斯卡最佳外语片的华语电影《卧虎藏龙》的英文为 *Crouching Tiger, Hidden Dragon*
考 同义 crouch = cower

crouch

类比 squat/蹲 to crouch/蹲 → countenance/面容 to face/脸 （同义）

★★ orator
['ɒrətə] *n.* 演说者，演讲者

变 oration *n.* 演说
记 orat-（oral）口语的 + -or
考 同义 orator = speaker
类比 oration/演说 to heard/听 → novel/小说 to read/读 （动宾）
articulate/口才好的 to orator/演讲者 → agile/灵活的 to acrobat/杂技演员 （人物及其特点）

★★ hint
[hɪnt] *v.* 暗示，线索

记 动物留下的脚印给打猎（hunt）的人一些线索（hint）
考 同义 hint = inkling
类比 hint/暗示 to advise/建议 → quibble/挑剔 to objection/反对 （＜程度）
nuance/细微差别 to subtle/微妙的 → hint/暗示 to indirect/间接的 （事物及其特点）

★ convoluted
[ˌkɒnvə'luːtɪd] *a.* 复杂的，费解的

记 因为涉及（involve）太多东西，所以显得复杂（convoluted）
考 同义 convoluted = twisted

★ substantial
[səb'stænʃl] *a.* 大量的，重要的

记 大量的（substantial）物质（substance）
考 同义 substantial = significant
注 substantial 这个单词的英文释义为：considerable in importance, value, degree, or amount。

★★ exclude
[ɪk'skluːd] *v.* 排除，排斥

变 exclusively *ad.* 专有地，排外地
考 同义 exclusively = entirely；exclude = keep out；ostracize = exclude
类比 disseminate/散播 to information/消息 → exclude/驱逐 to outcast/流浪者 （动宾）

★ stain
[steɪn] *n.* 污点，瑕疵

记 这个错误会在你身上留下（stay）永远的污点（stain）
考 类比 bruise/瘀青 to skin/皮肤 → stain/瑕疵 to fabric/织物 （事物及其部分）

☆ orator　　☆ hint　　☆ convoluted　　☆ substantial　　☆ exclude
☆ stain

pariah
[pəˈraɪə] n. 贱民

记 这个单词发音前半部分类似于 poor，因为 poor，所以被划归为贱民 (pariah)

考 类比　pariah/贱民　to　ostracism/放逐　⇒　idol/偶像　to　adulation/崇拜　（动宾）

complacent
[kəmˈpleɪsənt] a. 自满的，得意的

记 com- + place + nt：大家一起聚在 (con) 这个地方 (place)，让我觉得很得意 (complacent)

考 同义　complacent = satisfied

covet
[ˈkʌvɪt] v. 垂涎

记 闭 (cover) 嘴，不要总垂涎 (covet) 别人的东西

考 同义　covet = begrudge

注 covet 这个单词的英文释义为：to envy the possession or enjoyment of。

captain
[ˈkæptɪn] n. 船长

考 类比
coach/教练　to　team/队伍　⇒　captain/队长　to　platoon/排　（人物及其对象）
pilot/机长　to　airplane/飞机　⇒　captain/船长　to　ship/船　（人物及其对象）
team/队伍　to　captain/队长　⇒　republic/共和国　to　president/总统　（人物及其对象）

List | 61 words　　　★ 复习一下学过的单词！

☐ advocate	☐ exemplify	☐ hover	☐ sentry
☐ chain	☐ facsimile	☐ meager	☐ sprint
☐ churlish	☐ flurry	☐ novel	☐ sprout
☐ corrupt	☐ heap	☐ prudent	☐ tractable
☐ disburse	☐ hoist	☐ robust	☐ wood

SSAT词汇 List 63

★★★ pacify

['pæsɪfaɪ] v. 安慰，使平静

变 pacific a. 平静的，温和的；pacifist n. 和平主义者
记 pac-（peace）+ -ify：向往和平（peace）的人总是希望事态可以平静（pacify）
考 同义 pacific = placid；conciliate = pacify；soothe = pacify

类比
warmonger 好战者 to pacifist 和平主义者 ⇒ nobody 小人物 to mogul 大亨 （反义）
vegetarian 素食者 to meat 肉 ⇒ pacifist 和平主义者 to violence 暴力 （人物及其对象）
vegetarian 素食者 to meat 肉 ⇒ pacifist 和平主义者 to war 战争 （人物及其对象）
libertarian 自由主义者 to censorship 审查制度 ⇒ pacifist 和平主义者 to violence 暴力 （人物及其对象）

★ paternalism

[pə'tɜːnəlɪzəm] n. 家长式统治

记 parental 家长的 + -ism
考 同义 paternalism = parent instruction

★★ modify

['mɒdɪfaɪ] v. 修改，美化

记 mode 模式 + -ify
考 同义 modify = change

类比
defend 防守 to untenable 不可防守的 ⇒ modify 修改 to invariable 不变的 （反义）

注 关于"修改，美化"的单词在 SSAT 的习题中有很多，如：optimize，ameliorate，amend，rectify。

★★ creditable

['kredɪtəbl] a. 可信的

变 credulous a. 轻信的；incredible a. 难以置信的
记 credit 信用 + -able

考 同义　creditable = believable；creditable = plausible；credulous = gullible
　　　　incredible = extraordinary

★★ aptitude
['æptɪtjuːd] *n.* 天资

记　送给大家一句共勉的话：It is your attitude, not your aptitude that determines your altitude.（决定你人生高度的不是你的天资，而是你的态度。）

考 同义　aptitude = ability；capacity = aptitude

类比　ability 能力 → aptitude 能力 ⇒ barrier 障碍 → barricade 路障　（同义）

★ callow
['kæləʊ] *a.* 年轻无经验的

记　因为年经无经验（callow），所以四处跟别人学（follow）
考 同义　callow = immature

★ anesthetic
[ˌænɪs'θetɪk] *n.* 麻醉剂

记　因为服用麻醉剂（anesthetic），所以看什么都很美（aesthetic）
考 类比　anesthetic 麻醉剂 → pain 疼痛 ⇒ muffler 消音器 → noise 噪音　（事物及其用途）

★ amalgamate
[ə'mælgəmeɪt] *v.* 合并

记　这个词来自古法语，15 世纪刚进入英语时的意思是"汞化物"（a mixture of mercury and another metal），后来引申成"合并"的意思
考 同义　amalgamate = unite with

★ ooze
[uːz] *v.* 渗出，泄露

记　哎呀（oops），血渗出来（ooze）了
考 同义　ooze = exude；ooze = seep

★★★ steadfast
['stedfɑːst] *a.* 坚定的，不变的

记　因为待着不走（stay），所以显得很坚定（steadfast）
考 同义　stable = steadfast；constant = steadfast；staunch = steadfast；steadfast = resolute

类比　steadfast 坚定的 → firm 稳定的 ⇒ scarce 稀有的 → rare 稀有的　（同义）
　　　fickle 善变的 → steadfast 稳定的 ⇒ tempestuous 暴风雨般的 → peaceful 和平的　（反义）

nugget

['nʌgɪt] *n.* 金块

记 我们常吃的肯德基的少校鸡块即为 Nugget NBA 的丹佛掘金队即为 Denver Nuggets
考 同义 nugget = lump

nugget

peruse

[pəˈruːz] *v.* 细读，研读

记 per- 始终 + use：细读 (peruse) 一本好书，对你一生 (per) 有用 (use)
考 同义 peruse = read
类比 puncture 刺穿 to perforate 穿孔 ⇒ preview 预习 to peruse 精读 （同类）

grave

[greɪv] *a.* 严肃的，严重的

变 gravity *n.* 严肃；重力
记 勇敢的 (brave) 人即使在面对严重的 (grave) 事情时，也可以保持稳定
考 同义 grave = solemn
类比 torsion 转矩 to rotate 扭转 ⇒ gravity 重力 to pull 拉 （事物及其动作）
gravity 重力 to force 力 ⇒ oxygen 氧气 to element 元素 （种属）
obscure 朦胧的 to clarity 清楚 ⇒ grave 严肃的 to comedy 喜剧 （缺乏）
quixotic 狂想的 to practicality 实际 ⇒ frivolous 轻浮的 to gravity 严肃 （反义）

tedious

[ˈtiːdɪəs] *a.* 沉闷的

记 TED 的视频节目越来越无聊 (tedious) 了
考 同义 tedious = tiresome；tedious = wearisome；tedious = boring

aggregate

[ˈægrɪgət] *n.* 总计，合计

记 先隔离 (segregate)，再总计 (aggregate)
考 同义 aggregate = organization

meek

[miːk] *a.* 温顺的

记 上学途中，见到 (meet) 一只温顺 (meek) 的小猫
考 同义 meek = submissive
类比 copious 大量的 to abundant 大量的 ⇒ docile 温顺的 to meek 温顺的 （同义）

meek 温顺的 →to→ arrogant 傲慢的 ⇒ mean 小气的 →to→ prodigal 挥霍的 （反义）

canary

[kəˈneəri] n. 金丝雀

记 谐音：可耐（爱）；金丝雀（canary）是非常可耐（爱）的动物
考 类比 canary 金丝雀 →to→ yellow 黄色 ⇒ robin's eggs 知更鸟蛋 →to→ blue 蓝色 （事物及其特点）
注 这个题的思路有些复杂，canary 这个单词的英文释义为：a small yellow bird，而 robin's eggs 是蓝色的，在美国又被称为 Robin egg blue。

peacock

[ˈpiːkɒk] n. 孔雀

记 请记住 as proud as a peacock 是"自大，目中无人"的意思
考 类比 seal 海豹 →to→ fur 皮毛 ⇒ peacock 孔雀 →to→ feather 羽毛 （事物及其部分）

drivel

[ˈdrɪvl] v. 说傻话，胡言乱语

记 喝酒开车（drive），边开边胡乱骂（drivel）
考 同义 drivel = nonsense

heterogeneous

[ˌhetərəˈdʒiːniəs] a. 异类的，异种的

记 hetero- 相异的 + gene 基因 + -ous：由不同（hetero）基因（gene）组成的即为异类的（heterogeneous）
考 同义 heterogeneous = mixed

List | 62 words ★ 复习一下学过的单词！

☐ abrupt	☐ crouch	☐ forlorn	☐ pecuniary
☐ captain	☐ descend	☐ hint	☐ stain
☐ complacent	☐ diagnose	☐ murder	☐ substantial
☐ convoluted	☐ exacerbate	☐ orator	☐ sustenance
☐ covet	☐ exclude	☐ pariah	☐ terminate

☆ canary   ☆ peacock   ☆ drivel   ☆ heterogeneous

SSAT词汇 List 64

endow ★★
[ɪnˈdaʊ] v. 赋予，捐赠

- 同义：endow = bestow
- 类比：filch (偷窃) to pickpocket (扒手) ⇒ endow (给予) to benefactor (捐助者) （人物及其特点）
- 注：关于"给予，捐赠"的单词在SSAT的习题中有很多，如：bequeath, grant, confer。

cajole ★★★
[kəˈdʒoʊl] v. 哄骗，勾引

- 变：cajolery n. 诱骗
- 记：这个单词反过来的谐音是 joke，用一个笑话（joke）去哄骗（cajole）别人
- 同义：cajole = persuade
- 类比：wheedle (欺骗) to cajolery (诱骗) ⇒ deceive (欺骗) to subterfuge (诡计) （同义）
  lull (哄骗) to trust (相信) ⇒ cajole (欺骗) to compliance (顺从) （动作及其目的）
- 注：关于"哄骗"的单词在SSAT的习题中有很多，如：coax, hoax。

restore ★
[rɪˈstɔː] v. 恢复

- 变：restoration n. 恢复
- 同义：restore = fix；restoration = regeneration

veracious ★
[vəˈreɪʃəs] a. 诚实的，真实的

- 注意区分"诚实的"（veracious）和"贪婪的"（voracious）
- 同义：veracious = true

corporal ★
[ˈkɔːpərəl] n. 下士

- 记：谐音：靠谱：靠谱的下士（corporal）
- 类比：corporal (下士) to sergeant (中士) ⇒ joey (小袋鼠) to kangaroo (袋鼠) （＜程度）

☆ endow　　☆ cajole　　☆ restore　　☆ veracious　　☆ corporal

summit ★★★
['sʌmɪt] n. 顶点；峰会

记 夏天（summer）的顶点（summit）就是暑假
考 同义 zenith = summit；pinnacle = summit；summit = peak；summit = conference
注 关于"顶点"的单词在 SSAT 的习题中有很多，如：crest，acme。

agenda ★★
[ə'dʒendə] n. 议程表

记 导游（agent）不能随意改变旅游线路，必须按着议程表（agenda）走
考 同义 agenda = program；agenda = schedule

类比
odd 奇怪的 to agenda 议程表 ⇒ quirky 奇怪的 to schedule 时间表 （纵向）
itinerary 路线 to travel 旅行 ⇒ agenda 议程 to meeting 会议 （事物及其对象）
agenda 议程表 to meeting 会议 ⇒ blueprint 蓝图 to building 建筑 （事物及其对象）

placid ★★
['plæsɪd] a. 平静的，温和的

记 人们地震后受到安慰（placate），所以还算显得平静（placid）
考 同义 placid = quiet；pacific = placid；placid = calm；placid = peaceful

crucial ★★
['kruːʃl] a. 关键的，重要的

记 残忍（cruel）是做人很重要（crucial）的一个要素
考 同义 vital = crucial

类比
insignificant 不重要的 to crucial 重要的 ⇒ loose 松的 to tight 紧的 （反义）
permanent 永恒的 to everlasting 持久的 ⇒ urgent 紧急的 to crucial 至关重要的 （同义）

plunder ★
['plʌndə] n. 战利品

记 犯了大错（blunder），丢失了唾手可及的战利品（plunder）
考 同义 plunder = booty

meditation ★
[ˌmedɪ'teɪʃn] v. 考虑，沉思

记 吃了药（medication）让自己昏昏欲睡、无法思考（meditation）
考 同义 mediation = thought

★ prehensile
[ˌpriːˈhensaɪl] *a.* 善于抓住的，适于把握的

记　先理解（comprehension）课文，再把握（prehensile）重点
考　同义　prehensile = grasping

★ punch
[pʌntʃ] *v.* 拳打

记　找一帮（bunch）人去打架（punch）
考　类比　punch/拳打 to bleeding/流血 ⇒ overheat/使过热 to burn/燃烧 （因果）

★★★ yield
[jiːld] *v.* 屈服

变　unyielding *a.* 不屈的
考　同义　tenacious = unyielding；unyielding = relentless；concede = yield
　　　　　yield = surrender；succumb = yield
　　类比　devious/弯曲的 to circuitous/绕行的 ⇒ yield/屈服 to submit/服从 （同义）
注　关于"坚定的，顽固的"单词在 SSAT 的习题中有很多，如：adamant, determined, rigid, resolute, stubborn。

★★ batter
[ˈbætə] *n.* 面糊；击球手

变　battered *a.* 击垮的，被打的
记　对于小孩子来说，较好的（better）选择就是把食物打成面糊状（batter）喂他们
考　同义　battered = dilapidated
　　类比　drill/钻子 to hole/孔 ⇒ blender/搅拌器 to batter/面糊 （事物及其目的）

★ proficient
[prəˈfɪʃnt] *a.* 熟练的，精通的

记　我们简历上常写的"语言流利度"即为 language proficiency
考　同义　adept = proficient

★★ judicious
[dʒuːˈdɪʃəs] *a.* 明智的

记　judi-（judge）+ -cious：做出良好的判断，显得很明智（judicious）
考　同义　judicious = wise；judicious = sage
　　类比　sage/圣人 to judicious/明智的 ⇒ miser/小气鬼 to stingy/吝啬的 （人物及其特点）

☆ prehensile　　☆ punch　　☆ yield　　☆ batter　　☆ proficient
☆ judicious

★ revitalize
[riːˈvaɪtəlaɪz] v. 复活

- 记 re- + vital 有活力的 + -ize
- 考 同义 revitalize = bring back to life

★★★ genuine
[ˈdʒenjʊɪn] a. 真实的，诚恳的

- 记 他是一个真正的（genuine）天才（genius）
- 考 同义 sincere = genuine；authentic = genuine；genuine = bona fide
  （bona fide 这个拉丁词的释义为 made in good faith without fraud or deceit）

★★ scribble
[ˈskrɪbl] v. 乱写

- 记 scrib- 写 + -ble
- 考 类比 babble 乱说 to talk 说话 ⇒ scribble 乱涂 to write 写 （种属）
  mumble 含糊地说 to talk 说话 ⇒ scribble 乱涂 to write 写 （种属）

List | 63 words ★ 复习一下学过的单词！

□ aggregate	□ canary	□ meek	□ paternalism
□ amalgamate	□ creditable	□ modify	□ peacock
□ anesthetic	□ drivel	□ nugget	□ peruse
□ aptitude	□ grave	□ ooze	□ steadfast
□ callow	□ heterogeneous	□ pacify	□ tedious

☆ revitalize   ☆ genuine   ☆ scribble

SSAT词汇 List 65

★ exquisite
[ɪkˈskwɪzɪt] *a.* 精致的，优美的

记 老师要求（require）来现场（site）的同学都必须打扮得精致（exquisite）一些
考 同义　exquisite = elegant

★★ pious
[ˈpaɪəs] *a.* 虔诚的

变 impious *a.* 不虔诚的
记 现场有大量（copious）虔诚的（pious）基督徒
考 类比　impious 不虔诚的 to reverence 尊敬 ⇒ superficial 肤浅的 to depth 深度（缺乏）
　　　erudite 博学的 to pedantic 迂腐的 ⇒ pious 虔诚的 to sanctimonious 假装虔诚的（同义：正反向）

★★ summary
[ˈsʌməri] *n.* 总结

变 summarize *v.* 总结
考 类比　synopsis 大纲 to summary 概要 ⇒ sprint 疾跑 to race 赛跑（同义）
　　　summarize 总结 to shorten 使简短 ⇒ classify 分类 to put in order 整理（同义）

★ penitent
[ˈpenɪtənt] *a.* 后悔的

记 peni-（penny）潘妮 + tent：潘妮（penny）的帐篷（tent）被偷了，她非常后悔（penitent）没听朋友的劝告把帐篷藏起来
考 类比　penitent 忏悔者 to contrite 后悔的 ⇒ zealot 狂热者 to fanatical 狂热的（人物及其特点）
注 关于"后悔的"单词在 SSAT 的习题中有很多，如：rueful, regretted, repented, remorseful。

★★★ enigma
[ɪˈnɪgmə] *n.* 谜

变 enigmatic *a.* 神秘的
记 二战中德军应用于军事和外交的密码中，最为出名的即为 ENIGMA（意思为"谜"），在

卷福主演的电影《模仿游戏》中对这一情节有所体现

考 同义 enigma = puzzle; enigmatic = mysterious

类比 mystery 谜 — to — solve 解决 → enigma 谜 — to — understand 懂得 （动宾）

★★ mineral ['mɪnərəl] n. 矿物质

记 我们喝的矿泉水即为 mineral water

考 类比
coal 煤 — to — mineral 矿物 → gold 金 — to — metal 金属 （种属）

mineral 矿物 — to — quartz 石英 → gem 宝石 — to — sapphire 蓝宝石 （种属）

calcium 钙 — to — mineral 矿物质 → sugar 糖 — to — carbohydrate 碳水化合物 （种属）

botanist 植物学家 — to — plants 植物 → geologist 地质学家 — to — minerals 矿物 （人物及其对象）

★ stagnant ['stæɡnənt] a. 停滞的

变 stagnancy n. 停滞，迟钝

记 因为过于稳定（steadfast），所以停滞（stagnant）

考 类比 stagnant 静止的 — to — pond 池塘 → flowing 流动的 — to — stream 小溪 （事物及其特点）

★★★ drill [drɪl] n. 钻子；v. 钻孔

记 使用钻子（drill）要有技巧（skill）

考 类比
ore 矿石 — to — mine 开矿 → oil 油 — to — drill 钻孔 （动宾）

drill 钻子 — to — bore 孔 → blade 刀片 — to — cut 切 （事物及其用途）

mechanic 机械师 — to — surgeon 医生 → drill 钻子 — to — scalpel 手术刀 （纵向）

drill 钻子 — to — hole 孔 → blender 搅拌器 — to — batter 面糊 （事物及其目的）

dentist 牙医 — to — drill 钻子 → surgeon 医生 — to — scalpel 手术刀 （人物及其工具）

camera 相机 — to — photographer 摄影师 → drill 钻子 — to — dentist 牙医 （人物及其工具）

★ overbear [ˌəʊvə'beə] v. 压制，克服

变 overbearing a. 盛气凌人的

记 压制（overbear）熊（bear），导致熊都灭绝（over）了

考 同义 overbearing = tyrannical

类比 overcharge 索价过高 — to — pay 付钱 → overbear 压制 — to — obey 听话 （动作及其目的）

dearth
[dɜːθ] *n.* 缺乏，缺少

记 地球（earth）缺乏（dearth）很多资源
考 同义 dearth = lack；dearth = shortage
类比 dreary 沉闷的 to happy 快乐的 ⇒ dearth 缺少 to surplus 盈余 （反义）

dormant
[ˈdɔːmənt] *a.* 休止的，静止的

记 因为生命在于静止（dormant），所以我要天天躺在宿舍（dormitory）里
考 同义 dormant = inactive

aplomb
[əˈplɒm] *n.* 沉着冷静

记 把 aplomb 看作 a bomb：即使一颗炸弹打下来，他也依然显得沉着冷静（aplomb）
考 同义 aplomb = confidence

refrain
[rɪˈfreɪn] *v.* 限制

记 先限制（refrain）后抑制（restrain）
考 同义 refrain = abstain
类比 prohibited 限制的 to refrain 限制 ⇒ ridiculous 搞笑的 to laugh 笑 （同义）

compensation
[ˌkɒmpenˈseɪʃn] *n.* 赔偿

记 com- + pens- 钱 + -ation：所有钱放在一起，然后赔偿（compensation）给你
考 类比 compensation 赔偿 to injustice 不正义 ⇒ eraser 橡皮 to pencil 铅笔 （事物及其用途）

optimize
[ˈɒptəmaɪz] *v.* 使最优化

记 拉丁词根 optim 即为 the great goodness 之意
考 同义 optimize = make best of
类比 optimize 最优化 to effective 有效的 ⇒ ensure 确保 to certain 确定的 （同义）
注 关于"美化"的单词在 SSAT 的习题中有很多，如：perfect, ameliorate, modify, amend, rectify。

deceive
[dɪˈsiːv] *v.* 欺骗

变 deceit *n.* 欺骗；deceitful *a.* 欺骗的
记 谐音：弟媳妇：我和我弟媳妇一起欺骗（deceive）我弟弟
考 同义 deceive = mislead；gullible = easily deceived；hoodwink = deceive
fraudulent = deceitful；deceive = dupe

类比：

feign 伴装	to	deceive 欺骗	⇒ flee 逃跑	to	elude 逃避 （同义）
ruse 诡计	to	deceive 欺骗	⇒ diversion 消遣	to	amuse 娱乐 （事物及其用途）
lax 放松的	to	resolution 决心	⇒ deceitful 欺骗的	to	sincerity 真诚 （缺乏）
wheedle 欺骗	to	cajolery 甜言蜜语	⇒ deceive 欺骗	to	subterfuge 托词 （同义）
fidelity 忠诚	to	unfaithfulness 不真实	⇒ honesty 诚实	to	deceit 欺骗 （反义）
aboveboard 直率的	to	duplicity 口是心非	⇒ sincerity 真诚	to	deceitful 欺骗的 （缺乏）

★★★
contain

[kən'teɪn] v. 包含，包括

变 contained a. 包含的；container n. 容器

考 同义 contain = comprise；contained = held；vessel = container；receptacle = container

类比：jar 罐子 to contain 容纳 ⇒ pillar 柱子 to support 支撑 （事物及其用途）

★★
rooster

['ru:stə] n. 公鸡

记 一只公鸡（rooster）和一只虾（lobster）在玩游戏

考 类比：
- rooster 公鸡 to chicken 鸡 ⇒ chimpanzee 黑猩猩 to ape 猿 （种属）
- hen 母鸡 to rooster 公鸡 ⇒ waitress 女服务员 to waiter 男服务员 （相对）

★
snout

[snaʊt] n. 鼻子

记 可以和 nose 一起记

考 类比：snout 鼻子 to pig 猪 ⇒ muzzle 狗鼻子 to dog 狗 （动物及其部分）

★
equable

['ekwəbl] a. 平静的

记 判决很公正（equitable），所以原告和被告双方都很平静（equable）

考 同义 equable = calm

List | **64** words　　　　　　　　　　　★ 复习一下学过的单词！

☐ agenda	☐ endow	☐ plunder	☐ revitalize
☐ batter	☐ genuine	☐ prehensile	☐ scribble
☐ cajole	☐ judicious	☐ proficient	☐ summit
☐ corporal	☐ meditation	☐ punch	☐ veracious
☐ crucial	☐ placid	☐ restore	☐ yield

SSAT词汇 List 66

caustic
['kɔːstɪk] *a.* 尖刻的，腐蚀的

记 仙人掌（cactus）扎手，导致（cause）腐蚀性的（caustic）伤痛
考 同义 caustic = stinging
类比 pungent 刺鼻的 to odor 味道 → caustic 尖刻的 to comment 评论 （修饰）

hoax
[həʊks] *n.* 欺骗

记 hoax 和 coax 不仅长得像，而且都有"欺骗，哄骗"之意
考 同义 hoax = falsification
注 关于"欺骗"的单词在 SSAT 的习题中有很多，如：coax，cajole。

genre
['ʒɑːnrə] *n.* 体裁，种类

记 总的来说（general）这篇文章的体裁（genre）属于小说
考 同义 genre = category；genre = style；genre = type
类比 vegetarian 素食的 to cuisine 烹饪 → fantasy 奇幻小说 to genre 题材 （种属）
（fantasy 这个单词的英文释义为：a story or situation that someone creates from their imagination and that is not based on reality）
genre 体裁 to romance 冒险故事 → organism 有机体 to cell 细胞 （种属）
（romance 这个单词的英文释义为：a prose narrative treating imaginary characters involved in events remote in time or place and usually heroic, adventurous, or mysterious）

editor
['edɪtə] *n.* 编辑

考 类比 coroner 验尸官 to corpse 尸体 → editor 编辑 to text 文本 （人物及其对象）
mechanic 机械工 to car 汽车 → editor 编辑 to book 书 （人物及其对象）
manager 经理 to store 商店 → editor 编辑 to film 电影 （人物及其对象）
painter 画家 to brush 刷子 → editor 编辑 to pen 笔 （人物及其工具）

☆ caustic　　☆ hoax　　☆ genre　　☆ editor

conform ★★
[kənˈfɔːm] v. 符合，一致

- 变 nonconformist n. 不墨守成规者
- 记 经我确认 (confirm)，双方符合 (conform) 结婚要求
- 考 同义 harmonize = conform；maverick = nonconformist

ostracize ★★★
[ˈɒstrəsaɪz] v. 驱逐

- 记 这个单词来自古希腊语 ostrakon，表示"贝壳"的意思。彼时的雅典实行民主政治的政策，对于那些危害国家或不受欢迎的人，会被驱逐出这个国家。进行表决时，老百姓会把人名写在贝壳上，久而久之这个单词就引申出"驱逐"的意思
- 考 同义 ostracize = exclude
- 类比 accept (符合) to accede (同意) → ostracize (驱逐) to deport (放逐) （同义）
- 注 关于"驱逐，驱赶"的单词在 SSAT 的习题中有很多，如：exile, banish, expel, expulse。

desolate ★
[ˈdesələt] a. 贫瘠的，荒凉的

- 记 de- 加强 + sol- (sole) 单独的 + -ate：一生孤独 (sole)，所以荒凉 (desolate)
- 考 同义 desolate = barren；desolate = deserted；desolate = lifeless

predominant ★
[prɪˈdɒmɪnənt] a. 主要的，支配的

- 记 pre- 预先 + dominant 主要的
- 考 同义 predominant = prevalent

perceive ★★★
[pəˈsiːv] v. 察觉，感觉

- 变 perceptive a. 感知的，知觉的；perception n. 知觉，感觉
- 记 感觉 (perceive) 自己在生日那天会收到 (receive) 朋友们送的礼物
- 考 同义 perceive = observe；perceptive = sharp；perceptive = astute
- 类比
  - discern (识别) to perceptive (感知) → see (看见) to witness (目击)（同义）
  - perceive (察觉) to discern (识别) → ascertain (确定) to determine (决定)（同义）
  - perceptive (知觉的) to insight (洞察力) → austere (严峻的) to sternness (严厉)（同义）
  - perceptive (感知的) to discern (辨别) → persistent (坚持) to persevere (坚持)（同义）
  - thought (想法) to delusion (幻觉) → perception (感知) to hallucination (幻觉)（同义：正反向）

eminent ★★
[ˈemɪnənt] a. 杰出的，有名的

- 变 eminence n. 显赫，卓越

记 美国著名说唱歌手 Eminem 在中国也非常有名（eminent）
考 同义　eminent = renowned；eminence = high position

★ cursory　['kɜːsəri] *a.* 肤浅的，草率的

记 动不动就说脏话（curse）的人显得很肤浅（cursory）
考 同义　cursory = hasty
　　类比　cursory 草率的 to superficial 肤浅的 ⇒ desultory 散漫的 to aimless 无目标的（同义）

★★ dune　[djuːn] *n.* 沙丘

记 完成（done）沙丘（dune）的建造工作
考 类比　dune 沙丘 to sand 沙子 ⇒ wave 波浪 to water 水（组成）
　　　　tree 树木 to forest 森林 ⇒ sand 沙子 to dune 沙丘（组成）
　　　　yarn 纱线 to cloth 布 ⇒ sand 沙子 to dune 沙丘（组成）

★★★ mystery　['mɪstəri] *n.* 神秘

变 mysterious *a.* 神秘的
记 my + -stery (story)：我的（my）故事（story）就是神秘（mystery）
考 同义　enigmatic = mysterious；mysterious = inscrutable
　　类比　arbitrate 仲裁 to dispute 争论 ⇒ solve 解决 to mystery 谜（动宾）
　　　　mystery 谜 to solve 解决 ⇒ enigma 谜 to understand 懂得（动宾）
　　　　mysterious 神秘的 to understandable 易懂的 ⇒ obscure 模糊的 to clear 清晰的（反义）

★ stymie　['staɪmi] *v.* 阻碍，阻挠

记 谐音：四袋米：敌人想用四袋米收买我，以阻碍（stymie）我军的计划
考 同义　stymie = frustrate
注 关于"阻碍，阻挠"的单词在 SSAT 的习题中有很多，如：thwart, foil, hinder, impede。

★ qualm　[kwɑːm] *n.* 疑虑，不安

记 谐音：夸母：夸父前去追日，夸母略显不安（qualm）
考 同义　qualm = misgiving

★★★ benevolent　[bə'nevələnt] *a.* 仁慈的，亲切的

变 benevolence *n.* 仁慈，善行

考 同义 generous = benevolent；benevolent = kind

类比 philanthropic 仁慈的 to benevolence 仁慈 ⇒ miserly 吝啬的 to stinginess 吝啬 （同义）

★★★ jargon
['dʒɑ:gən] *n.* 行话，术语

记 谐音：榨干：同行之间用行话（jargon）榨干外行人的钱

考 同义 jargon = terminology；jargon = slang；jargon = vernacular

类比 jargon 术语 to vocabulary 词汇 ⇒ gossip 八卦 to talk 谈话 （种属）

★★★ patient
['peɪʃnt] *a.* 有耐心的；*n.* 病人

变 impatient *a.* 无耐心的；impatience *n.* 无耐心

考 类比 bashful 腼腆的 to socialize 社交 ⇒ impatient 无耐心的 to wait 等待 （缺乏）

cognizant 认知的 to awareness 意识 ⇒ restive 不安宁的 to impatience 急躁 （同义）

defendant 被告 to accusation 控告 ⇒ patient 病人 to treatment 治疗 （人物及其特点）

★ cistern
['sɪstən] *n.* 水箱

记 姐姐（sister）扛着个大水箱（cistern）

考 同义 cistern = water tank

★★ lull
[lʌl] *n.* 间歇，暂停；*v.* 使平静，使安静；哄骗

记 迟钝的（dull）人容易被人欺骗（lull）

考 同义 lull = temporary pause

类比 lull 欺骗 to trust 信任 ⇒ cajole 诱骗 to compliance 顺从 （动作及其目的）

注 关于"使平静"的单词在 SSAT 的习题中有很多，如：soothe, pacify, appease, conciliate.

List | **65** words ★ 复习一下学过的单词！

□ aplomb	□ dormant	□ mineral	□ refrain
□ compensation	□ drill	□ optimize	□ rooster
□ contain	□ enigma	□ overbear	□ snout
□ dearth	□ equable	□ penitent	□ stagnant
□ deceive	□ exquisite	□ pious	□ summary

☆ jargon ☆ patient ☆ cistern ☆ lull

SSAT词汇 List 67

★★★
acquiesce [ˌækwiˈes] *v.* 默许，勉强同意

记 ac- + quies- (quiet) + ce：acquiesce 的英文释义即为 to comply quietly
考 同义 acquiesce = agree；acquiesce = comply；acquiesce = accept；acquiesce = assent

★★
exile [ˈeksaɪl] *v.* 放逐，流放

记 以前遭流放 (exile) 的犯人是从宣武门这个出口 (exit) 出的
考 同义 exile = ostracize；exile = banish
类比 exile/放逐 to country/国家 → expel/驱逐 to school/学校 （空间）
注 关于"放逐"的单词在 SSAT 的习题中有很多，如：outcast, expel, expulse。

★
waiter [ˈweɪtə] *n.* 服务员

考 类比 waiter/服务员 to chef/主厨 → restaurant/餐馆 to kitchen/厨房 （纵向）
flight attendant/空乘 to plane/飞机 → waiter/服务员 to restaurant/餐馆 （空间）
hen/母鸡 to rooster/公鸡 → waitress/女服务员 to waiter/男服务员 （相对）

★
seminar [ˈsemɪnɑː] *n.* 研讨会

记 萨米 (Sammy) 在开研讨会 (seminar)
考 类比 seminar/研讨会 to concert/演唱会 → speech/演讲 to music/音乐 （纵向）

★
refractory [rɪˈfræktəri] *a.* 倔强的

记 re- 相反 + -fractory (factory)：和工厂 (factory) 对着 (re) 干的人都是倔强的 (refractory) 人
考 同义 stubborn = refractory

☆ acquiesce　　☆ exile　　☆ waiter　　☆ seminar　　☆ refractory

frivolous ★★★
['frɪvələs] *a.* 无聊的，轻佻的

记 fri- (free) + vol- (will) + ous：出于自由意志 (free will)，你可以认真，也可以轻佻 (frivolous)

考 同义 superficial = frivolous； frivolous = silly

类比
- quixotic 狂想的 to practicality 实际 → frivolous 轻浮的 to gravity 严肃 （反义）
- fundamental 重要的 to frivolous 轻浮的 → strange 奇怪的 to common 常见的 （反义）
- unkempt 蓬乱的 to neat 整洁的 → serious 严肃的 to frivolous 轻佻的 （反义）

注 frivolous 这个单词的英文释义为：If you describe someone as frivolous, you mean they behave in a silly or light-hearted way, rather than being serious and sensible。

silence ★★
['saɪləns] *n.* 安静

考 类比
- gold 金 to silence 沉默 → money 钱 to time 时间 （同义）
- darkness 黑暗 to light 亮光 → silence 安静 to sound 声音 （缺乏）
- uproar 喧嚣 to silence 安静 → rage 愤怒 to forbearance 容忍 （反义）

patent ★
['peɪtnt] *n.* 专利权

记 中国的很多父母 (parent) 都觉得对自己的孩子享有专利权 (patent)

考 类比 copyright 著作权 to book 书 → patent 专利权 to design 设计 （事物及其特点）

dam ★★
[dæm] *n.* 大坝

考 类比
- bandage 绷带 to blood 血 → dam 大坝 to flood 洪水 （事物及其用途）
- muffle 抑制 to noise 噪音 → dam 大坝 to flood 洪水 （事物及其用途）
- spider 蜘蛛 to web 网 → beaver 海狸 to dam 大坝 （动物）

（这个题的思路有些复杂：spider 可以造 web，而 beaver 可以造 dam）

cargo ★★★
['kɑːgəʊ] *n.* 货物

记 货物 (cargo) 装车 (car)，说走 (go) 就走 (go)

考 类比
- jettison 抛弃 to cargo 货物 → evict 逐出 to tenant 房客 （动宾）
- passenger 乘客 to bus 公车 → cargo 货物 to ship 船 （空间）

freighter 货船 to cargo 货物 ⇒ suitcase 手提箱 to clothing 衣服 （空间）

mangle
[ˈmæŋgl] *v.* 乱砍，损坏

记 不要损坏（mangle）丛林（jungle）里的东西
考 同义 mangle = mutilate

façade
[fəˈsɑːd] *n.* 建筑物的外表

记 fac-（face）+ -ade
考 类比 pretence 借口 to reason 理由 ⇒ façade 建筑物的外表 to appearance 外观 （种属）

milk
[mɪlk] *n.* 牛奶；*v.* 挤奶

考 类比
milk 牛奶 to sour 酸的 ⇒ bread 面包 to stale 馊的 （修饰）
awe 敬畏 to celebrity 名人 ⇒ milk 挤奶 to cow 牛 （动宾）
cow 牛 to milk 牛奶 ⇒ pig 猪 to bacon 咸猪肉 （事物及其原材料）
grape 葡萄 to wine 酒 ⇒ milk 牛奶 to cheese 奶酪 （事物及其原材料）
refrigerator 冰箱 to milk 牛奶 ⇒ library 图书馆 to book 书 （空间）

furious
[ˈfjʊəriəs] *a.* 激烈的，狂怒的

记 系列电影《速度与激情》的英文即为 Fast & Furious
考 同义 furious = fierce
类比 ravenous 贪婪的（>程度） to hunger 饥饿 ⇒ furious 狂怒的 to indignation 愤慨
despondent 极度沮丧的（>程度） to sad 伤心的 ⇒ furious 狂怒的 to angry 生气的

furious

esteem
[ɪˈstiːm] *v.* 尊敬

记 谐音：It's team：对于这个团队（It's team）的工人，我们一定要尊敬（esteem）
考 同义 esteem = venerate；esteem = respect
注 esteem 这个单词 "自尊" 的意思我们是很熟悉的，此处是熟词僻义。

stadium
[ˈsteɪdiəm] *n.* 体育场

记 "鸟巢" 的官方名称即为 National Stadium 国家体育场

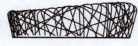
stadium

考 类比　motel to guests ⇒ stadium to crowd （空间）
　　　　旅馆　　客人　　　 体育场　　人群

expurgate ★   ['ekspəgeɪt] v. 删除，净化

记 expunge 和 expurgate 长相类似，意思也类似
考 同义　expurgate = cleanse；expurgate = delete

marquee ★   [mɑː'kiː] n. 天幕，华盖

记 mar 破坏 + -quee（queen）：不要破坏（mar）皇后（queen）头上的华盖（marquee）
考 同义　marquee = canopy
注 marquee 这个单词的英文释义为：a large tent, often with open sides, used chiefly for outdoor entertainment。

principal ★★★   ['prɪnsəpl] n. 校长

记 即使是校长（principal）也要遵守做事的规则和原理（principle）
考 类比　commander to decree ⇒ principal to discipline （人物及其对象）
　　　　长官　　命令　　　 校长　　纪律
　　　　principal to teacher ⇒ manager to cashier （人物及其对象）
　　　　校长　　老师　　　 经理　　收银员
　　　　sovereign to monarchy ⇒ principal to school （空间）
　　　　君主　　君主国　　　 校长　　学校
　　　　foreman to factory ⇒ principal to school （空间）
　　　　工头　　工厂　　　 校长　　学校

dilate ★   [daɪ'leɪt] v. 扩大，膨胀

记 因为推迟（delay）去医院，所以病人整个身体都膨胀（dilate）了
考 同义　dilate = enlarge
注 关于"扩大，膨胀"的单词在 SSAT 的习题中有很多，如：inflate, bloat, bulge。

List | 66 words　　　　　　　　　　　　　　★ 复习一下学过的单词！

□ benevolent	□ desolate	□ hoax	□ patient
□ caustic	□ dune	□ jargon	□ perceive
□ cistern	□ editor	□ lull	□ predominant
□ conform	□ eminent	□ mystery	□ qualm
□ cursory	□ genre	□ ostracize	□ stymie

☆ expurgate　　☆ marquee　　☆ principal　　☆ dilate

SSAT词汇 List 68

★ abode [əˈbəʊd] *n.* 住处，住所
记 用土砖（adobe）盖房子（abode）
考 同义 abode = home; abode = domicile

★ indefatigable [ˌɪndɪˈfætɪɡəbl] *a.* 不知疲倦的
考 同义 indefatigable = tireless

★ solicit [səˈlɪsɪt] *v.* 请求
记 solicit 这个单词还有 "招揽，兜售" 之意，所以在美国很多人为了防止有人上门推销，都会在门口贴一个牌子，上面写着 NO SOLICITING
考 同义 solicit = request

solicit

★★★ marsupial [mɑːˈsuːpɪəl] *a.* 有袋类动物
记 这个词来自于拉丁语 marsuppium，本意即为 "袋子"
考 类比
clam (蛤) to mollusk (软体动物) ⇒ kangaroo (袋鼠) to marsupial (有袋类动物) （种属）
spider (蜘蛛) to arachnid (蛛形纲动物) ⇒ kangaroo (袋鼠) to marsupial (有袋类动物) （种属）
crocodile (鳄鱼) to reptile (爬行类动物) ⇒ kangaroo (袋鼠) to marsupial (有袋类动物) （种属）

★ flagrant [ˈfleɪɡrənt] *a.* 明目张胆的
记 flagrant 是 "明目张胆的"，fragrant 是 "芳香的，愉悦的"
考 同义 flagrant = glaring

★ ambiguous [æmˈbɪɡjuəs] *a.* 模糊的
记 ambi- 二 + -guous (guess)：给你两个很类似的选项让你猜，诚心把你搞糊涂

（ambiguous）

考 同义 ambiguous = unclear

类比 correction 正确 —to→ erroneous 错误的 ⇒ clarification 澄清 —to→ ambiguous 模糊的 （缺乏）

evacuate [ɪˈvækjʊeɪt] v. 疏散，撤退

记 e- 朝外 + vacu- 空 + -ate：朝外弄空，即为疏散（evacuate）

考 同义 evacuate = empty out

类比 excavate 挖掘 —to→ dig 挖掘 ⇒ evacuate 疏散 —to→ empty 弄空 （同义）

forgery [ˈfɔːdʒəri] n. 伪造

记 忘记（forget）带真货，所以用假货（forgery）

考 类比 money 钱 —to→ counterfeit 假币 ⇒ genuine 真迹 —to→ art forgery 伪造 （反义）

cooperation 合作 —to→ collusion 共谋 ⇒ imitation 模仿 —to→ forgery 伪造 （同义：正反向）

gulf [gʌlf] n. 海湾

记 在海湾（gulf）打高尔夫（golf），别有一番风味

考 类比 bay 海湾 —to→ sea 海 ⇒ gulf 海湾 —to→ ocean 海洋 （空间）

cape 海角 —to→ continent 大陆 ⇒ gulf 海湾 —to→ ocean 海洋 （空间）

（这个题的思路有些复杂：对于 cape 我们可以这样理解：a large piece of land surrounded by water；对于 gulf 我们可以这样理解：a large area of sea enclosed by land）

impeccable [ɪmˈpekəbl] a. 无瑕疵的

记 im- 否定 + pecc- 拉丁词根"罪恶" + able：无罪恶的即为无瑕疵的（impeccable）

考 同义 impeccable = flawless

类比 impeccable 无瑕疵的 —to→ clean 干净的 ⇒ posh 时髦的 —to→ fancy 花哨的 （同义）

impeccable 无瑕疵的 —to→ fault 缺点 ⇒ unblemished 无缺点的 —to→ imperfection 不完美 （反义）

propel [prəˈpel] v. 推进

记 pro- 朝前 + -pel（pull）：朝前（pro）拉（pull），即为推进（propel）

考 同义 propel = project；push = propel

align ★

[əˈlaɪn] *v.* 排列，排成一行

- 记 谐音：a line
- 考 同义 align = straighten

anecdote ★

[ˈænɪkdəʊt] *n.* 轶事

- 记 谐音：安妮可逗了：给你讲个安妮的轶事（anecdote），因为安妮可逗了
- 考 类比 ditty/小曲 to oratorio/清唱剧 ⇒ anecdote/轶事 to novel/小说 （＜程度）

prohibit ★★★

[prəˈhɪbɪt] *v.* 阻止，禁止

- 变 prohibited *a.* 被禁止的
- 记 很多城市的地铁站入口会张贴一张写有"Dangerous Articles Prohibited（禁止危险物品）"的牌子
- 考 同义 forbid = prohibit；prohibit = illicit

  类比 prohibited/限制的 to refrain/限制 ⇒ ridiculous/搞笑的 to laugh/笑 （同义）

  prohibit/禁止 to allow/允许 ⇒ encourage/鼓励 to dissuade/劝阻 （反义）

repudiate ★★

[rɪˈpjuːdieɪt] *v.* 拒绝，否定

- 记 这个单词在拉丁语中最先指的是"拒绝对方的求爱"，16世纪进入英语之后被人引申为"离婚"，后来泛指被"逐出"一个家庭，最后有了今天"拒绝，否定"的意思
- 考 同义 repudiate = renounce

  类比 repudiate/否定 to negate/否定 ⇒ acknowledge/承认 to accept/接受 （同义）

  repudiate/否定 to deny/否定 ⇒ acknowledge/承认 to accept/接受 （同义）

mourn ★

[mɔːn] *v.* 哀悼，哀伤

- 记 这个词的名词形式为 mourning，发音和 morning 相同，可以记作：大早上（morning）到死者家中表示哀悼（mourning）
- 考 同义 grieve = mourn

nonchalant ★★

[ˈnɒnʃələnt] *a.* 冷漠的

- 记 江湖庸医（charlatan）对病人很冷漠（nonchalant）
- 考 同义 indifferent = nonchalant
- 注 关于"冷漠的"单词在 SSAT 的习题中有很多，如：aloof，detached，impassive，apathetic。

compromise ['kɒmprəmaɪz] v. 妥协

- 变 uncompromising a. 不妥协的
- 记 com- + promise：妥协（compromise）就是大家在一起（com）相互许诺（promise），彼此让步
- 考 同义 unflinching = uncompromising
- 类比 intransigent 不妥协的 to compromise 妥协 ⇒ dogged 顽强的 to surrender 投降 （反义）

blithe [blaɪð] a. 愉快的

- 记 因为有上帝保佑（bless），所以自己很快乐（blithe）
- 考 同义 blithe = carefree; blithe = cheerful; blithe = happy; blithe = gleeful
- 类比 prejudiced 有偏见的 to unbiased 无偏见的 ⇒ worry 担忧 to blithe 愉快的 （反义）
- 注 关于"愉快的"单词在 SSAT 的习题中有很多，如：jaunty, jovial, buoyant, jolly, jocund, jubilant, exhilarate, exultant, jocular, elated, lighthearted。

prickly ['prɪkli] a. 多刺的，易怒的

- 记 prick 刺 + ly：捡起（pick）地上的棍子朝你刺（prick）去，让你生气（prickly）
- 考 类比 knotty 棘手的 to difficult 困难的 ⇒ prickly 易怒的 to irritating 愤怒的 （同义）

List | **67** words ★ 复习一下学过的单词！

☐ acquiesce	☐ exile	☐ mangle	☐ refractory
☐ cargo	☐ expurgate	☐ marquee	☐ seminar
☐ dam	☐ façade	☐ milk	☐ silence
☐ dilate	☐ frivolous	☐ patent	☐ stadium
☐ esteem	☐ furious	☐ principal	☐ waiter

SSAT词汇 List 69

★ extraneous
[ɪkˈstreɪnɪəs] *a.* 外来的

记 因为是外来的（extraneous），所以略显多余（extra）
考 同义 extraneous = irrelevant

★ caucus
[ˈkɔːkəs] *n.* 干部会议

记 谐音：口渴死：开会（caucus）开了很久，口渴得要死
考 同义 caucus = meeting

★★ outline
[ˈaʊtlaɪn] *n.* 轮廓，大纲

考 同义 outline = contour

类比 outline 大纲 to document 文件 ⇒ sketch 缩略图 to picture 图画 （事物及其部分）
perimeter 周长 to figure 物体 ⇒ outline 轮廓 to object 物体 （事物及其部分）

★ shroud
[ʃraʊd] *n.* 裹尸布

记 尸体应该（should）用裹尸布（shroud）包裹起来
考 同义 shroud = veil

★★★ swarm
[swɔːm] *n.* 群

记 据说挤作一团（swarm）会比较暖和（warm）
考 同义 horde = swarm；swarm = flock

类比 archipelago 群岛 to island 岛 ⇒ swarm 蜂群 to bee 蜜蜂 （组成）
swarm 蜂群 to bees 蜜蜂 ⇒ drove 牛群 to cattle 牛 （组成）
hive 蜂房 to swarm 蜂群 ⇒ corral 畜栏 to herd 兽群 （空间）
throng 人群 to people 人 ⇒ swarm 一群虫子 to insects 昆虫 （同义）

☆ extraneous ☆ caucus ☆ outline ☆ shroud ☆ swarm

★
clamor
['klæmə] *n.* 喧闹

记 clam-（claim）要求 + -or：一群人在医院门口要讨个说法（claim），显得很喧闹（clamor）

考 同义 din = clamor；clamor = uproar

注 关于"喧闹"的单词在 SSAT 的习题中有很多，如：tumult, upheaval, loud cry, commotion。

★★
deter
[dɪ'tɜ:] *v.* 阻止，防止

记 下决心（determine）阻止（deter）这件事的发生

考 同义 deter = hinder；deter = discourage；deter = prevent

★★
antibiotic
[ˌæntɪbaɪ'ɒtɪk] *n.* 抗生素

记 anti- 反 + bio- 生命 + tic

考 类比 antibiotic 抗生素 to infection 感染 ⇒ antidote 解药 to poisoning 中毒 （事物及其对象）
antiseptic 防腐剂 to infection 感染 ⇒ antibiotic 抗生素 to bacteria 细菌 （事物及其对象）

★
wax
[wæks] *v.* 增大

记 麦克斯（Max）看着天上的月亮一点点增大（wax）

考 类比 wax 增大 to wane 变小 ⇒ advance 进步 to retreat 撤退 （反义）

★★
concise
[kən'saɪs] *a.* 简洁的

记 con- + cis- 切 + e：切掉所有多余的东西，所以显得很简洁（concise）

考 同义 concise = brief；concise = succinct；concise = short

注 关于"简洁的"单词在 SSAT 的习题中有很多，如：terse, laconic。

★★
perilous
['perələs] *a.* 危险的

考 同义 hazardous = perilous；perilous = dangerous

类比 perilous 危险的 to safe 安全的 ⇒ celebrated 著名的 to unknown 无名的 （反义）

★★
essential
[ɪ'senʃl] *a.* 重要的

考 同义 essential = indispensable；essential = requisite

类比 eliminate 删除 → to → optional 可选择的 → retain 保留 → to → essential 重要的 （纵向）

taboo 禁忌 → to → permissible 可允许的 → dispensable 可有可无的 → to → essential 重要的 （反义）

primate ['praɪmeɪt] n. 灵长类动物

记 人类是最主要的（primary）灵长类动物（primate）
考 类比 human 人类 → to → primate 灵长类动物 → snake 蛇 → to → reptile 爬行动物 （种属）

sporadic [spəˈrædɪk] a. 零星的，偶发的

记 spor-（sports）+ -adic（addict）有瘾的人：现在对体育（sports）上瘾的人（addict）很少（sporadic）
考 同义 irregular = sporadic；sporadic = intermittent；sporadic = fitful
注 关于"零星的"单词在 SSAT 的习题中有很多，如：infrequent，random。

mayhem [ˈmeɪhem] n. 混乱

记 发音类似于 may harm，由此可以联想到 mayhem
考 同义 mayhem = disorder

distort [dɪˈstɔːt] v. 扭曲

变 distortion n. 扭曲
记 我们常说的"哈哈镜"即为 distorting mirror
考 同义 distort = deform

类比 alter 更改 → to → distort 扭曲 → bump 碰撞 → to → collide 冲突 （同义）

image 图像 → to → distort 扭曲 → account 言论 → to → slant 故意歪曲 （动宾）

explicit 清晰的 → to → distortion 扭曲 → frank 坦诚的 → to → circumlocution 累赘陈述 （反义）

sapling [ˈsæplɪŋ] n. 树苗

记 四兄弟（sibling）一起负责种植一颗小树苗（sapling）
考 类比 sapling 树苗 → to → tree 树 → kitten 小猫咪 → to → cat 猫 （时间先后）

lieutenant 中尉 → to → private 下士 → tree 树 → to → sapling 树苗 （不同阶段）

☆ primate　　☆ sporadic　　☆ mayhem　　☆ distort　　☆ sapling

disdain

[dɪsˈdeɪn] v. 鄙视，蔑视

记 dis- + dai 戴 + n：法国贵族出门不戴帽子是会被别人鄙视（disdain）的
考 同义 disparage = disdain；disdain = contempt；disdain = disrespect

类比 sneer 嘲笑 to disdain 鄙视 ⇒ cringe 畏缩 to fear 害怕 （因果）

travesty

[ˈtrævəsti] n. 歪曲，滑稽模仿

记 四处走动（travel），歪曲（travesty）事实
考 同义 travesty = mockery

moist

[mɔɪst] a. 潮湿的；n. 潮湿

变 moisten v. 弄湿；moisture n. 湿度
记 中国大多数（most）南方城市都很潮湿（moist）
考 同义 dank = moist and chilly

类比
moist 潮湿的 to arid 干旱的 ⇒ sublime 崇高的 to deserted 被抛弃的 （反义）
abbreviate 缩短 to delete 删除 ⇒ moisten 弄湿 to flood 洪水 （<程度）
hydrophobia 恐水症 to moisture 水分 ⇒ acrophobia 恐高症 to height 高度 （反义）
humidifier 加湿器 to moisture 湿度 ⇒ furnace 炉子 to heat 热度 （事物及其用途）
pallid 苍白的 to color 颜色 ⇒ parched 烧焦的 to moisture 湿度 （缺乏）
blood 血 to human 人 ⇒ moist 潮湿 to cloud 云 （事物及其部分）

List | **68** words ★ 复习一下学过的单词！

□ abode	□ compromise	□ impeccable	□ prickly
□ align	□ evacuate	□ indefatigable	□ prohibit
□ ambiguous	□ flagrant	□ marsupial	□ propel
□ anecdote	□ forgery	□ mourn	□ repudiate
□ blithe	□ gulf	□ nonchalant	□ solicit

SSAT词汇 List 70

abash
[əˈbæʃ] v. 使困窘，使羞愧

记 因为鼻子上有灰（ash），所以我感到很窘迫（abash）
考 同义 abash = embarrass；abash = mortify
类比 abash 使困窘 to embarrassment 尴尬 → annoy 惹恼 to irritation 激怒 （同义）

assortment
[əˈsɔːtmənt] n. 混合物

记 混合物（assortment）即为各种各样（sort）的东西
考 同义 assortment = collection
注 关于"混合物"的单词在 SSAT 的习题中有很多，如：combination，mixture。

sincere
[sɪnˈsɪə] a. 真诚的

变 sincerity n. 真诚；sincerely ad. 真诚地；insincere a. 不真诚的
记 我们写信最后常说的"谨此问候"对应的英文即为 Yours Sincerely
考 同义 sincere = genuine；wholeheartedly = sincerely；hypocritical = insincere
类比
lax 放松 to resolution 决心 → deceitful 欺骗的 to sincerity 真诚 （缺乏）
friend 朋友 to animosity 敌意 → hypocrite 伪君子 to sincerity 真诚 （缺乏）
ostentation 卖弄 to simplicity 简单 → hypocrisy 虚伪 to sincerity 真诚 （反义）
aboveboard 光明正大的 to duplicity 不诚实 → sincerity 真诚 to deceitful 欺骗的 （反义）

harbinger
[ˈhɑːbɪndʒə] n. 先驱，预告

记 这个单词的读音很像"哈尔滨人"，所以可以记作：哈尔滨人都是先驱
考 同义 harbinger = messenger

planet
[ˈplænɪt] n. 行星

记 我计划（plan）去其他行星（planet）上居住

☆ abash　　☆ assortment　　☆ sincere　　☆ harbinger　　☆ planet

考 类比 moon 月球 →to→ satellite 卫星 ⇒ Mercury 水星 →to→ planet 行星 （纵向）
earth 地球 →to→ terrestrial 地球的 ⇒ planet 行星 →to→ celestial 天上的 （空间）
planet 行星 →to→ orbit 轨道 ⇒ bus 公车 →to→ route 路线 （空间）
planet solar 行星 →to→ system 太阳系 ⇒ horse 马 →to→ carousel 旋转木马 （空间）

★ deadlock ['dedlɒk] *n.* 僵局

记 dead + lock
考 同义 deadlock = impasse
　 类比 gridlock 交通堵塞 →to→ traffic 交通 ⇒ deadlock 僵局 →to→ negotiation 谈判 （事物及其特点）

★★★ profound [prə'faʊnd] *a.* 意义深远的

变 profundity *n.* 深刻，深奥
记 pro- 朝前 + found 建立：建立（found）起有深远意义的（profound）东西
考 同义 profound = deep；profound = insightful
　 类比 immaterial 不重要的 →to→ relevance 相关的 ⇒ superficial 肤浅的 →to→ profundity 深刻 （反义）
　 （relevance 这个单词的英文释义为：something's relevance to a situation or person is its importance or significance in that situation or to that person）

★ prance [prɑːns] *v.* 大步走

记 大步走（prance）在法国（France）的大街上
考 同义 prance = strut

★ unflinching [ʌn'flɪntʃɪŋ] *a.* 不退缩的

记 un- 否定 + flinch 退缩 + -ing
考 同义 unflinching = uncompromising；unflinching = fearless

★ oasis [əʊ'eɪsɪs] *n.* 绿洲

记 英国著名摇滚乐队（Oasis）
考 类比 desert 沙漠（缺乏） →to→ oasis 绿洲 ⇒ darkness 黑暗 →to→ lantern 灯笼

oasis

★★★ error ['erə] *a.* 错误

变 erroneous *a.* 错误的
考 同义 erroneous = incorrect；fallacy = error

类比　lapse 过失 —to→ error 错误　⇒　inkling 暗示 —to→ indication 指示　（<程度）

erroneous 错误的 —to→ correction 改正　⇒　ambiguous 模糊的 —to→ clarification 澄清　（反义）

prospector 勘探者 —to→ gold 金子　⇒　proofreader 校对者 —to→ error 错误　（人物及其对象）

☆ **spurn**　［spɜːn］ *v.* 蔑视

记　因为蔑视（spurn）对方，所以放火烧（burn）了对方的成果
考　同义　spurn = reject

☆☆ **prodigal**　[ˈprɒdɪɡl] *a.* 挥霍的

变　prodigious *a.* 巨大的，惊人的
记　pro- 朝前 + -digal（digital）：家里有很多数码（digital）产品，说明其很挥霍（prodigal）
考　同义　enormous = prodigious；extravagant = prodigal；wasteful = prodigal

类比　meek 温顺的 —to→ arrogant 傲慢的　⇒　mean 小气的 —to→ prodigal 挥霍的　（反义）

☆ **complete**　[kəmˈpliːt] *v.* 完成；*a.* 完全的

考　同义　absolute = complete

类比　borrow 借 —to→ return 还　⇒　begin 开始 —to→ complete 完成　（反义）

☆☆ **flee**　[fliː] *v.* 逃跑

记　跳蚤（flea）逃跑（flee）了
考　同义　flee = escape

类比　feign 伪装 —to→ deceive 欺骗　⇒　flee 逃跑 —to→ elude 逃避　（同义）

escape 逃跑 —to→ flee 逃跑　⇒　dismount 下车 —to→ alight 下车　（同义）

☆ **retard**　[rɪˈtɑːd] *v.* 延迟，减慢

记　你一伸腿绊倒了逃跑的罪犯，减慢（retard）了他的行动，警方决定给予你奖励（reward）
考　同义　retard = slow down

☆☆ **empathy**　[ˈempəθi] *n.* 移情作用

变　empathetic *a.* 移情作用的，同感的
记　e- 朝外 + path- 情感 + y
考　类比　ice 冰 —to→ cold 冷的　⇒　empathy 移情 —to→ caring 有同情心的　（事物及其特点）

★★★ advertise
['ædvətaɪz] v. 打广告

变 advertisement n. 广告；advertiser n. 广告商

考 类比
lobbyist 说客 to cause 事业 → advertiser 广告商 to product 产品 （人物及其对象）
billboard 广告牌 to advertisement 广告 → canvas 帆布 to painting 画 （空间）
customer 消费者 to advertise 广告 → soldier 士兵 to recruit 招募 （动作及其对象）

★ affiliation
[əˌfɪliˈeɪʃn] n. 附属，联盟

记 全国各地一系列的附属学校，英文均为 affiliated school

考 同义 affiliation = alliance

affiliation

★★★ grief
[ˈɡriːf] n. 悲痛，忧伤

变 grieve v. 悲伤，苦恼

记 天空飘来五个字"痛苦（grief）就一会（brief）"

考 同义 grieve = mourn

类比
celebrate 庆祝 to birth 出生 → grieve 悲伤 to death 死亡 （动宾）
ode 颂 to praise 赞扬 → elegy 挽歌 to grief 悲痛 （事物及其用途）
war 战争 to grief 悲痛 → peace 和平 to happiness 快乐 （事物及其特点）

List | 69 words ★ 复习一下学过的单词！

☐ antibiotic	☐ disdain	☐ moist	☐ shroud
☐ caucus	☐ distort	☐ outline	☐ sporadic
☐ clamor	☐ essential	☐ perilous	☐ swarm
☐ concise	☐ extraneous	☐ primate	☐ travesty
☐ deter	☐ mayhem	☐ sapling	☐ wax

SSAT词汇 List 71

★ grimace
[grɪ'meɪs] v. 扮鬼脸，做苦相

记 grim 冷酷的 + -ace (face)：冷酷的 (grim) 脸 (face) 上写满了痛苦 (grimace)
考 同义 grimace = sneer（这个题的思路有些复杂：grimace 这个单词的英文释义为：a facial expression usually of disgust, disapproval, or pain，而 sneer 这个单词的英文释义为：the smile or laugh with facial contortions that express scorn or contempt）

★★★ lubricant
['lu:brɪkənt] a. 润滑的；n. 润滑油

变 lubricate v. 使润滑
记 lu 露 + bric- (brick) 砖头 + -ant：有了露 (lu) 水的润滑 (lubricant)，砖头 (brick) 变得好移动了
考 同义 lubricant = slippery
类比 lubricant to slide → glue to adhere （事物及其用途）
　　　润滑油　　滑　　　胶水　　粘
　　　emollient to soften → oil to lubricate （动作及其目的）
　　　润肤剂　　变柔软　　油　　润滑
　　　lubricate to smoothly → muffle to quietly （动作及其目的）
　　　润滑　　　光滑地　　　蒙住　　安静地
　　　brine to preservative → grease to lubricant （动作及其目的）
　　　盐水　　防腐的　　　　油脂　　润滑的

★ nemesis
['neməsɪs] n. 报应，复仇

记 来自古希腊神话中的复仇女神涅墨西斯 (Nemesis)
考 同义 nemesis = revenge
类比 Nemesis to revenge → Athena to wisdom （同义）
　　　复仇女神　复仇　　雅典娜　智慧
　　　hostile to nemesis → fortified to stronghold （修饰）
　　　敌意的　　复仇　　加强的　　要塞

nemesis

注 Nemesis 指的本是古希腊神话中的复仇女神，但现在已经成为一个单词进入词典中

★ affluent
['æfluənt] a. 富裕的，丰富的

记 财大 (affluent) 气粗 (fluent)

考 同义 affluent = opulent；affluent = sufficient

类比 impecunious 贫穷的 to affluent 富裕的 → sober 清醒的 to intemperate 酗酒的 （反义）

★★ eccentric [ekˈsentrɪk] a. 古怪的

记 ec- 朝外 + -centric (center)：超过了 (ec) 这个正常圈 (center) 之外的，就显得很古怪 (eccentric)

考 同义 eccentric = irregular

类比 eccentric 古怪的 to odd 奇怪的 → splendid 灿烂的 to grand 宏伟的 （同义）

eccentric 古怪的 to idiosyncrasy 怪癖 → monotonous 单调的 to ennui 无聊 （同义）

★★★ victory [ˈvɪktəri] n. 胜利

变 victorious a. 胜利的

考 同义 conquest = victory

类比 poor 穷 to rich 富 → defeat 失败 to victory 胜利 （反义）

nomadic 流浪的 to wandering 漫游的 → victorious 胜利的 to winning 获胜的 （同义）

remuneration 报酬 to labor 劳动 → trophy 奖品 to victory 胜利 （事物及其对象）

celebration 庆祝 to victory 胜利 → argument 争论 to disagreement 不一致 （因果）

★★ gaggle [ˈɡæɡl] n. 鹅群

记 一群鹅 (gaggle) 在傻笑 (giggle)

考 类比 breed 一群狗 to dog 狗 → gaggle 鹅群 to goose 鹅 （组成）

wolf 狼 to pack 狼群 → goose 鹅 to gaggle 鹅群 （组成）

gaggle 鹅群 to goose 鹅 → school 鱼群 to fish 鱼 （组成）

★★★ ruthless [ˈruːθlɪs] a. 无情的，残忍的

记 ruth- (rule) + less：因为不 (less) 遵守规则 (rule)，所以被公司被无情 (ruthless) 开除

考 同义 merciless = ruthless；ruthless = brutal；ruthless = unsparing

类比 ruthless 残忍的 to mercy 仁慈 → naïve 幼稚的 to worldliness 世俗 （缺乏）

ruthless 无情的 to compassion 同情 → naïve 幼稚的 to sophistication 世故 （反义）

★ collapse [kəˈlæps] v. 倒塌

记 大学 (college) 宿舍突然倒塌 (collapse)

考 类比 potency 力量 — to — weaken 减弱 ⇒ volume 体积 — to — collapse 倒塌 （事物及其动作）
         allergic 过敏的 — to — sneeze 打喷嚏 ⇒ unstable 不稳定 — to — collapse 倒塌 （因果）

★★ sanctimonious   [ˌsæŋktɪˈməʊnɪəs] *a.* 假装虔诚的

记 sancti-（sanction）制裁 + -monious（admonish）劝告：劝告（admonish）那些假装虔诚的（sanctimonious）人，不忠诚就会受到制裁（sanction）

考 类比 audacious 胆大的 — to — boldness 胆大 ⇒ sanctimonious 假装虔诚的 — to — hypocrisy 虚伪 （同义）
         erudite 博学的 — to — pedantic 迂腐的 ⇒ pious 虔诚的 — to — sanctimonious 假装虔诚的 （同义：正反向）

★ renovation   [ˌrenəˈveɪʃn] *n.* 革新

记 re- + nov- 新 + ation
考 同义 revolution = renovation

★ blatant   [ˈbleɪtnt] *a.* 喧嚣的，公然的

记 老师公然（blatant）接受学生的贿赂，受到大家的一致批评（blame）
考 同义 blatant = obvious

★ napkin   [ˈnæpkɪn] *n.* 餐巾纸

记 绑架（kidnap）餐巾纸（napkin）
考 类比 doormat 门垫 — to — shoes 鞋 ⇒ napkin 餐巾纸 — to — mouth 嘴 （事物及其对象）

★ ethos   [ˈiːθɒs] *n.* 道德风貌

记 我们要尊重少数民族的（ethnic）道德风貌（ethos）
考 类比 ethos 道德风貌 — to — values 价值观念 ⇒ code 准则 — to — principles 准则 （同义）
注 ethos 这个单词的英文释义为：the disposition, character, or fundamental values peculiar to a specific person。

★ rival   [ˈraɪvəl] *n.* 对手

记 为了一条小河（river）的归属，河两岸的村民变成了对手（rival）
考 同义 rival = opponent

★★★ austere   [ɔːˈstɪə] *a.* 简朴的，严峻的，无装饰的

变 austerity *n.* 朴素，苦行
记 谐音：熬死 tear：形势严峻（austere），熬得我眼泪（tear）都出来了
考 同义 austere = severe；austere = plain；austerity = self-discipline

☆ sanctimonious   ☆ renovation   ☆ blatant   ☆ napkin   ☆ ethos
☆ rival   ☆ austere

类比　austere to style ⇒ controlled to movement　（修饰）
　　　简朴的　　造型　　　受约束的　　行为

pedantic [pɪˈdæntɪk] *a.* 迂腐的

记 谐音：皮蛋：总喝皮蛋瘦肉粥的人会比较迂腐（pedantic）
考 类比　erudite to pedantic ⇒ pious to sanctimonious　（同义：正反向）
　　　博学的　迂腐的　　　虔诚的　假装虔诚的

boon [buːn] *n.* 福利，福气

记 传说做梦摸月亮（moon）会比较有福气（boon）
考 同义　boon = gift

recalcitrant [rɪˈkælsɪtrənt] *a.* 叛逆的，反抗的，顽强的

记 re- 反 + calc- 石头 + itrant：他反过来用石头砸你，说明他很叛逆（recalcitrant）
考 同义　stubborn = recalcitrant
　 类比　recalcitrant to obedience ⇒ insolent to respect　（反义）
　　　　叛逆的　　　顺从　　　　无礼的　　尊敬
　　　　refined to vulgar ⇒ submissive to recalcitrant　（反义）
　　　　有教养的　粗俗的　　顺从的　　　叛逆的

abundant [əˈbʌndənt] *a.* 丰富的

变 abundance *n.* 充裕
记 谐音：a 一 + bund 谐音"帮"：一帮一帮地出现，即为很多的（abundant）
考 同义　profusion = abundance；abundant = bounteous；abundant = opulent
　　　　abounding = abundant
　 类比　copious to abundant ⇒ docile to meek　（同义）
　　　　大量的　　大量的　　　温顺的　温顺的
　　　　famine to abundance ⇒ poverty to wealth　（反义）
　　　　饥荒　　大量　　　　贫穷　　财富
　　　　meager to abundant ⇒ decrepit to robust　（反义）
　　　　缺乏的　　大量的　　衰老破旧的　强健的
注 关于"丰富的，大量的"单词在 SSAT 的习题中有很多，如：ample, plentiful。

List | 70 words　　　　　　　　　　　★ 复习一下学过的单词！

□ abash	□ deadlock	□ harbinger	□ profound
□ advertise	□ empathy	□ oasis	□ retard
□ affiliation	□ error	□ planet	□ sincere
□ assortment	□ flee	□ prance	□ spurn
□ complete	□ grief	□ prodigal	□ unflinching

☆ pedantic　　☆ boon　　☆ recalcitrant　　☆ abundant

SSAT词汇 List 72

supplant
[səˈplɑːnt] v. 取代，排挤掉
- 记 种植新的植物（plant），取代（supplant）旧的植物（plant）
- 考 同义 supplant = displace

calamity
[kəˈlæmɪti] n. 灾难
- 变 calamitous a. 灾难的
- 记 cal-（call）+-amity（almighty）全能神：遇到灾难（calamity）想到给全能神（almighty）打电话（call）
- 考 同义 catastrophe = calamity

类比
- problem 问题 to calamity 灾难 → meal 饭 to banquet 酒宴 （<程度）
- ordeal 折磨 to calamity 灾难 → transplant 迁移 to reorient 再调整 （同义）
- crafty 狡猾的 to cunning 狡猾的 → tragic 悲剧的 to calamitous 灾难性的 （同义）
- cavernous 洞穴状的 to hollow 空的 → calamitous 灾难的 to unfortunate 不幸的 （同义）

deluge
[ˈdeljuːdʒ] n. 洪水；v. 压倒
- 记 打开阀门，洪水（deluge）泄露（divulge）出来
- 考 同义 deluge = overwhelm；deluge = flood；deluge = torrent

类比
- drip 水滴 to deluge 洪水 → smolder 闷烧 to blaze 燃烧 （<程度）
- sprinkle 喷洒 to deluge 洪水 → flurry 小风 to blizzard 暴风雪 （<程度）

plaudit
[ˈplɔːdɪt] n. 喝彩，赞美
- 记 谐音 applaud it
- 考 同义 praise = plaudit

saga
[ˈsɑːɡə] n. 传说，冒险故事
- 变 sagacity n. 睿智，智敏

☆ supplant ☆ calamity ☆ deluge ☆ plaudit ☆ saga

记 这个单词本是"传说，冒险"的意思，主要描述在冰岛定居的挪威国王的历史和早期日耳曼英雄的神话传说
考 同义 sagacity = wisdom

类比 saga/冒险故事 to story/故事 ⇒ lullaby/摇篮曲 to song/歌曲 （种属）

★ suffuse
[sə'fjuːz] v. 充满

记 因为充满（suffuse），所以满溢（sufficient）
考 同义 suffuse = imbue

★★★ anthology
[æn'θɒlədʒi] n. 选集

记 注意区分"选集"anthology 和"人类学"anthropology
考 类比
journal/期刊 to article/文章 ⇒ anthology/诗集 to poem/古诗 （组成）
medley/混合曲 to song/歌曲 ⇒ anthology/选集 to story/故事 （组成）
song/歌曲 to playlist/播放列表 ⇒ poem/古诗 to anthology/诗集 （组成）
essay/文章 to paragraph/段落 ⇒ anthology/作品集 to works/作品 （组成）
lexicon/词典 to words/单词 ⇒ anthology/作品集 to works/作品 （组成）
anthology/作品集 to lexicon/词典 ⇒ works/作品 to words/单词 （纵向）

★★★ sluggish
['slʌgɪʃ] a. 萧条的，懒惰的

记 市场萧条（sluggish）到坐飞机都不能免费托运行李箱（luggage）了
考 同义 sluggish = slow; sluggish = listless

类比 torpid/不活泼的 to sluggish/懒惰的 ⇒ comic/好笑的 to funny/搞笑的 （同义）

★★ lavish
['lævɪʃ] a. 丰富的，过分大方的

记 lav- 古法语词根表示"水"，原指"花钱如流水一般地奢侈"
考 同义 munificent = lavish; lavish = extravagant; fete = lavish party

类比 sufficient/充足的 to plentiful/大量的 ⇒ adequate/充足的 to lavish/丰富的 （纵向）

★ hybrid
['haɪbrɪd] a. 混合的

记 著名摇滚乐队林肯公园（Linkin Park）的第一张专辑就叫《混合理论》（Hybrid Theory）
考 类比 purebred/纯种的（反义） to hybrid/混合的 ⇒ pedigreed/纯的 to mongrel/杂交的

hybrid

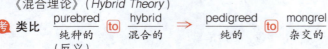

impede

[ɪmˈpiːd] *v.* 妨碍，阻碍

变 impediment *n.* 妨碍，阻碍
记 im- (in) + ped- 脚 + e：脚 (ped) 朝内 (in) 放，阻碍 (impede) 别人通行
考 同义 obstacle = impediment；impediment = hindrance；impede = block

类比 obstruct / 妨碍 to impede / 阻碍 ⇒ impenetrable / 不能通过的 to impervious / 无法入侵的 （同义）

注 关于"阻碍"的单词在 SSAT 的习题中有很多，如：thwart, foil, prevent, hinder, frustrate。

annihilate

[əˈnaɪəleɪt] *v.* 歼灭，战胜

记 an + nihil- 无，零 + ate：歼灭 (annihilate) 敌人，使其什么都不剩
考 同义 annihilate = obliterate

pugilist

[ˈpjuːdʒɪlɪst] *n.* 拳击手

记 pugi 普吉岛 + list 名单：他是普吉岛 (pugi) 警察黑名单 (list) 上的地下拳手 (pugilist)
考 同义 pugilist = fighter

类比 pugilist / 拳击手 to boxing / 拳击 ⇒ cartographer / 地图编辑者 to map / 地图 （人物及其对象）

fulfill

[fʊlˈfɪl] *v.* 履行，实现

变 fulfillment *n.* 履行，实现
记 ful- (full) 满 + fill 满
考 同义 fulfill = accomplish

类比 ambition / 雄心 to accomplishment / 成就 ⇒ craving / 渴望 to fulfillment / 实现 （时间先后）

knack

[næk] *n.* 本领

记 敲 (knock) 开师傅家的门，拜师学艺 (knack)
考 同义 knack = ability

contradict

[ˌkɒntrəˈdɪkt] *v.* 矛盾

变 contradiction *n.* 矛盾
记 contra- (against) + dict- 说话：两人反着 (against) 说话，产生矛盾 (contradict)
考 同义 contradiction = paradox

类比 contradict / 矛盾 to opposition / 相反 ⇒ comply / 顺从 to obedience / 听话 （同义）

earnestness / 认真 to ingenuousness / 率直 ⇒ contradiction / 矛盾 to opposition / 反对 （同义）

☆ impede ☆ annihilate ☆ pugilist ☆ fulfill ☆ knack
☆ contradict

beneficial ★★★

[ˌbenɪˈfɪʃl] *a.* 有好处的

变 beneficent *a.* 慈善的，善行的；benefit *v.* 对……有益；benefactor *n.* 做好事者

考 同义 beneficent = merciful；beneficent = bountiful；benefit = assist；beneficial = salutary
benefactor = contributor；benefactor = supporter

类比 filch (to) pickpocket ⇒ endow (to) benefactor （人物及其特点）
偷窃　　　扒手　　　　给予　　　捐助者

miser (to) generous ⇒ benefactor (to) stingy （反义）
小气鬼　　大方的　　　捐赠者　　　吝啬

注 关于"有益的，有利的"单词在 SSAT 的习题中有很多，如：favorable，profitable，propitious，valuable，advantageous。

pernicious ★★

[pəˈnɪʃəs] *a.* 有毒的

记 谐音：泼你：用有毒的（pernicious）液体泼你一身
考 同义 pernicious = harmful

类比 pernicious (to) benign ⇒ obligatory (to) optional （反义）
有毒的　　良性的　　　必需的　　可选择的

spouse ★

[spaʊz] *n.* 配偶

记 买房（house）是找媳妇（spouse）的前提
考 类比 marital (to) spouse ⇒ fraternal (to) brother （同义）
婚姻的　　配偶　　　兄弟般的　　兄弟

reptile ★★★

[ˈreptaɪl] *n.* 爬行动物

考 类比 dodo (to) bird ⇒ dinosaur (to) reptile （种属）
渡渡鸟　　鸟　　　恐龙　　　爬行动物

human (to) primate ⇒ snake (to) reptile （种属）
人类　　灵长类动物　　蛇　　　爬行动物

frog (to) amphibian ⇒ dinosaur (to) reptile （种属）
青蛙　　两栖动物　　　恐龙　　　爬行动物

crocodile (to) reptile ⇒ kangaroo (to) marsupial （种属）
鳄鱼　　爬行类动物　　袋鼠　　　有袋类动物

List | **71** words　　　　　　　　★ 复习一下学过的单词！

□ abundant	□ collapse	□ lubricant	□ renovation
□ affluent	□ eccentric	□ napkin	□ rival
□ austere	□ ethos	□ nemesis	□ ruthless
□ blatant	□ gaggle	□ pedantic	□ sanctimonious
□ boon	□ grimace	□ recalcitrant	□ victory

SSAT词汇 List 73

★★ recluse
[rɪˈkluːs] *n.* 隐士

变 reclusive *a.* 隐居的
记 re- + -cluse (close): 重复 (re) 把自己关 (close) 起来的人即为隐士 (recluse)
考 类比 reclusive 隐居的 to sociable 好社交的 → taciturn 沉默的 to chatty 爱聊天的 (反义)
recluse 隐士 to publicity 公开 → anarchist 无政府主义者 to order 规则 (人物及其对象)

★ banish
[ˈbænɪʃ] *v.* 放逐,驱逐

记 不仅他的作品在本国被禁止 (ban),而且他本人也被驱逐 (banish)
考 同义 banish = remove; exile = banish
类比 evict 驱逐 to residence 住宅 → banish 驱逐 to country 国家 (动作及其对象)

★ prerogative
[prɪˈrɒɡətɪv] *n.* 特权

记 原指在古罗马社会中第一拨实行投票的群体,因为罗马人认为第一拨投票的人很重要,应该拥有"特权"
考 同义 prerogative = choice

★★★ enormous
[ɪˈnɔːməs] *a.* 巨大的

记 e- 朝外 + norm- (normal) + ous:超过标准号即为巨大的 (enormous)
考 同义 enormous = prodigious; enormous statue = colossus; tremendous = enormous
类比 enormous 巨大的 to miniscule 极小的 → eradicate 根除 to establish 建立 (反义)
enormous 巨大的 to colossal 巨大的 → fundamental 基础的 to rudimentary 基础的 (同义)

★ aggrandize
[əˈɡrændaɪz] *v.* 增大,夸张

变 aggrandizement *n.* 增大,夸张

☆ recluse ☆ banish ☆ prerogative ☆ enormous ☆ aggrandize

记 ag- 加强 + grand 宏伟的，壮大的 + -ize
考 同义 aggrandizement = exaggeration
类比 aggrandize 增大 to increase 增加 ⇒ desiccate 变干 to dryness 干燥 （同义）

★ precarious [prɪˈkeərɪəs] a. 危险的，不确定的

记 pre- 提前 + cari- (care) + -ous：因为太危险 (precarious)，所以需要提前 (pre) 关心 (care)
考 类比 precarious 危险的 to safe 安全的 ⇒ muddy 模糊的 to clear 清楚的 （反义）

★★ phenomenon [fɪˈnɒmɪnən] n. 现象

变 phenomenal a. 现象级的，显著的
记 ph + -enomenon (enormous)：这个池塘 pH 值很大 (enormous)，是个奇怪的现象 (phenomenon)
考 同义 phenomenon = occurrence；phenomenal = extraordinary

★ tolerate [ˈtɒləreɪt] v. 容忍

考 同义 tolerate = allow

★★★ mirror [ˈmɪrə] n. 镜子；v. 模仿

考 同义 imitate = mirror
类比
window 窗户 to wall 墙 ⇒ mirror 镜子 to car 车 （空间）
pane 窗格 to window 窗户 ⇒ mirror 镜子 to dresser 梳妆台 （组成）
anvil 铁砧 to heavy 重的 ⇒ mirror 镜子 to smooth 光滑的 （修饰）
mirror 镜子 to reflection 反射 ⇒ bicycle 自行车 to ride 骑 （事物及其用途）
lens 镜片 to spectacles 眼镜 ⇒ mirror 镜子 to dresser 梳妆台 （事物及其部分）

★ highwayman [ˈhaɪweɪmən] n. 强盗

考 同义 highwayman = robber

★★★ obedient [əˈbiːdɪənt] a. 顺从的，服从的

变 obedience n. 顺从，服从；disobedient a. 不服从的
记 obedient 的动词形式是我们熟悉的 obey
考 同义 docile = obedient；amenable = obedient
类比 frugal 节俭的 to spending 花费 ⇒ unruly 不守规矩的 to obedient 听话的 （反义）

obedience 听话	to	submissiveness 顺从	⇒	outset 开始	to	commencement 开始	（同义）
contradict 矛盾	to	opposition 相反	⇒	comply 顺从	to	obedience 听话	（同义）
recalcitrant 叛逆的	to	obedience 听话的	⇒	insolent 傲慢的	to	respect 尊敬	（反义）
adept 熟练的	to	unskilled 不熟练的	⇒	mischievous 淘气的	to	obedient 顺从的	（反义）
fractious 易怒的	to	obedience 不听话	⇒	rigid 僵硬的	to	adaptability 适应性	（缺乏）
disobedient 不服从的	to	compliance 顺从	⇒	inconsistent 不一致的	to	dependability 可靠性	（反义）

★

cupidity

[kjuːˈpɪdɪti] *n.* 贪心，贪婪

记 cupidity 来自于"爱神丘比特"（cupid），大家可以想象他是一个贪婪的家伙
考 同义 cupidity = avarice

类比 cupidity 贪婪 to voracious 贪婪的 ⇒ humility 谦虚 to modest 谦虚的 （同义）

★★★

stealth

[stelθ] *n.* 绝密，秘密

变 stealthy *a.* 秘密的
记 医院对于病人的健康（health）状况持保密（stealth）态度
考 同义 stealthy = concealed

类比 burglar 盗贼 to stealth 鬼鬼祟祟 ⇒ miser 吝啬鬼 to greed 贪婪 （人物及其特点）

disingenuous 狡猾的 to craftiness 狡猾 ⇒ surreptitious 秘密的 to stealth 秘密 （同义）

注 关于"秘密的"单词在 SSAT 的习题中有很多，如：covert, furtive, clandestine, surreptitious。

★★★

appease

[əˈpiːz] *v.* 使平息，使满足

记 ap- + -pease（peace）：平息（appease）事端，以达到和平（peace）状态
考 同义 satisfy = appease; appease = mitigate; conciliate = appease

类比 appease 安抚 to anger 生气 ⇒ enlighten 启发 to ignorance 无知 （因果）

注 关于"平息，安慰"的单词在 SSAT 的习题中有很多，如：soothe, calm, pacify, mollify, lull, quell。

★

facet

[ˈfæsɪt] *n.* 方面，表面

记 你的脸（face）只能代表你这个人的表面（facet）而已
考 同义 facet = aspect

blender ★★
['blendə] v. 搅拌机

记 借出方 (lender) 借给你一个搅拌机 (blender)

考 类比 drill 钻子 to hole 孔 → blender 搅拌器 to batter 面糊 （事物及其目的）

chisel 凿子 to carving 雕刻 → blender 搅拌机 to mixing 混合 （事物及其目的）

condescend ★
[ˌkɒndɪˈsend] v. 屈尊，俯就

变 condescending a. 屈尊的

记 con- + descend 下降：大家都放下身段，即为屈尊 (condescend)

考 同义 condescend = stoop; condescending = superior

类比 condescending 屈尊的 to respect 尊敬 → merciless 无情的 to compassion 同情 （反义）

注 关于"家长的，居高临下的"单词在 SSAT 的习题中有很多，如：paternalistic, patronizing, dismissive, oppressive。

automobile ★★
[ˈɔːtəməʊbiːl] n. 汽车

考 类比 bush 灌木丛 to shrub 灌木丛 → car 车 to automobile 汽车 （同义）

rife ★★
[raɪf] a. 普遍的，流行的

记 中国在婚姻方面普遍的 (rife) 做法是一夫一妻 (wife) 制

考 同义 rife = widespread

crafty ★★
[ˈkrɑːfti] a. 狡猾的

记 用狡猾的 (crafty) 手段溜上飞机 (aircraft)

考 同义 crafty = sly; crafty = wily

类比 crafty 狡猾的 to cunning 狡猾的 → tragic 悲剧的 to calamitous 灾难性的 （同义）

List | 72 words ★ 复习一下学过的单词！

□ annihilate	□ deluge	□ lavish	□ saga
□ anthology	□ fulfill	□ pernicious	□ sluggish
□ beneficial	□ hybrid	□ plaudit	□ spouse
□ calamity	□ impede	□ pugilist	□ suffuse
□ contradict	□ knack	□ reptile	□ supplant

☆ blender ☆ condescend ☆ automobile ☆ rife ☆ crafty

SSAT词汇 List 74

★ feral
['fɪərəl] *a.* 野生的，凶猛的

记 野生（feral）动物都好凶猛（fierce）
考 类比　feral/野生的 to domestication/驯养 → crude/粗鲁的 to refinement/文雅　（反义）

★★ seal
[si:l] *n.* 海豹；*v.* 密封

变 sealed *a.* 密封的
记 美国海豹突击队取 Sea（海）、Air（空）、Land（陆）之意构成英文 SEAL
考 类比　seal/海豹 to fur/皮毛 → peacock/孔雀 to feather/羽毛　（事物及其部分）
　　　　capacious/宽敞的 to cramped/狭窄的 → agape/张开的 to sealed/封着的　（反义）

★ cheat
[tʃi:t] *v.* 欺骗

考 同义　cheat = bilk；cheat = swindle；adulterate = cheat

★ poise
[pɔɪz] *n.* 平衡，镇定；*v.* 使平衡

记 站好了（poise），摆个 POSE 来拍照
考 同义　poise = equilibrium

★★★ gem
[dʒem] *n.* 宝石

记 交通堵塞（jam）导致抢劫了宝石（gem）的劫匪无法脱逃
考 类比　rose/玫瑰 to plant/植物 → emerald/绿宝石 to gem/宝石　（种属）
　　　　gem/宝石 to turquoise/绿松石 → flower/花 to violet/紫罗兰　（种属）
　　　　mineral/矿物 to quartz/石英 → gem/宝石 to sapphire/蓝宝石　（种属）

shoe 鞋 → moccasin 软帮鞋　⇒　gem 宝石 → ruby 红宝石　（种属）

gem 宝石 → stone 石头　⇒　jewel 珠宝 → rock 石头　（种属）

（这个题的思路有些复杂：gem 是一种加工过后的 stone，而 jewel 则是一种加工过后的 rock）

★★★ soothe　[suːð] v. 安慰，缓和

变 soothing a. 安慰的

记 对自己的熊孩子恨得咬牙切齿（tooth），但还要安慰（soothe）自己说他只是个孩子

考 同义　soothe = calm；soothe = pacify；soothe = placate

类比　irk 使烦恼 → soothing 安慰的　⇒　support 支持 → undermining 暗中破坏的　（反义）

★★ sartorial　[sɑːˈtɔːriəl] a. 裁缝的

记 sar-（sir）+ -totial（tailor）：这位先生（sir）是个裁缝（tailor），所以他做一些裁缝的（sartorial）活

考 类比　pecuniary 金钱的 → money 钱　⇒　sartorial 裁缝的 → sew 缝　（同义）

culinary 厨房的 → cook 做饭　⇒　sartorial 裁缝的 → sew 缝　（事情及动作）

★ poll　[pəʊl] v. 投票，选举

记 拉（pull）着朋友一起去投票（poll）

考 同义　poll = survey

★★ obdurate　[ˈɒbdjʊərət] a. 顽固的，固执的

记 ob- 相反 + dur-（during）+ -ate：顽固（obdurate）的人婚姻都不会长久（during）

考 同义　obdurate = stubborn；adamant = obdurate

★ monologue　[ˈmɒnəlɒɡ] n. 独白

记 mono- 一个 + -logue（language）：一个人的语言即为独白（monologue）

考 类比　aria 咏叹调 → opera 歌剧　⇒　monologue 独白 → play 戏剧　（种属）

monologue 独白 → speech 演讲　⇒　solo 独奏 → play 表演　（种属）

actor 演员 → monologue 独白　⇒　dancer 舞者 → solo 独舞　（人物及其动作）

ungainly

[ʌnˈgeɪnli] *a.* 笨拙的，不雅的

记 un- + gain + -ly：参加比赛，一无所获，显得很笨拙（ungainly）

考 同义 ungainly = clumsy；ungainly = inept

类比 timeless 永恒的 to ephemeral 短暂的 ⇒ ungainly 笨拙的 to dexterous 敏捷的 （反义）

drought

[ˈdraʊt] *n.* 干旱

记 长期不下雨带来（brought）了干旱（drought）

考 类比 drought 干旱 to rain 下雨 ⇒ famine 饥荒 to nourishment 营养 （缺乏）

famine 饥荒 to food 食物 ⇒ drought 干旱 to water 水 （缺乏）

flood 洪水 to drought 干旱 ⇒ rich 富有的 to poor 穷的 （反义）

desist

[dɪˈzɪst] *v.* 停止

记 我坚持（insist）这次会议应该立即停止（desist）

考 类比 desist 停止 to cease 停止 ⇒ resist 抵制 to oppose 反对 （同义）

calligrapher

[kəˈlɪgrəfə] *n.* 书法家

记 谐音：凯丽（Kelly）+ graph- 写：Kelly 字写得很好，她是一位书法家（calligrapher）

考 类比 painter 画家 to brush 刷子 ⇒ calligrapher 书法家 to pen 笔 （人物及其工具）

corral

[kəˈrɑːl] *n.* 畜栏

记 畜栏（corral）里有好多胡萝卜（carrot）

考 类比 hive 蜂房 to swarm 蜂群 ⇒ corral 畜栏 to herd 兽群 （空间）

abscond

[əbˈskɒnd] *v.* 潜逃

记 潜逃（abscond）的时候不能耽误一分一秒（second）

考 同义 abscond = leave

类比 abscond 潜逃 to depart 离开 ⇒ lurk 潜伏 to wait 等待 （同义：正反向）

sword

[sɔːd] *n.* 剑

记 说话（word）不雅，如刀剑（sword）般伤人

考 类比
sword 剑 to sheath 剑鞘 ⇒ coin 硬币 to pocket 口袋 （空间）
sword 剑 to fence 击剑 ⇒ glove 手套 to box 拳击 （事物及其部分）
sword 剑 to dueling 决斗 ⇒ pen 钢笔 to writing 写作 （事物及其用途）

★★ resist [rɪˈzɪst] v. 抵制，抵抗

考 同义 withstand = resist
类比
lazy 懒惰的 to inert 惰性的 ⇒ resist 抵制 to refuse 拒绝 （同义）
desist 停止 to cease 停止 ⇒ resist 抵制 to oppose 反对 （同义）

★ deck [dek] n. 一副牌

记 桌子（desk）上放着一副牌（deck）
变 类比
member 成员 to team 队伍 ⇒ card 纸牌 to deck 一副牌 （组成）
card 卡片 to deck 一副牌 ⇒ note 音符 to symphony 交响乐 （组成）

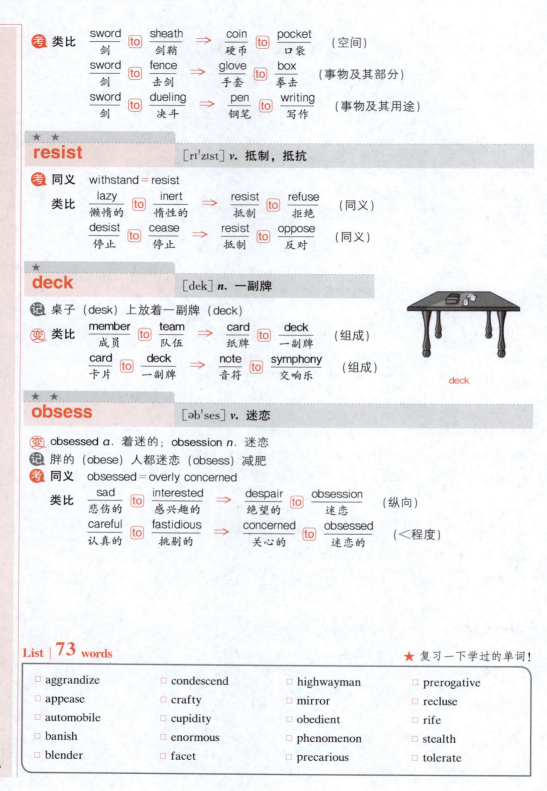
deck

★★ obsess [əbˈses] v. 迷恋

变 obsessed a. 着迷的；obsession n. 迷恋
记 胖的（obese）人都迷恋（obsess）减肥
考 同义 obsessed = overly concerned
类比
sad 悲伤的 to interested 感兴趣的 ⇒ despair 绝望的 to obsession 迷恋 （纵向）
careful 认真的 to fastidious 挑剔的 ⇒ concerned 关心的 to obsessed 迷恋的 （＜程度）

List | 73 words ★ 复习一下学过的单词！

- aggrandize
- appease
- automobile
- banish
- blender
- condescend
- crafty
- cupidity
- enormous
- facet
- highwayman
- mirror
- obedient
- phenomenon
- precarious
- prerogative
- recluse
- rife
- stealth
- tolerate

SSAT词汇 List 75

dynamic
[daɪˈnæmɪk] *a.* 动力的，有活力的
记 dy-（die）+ nam-（name）+ ic：死（die）后名（name）声大作，比生前更有活力（dynamic）
考 同义 dynamic = vital

discursive
[dɪˈskɜːsɪv] *a.* 散漫的，离题的
记 论文（discourse）写得有点离题（discursive）
考 类比 discursive 离题的 to focus 焦点 ⇒ verbose 啰嗦的 to brevity 简洁 （缺乏）

solo
[ˈsəʊləʊ] *n.* 独奏
变 soloist *n.* 独奏者
考 同义 soloist = performer
类比 monologue 独白 to speech 演讲 ⇒ solo 独奏 to play 表演 （种属）
actor 演员 to monologue 独白 ⇒ dancer 舞者 to solo 独舞 （人物及其动作）

insinuate
[ɪnˈsɪnjueɪt] *v.* 暗示
记 她暗示（insinuate）我，我的女朋友待人不真诚（insincere）
考 同义 insinuate = hint
类比 infiltrate 渗入 to enter 进入 ⇒ insinuate 暗示 to say 说话 （＜程度）
注 关于"暗示"的单词在 SSAT 的习题中有很多，如：imply, innuendo, allude。

flammable
[ˈflæməbl] *a.* 易燃的
变 inflammable *a.* 易燃的；inflammatory *a.* 煽动的
记 flamma-（flame）火焰 + -able
考 同义 incendiary = inflammatory

类比　fragile 脆弱的 — to — break 打碎　⇒　flammable 易燃的 — to — burn 燃烧　（因果）

　　　flammable 易燃的 — to — inflammable 易燃的　⇒　impartial 公正的 — to — disinterested 公正的　（同义）

★★ limber　['lɪmbə] a. 柔软的，敏捷的

记　身手敏捷（limber）是一个合格的爬山者（climber）的前提
考　同义　limber = supple；limber = soft

★★ fortify　['fɔːtɪfaɪ] v. 加强

变　fortified a. 加强的
记　加强（fortify）城堡（fort）外围建设
考　同义　fortify = strengthen

类比　abbreviate 缩短 — to — short 短的　⇒　fortify 加强 — to — strong 强壮的　（因果）

　　　hostile 敌意的 — to — nemesis 复仇　⇒　fortified 加强的 — to — stronghold 要塞　（修饰）

★ pit　[pɪt] n. 地洞；核

记　地洞（pit）里有只猪（pig）
考　同义　abyss = pit

类比　core 苹果核 — to — apple 苹果　⇒　pit 桃核 — to — peach 桃子　（空间）

★★★ condole　[kən'dəul] v. 慰问，吊唁

变　condolence n. 哀悼
记　给仇人的家属送去慰问（condole），得到了仇人的宽恕（condone）
考　同义　condolence = comfort；condolence = sympathetic response

类比　condolence 哀悼 — to — grief 悲痛　⇒　commendation 赞扬 — to — success 成功　（因果）

注　关于"同情"的单词在 SSAT 的习题中有很多，如：compassion，forgiveness。

★★ auditorium　[ɔːdɪ'tɔːrɪəm] n. 礼堂

记　audi- 听：在礼堂（auditorium）听演讲
考　类比　auditorium 礼堂 — to — lecture 讲座　⇒　theater 剧场 — to — concert 演唱会　（空间）

　　　gymnasium 体育馆 — to — games 运动　⇒　auditorium 礼堂 — to — production 产品　（空间）

★ capitulate [kəˈpɪtʃʊleɪt] v. 投降

- 记 船长（capitan）被抓，船员只好对海盗投降（capitulate）
- 考 同义 capitulate = surrender
  - 类比 capitulate 投降 to surrender 认输 ⇒ remonstrate 抗议 to protest 抗议 （同义）

★★ insipid [ɪnˈsɪpɪd] a. 清淡的，无趣的

- 记 in + sip 小口喝 + id：小口喝酒，觉得清淡无味（insipid）
- 考 同义 insipid = dull
  - 类比 insipid 平淡的 to spirit 精神 ⇒ free 自由的 to restraint 限制 （缺乏）
  - insipid 清淡的 to food 食物 ⇒ banal 平庸的 to conversation 谈话 （修饰）
  - dull 无聊的 to insipid 清淡的 ⇒ diverting 有趣的 to entertaining 娱乐的 （同义）

★★★ prevail [prɪˈveɪl] v. 盛行，战胜

- 变 prevalent a. 流行的，普遍的；prevailing a. 流行的，盛行的
- 考 同义 prevail = triumph；prevail = win；predominant = prevalent
  prevalent = widespread；prevailing = dominant

★ brook [brʊk] n. 小河

- 记 布鲁克林（Brooklyn）区有一条小河（brook）
- 考 类比 lake 湖 to pond 池塘 ⇒ river 河流 to brook 小河 （>程度）
- 注 关于"小河"的单词在 SSAT 的习题中有很多，如：creek, rill。

★ insulate [ˈɪnsjʊleɪt] v. 隔离

- 记 这个明星自动隔离（insulate）了外界对他的所有不利评价（insult）
- 考 类比 fan 电扇 to circulate 流通 ⇒ wall 墙 to insulate 隔离 （事物及其动作）

★ lapel [ləˈpel] n. 翻领

- 记 这件衣服的商标（label）被贴在翻领（lapel）的位置
- 考 类比 lapel 西服翻领 to chest 胸 ⇒ cuff 袖口 to arm 胳膊 （空间）

lapel

appeal ★
[əˈpiːl] v. 请求

记 在婚礼上出现（appear）了一个不速之客，请求（appeal）新娘不要嫁给新郎
考 同义　appeal = plea

cantankerous ★★★
[kænˈtæŋkərəs] a. 脾气坏的

记 谐音：开坦克的：看，坦克都开上了，这人的脾气还是很坏（cantankerous）
考 同义　cantankerous = irascible
注 关于"脾气不好的"单词在 SSAT 的习题中有很多，如：irritable, choleric, enraged, irate。

atone ★
[əˈtəʊn] v. 赎罪，弥补

变 atonement n. 赎罪
记 古有负荆请罪，今有负石（stone）请罪（atone）
　 2007 年奥斯卡最佳影片（提名）为 Atonement
考 同义　atone = repent
类比　atonement 弥补 to amendment 改善 ⇒ edifice 大建筑 to impressive structure 大建筑　（同义）

atone
2007 奥斯卡最佳影片

secure ★★★
[sɪˈkjʊə] a. 安全的；v. 保护

变 security n. 安全；insecurity n. 不安全
考 同义　capture = secure；secure = safe；impregnable = secure
类比　threat 威胁 to insecurity 不安全 ⇒ horror 恐惧 to fear 害怕　（因果）
　　　harness 马具 to secure 保护 ⇒ girder 大梁 to support 支撑　（事物及其用途）
　　　security 保安 to guard building 大楼 ⇒ keeper 看守人 to lighthouse 灯塔　（人物及其对象）

List | 74 words　　　　　　　　　　　　　★ 复习一下学过的单词！

- abscond
- calligrapher
- cheat
- corral
- deck
- desist
- drought
- feral
- gem
- monologue
- obdurate
- obsess
- poise
- poll
- resist
- sartorial
- seal
- soothe
- sword
- ungainly

SSAT词汇 List 76

ounce
[aʊns] *n.* 盎司

记 可以通过对应的发音来记忆
考 类比 gram 克 to ounce 盎司 ⇒ meter 米 to mile 英里 (同类)

confidential
[ˌkɒnfɪˈdenʃl] *a.* 机密的

变 confide *v.* 吐露，委托
记 虽然我很自信（confident）这件事是真的，但我依旧对此事保密（confidential）
考 同义 confide = entrust；confidential = secret
类比 ambitious 雄心的 to determined 坚决的 ⇒ confidential 机密的 to private 私人的 (同义)

masterpiece
[ˈmɑːstəpiːs] *n.* 杰作

记 大师（master）的一张纸（piece）也是杰作（masterpiece）
考 类比 artist 艺术家 to masterpiece 杰作 ⇒ author 作者 to bestseller 畅销书 (人物及其对象)
artist 艺术家 to masterpiece 杰作 ⇒ seamstress 女裁缝 to quilt 被子 (人物及其对象)

fluctuate
[ˈflʌktʃueɪt] *v.* 波动，摇摆

变 fluctuation *n.* 起伏，波动
记 flu-（flow）+ tuate：水流（flow）在波动（fluctuate）
考 同义 fluctuate = waver；fluctuate = vacillate

annotation
[ˌænəʊˈteɪʃn] *n.* 注释，注解

记 an + not-（note）+ ation：把别人的笔记（note）当作注解（annotation）
考 同义 annotation = explanation；annotation = textual comment

☆ ounce　　☆ confidential　　☆ masterpiece　　☆ fluctuate　　☆ annotation

poison ★★★ ['pɔɪzn] v. 中毒

- 变 poisonous a. 有毒的；poisoning n. 中毒
- 考 同义 poisonous = toxic

类比
- poison 毒药 to toxic 有毒的 ⇒ sugar 糖 to sweet 甜的 （修饰）
- strip 条纹 to zebra 斑马 ⇒ poison 毒 to cobra 眼镜蛇 （事物及其特点）
- poison 毒药 to skull and crossbone 头骨骷髅形 ⇒ love 爱 to heart 心形 （修饰）
- antibiotic 抗生素 to infection 感染 ⇒ antidote 解药 to poisoning 中毒 （事物及其用途）

fraud ★ [frɔːd] n. 骗子，欺骗

- 变 fraudulent a. 欺骗性的；defraud v. 欺骗
- 记 弗洛伊德 (Freud) 是个骗子 (fraud)
- 考 同义 fraud = deception；embezzle = defraud；fraudulent = deceitful

prolong ★★ [prə'lɒŋ] v. 延长

- 记 pro- 朝前 + long
- 考 同义 prolong = lengthen

类比
- prolong 延长 to time 时间 ⇒ expand 扩大 to space 空间 （动宾）

infirmary ★ [ɪn'fɜːməri] n. 医务室

- 记 有一次我课上说医务室的英文是 infirmary，学生问我："老师，为什么还专门给义乌市找个对应的英文啊？是因为它们小商品比较火吗？"
- 考 同义 infirmary = dispensary

annul ★ [ə'nʌl] v. 取消，废除

- 记 an- + -nul 无效，零：今天的德语中的"无效"依旧用这个词表示
- 考 同义 annul = cancel

imperious ★ [ɪm'pɪəriəs] a. 专横的，傲慢的

- 记 im- (in) + -perious (period)：这个演员当年拍戏期间 (period) 非常傲慢 (imperious)
  傲慢的 (imperious) 人不管别人如何评价，他都不受其影响 (impervious)

- 考 同义 ceremonious = imperious

schism
★

['skɪzəm] *n.* 分裂

📝 sch-（school）+ -ism：学校（school）里的很多小派别（ism）间产生了分裂（schism）

🔍 类比 fracture/骨折 to bone/骨头 ⇒ schism/分裂 to church/教堂 （事物及其动作）

agony
★★★

['ægəni] *n.* 极大痛苦

🔄 agonize *v.* 使痛苦；agonizing *a.* 苦恼的

📝 谐音：爱过你：因为爱过你，所以现在分手觉得十分痛苦（agony）

🔍 同义 anguish = agonize；excruciating = agonizing

类比 mirth/欢乐 to misery/痛苦 ⇒ bliss/极乐 to agony/痛苦 （反义）

daydream/白日梦 to hallucination/幻觉 ⇒ pain/痛苦 to agony/极大痛苦 （<程度）

inconsistent
★

[ˌɪnkən'sɪstənt] *a.* 不一致的，前后矛盾的

📝 in-否定 + consistent 一致的

🔍 同义 erratic = inconsistent

类比 disobedient/不服从的 to compliance/顺从 ⇒ inconsistent/不一致的 to dependability/可靠性 （反义）

intimidate
★

[ɪn'tɪmɪdeɪt] *v.* 威胁

📝 竟然被自己的好友（intimate）给威胁（intimidate）了，感觉很生气

🔍 类比 intimidate/恐吓 to daunt/恐吓 ⇒ dismay/使惊慌 to horrify/使恐惧 （同义）

brandish/挥舞 to threat/威胁 ⇒ browbeat/恫吓 to intimidate/威胁 （动作及其目的）

berate
★★★

[bɪ'reɪt] *v.* 严责，申斥

📝 评估（rate）没达标，所以被批评（berate）

🔍 同义 berate = criticize；scold = berate；berate = chide

类比 berate/严责 to criticize/批评 ⇒ goad/激励 to urge/催促 （同义）

📌 关于"批评"的单词在 SSAT 的习题中有很多，如：reprimand, censure, reproach, disparage。

scurry
★★

['skʌri] *v.* 疾跑

📝 她快速跑去（scurry）饭店吃咖喱（curry）

同义 scurry = hurry

类比 walk 走路 to scurry 快走 ⇒ jog 慢跑 to sprint 快跑 （<程度）

★★★ archipelago [ˌɑːkɪˈpeləɡəʊ] n. 群岛

记 arch 弧 + ipelago 谐音：拍个够：站在呈现出弧（arch）形的群岛（archipelago）前让你拍照一次拍个够

考 类比
archipelago 群岛 to island 岛 ⇒ swarm 蜂群 to bee 蜜蜂 （组成）
juror 陪审团成员 to jury 陪审团 ⇒ island 岛 to archipelago 群岛 （组成）
link 一个链条 to chain 链条 ⇒ island 岛 to archipelago 群岛 （组成）

★ ponderous [ˈpɒndərəs] a. 笨重的

记 谐音：胖得要死

考 同义 ponderous = heavy

类比 ponderous 笨重的 to heavy 重的 ⇒ deferential 恭敬的 to respectful 尊敬的 （同义）

★ lenient [ˈliːnɪənt] a. 宽大的，仁慈的

记 谐音：列宁：据说列宁是个很仁慈的（lenient）人

考 类比 lenient 宽大的 to permissive 许可的 ⇒ chummy 亲密的 to familiar 熟悉的 （同义）

List | 75 words　　　　★ 复习一下学过的单词！

☐ appeal	☐ capitulate	☐ fortify	☐ limber
☐ atone	☐ condole	☐ insinuate	☐ pit
☐ auditorium	☐ discursive	☐ insipid	☐ prevail
☐ brook	☐ dynamic	☐ insulate	☐ secure
☐ cantankerous	☐ flammable	☐ lapel	☐ solo

alter
★★

['ɔːltə] v. 改变，更改

变 alteration n. 改变
记 我警告（alert）你，别乱更改（alter）这个房间家具的摆设
考 同义 alter = change；modify = alter

类比
alter 改变 to revise 修改 ⇒ discard 抛弃 to delete 删除 （同义）
alter 更改 to distort 扭曲 ⇒ bump 碰撞 to collide 冲突 （同义）
transition 转变 to alteration 改变 ⇒ start 开始 to initiation 开始 （同义）

adamant
★★

['ædəmənt] a. 坚定的

记 亚当（Adam）是个意志坚定的（adamant）孩子
考 同义 adamant = unbreakable；adamant = stubborn；adamant = obdurate
注 关于"坚定的"单词在 SSAT 的习题中有很多，如：determined，rigid，resolute，unyielding。

casualty
★

['kæʒʊəlti] n. 伤亡人员

记 过马路的时候过于随意（casual），结果变成伤亡人员（casualty）之一
考 类比 casualty 伤亡人员 to injury 受伤 ⇒ pioneer 拓荒者 to settlement 定居 （人物及其特点）
（pioneer 这个单词的英文释义为：one of the first to settle in a territory）

emphatic
★

[ɪm'fætɪk] a. 强调的

记 这个单词的名词形式是我们熟悉的 emphasis，动词形式则是 emphasize
考 同义 emphatic = forceful

confirm
★★★

[kən'fɜːm] v. 确认

变 confirmation n. 确认

考 同义 confirm = certify; confirm = corroborate; confirmation = corroboration

类比 confirm 确认 `to` deny 否认 ⇒ accept 接受 `to` reject 拒绝 （反义）

★ pledge
[pledʒ] *v.* 保证，许诺

记 谐音：破烂纸：把自己的许诺（pledge）写在一张破烂纸上
考 同义 pledge = vow

★★★ obvious
[ˈɒbviəs] *a.* 明显的

考 同义 blatant = obvious; obvious = conspicuous; obvious = overt; obvious = apparent

类比 hidden 隐藏 `to` obvious 公开的 ⇒ reserved 矜持的 `to` rambunctious 喧闹的 （反义）

★ canter
[ˈkæntə] *v.* 慢跑

记 这个单词来自于 Geofrey Chaucer 的《坎特伯雷故事集》（Canterbury），讲的是 29 个伦敦人去坎特伯雷朝圣的故事，由此有了 canter 这个单词

考 类比 canter 慢跑 `to` gallop 快跑 ⇒ jog 慢跑 `to` sprint 快跑 （＜程度）

★★★ gully
[ˈgʌli] *n.* 冲沟，水沟

记 谐音：咖喱：在印度，人们总把吃不完的咖喱汁倒在门口，久而久之就形成了水沟（gully）

考 类比
canyon 峡谷 `to` gully 冲沟 ⇒ chasm 裂口 `to` groove 凹槽 （同义）
gully 水沟 `to` canyon 峡谷 ⇒ crack 裂缝 `to` chasm 裂口 （同义）
erosion 侵蚀 `to` gully 水沟 ⇒ excavation 挖掘 `to` mine 矿 （因果）

★ fraction
[ˈfrækʃn] *n.* 小部分

记 他大闹机场的行为（action）只代表了一小部分（fraction）人
考 同义 fraction = piece

★★ instigate
[ˈɪnstɪɡeɪt] *v.* 煽动

变 instigator *n.* 煽动者
记 煽动（instigate）社交网站 instagram 上的网友抵制毒品
考 同义 instigate = foment; instigate = provoke; incite = instigate

discard ★

[dɪˈskɑːd] *v.* 抛弃

考 同义 discard = reject

类比 discard 丢弃 → delete 删除 ⇒ alter 更改 → revise 修改 （同义）

nomad ★★★

[ˈnəʊmæd] *n.* 游牧民，流浪者

变 nomadic *a.* 游牧的，流浪的

记 一个游牧者（nomad）只是喜欢到处转转，他并没有（no）疯（mad）

考 同义 itinerant = nomadic；nomad = wanderer

类比
- band 群体 → nomad 游牧者 ⇒ colony 种群 → artist 艺术家 （组成）
- standee 站票者 → seat 座位 ⇒ nomad 游牧民 → home 家 （人物及其特点）
- nomadic 流浪的 → wandering 漫游的 ⇒ victorious 胜利的 → winning 获胜的 （同义）
- loudmouth 高声讲话的人 → boisterous 喧闹的 ⇒ nomad 流浪者 → wandering 流浪的 （人物及其特点）

illuminate ★★

[ɪˈluːmɪneɪt] *v.* 照亮

变 illumination *n.* 照亮

记 il- 加强 + lumin-（lumen）流明 + -ate：光照单位——流明的存在就是为了照亮（illuminate）

考 同义 illuminate = light；illuminate = enlighten

类比
- siren 警报 → warning 警告 ⇒ light 光 → illumination 照亮 （事物及其目的）
- apron 围裙 → protect 保护 ⇒ lamp 灯 → illuminate 照亮 （事物及其用途）

sullen ★★

[ˈsʌlən] *a.* 愠怒的

记 他因自己的堕落（fallen）而生气（sullen）

考 同义 sulky = sullen

类比 lucid 清晰的 → clear 清楚的 ⇒ sullen 愠怒的 → gloomy 沮丧的 （同义）

vivacious ★★

[vɪˈveɪʃəs] *a.* 活泼的

记 viva-（vivid）+ cious：因为生动（vivid），所以活泼（vivacious）

考 同义 vivacious = animated；lively = vivacious

类比 vivacious 活泼的 → lively 活跃的 ⇒ loquacious 话多的 → talkative 话多的 （同义）

abstract ★★

['æbstrækt] *a.* 抽象的；*n.* 摘要

考 同义　abstract = theoretical

类比　scene 一幕戏 — to — play 戏 ⇒ thesis 论点 — to — abstract 摘要 （组成）

abstract 抽象的 — to — concrete 具体的 ⇒ stubborn 倔强的 — to — flexible 灵活的 （反义）

solvent ★

['sɒlvənt] *n.* 溶液；*a.* 有偿付能力的

变　insolvent *a.* 破产的
记　老赖说这件事好解决（solve），他还钱（solvent）就行了
考 同义　insolvent = bankrupt

类比　solvent 溶液 — to — dissolve 溶解 ⇒ clipper 剪刀 — to — trim 修剪 （事物及其动作）

illiterate ★★

[ɪˈlɪtərət] *a.* 文盲的

记　il- 否定 + literate 受到过教育的
考 同义　illiterate = unlettered；illiterate = unable to read

recede ★★

[rɪˈsiːd] *v.* 后退，撤回

记　re- 向后 + ced- 走路 + e
考 同义　retreat = recede；recede = draw back

类比　recede 撤退 — to — retreat 撤退 ⇒ depict 描绘 — to — portray 描绘 （同义）

List | 76 words　　★ 复习一下学过的单词！

□ agony	□ confidential	□ infirmary	□ poison
□ annotation	□ fluctuate	□ intimidate	□ ponderous
□ annul	□ fraud	□ lenient	□ prolong
□ archipelago	□ imperious	□ masterpiece	□ schism
□ berate	□ inconsistent	□ ounce	□ scurry

SSAT词汇 List 78

★★ munificent
[mjuːˈnɪfɪsnt] *a.* 慷慨的，丰厚的

记 房子很壮丽（magnificent），房子的主人很慷慨（munificent）
考 同义 munificent = plentiful； lavish = munificent

★★★ vigilant
[ˈvɪdʒɪlənt] *a.* 警惕的，警觉的

记 弗吉尼亚州（Virginia）是美国最有警惕性的（vigilant）一个州
考 同义 vigilant = observant； vigilant = alert； vigilant = watchful
类比 vigilant 警觉的 to careful 仔细的 ⇒ meticulous 一丝不苟的 to thorough 周密的 （>程度）
注 关于"警惕的，警觉的"单词在SSAT的习题中有很多，如：wary, cautious, attentive。

★★★ superficial
[ˌsuːpəˈfɪʃl] *a.* 肤浅的

记 super 超级 + fici-（face）脸 + al：这个人找对象看脸，说明很肤浅（superficial）
考 同义 superficial = without depth； superficial = frivolous
类比
cursory 草率的 to superficial 肤浅的 ⇒ desultory 散漫的 to aimless 无目标的 （同义）
impious 不虔诚的 to reverence 尊敬 ⇒ superficial 肤浅的 to depth 深度 （缺乏）
immaterial 不重要的 to relevance 相关的 ⇒ superficial 肤浅的 to profundity 深刻 （反义）
（relevance 这个单词的英文释义为：something's relevance to a situation or person is its importance or significance in that situation or to that person）

★★ offense
[əˈfens] *n.* 进攻，冒犯

变 offend *v.* 进攻； offensive *a.* 冒犯的
记 篮球场上的事，不是进攻（offense）就是防守（defense）
考 同义 offend = affront； offensive = repugnant
类比
exalt 赞扬 to criticize 批评 ⇒ compliment 赞美 to offend 冒犯 （反义）
attack 攻击 to protect 保护 ⇒ offense 进攻 to defense 防卫 （反义）

☆ munificent　　☆ vigilant　　☆ superficial　　☆ offense

irascible ★
[ɪˈræsəbl] a. 易怒的

- 记 irasc-(eraser) + -ible：他的作业被别人用橡皮（eraser）擦掉了，所以他很生气（irascible）
- 考 同义 cantankerous = irascible；irascible = grumpy
- 注 关于"易怒的"单词在 SSAT 的习题中有很多，如：irritable, choleric, enraged, irate。

uproar ★★★
[ˈʌprɔː] n. 骚动，喧嚣

- 变 uproarious a. 骚动的，喧嚣的
- 记 up 上 + roar 咆哮：朝天（up）咆哮（roar），引起骚动（uproar）
- 考 同义 boisterous = uproarious；uproar = loud cry
- 类比 uproar (喧嚣) to silence (安静) → rage (愤怒) to forbearance (容忍) （反义）
  amusing (搞笑的) to uproarious (喧闹的) → interesting (有趣的) to mesmerizing (令人着迷的) （<程度）
- 注 关于"喧闹"的单词在 SSAT 的习题中有很多，如：tumult, upheaval, commotion。

hyperbole ★★★
[haɪˈpɜːbəli] n. 夸张的语句

- 记 hyper-(super) + -bole (bowl)：评论员用夸张的语句（hyperbole）评价着超级碗（Super Bowl）
- 考 同义 hyperbole = exaggeration；hyperbole = exaggerated expression
  hyperbole = overstatement
- 类比 hyperbole (夸张) to exaggeration (夸张) → ornament (装饰) to decoration (装饰) （同义）
  caricature (漫画) to drawing (画) → hyperbole (夸张言辞) to statement (言论) （>程度）
  caricature (漫画) to portrait (画) → hyperbole (夸张言辞) to statement (言论) （>程度）

venerate ★★★
[ˈvenəreɪt] v. 尊敬

- 变 venerable a. 值得尊敬的；veneration n. 尊敬，崇拜；venerated a. 尊敬的
- 记 对于老兵（veteran）我们要尊敬（venerate）
- 考 同义 venerable = respectable；esteem = venerate
- 类比 venerated (尊敬的) to despise (鄙视) → bored (无聊的) to engage (吸引) （反义）
  respect (尊敬) to veneration (尊敬) → hate (讨厌) to abomination (厌恶) （同义）

potent ★★★
[ˈpəʊtnt] a. 强有力的

- 变 potency n. 力量
- 记 有势力的（potent）人从小就能显示出巨大的潜力（potential）
- 考 同义 potent = powerful；potency = strength
- 类比 potency (力量) to weaken (减弱) → volume (体积) to collapse (倒塌) （事物及其动作）

voracious 贪婪的 to gluttonous 贪吃的 → potent 强有力的 to strong 强壮的 （同义）

horn
[hɔːn] *n.* 喇叭；角

考 类比
horn 喇叭 to blow 吹 → harp 竖琴 to pluck 弹 （动宾）
trumpet 小号 to horn 喇叭 → tambourine 小手鼓 to drum 鼓 （种属）
cherub 天使 to wings 翅膀 → imp 小恶魔 to horns 角 （人物及其特点）

anomalous
[əˈnɒmələs] *a.* 异常的

记 a- 相反 + nomal-（normal）+ -ous
考 同义 preternatural = anomalous

sapphire
[ˈsæfaɪə] *n.* 蓝宝石

记 sapp-（sap）树液 + hire 雇用：雇用（hire）人去从树液（sap）里榨取出蓝宝石（sapphire）
考 类比
mineral 矿物 to quartz 石英 → gem 宝石 to sapphire 蓝宝石 （种属）
emerald 绿宝石 to green 绿色 → sapphire 蓝宝石 to blue 蓝色 （事物及其特点）

aloof
[əˈluːf] *a.* 冷漠的

记 一个人高高地站在房顶（roof）上，显得很冷漠（aloof）
考 同义 aloof = reserved; aloof = apart; aloof = distant
aloof = uninvolved; indifferent = aloof

detain
[dɪˈteɪn] *v.* 拘留，扣留

变 detainment *n.* 扣留，拘留
记 拘留（detain）犯人之前需要先了解其犯罪的细节（detail）
考 类比
confine 限制 to prisoner 囚犯 → detain 拘留 to suspect 嫌疑犯 （动宾）
kidnap 绑架 to detainment 拘留 → extortion 勒索 to retribution 惩罚 （因果）

infection
[ɪnˈfekʃn] *n.* 感染

变 infectious *a.* 感染的
记 手术倒是成功了，美（perfection）中不足的是病人术后的感染（infection）
考 同义 infectious = contagious
类比 antibiotic 抗生素 to infection 感染 → antidote 解药 to poisoning 中毒 （事物及其用途）

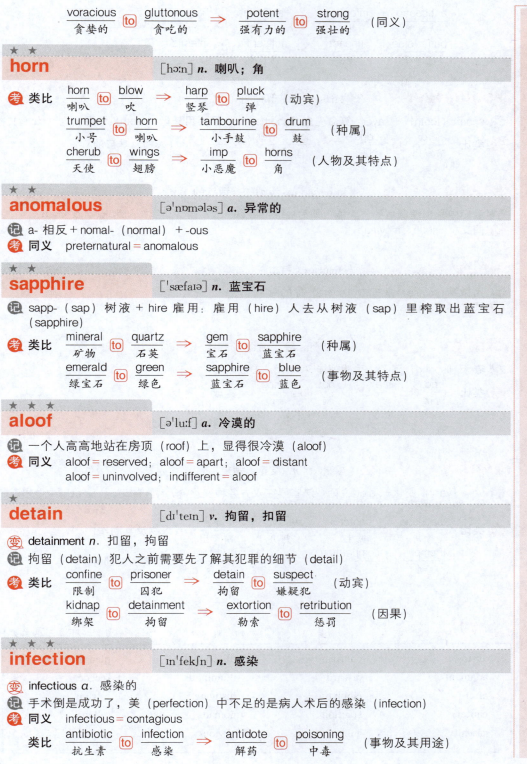

| antiseptic 防腐剂 | to | infection 感染 | → | antibiotic 抗生素 | to | bacteria 细菌 | （事物及其用途） |
| buffer side 缓冲面 | to | impact 撞击 | → | antiseptic 防腐剂 | to | infection 感染 | （事物及其用途） |

★ soothsayer ['suːθseɪə] n. 算命者

记 sooth- (tooth) + sayer：算命先生 (soothsayer) 是个用牙齿 (tooth) 说话的人 (sayer)

考 类比 juror 陪审团 to judge 判断 → soothsayer 算命者 to predict 预言 （人物及其目的）

★ kinetic [kɪ'netɪk] a. 运动的，活跃的

记 我们中学物理课上的"势能"即为 potential energy，而"动能"则为 kinetic energy
考 同义 kinetic = moving

★ smite [smaɪt] v. 打击

记 用微笑 (smile) 来打击 (smite) 你的对手
考 同义 smite = strike

★ string [strɪŋ] n. 线，细绳

记 春天 (spring) 到了，手拽细绳 (string) 去放风筝

考 类比 grid 网格 to line 线 → net 网 to string 细绳 （组成）
wick 灯芯 to torch 火炬 → string 弦 to harp 竖琴 （事物及其部分）

★★ verdict ['vɜːdɪkt] n. 结论，裁定

记 ver- (vary) 变化 + -dict 说话：法官要在双方各种变化 (vary) 的话语 (dict) 中做出裁定 (verdict)

考 类比 diagnose 诊断 to doctor 医生 → verdict 判决 to jury 陪审团 （人物及其动作）
triumph 胜利 to competition 比赛 → verdict 裁定 to trial 审讯 （事物及其部分）

List | 77 words   ★ 复习一下学过的单词！

☐ abstract	☐ confirm	☐ illiterate	☐ pledge
☐ adamant	☐ discard	☐ illuminate	☐ recede
☐ alter	☐ emphatic	☐ instigate	☐ solvent
☐ canter	☐ fraction	☐ nomad	☐ sullen
☐ casualty	☐ gully	☐ obvious	☐ vivacious

SSAT词汇 List 79

★★ meddle
['medl] v. 管闲事

变 meddling a. 管闲事的；meddlesome a. 爱管闲事的
记 站在中间（middle）管闲事（meddle）
考 同义 meddlesome = nosy；meddling = officious；interfere = meddle

★★ enthrall
[ɪn'θrɔːl] v. 迷住，着迷

记 2008 年陈凯歌的电影《梅兰芳》的英文翻译即为 Forever Enthralled
考 同义 enthrall = captivate；enthrall = engross；enthrall = fascinate

Forever Enthralled
enthrall

★ dismiss
[dɪz'mɪs] v. 解雇

考 类比 consider（考虑）to dismiss（解雇） → reflect（反射）to absorb（吸收） （反义）
         impeach（起诉）to dismiss（解雇） → arraign（传讯）to indict（起诉） （动作先后）

★ wispy
['wɪspi] a. 脆弱的

记 喝威士忌（Whisky）太多，所以身体很脆弱（wispy）
考 同义 wispy = fragile；wispy = slight

★ intact
[ɪn'tækt] a. 完整的

记 in- 否定 + -tact（touch）：没有被外人接触，依旧保持完整（intact）
考 同义 intact = unaffected

★ marathon
['mærəθən] n. 马拉松

记 marathon 原为希腊一地名，1896 年在首届奥运会中被引入，中文的马拉松三字即为英文的音译
考 类比 sprint（快跑）to speed（速度） → marathon（马拉松）to endurance（耐力） （事物及其特点）

☆ meddle ☆ enthrall ☆ dismiss ☆ wispy ☆ intact
☆ marathon

sleep → hibernation ⇒ race → marathon （种属）
睡觉　　冬眠　　　　比赛　　马拉松

appliance [əˈplaɪəns] n. 器具，装置

记 我们中国的"苏宁电器"英文即为 Suning Appliance

考 类比 root → tree ⇒ switch → appliance （种属）
　　　　根　　　树　　　　开关　　　器具
　　　　toaster → appliance ⇒ spoon → tableware （种属）
　　　　烤面包机　　器具　　　　勺　　　　餐具

appliance

pane [peɪn] n. 窗玻璃

记 把刀插在窗格（pane）上，让窗格也感到疼（pain）

考 类比 sheet → paper ⇒ pane → glass （同义）
　　　　薄片　　纸　　　　窗玻璃　玻璃
　　　　pane → window ⇒ mirror → dresser （组成）
　　　　窗玻璃　窗户　　　镜子　　　梳妆台
　　　　pane → window ⇒ prong → fork （组成）
　　　　窗玻璃　窗户　　　叉子上的齿　叉子
　　　　pane → window ⇒ lens → spectacles （组成）
　　　　窗玻璃　窗户　　　镜片　　眼镜

affection [əˈfekʃn] n. 喜爱，感情

变 affectionate a. 深情的
记 注意区分"装模作样"affectation 和"感情"affection
考 同义 affinity = affection
　　类比 affectionate → loving ⇒ considerate → courteous （同义）
　　　　充满爱的　　亲爱的　　考虑周到的　有礼貌的
　　（courteous 这个单词的英文释义为：marked by respect for and consideration of others）

proverb [ˈprɒvɜːb] n. 谚语

变 proverbial a. 谚语的，众所周知的
记 pro- 朝前 + verb 动词：圣人的嘴朝前（pro）一动，蹦出来的词（verb）就成为谚语（proverb）
考 同义 adage = proverb；maxim = proverb
　　类比 cautious → impulsive ⇒ secretive → proverbial （反义）
　　　　谨慎的　　冲动的　　　秘密的　　众所周知的

envious [ˈenviəs] a. 嫉妒的

考 同义 envious = jealous

chronic
★

['krɒnɪk] *a.* 慢性的，长期的

记 这个词来自希腊时间之神（Chronos）
考 同义 chronic = persistent

类比 recurrent 周期性的 —to→ dream 梦 ⇒ chronic 慢性的 —to→ illness 疾病 （修饰）

chronic 长期的 —to→ habitual 习惯的 ⇒ acute 激烈的 —to→ intense 强烈的 （同义）

object
★★★

[əbˈdʒekt] *v.* 反对；*n.* 物体

变 objective *a.* 客观的；objective *n.* 目的；objection *n.* 反对
考 同义 impartial = objective；objective = intention；objective = purpose

类比 hint 暗示 —to→ advise 建议 ⇒ quibble 挑剔 —to→ objection 反对 （＜程度）

incantation 咒语 —to→ word 话语 ⇒ talisman 护身符 —to→ object 物品 （种属）

object 物体 —to→ still life 静物 ⇒ person 人物 —to→ portrait 肖像画 （种属）

perimeter 周长 —to→ figure 物体 ⇒ outline 轮廓 —to→ object 物体 （事物及其部分）

border 边界 —to→ country 国家 ⇒ perimeter 周长 —to→ object 物体 （事物及其部分）

assert
★★

[əˈsɜːt] *v.* 断言，主张，声称

变 assertive *a.* 肯定的，独断的
记 维护（assert）自己国家的沙漠（desert）不被侵犯
考 同义 assert = declare；allege = to assert without proof

类比 belligerent 好战的 —to→ assertive 独断的 ⇒ despairing 绝望的 —to→ discouraged 气馁的 （＞程度）

（assertive 这个单词的英文释义为：aggressively self-assured）

synchronize
★

[ˈsɪŋkrənaɪz] *v.* 使同步，使同时发生

记 syn- 相同 + chron- 时间 + -ize
考 同义 synchronize = unify

drastic
★

[ˈdræstɪk] *a.* 激烈的，猛烈的

记 drastic 可以和 dramatic 放在一起记
考 同义 drastic = extreme

clumsy ★★★
['klʌmzi] a. 笨拙的

- 变 clumsiness n. 笨拙
- 记 腰上有个肿块（lump），所以走起路来显得很笨拙（clumsy）
- 考 同义 ungainly = clumsy

类比：
- satiated 满足的 to hunger 饥饿的 → adroit 敏捷的 to clumsiness 笨拙 （反义）
- somnolent 催眠的 to wakeful 醒着的 → graceful 优雅的 to clumsy 笨拙的 （反义）
- idle 闲置的 to employed 被雇用的 → graceful 优雅的 to clumsy 笨拙的 （反义）
- lummox 笨拙的人 to clumsy 笨拙的 → egotist 自私者 to conceited 自负的 （人物及其特点）

relish ★★
['relɪʃ] n. 开胃小菜，调味料；v. 喜爱

- 记 熟食店（deli）里面有很多开胃菜（relish）
- 考 类比：
  - initiate 开始 to conclude 结束 → relish 喜爱 to detest 憎恶 （反义）
  - relish 调味品 to pickles 泡菜 → salsa 萨尔萨酱 to tomatoes 西红柿 （同类）

phonetics ★
[fə'netɪks] n. 语音学

- 记 打电话（phone）向别人请教语音学（phonetics）的知识
- 考 类比：semantics 语义学 to meaning 意思 → phonetics 语音学 to sound 发音 （事物及其用途）

spear ★
[spɪə] n. 矛

- 变 spearhead n. 带头，先锋
- 记 用矛（spear）去戳面前的这个梨（pear）
- 考 同义 spearhead = pioneer

类比：spear 矛 to bludgeon 棍棒 → lathe 车床 to vise 虎钳 （同类）

List | **78 words**　　　　　　　　　　　　　　　　★ 复习一下学过的单词！

□ aloof	□ infection	□ potent	□ superficial
□ anomalous	□ irascible	□ sapphire	□ uproar
□ detain	□ kinetic	□ smite	□ venerate
□ horn	□ munificent	□ soothsayer	□ verdict
□ hyperbole	□ offense	□ string	□ vigilant

SSAT词汇 List 80

bard
[bɑːd] n. 游吟诗人

记 游吟诗人（bard）蓄胡子（beard）
考 类比 virtuoso / 行家 to music / 音乐 ⇒ bard / 游吟诗人 to poetry / 诗 （人物及其对象）
（virtuoso 这个单词的英文释义为：a virtuoso is someone who is extremely good at something，especially at playing a musical instrument）

canvass
['kænvəs] n. 调查

记 注意区分"调查" canvass 和"帆布" canvas
考 同义 canvass = survey

hypocrisy
[hɪ'pɒkrəsi] n. 虚伪，伪善

变 hypocrite n. 伪君子；hypocritical a. 虚伪的
记 hypo- 背后 + -crisy（criticize）：总暗地里（hypo）批评（criticize）别人，显得很虚伪（hypocrisy）
考 同义 hypocritical = insincere
类比 ostentation / 卖弄 to simplicity / 简单 ⇒ hypocrisy / 虚伪 to sincerity / 真诚 （反义）
friend / 朋友 to animosity / 敌意 ⇒ hypocrite / 伪君子 to sincerity / 真诚 （缺乏）
audacious / 胆大的 to boldness / 胆大 ⇒ sanctimonious / 假装虔诚的 to hypocrisy / 虚伪 （同义）
注 关于"虚伪"的单词在 SSAT 的习题中有很多，如：phony, insincerity。

inspire
[ɪn'spaɪə] v. 鼓舞，激励

变 inspiring a. 激励人心的；inspiration n. 灵感，鼓舞
记 鼓舞（inspire）让你有精神（spirit）
考 同义 incentive = inspiration
类比 sponsor / 赞助商 to funding / 赞助 ⇒ muse / 缪斯 to inspiration / 灵感 （人物及其对象）

☆ bard　　☆ canvass　　☆☆ hypocrisy　　☆☆☆ inspire

anthem 圣歌 to inspire 激励 → shuttle 班车 to transport 运输 （事物及其用途）

impressive 使人钦佩的 to inspiring 激励的 → derogatory 贬低的 to critical 批评的 （同义）

persevere ★★★
[ˌpɜːsɪˈvɪə] v. 坚持，不屈不挠

变 persevering a. 不屈不挠的；perseverance n. 坚持不懈；perseverant a. 坚持的
记 这个老师始终坚持（persevere）严厉（severe）对待学生
考 同义 perseverance = determination

类比
perceptive 有知觉的 to discern 识别 → persistent 坚持的 to persevere 坚持 （同义）
recurrence 循环发生的 to periodic 周期的 → determination 决心 to persevering 不屈不挠的 （同义）

注 关于"不屈不挠的"单词在 SSAT 的习题中有很多，如：tenacious, unswerving, steadfast。

crutch ★
[krʌtʃ] n. 拐杖

记 车祸（crash）之后，你需要一副拐杖（crutch）
考 类比
vision 视力 to lens 镜片 → mobility 移动 to crutches 拐杖 （事物及其用途）
goggle 护目镜 to vision 视力 → crutch 拐杖 to motion 移动 （事物及其用途）

debris ★
[ˈdeɪbriː] n. 碎片，残骸

记 这个单词的发音需要注意，其中 s 是不发音的
考 同义 debris = wreckage；debris = rubble

mortify ★★★
[ˈmɔːtɪfaɪ] v. 使屈辱

变 mortified a. 窘迫的
记 受到屈辱（mortify）之后，一开始很生气，慢慢地就缓和（mollify）了下来
考 同义 mortify = humiliate；mortify = embarrass；abash = mortify

adroit ★★
[əˈdrɔɪt] a. 敏捷的，灵巧的

记 在底特律（Detroit）开车的司机都必须得身手敏捷（adroit）
考 同义 dexterous = adroit

类比
adroit 敏捷的 to nimbleness 敏捷 → crooked 弯曲的 to hook 钩子 （同义）
adroit 敏捷的 to motion 行动 → articulate 口齿清晰的 to speech 演讲 （修饰）
satiated 满足的 to hunger 饥饿 → adroit 敏捷的 to clumsiness 笨拙 （反义）

weary

[ˈwɪəri] *a.* 疲倦的，厌烦的

- 变 wearisome *a.* 使疲倦的，使厌烦的；weariness *n.* 疲倦，厌烦
- 记 总穿（wear）一件相同的衣服，给人一种厌倦（weary）感
- 考 同义 tedious = wearisome；fatigue = weariness

propensity

[prəˈpensɪti] *n.* 倾向

- 记 因为花费（expense）超标，所以投资商有撤资的倾向（propensity）
- 考 同义 propensity = proclivity；propensity = penchant；predilection = propensity
- 注 有一个奇怪但有趣的现象，英语中表"倾向，趋向"的单词好多都以字母 p 开头，如：proclivity，preference，penchant，predilection。

destitute

[ˈdestɪtjuːt] *a.* 赤贫的

- 记 这个机构（institute）比较穷（destitute）
- 考 同义 destitute = poor；destitute = indigent；destitute = impoverished

类比 destitute 穷的 to money 钱 ⇒ confident 自信的 to doubt 怀疑（缺乏）

lawn

[lɔːn] *n.* 草地，草坪

- 记 法律（law）规定，不得踩草坪（lawn）

考 类比 mow 割 to lawn 草 ⇒ prune 修建 to tree 树（动宾）

meadow 牧场 to lawn 草地 ⇒ lake 湖 to swimming pool 游泳池 （＞程度）

rouse

[raʊz] *v.* 唤醒，觉醒

- 记 王子手中玫瑰花（rose）的香气，唤醒（rouse）了熟睡中的公主
- 考 同义 rouse = awake；incite = rouse

sober

[ˈsəʊbə] *a.* 清醒的，未醉的

- 变 sobriety *n.* 清醒，冷静
- 记 关于 sober，Winston Churchill 有个著名的笑话可以帮助大家记忆。一位女士批评 Winston Churchill："Your are drunk."而 Churchill 反击道："Madam, you are ugly and in the morning. I'm gonna be sober."
- 考 同义 sober = not drunk

类比 sober 未醉的 to intemperate 酗酒的 ⇒ impecunious 贫穷的 to affluent 富裕的 （反义）

haphazard

[hæpˈhæzəd] *a.* 随意的，无序的

- 变 hazardous *a.* 危险的

记 因为过于随意（haphazard），所以导致危险（hazard）
考 同义 hazardous = perilous; haphazard = random; haphazard = casual

creed ★
[kriːd] n. 信条，教义

记 他的人生信条（creed）就是时刻保持贪婪（greed）
考 同义 creed = belief

evict ★★
[ɪˈvɪkt] v. 驱逐，逐出

记 维克多（Victor）被驱逐（evict）出境
考 同义 oust = evict

类比
- jettison 抛弃 to cargo 货物 ⇒ evict 逐出 to tenant 房客 （动宾）
- evict 驱逐 to residence 住宅 ⇒ banish 驱逐 to country 国家 （动宾）
- evict 驱逐 to admit 允许进入 ⇒ malfunction 出故障 to operate 启动 （反义）

interfere ★★
[ˌɪntəˈfɪə] v. 干涉，打扰

记 这个公司允许随意进入（enter），所以工作人员经常遭到打扰（interfere）
考 同义 interfere = intervene; interfere = meddle

uprising ★★★
[ˈʌpraɪzɪŋ] n. 起义

记 up 朝上 + rising 升起
考 类比
- extinguish 熄灭 to fire 火 ⇒ quell 平息 to uprising 起义 （动宾）
- quell 平息 to uprising 起义 ⇒ crush 镇压 to riot 暴乱 （动宾）
- uprising 起义 to revolution 革命 ⇒ spark 火花 to fire 火 （<程度）

List | 79 words　　　　　　　　　　　　　★ 复习一下学过的单词！

☐ affection　　☐ dismiss　　☐ marathon　　☐ proverb
☐ appliance　　☐ drastic　　☐ meddle　　☐ relish
☐ assert　　☐ enthrall　　☐ object　　☐ spear
☐ chronic　　☐ envious　　☐ pane　　☐ synchronize
☐ clumsy　　☐ intact　　☐ phonetics　　☐ wispy

SSAT词汇 List 81

reticent
['retɪsnt] *a.* 沉默的

记 这个小姑娘单纯（innocent）且不爱说话（reticent）
考 同义 reticent = reserved；reticent = un-talkative

bellow
['beləʊ] *v.* 吼叫

记 冲自己的小伙伴（fellow）吼叫（bellow）
考 类比 whisper 私语 to bellow 吼叫 ⇒ suggest 建议 to command 命令 （<程度）

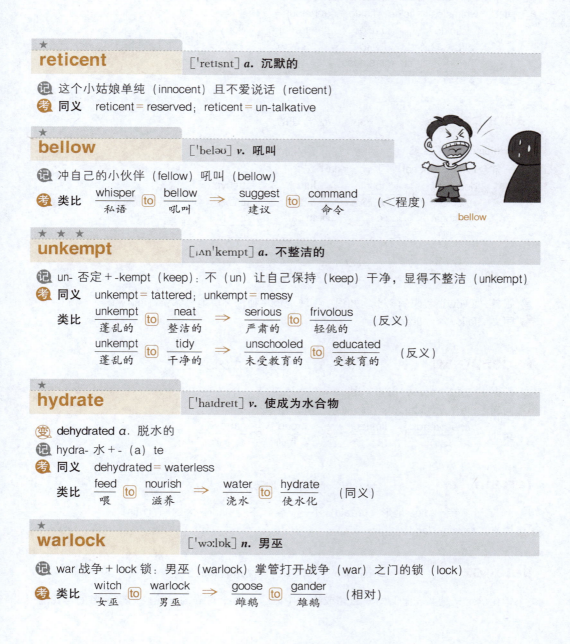
bellow

unkempt
[ˌʌn'kempt] *a.* 不整洁的

记 un- 否定 + -kempt（keep）：不（un）让自己保持（keep）干净，显得不整洁（unkempt）
考 同义 unkempt = tattered；unkempt = messy
类比 unkempt 蓬乱的 to neat 整洁的 ⇒ serious 严肃的 to frivolous 轻佻的 （反义）
unkempt 蓬乱的 to tidy 干净的 ⇒ unschooled 未受教育的 to educated 受教育的 （反义）

hydrate
['haɪdreɪt] *v.* 使成为水合物

变 dehydrated *a.* 脱水的
记 hydra- 水 + -(a)te
考 同义 dehydrated = waterless
类比 feed 喂 to nourish 滋养 ⇒ water 浇水 to hydrate 使水化 （同义）

warlock
['wɔːlɒk] *n.* 男巫

记 war 战争 + lock 锁：男巫（warlock）掌管打开战争（war）之门的锁（lock）
考 类比 witch 女巫 to warlock 男巫 ⇒ goose 雌鹅 to gander 雄鹅 （相对）

☆ reticent　　☆ bellow　　☆ unkempt　　☆ hydrate　　☆ warlock

revival
[rɪˈvaɪvl] *n.* 复兴，复活

记 幸存者（survival）让自己当年的遭遇重新（revival）回到大众视野
考 同义 revival = renaissance

fickle
[ˈfɪkl] *a.* 变化无常的

记 硬币中只有五毛（nickel）硬币是用镍制作的，和其余硬币不同，显得变化无常（fickle）
考 同义 whimsical = fickle；fickle = capricious

类比 fickle 变化无常的 —to— change 变化 ⇒ fretful 焦躁的 —to— worry 担忧 （同义）

fickle 多变的 —to— steadfastness 稳定 ⇒ tempestuous 暴乱的 —to— peace 和平 （反义）

rational
[ˈræʃnəl] *a.* 合理的

变 irrational *a.* 不合理的
记 一条合理的（rational）国（national）法
考 类比 deduction 推论 —to— rational 合理的 ⇒ hunch 直觉 —to— intuitive 直觉的 （同义）

irrational 不合理的 —to— logic 逻辑 ⇒ unethical 不道德的 —to— morality 道德 （缺乏）

fallow
[ˈfæləʊ] *a.* 休耕的

记 跟着（follow）我来学习土地知识：哪块地该耕种，哪块地该休耕（fallow）
考 同义 fallow = unused

widespread
[ˈwaɪdspred] *a.* 普遍的，广泛的

记 wide 广泛的 + spread 分散
考 同义 rife = widespread；prevalent = widespread

类比 widespread 广泛的 —to— limited 限制的 ⇒ broad 宽广的 —to— narrow 狭窄的 （反义）

terrain
[təˈreɪn] *n.* 地形，地势

记 ter 谐音：特 + rain：地形（terrain）不好，常年下特（ter）大的雨（rain）
考 同义 terrain = land

paradox
[ˈpærədɒks] *n.* 悖论，似是而非的论点

记 悖论的定义是：表面上同一命题或推理中隐含着两个对立的结论。比较著名的悖论有

"说谎者悖论（Liar Paradox）""祖父悖论（Grandfather Paradox）"。
考 同义　contradiction = paradox

★★ legible
['ledʒəbl] *a.* 清晰的，易读的

变 illegible *a.* 难以辨认的；legibility *n.* 易读性
记 合法的（legal）文档应清晰易读（legible）
考 同义　legible = easy to read

类比　illegible 难以辨认的 **to** read 读 ⇒ invisible 不可视的 **to** see 看 （缺乏）
　　　articulate 口齿清晰的 **to** speaking 说话 ⇒ legible 清晰易辨的 **to** writing 书写 （修饰）
　　　articulateness 口齿清晰 **to** speech 演讲 ⇒ legibility 易读 **to** handwriting 书写 （修饰）

★★ barrage
['bærɑːʒ] *v.* 以密集炮火进攻

记 我们常说的出现在视频里的"弹幕"英文即为 barrage
考 同义　barrage = attack

★ evident
['evɪdənt] *a.* 明显的

考 同义　evident = clear

★ torrid
['tɒrɪd] *a.* 酷热的

记 天气酷热（torrid），汗如雨下（torrent）
　　 因为天气酷热（torrid），所以连小狗都不活泼（torpid）了
考 类比　warm 暖和的 **to** torrid 酷热的 ⇒ cold 冷的 **to** frozen 冻冰的 （＜程度）

★★★ contempt
[kən'tempt] *v.* 轻视，蔑视

记 不要总试图（attempt）去鄙视（contempt）别人
考 同义　contempt = disdain；haughty = contemptuous

类比　mock 嘲笑 **to** derision 嘲笑 ⇒ despise 鄙视 **to** contempt 鄙视 （同义）
　　　contempt 鄙视 **to** sneer 嘲笑 ⇒ displeasure 不愉快 **to** frown 皱眉 （同义）
　　　contempt 鄙视 **to** disrespect 不敬 ⇒ hatred 厌恶 **to** dislike 不喜欢 （＞程度）

strive

[straɪv] *v.* 努力，奋斗

记 注意区分"努力"（strive）和"繁荣"（thrive）
考 同义 strive = try hard; endeavor = strive

类比 strive 力争 to attain 达到 ⇒ sidestep 回避 to avoid 避免 （同义）

thesis

[ˈθiːsɪs] *n.* 论文；论点

考 同义 thesis = paper

类比 thesis 论文 to appendix 附录 （事物及其部分）
scene 一幕戏 to play 戏 ⇒ thesis 论点 to abstract 摘要 （组成）
point 观点 to argument 论证 ⇒ theme 主题 to thesis 论文 （事物及其部分）

treachery

[ˈtretʃəri] *n.* 背叛，叛变

记 这个老师（teacher）背叛（treachery）了自己的原单位
考 同义 treachery = perfidy

List | 80 words ★复习一下学过的单词！

□ adroit	□ debris	□ inspire	□ propensity
□ bard	□ destitute	□ interfere	□ rouse
□ canvass	□ evict	□ lawn	□ sober
□ creed	□ haphazard	□ mortify	□ uprising
□ crutch	□ hypocrisy	□ persevere	□ weary

SSAT词汇 List 82

remonstrate
['remənstreɪt] v. 抗议

记 对这个不公正的判决，我表示（demonstrate）抗议（remonstrate）

考 类比 capitulate（认输）to surrender（投降）⇒ remonstrate（抗议）to protest（反对）（同义）

skeleton
['skelɪtn] n. 骨骼，骨架

记 英文谚语"a skeleton in the closet"即为中文的"家丑不可外扬"

考 类比 skeleton（骨架）to animal（动物）⇒ framing（框架）to building（建筑物）（事物及其部分）

类比 skeleton（骨架）to mammal（哺乳动物）⇒ trunk（树干）to tree（树）（事物及其部分）

类比 frame（框架）to building（建筑物）⇒ skeleton（骨架）to body（身体）（事物及其部分）

therapeutic
[ˌθerə'pjuːtɪk] a. 治疗的，治愈的

记 这个单词的名词形式是 therapy，意为"治疗"；其表示人的名词为 therapist，意为"治疗师"。曾经看过一看电影，男主角把 therapist 看成了 the rapist

考 同义 therapeutic = curative

superimpose
[ˌsuːpərɪm'pəʊz] v. 添加

记 super- 上 + impose 强加：添加（superimpose）其实就是强加（impose）别人之上（super）

考 同义 lay over = superimpose；superimpose = place on top of

retreat
[rɪ'triːt] v. 撤退

考 同义 retreat = recede

类比 wax（增大）to wane（变小）⇒ advance（进步）to retreat（撤退）（反义）

recede (撤退) to retreat (撤退) → depict (描绘) to portray (描绘) （同义）
forward (向前的) to backward (向后的) → assault (攻击) to retreat (撤退) （反义）

★ xenophobia

[ˌzenəˈfəubiə] *n.* 老外恐惧症，陌生人恐惧症

记 xeno- 外国的 + phobia 恐惧症
考 类比 xenophobia (老外恐惧症) to foreigner (外国人) → acrophobia (恐高症) to height (高度) （事物及其对象）

★ lacerated

[ˈlæsəreɪtɪd] *a.* 割裂的，撕碎的

记 lacer- (laser) 激光 + -ated：用激光 (lacer) 来割裂 (lacerated) 玻璃
考 类比 decadent (颓废的) to decayed (腐烂的) → lacerated (撕裂的) to tore (撕开的) （同义）

★★ impact

[ˈɪmpækt] *n.* 影响，撞击

考 同义 impact = collision
  类比 buffer (缓冲区) to impact (冲击力) → armor (盔甲) to hit (击打) （事物及其用途）
       buffer side (缓冲面) to impact (影响) → antiseptic (防腐剂) to infection (感染) （事物及其用途）

★ intersect

[ˌɪntəˈsekt] *v.* 相交，交集

变 intersection *n.* 十字路口
记 inter- 两者之间 + -sect (section) 部分
考 同义 intersect = converge
  类比 intersection (十字路口) to streets (街道) → junction (交汇处) to highways (高速路) （空间）

★★ garment

[ˈɡɑːmənt] *n.* 衣物

记 政府 (government) 按期给穷人发放衣物 (garment)
考 类比 clothe (衣物) to garment (衣物) → arm (武器) to weapon (武器) （同义）
       wear (穿) to garment (衣服) → drink (喝) to beverage (饮料) （动宾）

prestige
[preˈstiːʒ] *n.* 威望，名气

- 记 pre- 提前 + -stige（stage）：小孩早早（pre）登上舞台（stage）就是为了出名（prestige）
- 考 同义 prestige = status；prestige = respect

dawdle
[ˈdɔːdl] *v.* 混日子，游手好闲

- 记 谐音：兜兜：整天游手好闲（dawdle）、四处兜兜风
- 考 同义 dawdle = waste time；dawdle = linger

despot
[ˈdespɒt] *n.* 暴君

- 记 de- 否定 + spot：因为他是暴君（despot），所以要把他安排在不好的（de）位置（spot）
- 考 同义 despot = tyrant；despot = dictator

metal
[ˈmetl] *n.* 金属

- 记 奖牌（medal）是由金属（metal）做成的
- 考 类比 coal/煤 to mineral/矿物 ⇒ gold/金 to metal/金属 （种属）
  iron/铁 to metal/金属 ⇒ granite/花岗岩 to rock/石头 （种属）
  steel/钢 to metal/金属 ⇒ iron/铁 to ore/矿石 （纵向）
  （这个题的思路有些复杂：用 iron 可以炼出 steel，用 ore 可以炼出 metal）

etiquette
[ˈetɪket] *n.* 礼节，礼仪

- 记 进门出示门票（ticket）是一种基本礼仪（etiquette）
- 考 同义 etiquette = manners

bias
[ˈbaɪəs] *n.* 偏见

- 变 biased *a.* 有偏见的；unbiased *a.* 公正的
- 记 谐音 buy us：因为我曾经被他们收买（buy us），所以我现在对他们有偏见（bias）
- 考 同义 prejudiced = biased；bias = preference
- 类比 prejudiced/有偏见的 to unbiased/无偏见的 ⇒ worried/担忧的 to blithe/愉快的 （反义）

intimate
[ˈɪntɪmeɪt] *n.* 好友，至交；*a.* 亲密的

- 记 in + timate（teammate）：都在（in）一个球队，所以队员们（teammate）都是至交（intimate）

考 同义 intimate = friendly; intimate = confidant

类比 beautiful/美丽的 to sublime/壮丽的 → intimate/亲密的 to romantic/浪漫的 （同义）

★ exuberant
[ɪgˈzjuːbərənt] a. 繁茂的，热情洋溢的

记 即使这个饭店价格略高（exorbitant），但它每天依旧很热闹（exuberant）

考 同义 exuberant = enthusiastic

★★★ plain
[pleɪn] a. 朴素的，简单的

考 同义 simple = plain; austere = plain; conspicuous = plain as day（显眼的，非常明显的）

类比 decorate/装饰 to plain/普通的 → cook/煮 to raw/生的 （动宾）

plain/朴素的 to luxurious/奢侈的 → still/静止的 to energetic/精力旺盛的 （反义）

★★★ aesthetic
[iːsˈθetɪk] a. 美学的

变 aesthete n. 唯美主义者

记 因为服用麻醉剂（anesthetic），所以看什么都很美（aesthetic）

考 同义 aesthetic = beautiful; aesthete = connoisseur
(connoisseur 这个单词的英文释义为：one who understands the details, technique, or principles of an art)

类比 beauty/美丽 to aesthete/审美家 → pleasure/快乐 to hedonist/享乐主义者 （人物及其对象）

List | **81** words   ★ 复习一下学过的单词！

□ barrage	□ fickle	□ reticent	□ torrid
□ bellow	□ hydrate	□ revival	□ treachery
□ contempt	□ legible	□ strive	□ unkempt
□ evident	□ paradox	□ terrain	□ warlock
□ fallow	□ rational	□ thesis	□ widespread

☆ exuberant　　☆ plain　　☆ aesthetic

SSAT词汇 List 83

★★ opulent
['ɒpjʊlənt] *a.* 丰富的，富裕的

记 注意区分"肥胖的" corpulent 和"富裕的" opulent
考 同义 opulent = rich；affluent = opulent；abundant = opulent

★★★ amiable
['eɪmɪəbl] *a.* 和蔼可亲的

记 ami- 是拉丁词根，表示"爱"
考 同义 amiable = friendly；congenial = amiable

类比
amiable 和蔼的 to genial 友好的 ⇒ baggy 袋状的 to loose 松散的 （同义）
industrious 勤奋的 to pupil 学生 ⇒ amiable 友好的 to neighbor 邻居 （修饰）
amiable 和蔼的 to grumpy 脾气坏的 ⇒ friendly 友好的 to surly 乖戾的 （反义）
happiness 快乐 to sadness 悲伤 ⇒ amiable 和蔼可亲的 to antagonistic 对抗的 （反义）

注 关于"友好的"单词在 SSAT 的习题中有很多，如：genial, gentle, amicable, affable, intimate。

★ gauntlet
['gɔːntlɪt] *n.* 金属手套

记 姑姑（aunt）让（let）我戴上金属手套（gauntlet），以保护自己
考 类比
gauntlet 金属手套 to glove 手套 ⇒ helmet 头盔 to hat 帽子 （种属）
gauntlet 金属手套 to hand 手 ⇒ visor 面甲 to face 脸 （空间）

gauntlet

★ jewel
['dʒuːəl] *n.* 宝石，珠宝

变 jeweler *n.* 珠宝商；jewelry *n.* 珠宝总称
考 类比
baker 烘焙师 to bread 面包 ⇒ jeweler 珠宝商 to pendant 挂坠 （人物及其对象）
ring 戒指 to jewelry 珠宝 ⇒ dresser 梳妆台 to furniture 家具 （种属）

gem → stone ⇒ jewel → rock （种属）
宝石　　石头　　珠宝　　石头

（这个题的思路有些复杂：gem 是一种加工过后的 stone，而 jewel 则是一种加工过后的 rock）

★★★ gluttony ['glʌtni] n. 贪吃，暴饮暴食

变 glutton n. 贪吃者；gluttonous a. 贪吃的
记 上帝说人类的七宗罪之一就是 gluttony
考 同义　voracious = gluttonous；ravenous = gluttonous；gourmand = glutton

类比
glutton → moderation ⇒ scoundrel → virtue （缺乏）
贪吃者　　节制　　　　恶棍　　　道德

avarice → money ⇒ gluttony → food （动作及其对象）
贪婪　　　钱　　　暴饮暴食　　食物

voracious → gluttonous ⇒ potent → strong （同义）
贪婪的　　　贪吃的　　　强有力　强壮的

pugnacious → fight ⇒ gluttonous → eat （动作及其情感）
好斗的　　　打架　　贪吃的　　　吃

glutton → voracious ⇒ stickler → fussy （人物及其特点）
贪吃者　　贪婪的　　　坚持细节者　挑剔的

gluttony

★ unscrupulous [ʌn'skruːpjʊləs] a. 肆无忌惮的

记 un- + scrupulous 谨慎的
考 同义　unscrupulous = unprincipled

类比
conscientious → ethical ⇒ immoral → unscrupulous （同义）
认真的　　　　有道德的　　不道德的　肆无忌惮的

★★★ note [nəʊt] n. 音符

考 类比
letter → novel ⇒ note → symphony （组成）
字母　　小说　　音符　交响乐

note → chord ⇒ tone → scale （组成）
音符　和弦　　音调　音阶

card → deck ⇒ note → symphony （组成）
卡片　一副牌　音符　交响乐

word → language ⇒ note → music （组成）
单词　语言　　　音符　音乐

注 note 这个单词"笔记"的意思我们很熟悉，这里是熟词僻义。

★★ aroma [ə'rəʊmə] n. 芳香

变 aromatic a. 芳香的
记 a + roma 罗马：啊(a)，罗马(roma)，你好芳香(aroma)啊
考 类比
palatable → delicious ⇒ aromatic → fragrant （同义）
好吃的　　好吃的　　芳香的　芳香的

putrid → garbage ⇒ aromatic → spice （事物及其特点）
臭的　　垃圾　　　芳香的　香料

注 关于"芳香"的单词在 SSAT 的习题中有很多，如：savory，spicy，redolent，balmy，perfumed。

buffoon ★★
[bəˈfuːn] *n.* 丑角

变 buffoonery *n.* 滑稽，插科打诨
记 小丑（buffoon）的衣服钮扣（button）总是扣不整齐
考 同义 buffoon = fool

类比
harpoon 鱼叉 to whaling 捕鱼 ⇒ buffoon 小丑 to clowning 滑稽表演 （事物及其对象）
affectation 装模作样 to behavior 行为 ⇒ buffoonery 滑稽 to action 行为 （同义：正反向）

owl ★★
[aʊl] *n.* 猫头鹰

记 猫头鹰（owl）狂叫（howl）
考 类比
owl 猫头鹰 to hoot 呼呼 ⇒ snake 蛇 to hiss 嘶嘶 （事物及其动作）
owl 猫头鹰 to wisdom 智慧 ⇒ pig 猪 to indolence 懒惰 （动物）
owl 猫头鹰 to wisdom 智慧 ⇒ ant 蚂蚁 to diligence 勤奋 （动物）

pugnacious ★★
[pʌɡˈneɪʃəs] *a.* 好斗的，好战的

记 火药味（pungent）四射，好斗的（pugnacious）双方开始动起手来
谐音 胖哥：如果你叫他胖哥，所以好斗的（pugnacious）他就会和你动起手来
考 同义 pugnacious = belligerent

类比
licentious 放纵的 to morality 道德 ⇒ pugnacious 好斗的 to amiability 友善 （缺乏）
pugnacious 好斗的 to fight 打架 ⇒ gluttonous 贪吃的 to eat 吃 （动作及其情感）

admonish ★★★
[ædˈmɒnɪʃ] *v.* 告诫，劝告

变 admonishment *n.* 警告
记 ad- 加强 + -monish（monitor）：班长（monitor）警告（admonish）你要好好学习，不要闹事
考 同义 admonish = caution

类比
spat 口角 to brawl 争吵 ⇒ admonish 警告 to condemn 定罪 （＜程度）
distinction 区别 to nuance 小差别 ⇒ castigation 惩罚 to admonishment 警告 （＞程度）

wave ★★★
[weɪv] *n.* 波涛；*v.* 挥舞

考 类比
hurricane 飓风 to breeze 微风 ⇒ tidal wave 浪潮 to ripple 涟漪 （＞程度）
dune 沙丘 to sand 沙子 ⇒ wave 波浪 to water 水 （组成）

flap 振动	to	wing 翅膀	⇒	wave 挥手	to	hand 手	（动宾）
mountain 山	to	peak 顶峰	⇒	wave 波涛	to	crest 浪尖	（事物及其部分）
darkness 黑暗	to	eclipse 日食	⇒	tidal wave 浪潮	to	tsunami 海啸	（事物及其部分）
sky 天空	to	clouds 云	⇒	ocean 海洋	to	wave 波浪	（空间）
surfboard 冲浪板	to	wave 波浪	⇒	skateboard 滑板	to	pavement 人行道	（空间）

★★★ symphony ['sɪmfəni] n. 交响乐

记 sym-（same）+ -phony 声音：交响乐（symphony）就是所有声音（phony）同时（same）响起

考 类比

epic 史诗	to	haiku 俳句	⇒	symphony 交响乐	to	ditty 小调	（>程度）
epic 史诗	to	haiku 俳句	⇒	symphony 交响乐	to	song 歌曲	（>程度）
letter 字母	to	novel 小说	⇒	note 音符	to	symphony 交响乐	（组成）
card 卡片	to	deck 一副牌	⇒	note 音符	to	symphony 交响乐	（组成）
movement 乐章	to	symphony 交响乐	⇒	act 幕	to	play 演出	（组成）
symphony 交响乐	to	instrumentalist 乐器演奏者	⇒	play 戏	to	actor 演员	（人物及其对象）
symphony 交响乐	to	instrumentalist 乐器演奏者	⇒	ballet 芭蕾	to	dancer 舞蹈家	（人物及其对象）
movement 乐章	to	symphony 交响乐	⇒	chapter 章节	to	book 书	（组成）
epilogue 结语	to	novel 小说	⇒	finale 终曲	to	symphony 交响乐	（事物及其部分）
epilogue 结语	to	book 书	⇒	finale 终曲	to	symphony 交响乐	（事物及其部分）

★★ culinary ['kʌlɪnəri] a. 厨房的，烹饪的

记 用厨房的（culinary）东西来做咖喱（curry）

考 类比

pecuniary 金钱的	to	money 钱	⇒	culinary 烹饪的	to	cookery 烹饪术	（同义）
culinary 厨房的	to	cook 做饭	⇒	sartorial 裁缝的	to	sew 缝	（同义）
literary 文学的	to	writing 写作	⇒	culinary 烹饪的	to	cooking 做饭	（同义）

★ intransigent [ɪn'trænsɪdʒənt] a. 不妥协的

记 in + trans- 转换 + igent：不妥协的（intransigent）意味不（in）轻易转换（trans）自己

考 类比　intransigent 不妥协的 — to — compromise 妥协　⇒　dogged 顽强的 — to — surrender 投降　（反义）

conceal　[kənˈsiːl] v. 隐藏

- 变　concealed a. 隐藏的
- 记　con- + -ceal (seal) 封：全都 (con) 封住 (seal) 了即为隐藏 (conceal)
- 考　同义　stealthy = concealed; concealed = incognito

类比　
conceal 隐藏 — to — reveal 显现　⇒　ascend 上升 — to — descend 下降　（反义）
announce 宣布 — to — inform 通知　⇒　wrap 包装 — to — conceal 隐藏　（动作及其目的）
barrier 障碍 — to — obstruct 阻碍　⇒　camouflage 伪装 — to — conceal 隐藏　（事物及其用途）
preserve 保存 — to — store 贮藏　⇒　wrap 包装 — to — conceal 隐藏　（事物及其用途）

ulcer　[ˈʌlsə] n. 溃疡

- 记　叔叔 (uncle) 得了口腔溃疡 (ulcer)
- 考　同义　ulcer = canker

caterpillar　[ˈkætəpɪlə] n. 毛毛虫

- 记　cater 迎合 + pillar 柱子：想象毛毛虫 (caterpillar) 在柱子上爬，好像在迎合 (cater) 柱子 (pillar)
- 考　类比　
tadpole 蝌蚪 — to — frog 青蛙　⇒　caterpillar 毛毛虫 — to — butterfly 蝴蝶　（时间先后）
butterfly 蝴蝶 — to — caterpillar 毛毛虫　⇒　blossom 花朵 — to — bud 花蕾　（时间先后）

cluster　[ˈklʌstə] n. 群，簇，星群

- 记　星群 (cluster) 闪亮 (luster)
- 考　类比　star 星星 — to — cluster 星群　⇒　tree 树 — to — clump 树丛　（组成）

List | 82 words　★ 复习一下学过的单词！

- aesthetic
- bias
- dawdle
- despot
- etiquette
- exuberant
- garment
- impact
- intersect
- intimate
- lacerated
- metal
- plain
- prestige
- remonstrate
- retreat
- skeleton
- superimpose
- therapeutic
- xenophobia

☆ conceal　　☆ ulcer　　☆ caterpillar　　☆ cluster

SSAT词汇 List 84

finale
[fɪˈnɑːli] *n.* 终曲

记 终曲（finale）就是演出中最后的（final）歌曲
考 类比
- epilogue (结语) to book (书) → finale (终曲) to symphony (交响乐) （事物及其部分）
- epilogue (结语) to novel (小说) → finale (终曲) to symphony (交响乐) （事物及其部分）
- finale (终曲) to opera (歌剧) → epilogue (尾声) to play (戏剧) （事物及其部分）
- dessert (饭后甜点) to meal (饭) → finale (终曲) to performance (表演) （事物及其部分）

vertical
[ˈvɜːtɪkl] *a.* 垂直的

记 英语中在说一个人矮的时候有这么一个委婉的说法：vertically challenged
考 类比
- vertical (垂直的) to horizontal (水平的) → erect (竖直的) to prone (俯卧) （反义）

delight
[dɪˈlaɪt] *n.* 高兴

考 类比
- grin (露齿笑) to delight (高兴) → frown (皱眉) to dismay (沮丧) （动作及其情感）
- frown (皱眉) to disgust (恶心) → grin (露齿笑) to delight (高兴) （动作及其情感）

pest
[pest] *n.* 害虫

记 谐音 拍死它：遇到害虫（pest）就要去拍死它
考 类比
- pest (害虫) to annoying (烦人的) → plateau (高原) to level (水平的) （事物及其特点）
- hoe (锄头) to weed (草) → insecticide (杀虫剂) to pest (害虫) （事物及其对象）

disposition
[ˌdɪspəˈzɪʃn] *n.* 性情，态度

记 因为职位（position）降低，所以性情（disposition）大变
考 同义 attitude = disposition

turbulent
[ˈtɜːbjʊlənt] *a.* 骚乱的

记 来自"涡轮机" turbine
考 同义 turbulent = violent；turbulent = disordered

duplicate
[ˈdjuːplɪkeɪt] *a.* 复制的

记 非法的复制品（duplicate）被警方查获，公司老板也受到牵连（implicate）
考 同义 duplicate = identical；facsimile = duplicate

scatter
[ˈskætə] *v.* 分散，散播

记 斯科特（Scott）命令手下的警察分散开来（scatter）
考 类比
drop 掉 to scatter 散播 ⇒ down 朝下 to around 四周 （纵向）
gather 聚集 to scatter 分散 ⇒ attract 吸引 to repel 排斥 （反义）
spread 散播 to scatter 分散 ⇒ separate 分开 to distribute 分开 （同义）

nurture
[ˈnɜːtʃə] *v.* 培养，养育；*n.* 培养

记 一个民族的文化（culture）需要慢慢培养（nurture）
考 同义 nurture = cultivate
类比
animal 动物 to nature 自然 ⇒ baby 孩子 to nurture 培养 （事物及其特性）
nature 自然 to nurture 培养 ⇒ congenital 先天的 to acquired 后天习得的 （纵向）

abyss
[əˈbɪs] *n.* 深渊

记 谐音：俺必死：掉入深渊（abyss），俺必死无疑
考 同义 abyss = hole；abyss = pit；abyss = gorge

address
[əˈdres] *v.* 演说，演讲

考 同义 address = speak to
类比
sweat suit 运动套装 to uniform 制服 ⇒ chat 聊天 to address 演说 （种属）
注 address 这个单词"地址"的意思我们很熟悉，此处为熟词僻义。

trample
['træmpl] v. 踩踏

记 寺庙（temple）发生了踩踏（trample）事件
考 同义 trample = tread

dejected
[dɪ'dʒektɪd] a. 沮丧的，灰心的

记 因为被拒绝（rejected），所以很沮丧（dejected）
考 类比 dejected 沮丧的 to sanguine 乐观的 ⇒ ignorant 无知的 to ingenious 机灵的 （反义）

parody
['pærədi] n. 诙谐的模仿，恶搞

记 鹦鹉（parrot）总喜欢诙谐地模仿（parody）人类
考 类比 immense 巨大的 to narrow 狭窄的 ⇒ sad movie 悲伤电影 to parody 恶搞 （反义）

canoe
[kə'nu:] n. 独木舟

记 我能（can）划独木舟（canoe）
考 类比 canoe 独木舟 to river 河流 ⇒ train 火车 to track 轨道 （空间）
canoe 独木舟 to boat 船 ⇒ truck 卡车 to automobile 汽车 （种属）

ephemeral
[ɪ'femərəl] a. 短暂的

记 ephemera 本意指的是"蜉蝣"，这是大自然中生命最短的生物，很少有能活过一天的，因此引申出"短暂的"意思
考 同义 ephemeral = fleeting
类比 timeless 永恒的 to ephemeral 短暂的 ⇒ ungainly 笨拙的 to dexterous 敏捷的 （反义）
animate 有生命力的 to living 活着的 ⇒ ephemeral 短暂的 to unendurable 不能持久的 （同义）

canal
[kə'næl] n. 运河

记 京杭大运河的英文即为 the Beijing-Hangzhou Grand Canal
考 类比 canal 运河 to waterway 水道 ⇒ reservoir 蓄水池 to lake 湖 （种属）
canal 运河 to river 河流 ⇒ mine 矿 to cavern 洞穴 （人工和自然）

exact [ɪgˈzækt] *a.* 准确的，精确的

变 exacting *a.* 严格的，苛求的
考 同义 exact = precise; exacting = meticulous

类比 exacting 苛求的 to demanding 苛求的 ⇒ extracting 拔出的 to removing 移动的 （同义）

perfectionist 完美主义者 to exacting 苛求的 ⇒ extrovert 外向者 to outgoing 外向的 （人物及其特点）

voracious [vəˈreɪʃəs] *a.* 贪婪的，贪吃的

记 注意区分"诚实的" veracious 和"贪婪的" voracious
考 同义 voracious = gluttonous

类比 cupidity 贪婪 to voracious 贪婪的 ⇒ humility 谦虚 to modest 谦虚的 （同义）

voracious 贪婪的 to gluttonous 贪吃的 ⇒ potent 强有力的 to strong 强壮的 （同义）

voracious 贪婪的 to food 食物 ⇒ greedy 贪婪的 to money 钱 （事物及其对象）

glutton 贪吃者 to voracious 贪婪的 ⇒ stickler 坚持细节者 to fussy 挑剔的 （人物及其特点）

medley [ˈmedli] *n.* 混合曲，串烧

记 混合曲（medley）就是很多歌曲（melody）串在一起
考 类比 song 歌曲 to medley 混合曲 ⇒ picture 图画 to collage 剪贴画 （组成）

medley 混合曲 to song 歌曲 ⇒ anthology 选集 to story 故事 （组成）

List | **83** words ★ 复习一下学过的单词！

- admonish
- amiable
- aroma
- buffoon
- caterpillar
- cluster
- conceal
- culinary
- gauntlet
- gluttony
- intransigent
- jewel
- note
- opulent
- owl
- pugnacious
- symphony
- ulcer
- unscrupulous
- wave

☆ exact　　☆ voracious　　☆ medley

SSAT词汇 List 85

★★ riot
['raɪət] *n.* 暴乱

记 反动派始终认为自己的暴乱（riot）是正确的（right）

考 类比 crush（镇压）to riot（暴乱）⇒ quell（平息）to uprising（起义）（动宾）
crush（镇压）to riot（暴乱）⇒ extinguish（熄灭）to fire（火）（动宾）

★★ conciliate
[kən'sɪlieɪt] *v.* 安抚，抚慰

记 委员会（council）里的人相互抚慰（conciliate）
考 同义 conciliate = pacify；conciliate = appease
注 关于"安抚，安慰"的单词在 SSAT 的习题中有很多，如：sooth, calm, mollify, lull, quell。

★★ incite
[ɪn'saɪt] *v.* 煽动，刺激

记 受到别人煽动（incite），他反而显得很兴奋（excite）
考 同义 incite = provoke；incite = rouse；incite = instigate

★ capital
['kæpɪtəl] *a.* 重要的

考 同义 primary = capital
注 capital 这个单词"首都"的意思我们很熟悉，此处为熟词僻义。

★★★ vex
[veks] *v.* 使烦恼

记 性（sex）骚扰让人烦恼（vex）
考 同义 badger = vex；harass = vex；irritate = vex
类比 vex（使烦恼）to fret（烦恼）⇒ amuse（娱乐）to divert（娱乐）（同义）
swipe（偷窃）to pilfer（偷窃）⇒ provoke（激怒）to vex（使烦恼）（同义）
（swipe 这个单词的英文释义为：to steal; filch）

☆ riot　　☆ conciliate　　☆ incite　　☆ capital　　☆ vex

adversary ★★ ['ædvəsəri] *n.* 对手，敌人

- 记 广告（advertise）是家长在教育孩子时所面对的最大对手（adversary）
- 考 同义 adversary = opponent

  类比
  - adversary 敌人 to enmity 敌意 ⇒ underdog 失败者 to sympathy 同情 （人物及其特点）
  - neighbor 邻居 to proximity 接近 ⇒ adversary 反对者 to opposition 反对 （人物及其特点）
  - disinterested 公正的 to favoritism 偏袒 ⇒ adversarial 对抗的 to cooperativeness 合作 （反义）

supervisor ★ ['suːpəvaɪzə] *n.* 监督人，管理者

- 记 super- 在……上 + vis- 看 + -or 人：总高高在上看着别人的人，即为监督人（supervisor）
- 考 类比
  - parent 父母 to child 孩子 ⇒ supervisor 监督者 to employee 员工 （人物及其对象）

acclaim ★ [ə'kleɪm] *v.* 欢呼，称赞

- 记 高喊（exclaim）赞美（acclaim）别人的话
- 考 同义 acclaim = compliment
- 注 关于"赞扬"的单词在 SSAT 的习题中有很多，如：eulogy, commend, accolade。

elude ★★ [ɪ'luːd] *v.* 逃避，躲避

- 变 elusive *a.* 逃避的，难懂的
- 记 故意排除（exclude）事实，实则为了逃避（elude）法律责任
- 考 同义 evade = elude；impenetrable = elusive

  类比
  - feign 躲避 to deceive 欺骗 ⇒ flee 逃跑 to elude 逃避 （同义）

disprove ★ [ˌdɪs'pruːv] *v.* 反驳

- 记 dis- + prove：证明……是虚假的，即为反驳
- 考 同义 disprove = refute

quake ★★ [kweɪk] *n.* 震动

- 变 earthquake *n.* 地震
- 考 同义 quake = shake

  类比
  - tremor 震动 to earthquake 地震 ⇒ wind 风 to tornado 龙卷风 （<程度）
  - tremor 震动 to earthquake 地震 ⇒ misdemeanor 轻罪 to felony 重罪 （<程度）

apprehend ★★★

[ˌæprɪˈhend] v. 理解；忧虑

变 apprehensive a. 忧虑的，不安的
记 知道（apprehend）得越多就越感到忧虑（apprehensive）
考 同义 apprehend = understand; apprehensive = worried; apprehensive = doubtful
apprehensive = fearful

类比 comprehensive (广泛的) to inclusive (包含的) → apprehensive (忧虑的) to uneasy (不自在的)（同义）

elevator ★★

[ˈelɪveɪtə] n. 电梯

变 elevate v. 提升，提高
记 我们常坐的直上直下的电梯，在美国叫 lift，在英国就叫 elevator
考 同义 exalt = elevate

类比 house (房子) to stairs (楼梯) → building (楼房) to elevator (电梯)（空间）
lucid (明晰的) to pellucid (明晰的) → lofty (崇高的) to elevated (高尚的)（同义）

jury ★★★

[ˈdʒʊəri] n. 陪审团

变 juror n. 陪审员
记 法官要保证陪审团（jury）成员不受伤害（injury）
考 类比 judge (法官) to jury (陪审团) （人物及其对象）
juror (陪审团成员) to jury (陪审团) → island (岛屿) to archipelago (群岛)（组成）
diagnose (诊断) to doctor (医生) → verdict (裁定) to jury (陪审团)（人物及其动作）

valley ★★

[ˈvæli] n. 山谷，峡谷

记 北京著名的景点"欢乐谷"英文为：Happy Valley；美国著名的景点"科罗拉多大峡谷"英文为：Grand Valley

valley

考 类比 negative (消极的) to positive (积极的) → valley (峡谷) to mountain (山)（反义）
mountain (山) to valley (峡谷) → genius (天才) to idiot (蠢人)（反义）

potable ★★

[ˈpəʊtəbl] a. 可饮用的

记 pot 壶，盆 + -able：可饮用的（potable）即为能（able）用盆（pot）喝的

考 类比 potable (可饮用的) to water (水) → edible (可食用的) to vegetable (蔬菜)（修饰）

| potable 可饮用的 | to | drink 喝 | ⇒ | tangible 可触知的 | to | touch 接触 | （同义） |

raucous ★★

[ˈrɔːkəs] *a.* 沙哑的，刺耳的

- 记 声音沙哑的（raucous）浣熊（racoon）
- 考 同义 raucous = hoarse；harsh = raucous

| 类比 | raucous 刺耳的 | to | quiet 安静的 | ⇒ | shelter 庇护 | to | exposure 暴露 | （反义） |

impassive ★

[ɪmˈpæsɪv] *a.* 冷漠的

- 记 陷入僵局（impasse），路人冷漠（impassive）、不予帮助
- 考 同义 impassive = unfeeling；impassive = passionless
- 注 关于"冷漠的"单词在 SSAT 的习题中有很多，如：aloof, detached, indifferent, apathetic, nonchalant。

bulwark ★★

[ˈbʊlwək] *n.* 堡垒；*v.* 保护

- 记 bul-（bull）+ -wark（work）：公牛（bull）的工作（work）就是代替狗来保护（bulwark）堡垒（bulwark）
- 考 同义 bulwark = protection

| 类比 | bulwark 堡垒 | to | protect 保护 | ⇒ | coil 线圈 | to | gyrate 旋转 | （事物及其特点） |

umbrella ★★★

[ʌmˈbrelə] *n.* 雨伞

考 类比
cane 手杖	to	umbrella 雨伞	⇒	old 老人	to	rain 雨	（纵向）
umbrella 雨伞	to	soak 浸透	⇒	shield 盾牌	to	wound 受伤	（缺乏）
rain 雨	to	umbrella 雨伞	⇒	draft 穿堂风	to	door 门	（事物及其用途）
pole 柱子	to	tent 帐篷	⇒	rib 伞骨	to	umbrella 雨伞	（事物及其部分）

List | **84** words   ★ 复习一下学过的单词！

- □ abyss
- □ address
- □ canal
- □ canoe
- □ dejected
- □ delight
- □ disposition
- □ duplicate
- □ ephemeral
- □ exact
- □ finale
- □ medley
- □ nurture
- □ parody
- □ pest
- □ scatter
- □ trample
- □ turbulent
- □ vertical
- □ voracious

SSAT词汇 List 86

skyscraper
['skaɪskreɪpə] n. 摩天大楼

考 类比 skyscraper to building → redwood to tree （种属）
　　　　摩天大楼　　建筑物　　　红木树　　树
　　　bone to mammal → girder to skyscraper （事物及其部分）
　　　骨头　　哺乳动物　　大梁　　摩天大楼

lessen
['lesn] v. 减弱

考 同义 lessen = dwindle
　类比 clasp to release → boost to lessen （反义）
　　　紧扣　　释放　　　推动　　减弱

sow
[saʊ] v. 播种；n. 母猪

记 慢慢（slow）地播种（sow）
考 同义 sow = pig
　类比 sow to reap → crawl to walk （时间先后）
　　　播种　　收获　　爬　　走
　　　prune to plant → sow to earth （动宾）
　　　修剪　　植物　　播种　　土地

vacuum
['vækjʊəm] n. 真空

记 vac- 空 + -uum
考 类比 paragon to epitome → vacuum to void （同义）
　　　模范　　典型　　　真空　　真空

accomplish
[ə'kʌmplɪʃ] v. 完成，实现

变 accomplishment n. 完成，成就
考 同义 fulfill = accomplish
　类比 present to birthday → reward to accomplishment （因果）
　　　礼物　　生日　　　奖励　　成就
　　　ambition to accomplishment → craving to fulfillment （时间先后）
　　　雄心　　成就　　　　　　　渴望　　实现

注 关于"完成，实现"的单词在 SSAT 的习题中有很多，如：finish, achieve, realize。

violin ★★
[ˌvaɪəˈlɪn] *n.* 小提琴

变 violinist *n.* 小提琴家

记 朱自清在《荷塘月色》中这样描写：月光是隔了树照过来的，高处丛生的灌木，落下参差的斑驳的黑影，峭楞楞如鬼一般；弯弯的杨柳的稀疏的倩影，却又像是画在荷叶上。塘中的月色并不均匀；但光与影有着和谐的旋律，如梵婀玲上奏着的名曲。结尾处的"梵婀玲"即为英文 violin 的发音直译

考 类比
ax 大斧头 to hatchet 小斧头 ⇒ cello 大提琴 to violin 小提琴 （＞程度）
brush 刷子 to painter 油漆匠 ⇒ bow 弓 to violinist 小提琴家 （人物及其工具）

waive ★
[weɪv] *v.* 放弃，搁置

记 我（I）放弃（waive）了和海浪（wave）的斗争
考 同义 waive = postpone；waive = relinquish；waive = give up

poignant
[ˈpɔɪnjənt] *a.* 尖锐的，深刻的

记 文章尖锐（poignant）且直击要害（point）
考 类比
pungent 辛辣的 to flavor 口味 ⇒ poignant 尖锐的 to criticism 批评 （修饰）
pungent 刺激性的 to flower 花 ⇒ poignant 辛酸的 to emotion 情感 （修饰）
pungent 刺激性的 to flower 花 ⇒ poignant 辛酸的 to speech 演讲 （修饰）

注 关于"尖锐的"单词在 SSAT 的习题中有很多，如：piquant, sharp, flavorful。

canine ★★★
[ˈkeɪnaɪn] *a.* 犬的

记 ca-（cat）+ nine：猫（cat）有九（nine）条命，所以它不怕狗（canine）
考 类比
bird 鸟 to avian 鸟的 ⇒ dog 狗 to canine 犬的 （种属）
canine 犬的 to dog 狗 ⇒ feline 猫的 to cat 猫 （种属）
shrubbery 灌木 to vegetation 植被 ⇒ wolf 狼 to canine 犬的 （种属）
Dalmatian 斑点狗 to canine 犬的 ⇒ tabby 斑猫 to feline 猫科的 （种属）

thicket ★
[ˈθɪkɪt] *n.* 灌木丛

记 茂密的（thick）灌木丛（thicket）
考 类比
thicket 灌木丛 to shrubs 灌木 ⇒ grove 小树林 to trees 树木 （组成）

☆ violin　　☆ waive　　☆ poignant　　☆ canine　　☆ thicket

★★★ odor

['əʊdə] *n.* 气味

变 odorless *a.* 无味的
记 因为你身上有味道（odor），所以老师命令（order）你赶紧回家洗澡
考 类比
reek 臭味 to odor 味道 ⇒ blare 巨响 to sound 声音 （种属）
pungent 刺鼻的 to odor 味道 ⇒ caustic 尖刻的 to comment 评论 （修饰）
pungent 刺鼻的 to odor 味道 ⇒ intense 强烈的 to emotion 情感 （修饰）
odor 臭味 to stench 恶臭 ⇒ sad 伤心的 to tragic 悲剧的 （<程度）
porcupine 豪猪 to quill 刚毛 ⇒ skunk 臭鼬 to odor 气味 （事物及其特点）
amorphous 无形的 to shape 形状 ⇒ odorless 无气味的 to scent 气味 （缺乏）

★★ jeer

[dʒɪə] *v.* 嘲笑，戏弄

记 开宝马的人嘲笑（jeer）开吉普车（jeep）的人
考 同义 jeer = ridicule; jeer = scoff; jeer = mock

★ sap

[sæp] *n.* 树液

记 大树的树液（sap）被诗人比喻成大树伤心的（sad）眼泪
考 类比 sap 树液 to plant 植物 ⇒ blood 血 to animal 动物 （事物及其部分）

★★★ shell

[ʃel] *n.* 壳

变 shellfish *n.* 甲壳类动物
记 卖（sell）贝壳（shell）喽
考 类比
shell 壳 to nut 坚果 ⇒ hull 船体 to ship 船 （事物及其部分）
egg 鸡蛋 to shell 蛋壳 ⇒ banana 香蕉 to peel 香蕉皮 （事物及其部分）
shellfish 甲壳类动物 to lobster 虾 ⇒ poultry 禽类 to chicken 小鸡 （种属）

★ habit

['hæbɪt] *n.* 习惯

变 habitual *a.* 习惯的
考 同义 frequent = habitual
类比 habit 习惯 to individual 个人 ⇒ custom 习俗 to society 社会 （事物及其对象）

grant ★★★

[grɑːnt] v. 给予；同意

记 给予（grant）你一幢宏伟的（grand）房子

考 同义 confer = grant; concede = grant; bequeath = grant; grant = give

类比 sequester (隔绝) to reveal (显露) ⇒ grant (同意) to deny (否认) （反义）

注 关于"给予"的单词在 SSAT 的习题中有很多，如：endow, bestow。

wheedle ★★

['wiːdl] v. 以甜言蜜语诱骗，哄骗

记 容嬷嬷先好言诱骗（wheedle）你过来，不听话就拿针（needle）扎你

考 同义 wheedle = coax

类比 wheedle (欺骗) to cajolery (诱骗) ⇒ deceive (欺骗) to subterfuge (诡计) （同义）

注 关于"哄骗"的单词在 SSAT 的习题中有很多，如：cajole, coax, hoax。

obsolete ★★

['ɒbsəliːt] a. 陈旧的，过时的

记 现在还使用诺基亚手机绝对（absolute）是过时的（obsolete）表现

考 同义 obsolete = old-fashioned

类比 tentative (踌躇的) to unwilling (不情愿的) ⇒ outdated (过时的) to obsolete (过时的) （同义）

obsolete (过时的) to disuse (停止使用) ⇒ chaotic (混乱的) to confusion (困惑) （同义）

（chaotic 这个单词的英文释义为：a state of utter confusion）

alp ★

[ælp] n. 高山

记 阿尔卑斯山（Alps）

考 类比 boulevard (林荫大道) to lane (小巷) ⇒ alp (高山) to hill (小山) （>程度）

oblige ★★

[ə'blaɪdʒ] v. 迫使，使有义务做

变 obliged a. 有责任的；obligatory a. 义务的，必须的

记 ob- 相反 + -lige (like)：不（ob）喜欢（like）前夫的孩子，但是有义务（oblige）照顾

考 同义 obliged = bound; obligatory = required

类比 pernicious (有毒的) to benign (良性的) ⇒ obligatory (必须的) to optional (可选择的) （反义）

List | 85 words

★复习一下学过的单词！

- [ ] acclaim
- [ ] conciliate
- [ ] incite
- [ ] riot
- [ ] adversary
- [ ] disprove
- [ ] jury
- [ ] supervisor
- [ ] apprehend
- [ ] elevator
- [ ] potable
- [ ] umbrella
- [ ] bulwark
- [ ] elude
- [ ] quake
- [ ] valley
- [ ] capital
- [ ] impassive
- [ ] raucous
- [ ] vex

SSAT词汇 List 87

★ coroner ['kɒrənə] n. 验尸官

记 可怜的验尸官（coroner）只能在角落（corner）里工作

考 类比 surgeon 医生 to hospital 医院 → coroner 验尸官 to morgue 停尸房 （空间）
coroner 验尸官 to corpse 尸体 → editor 编辑 to text 文本 （人物及其对象）

★ thwart [θwɔːt] v. 挫败

记 在战争（war）中挫败（thwart）敌人

考 类比 flit 掠过 to dart 飞过 → foil 挫败 to thwart 挫败 （同义）

★★★ downpour ['daʊnpɔː] n. 倾盆大雨

记 down 下 + pour 流出

考 类比 flurry 阵风 to blizzard 暴风雪 → drizzle 毛毛雨 to downpour 大雨 （<程度）
breeze 微风 to wind 风 → drizzle 毛毛雨 to downpour 大雨 （<程度）
drizzle 毛毛雨 to downpour 大雨 → kindle 点燃 to blaze 燃烧 （<程度）

★★★ direct [dɪˈrekt] a. 直接的

变 director n. 导演；indirect a. 不直接的；direction n. 方向；directive n. 指示，指令

考 同义 succinct = direct; injunction = directive

类比 meander 蜿蜒前进 to direction 方向 → babble 乱说 to meaning 意义 （缺乏）
aimless 漫无目的的 to direction 方向 → reckless 鲁莽的 to caution 谨慎 （缺乏）
nuance 细微差别 to subtle 微妙的 → hint 暗示 to indirect 不直接的 （事物及其特点）

356 ☆ coroner ☆ thwart ☆ downpour ☆ direct

program → computer ⇒ direction → compass （事物及其特点）
程序　　电脑　　　 方向　　 指南针

choreographer → dancers ⇒ director → actors （人物及其对象）
编舞　　　　 舞蹈家　　　导演　　演员

coach → player ⇒ director → actor （人物及其对象）
教练　　运动员　　导演　　演员

director → actor ⇒ conductor → musician （人物及其对象）
导演　　演员　　　指挥　　　音乐家

conductor → orchestra ⇒ director → cast （人物及其对象）
指挥　　　管弦乐队　　导演　　全体演员

director → script ⇒ conductor → score （人物及其对象）
导演　　脚本　　　指挥家　　乐谱

producer → TV program ⇒ director → movie （人物及其对象）
制片人　　电视节目　　　导演　　电影

embellishment → decorative ⇒ circumlocution → indirect （同义）
装饰　　　　　装饰性的　　　累赘陈述　　　　不直接的

★★ dubious

['dju:bɪəs] *a.* 怀疑的

- 记 dub- (doubt) + -ious
- 考 同义 dubious = doubtful

类比 dubious → doubtful ⇒ questionable → uncertain （同义）
　　 怀疑的　　怀疑的　　　有疑问的　　　不确定的

　　 mettlesome → courage ⇒ dubious → suspiciousness （同义）
　　 有精神的　　勇气　　　可疑的　　怀疑

★ abandon

[ə'bændən] *v.* 抛弃，放弃

- 记 这个单词是所有按字母排序的词汇书开篇的第一个，如果这个你都不认识，就不用往下看了
- 考 同义 desert = abandon

★ trickle

['trɪkl] *n.* 细流，涓流

- 记 恶作剧 (trick) 般地把涓涓细流 (trickle) 倒在你头上
- 考 类比 trickle → flow ⇒ flicker → blaze （＜程度）
　　 涓流　　水流　　闪烁　　火焰

　　 trickle → flow ⇒ morsel → bite （＜程度）
　　 涓流　　水流　　一小口食物　一口食物

★ opinionated

[ə'pɪnɪəneɪtɪd] *a.* 固执己见的

- 变 opinion *n.* 观点
- 记 因为总是坚持自己的观点 (opinion)，所以被人称为固执的 (opinionated)
- 考 同义 opinionated = dogmatic

类比 conviction → opinion ⇒ reverence → admiration （＞程度）
　　 信念　　　观点　　　尊敬　　　羡慕

☆ dubious　　☆ abandon　　☆ trickle　　☆ opinionated

magnitude ★

[ˈmægnɪtjuːd] *n.* 大小，量级

记 magn-（magnet）磁铁 + -itude（attitude）：据说磁铁（magnet）可以用来预测地震，也可以这样记：磁铁（magnet）的态度（attitude）预测了地震的量级（magnitude）

考 同义 magnitude = quantity

类比 magnitude（震级）to earthquake（地震）→ decibel（分贝）to sound（声音）（修饰）

monsoon ★

[mɒnˈsuːn] *n.* 雨季，大雨

记 mon-（moon）+ soon：看到月亮（moon），你就知道很快（soon）就是梅雨季节（monsoon）了

考 类比 rain（雨）to monsoon（大雨）→ wind（风）to hurricane（飓风）（＜程度）

epiphany ★

[ɪˈpɪfəni] *n.* 顿悟

记 本意指每年1月6日的主显节，纪念贤士朝拜耶稣

考 同义 epiphany = realization

melt ★★

[melt] *v.* 熔化，融化

变 molten *a.* 熔化的

记 大雪融化（melt），蛇开始脱皮（molt）

考 同义 molten = liquefied

类比 congeal（凝结）to solid（固体）→ melt（融化）to liquid（液体）（事物及其特点）

snow（雪）to melt（融化）→ cement（水泥）to harden（变硬）（事物及其动作）

注 molten 是 melt 的过去分词，而跟 molt 没关系

chagrin ★★

[ˈʃægrɪn] *n.* 懊恼，失望

记 cha 茶 + grin 咧嘴笑：喝了口很贵的茶（cha），虽然失望（chagrin），但是依旧要面带微笑（grin）

考 同义 chagrin = embarrassment；chagrin = humiliation

注 chagrin 这个单词的英文释义为：a keen feeling of mental unease, as of humiliation or embarrassment。

shun ★★★

[ʃʌn] *v.* 避开

记 大夏天要避开（shun）阳光（sun）的直射

考 同义 avoid = shun

类比 shun（躲避）to embrace（接受）→ shrink（退缩）to pounce（猛扑）（反义）

outcast 流浪者 — to — shun 躲避 ⇒ idol 偶像 — to — worship 崇拜　（人物及其特点）

communicate ［kəˈmjuːnɪkeɪt］ v. 交流

变 communication n. 交流
考 类比
speak 说话 — to — communication 交流 ⇒ walk 走路 — to — locomotion 移动　（同义）
express 表达 — to — state 说话 ⇒ communicate 交流 — to — write 写字　（种属）
telepathy 心灵感应 — to — communicate 交流 ⇒ telecast 电视广播 — to — send 发送　（事物及其动作）

filch ［fɪltʃ］ v. 窃取，偷窃

记 让你去取（fetch）东西而不是去偷（filch）东西
考 类比
filch 偷窃 — to — pilfer 偷窃 ⇒ fidget 坐立不安 — to — squirm 蠕动　（同义）
filch 偷窃 — to — pickpocket 扒手 ⇒ endow 给予 — to — benefactor 捐助者　（人物及其动作）

trumpet ［ˈtrʌmpɪt］ n. 喇叭，小号

记 吹起胜利（triumph）的小喇叭（trumpet）
考 类比
cello 大提琴 — to — viola 中提琴 ⇒ tuba 大号 — to — trumpet 小号　（>程度）
trumpet 小号 — to — horn 喇叭 ⇒ tambourine 小手鼓 — to — drum 鼓　（种属）
strum 弹奏 — to — banjo 班卓琴 ⇒ blow 吹 — to — trumpet 喇叭　（动宾）

orbit ［ˈɔːbɪt］ n. 轨道

记 兔子（rabbit）沿着轨道（orbit）跑
考 同义 revolution = orbit
类比
planet 行星 — to — orbit 轨道 ⇒ bus 公车 — to — route 路线　（空间）
pinnacle 顶峰 — to — mountain 山 ⇒ apogee 最高点 — to — orbit 轨道　（空间）

groove ［gruːv］ n. 凹槽

记 想当年在国内红极一时的德国"舞动精灵"乐队的英文即为 Groove Coverage
考 类比
canyon 峡谷 — to — gully 冲沟 ⇒ chasm 裂口 — to — groove 凹槽　（同义）
groove 凹槽 — to — record 唱片 ⇒ wrinkle 皱纹 — to — face 脸　（空间）

☆ communicate　☆ filch　☆ trumpet　☆ orbit　☆ groove

★★★ amphibian [æmˈfɪbiən] *n.* 两栖动物

记 amphi- (ambi) 二 + bi- (bio) 生命 + an：两栖动物 (amphibian) 有两个生命 (bio)

考 类比
frog 青蛙 to amphibian 两栖动物 ⇒ dinosaur 恐龙 to reptile 爬行动物 （种属）
frog 青蛙 to amphibian 两栖动物 ⇒ whale 鲸 to mammal 哺乳动物 （种属）
frog 青蛙 to amphibian 两栖动物 ⇒ human 人 to mammal 哺乳动物 （种属）
amphibian 两栖动物 to frog 青蛙 ⇒ rodent 啮齿类动物 to beaver 海狸 （种属）
aeronautics 航空学 to science 科学 ⇒ salamander 火蜥蜴 to amphibian 两栖动物 （种属）

List | **86** words ★ 复习一下学过的单词！

☐ accomplish	☐ jeer	☐ poignant	☐ thicket
☐ alp	☐ lessen	☐ sap	☐ vacuum
☐ canine	☐ oblige	☐ shell	☐ violin
☐ grant	☐ obsolete	☐ skyscraper	☐ waive
☐ habit	☐ odor	☐ sow	☐ wheedle

SSAT词汇 List 88

tirade
[taɪˈreɪd] *n.* 激烈的长篇演说

记 他希望自己用一篇演讲（tirade）来打动别的国家同意进行贸易（trade）往来

考 类比 tirade 激烈的长篇演说 to speech 演讲 ⇒ feature 专题文章 to article 文章 （种属）

★★★ perpetual
[pəˈpetʃuəl] *a.* 永久的

变 perpetuity *n.* 永恒

记 我们熟悉的"永动机"的英文即为 perpetual motion machine

考 同义 perpetual = unending；perpetual = continuous

类比 perpetual 永久的 to continuous 持续的 ⇒ invincible 战无不胜的 to unbeatable 无敌的 （同义）

perpetuity 永恒 to impermanence 短暂 ⇒ interminable 无休止的 to occasional 偶然的 （反义）

★ verge
[vɜːdʒ] *n.* 接近，边缘

记 这年头，诗歌（verse）处于灭绝边缘（verge）

考 同义 verge = threshold

注 verge 这个单词的英文释义为：brink, threshold。

★★ wane
[weɪn] *v.* 衰落，变小

记 年纪增大，酒（wine）量变小（wane）

考 同义 ebb = wane；wane = diminish

类比 wax 增大 to wane 变小 ⇒ advance 进步 to retreat 撤退 （反义）

★★★ extol
[ɪkˈstəʊl] *v.* 颂扬，赞美

记 ex- 朝外 + -tol（tall）：朝外（ex）把你往高了说即为颂扬（extol）

考 同义 extol = praise highly；extol = commend

☆ tirade   ☆ perpetual   ☆ verge   ☆ wane   ☆ extol

361

类比　flare to shine → extol to praise　（＞程度）
　　　闪耀　　发光　　赞美　　表扬
　　　regale to entertain → extol to praise　（＞程度）
　　　盛情款待　款待　　赞美　　表扬

coil　[kɔɪl] v. 盘绕，缠绕

记 在鸡腿外面缠绕（coil）一层面糊，然后放进煮（boil）沸的油（oil）里炸
考 类比　fold to blanket → coil to rope　（动宾）
　　　折叠　　毯子　　缠绕　　绳子
　　　bulwark to protect → coil to gyrate　（事物及其特点）
　　　堡垒　　保护　　线圈　　旋转

callous　['kæləs] a. 无情的，麻木的

记 这个单词来自（callus），指的是手上起的茧，久而久之引申成"无情的，麻木的"意思
考 同义　callous = insensitive

jest　[dʒest] v. 嘲笑

记 嘲笑（jest）别人最好（best）的方式就是用行动来说话
考 类比　riddle to puzzlement → jest to laughter　（因果）
　　　迷　　困惑　　嘲笑　　笑声

analyze　['ænəlaɪz] v. 分析

变 analysis n. 分析；analyst n. 分析家
考 同义　analysis = diagnosis
　　类比　book to read → data to analyze　（动宾）
　　　　书　　读　　数据　　分析
　　　　summarize to analyze → shorten to understand　（纵向）
　　　　总结　　分析　　缩短　　懂得
　　　　altercation to argument → analysis to break down　（同义）
　　　　争论　　争论　　分析　　分解
　　　　tourist to sightseeing → analyst to examining　（人物及其动作）
　　　　游客　　观光　　分析家　　检测

sketch　[sketʃ] n. 素描，缩略图

记 这是斯沃琪（swatch）手表最初的缩略图（sketch）
考 类比　sketch to draw → skim to read　（种属）
　　　缩略图　画　　略读　　读
　　　outline to document → sketch to picture　（事物及其部分）
　　　大纲　　文件　　缩略图　　图画

★★★ persistent

[pə'sɪstənt] *a.* 固执的，坚持的

- 变　persist *v.* 坚持
- 记　persistent 和 insistent 意思相同，均为"坚持的"
- 考　同义　persist = continue; persist = endure; chronic = persistent; determined = persistent
  persistent = tenacious

  类比　perceptive (感知的) to discern (辨别) ⇒ persistent (坚持的) to persevere (坚持) （同义）

  persistent (固执的) to obstinate (固执的) ⇒ valiant (勇敢的) to brave (勇敢的) （同义）

★ devour

[dɪ'vaʊə] *v.* 吞食

- 记　魔鬼（devil）吞食（devour）了我们的食物
- 考　类比　snack (吃零食) to devour (吞食) ⇒ push (推) to shove (强推) （<程度）

  consume (消耗) to devour (吞食) ⇒ suspend (暂缓工作) to expel (驱逐) （<程度）

★ submerge

[səb'mɜːdʒ] *v.* 淹没

- 记　sub- 下 + merge 谐音：没之；淹没（submerge）即为用水淹没之（merge）
- 考　同义　immerse = submerge

★ legend

['ledʒənd] *n.* 图例

- 考　类比　legend (图标) to map (地图) ⇒ key (图标) to chart (图表) （空间）
- 注　legend 这个单词"传奇"的意思我们很熟悉，此处为熟词僻义。

★★★ moderate

['mɒdəreɪt] *a.* 温和的，适度的；*v.* 减轻，节制

- 变　moderation *n.* 节制
- 记　现代（modern）人在饮食方面都很不节制（moderate）
- 考　同义　moderate = temperate; reasonable = moderate; moderate = not extreme

  类比　glutton (贪吃者) to moderation (节制) ⇒ scoundrel (恶棍) to virtue (道德) （缺乏）

  remiss (怠慢的) to dutifulness (负责) ⇒ intemperate (放纵的) to moderation (节制) （反义）

  dispassionate (公平的) to partisanship (党派性) ⇒ intemperate (放纵的) to moderation (节制) （反义）

- 注　关于"减轻，节制"的单词在 SSAT 的习题中有很多，如：abate, alleviate, assuage, dampen, mitigate。

kitten ['kɪtn] n. 小猫

记 Kitten 是我们常说的 Hello Kitty 中 Kitty 的另外一种写法

考 类比 kitten/小猫 to cat/猫 ⇒ foal/小马 to horse/马 （成长过程）
kitten/小猫 to cat/猫 ⇒ puppy/小狗 to dog/狗 （成长过程）
kitten/小猫 to cat/猫 ⇒ child/小孩 to adult/成人 （成长过程）

doleful ['dəʊlful] a. 悲哀的

记 因为一个人（sole）过日子，所以很悲哀（doleful）
考 同义 doleful = joyless；doleful = sad

morose [məˈrəʊs] a. 郁闷的，孤僻的

记 mo 没 + rose 玫瑰：因为情人节当天没有收到玫瑰花，所以很郁闷（morose）
考 类比 morose/郁闷的 to cheerful/开心的 ⇒ hygienic/卫生的 to contaminated/污染的 （反义）

vend [vend] v. 出售

记 我们常见的自动售货机即为 vending machine
考 同义 vend = sell

barley ['bɑːli] n. 大麦

记 我们这个地方几乎不（barely）产大麦（barley）
考 类比 barley/大麦 to bread/面包 ⇒ egg/鸡蛋 to omelet/煎蛋卷 （成分）
barley/大麦 to grain/一粒大麦 ⇒ wine/酒 to drop/一滴酒 （组成）

List | 87 words　　　　　　　　　　★ 复习一下学过的单词！

□ abandon	□ direct	□ groove	□ orbit
□ amphibian	□ downpour	□ magnitude	□ shun
□ chagrin	□ dubious	□ melt	□ thwart
□ communicate	□ epiphany	□ monsoon	□ trickle
□ coroner	□ filch	□ opinionated	□ trumpet

SSAT词汇 List 89

indolent
[ˈɪndələnt] *a.* 懒惰的
记 这些人既懒惰（indolent）又傲慢（insolent）
考 同义 indolent = languid; indolent = lazy

talon
[ˈtælən] *n.* 爪子
记 鹰在美发沙龙（salon）里做美爪（talon）
考 类比 talon/爪子 to bird/鸟 ⇒ gill/鱼鳃 to fish/鱼 （事物及其部分）
cat/猫 to claw/爪 ⇒ eagle/鹰 to talon/爪 （事物及其部分）

aboriginal
[ˌæbəˈrɪdʒənəl] *a.* 土著的，原始的
记 原始的（aboriginal）这个单词里面包含一个原始的（original）
考 同义 aboriginal = primordial
类比 pandemic/大流行病 to endemic/地方性疾病 ⇒ universal/宇宙的 to aboriginal/当地的 （＞程度）

evade
[ɪˈveɪd] *v.* 躲避，逃避
变 evasion *n.* 逃避，躲避
记 To evade or invade, that is a question.
考 同义 evade = sidestep; evade = elude; evade = escape; evade = shirk
evasion = avoidance

reflex
[ˈriːfleks] *n.* 反应
记 看到自己倒影（reflection）的第一反应（reflex）就是"我为啥那么帅"
考 类比 reflex = instinctive reaction

grid
[ɡrɪd] *n.* 网格，格子
记 大街上随处可见的国家电网的英文为 State Grid

grid

☆ indolent   ☆ talon   ☆ aboriginal   ☆ evade   ☆ reflex
☆ grid

考 类比　grid→line ⇒ circle→arc　（组成）
　　　网格　线　　圆　　弧

　　　grid→line ⇒ net→string　（组成）
　　　网格　线　　网　细绳

★★★ irritate ['ɪrɪteɪt] v. 激怒

变　irritation n. 激怒；irritating a. 愤怒的
记　洗车的时候不小心冲洗（irrigate）了别人家晾晒的床单，激怒（irritate）了人家
考　同义　vex = irritate；irritate = exasperate；annoy = irritate

　　类比　noise→irritate ⇒ music→calm　（事物及其动作）
　　　　　噪音　激怒　　音乐　使平静

　　　　　abash→embarrassment ⇒ annoy→irritation　（同义）
　　　　　使困窘　尴尬　　　　　惹恼　激怒

　　　　　knotty→difficult ⇒ prickly→irritating　（同义）
　　　　　棘手的　困难的　　易怒的　易怒的

注　关于"激怒"的单词在 SSAT 的习题中有很多，如：provoke，stir，annoy，ire。

★★ natal ['neɪtl] a. 出生的，新生的

记　新出生的（natal）女孩子起名叫娜塔莉（Natalie）
考　同义　natal = refer to the birth

　　类比　natal→birth ⇒ fatal→demise　（同义）
　　　　　新生的　出生　致命的　死亡

注　关于"新生的"单词在 SSAT 的习题中有很多，如：innate，inherent，congenital。

★★ frame [freɪm] n. 框架

记　有名气（fame）的人照片都放在相框（frame）里
考　同义　frame = chassis

　　类比　frame→building ⇒ skeleton→body　（事物及其部分）
　　　　　框架　建筑物　　骨架　身体

　　　　　picture→frame ⇒ diamond→setting　（空间）
　　　　　图画　框架　　　钻石　放钻石的支架

★ onerous ['əʊnərəs] a. 繁重的

记　工作繁重（onerous），身体虚弱，是得病的先兆（ominous）
考　同义　onerous = exceedingly difficult

★★★ endeavor [en'devə] v. 努力；n. 努力

记　美国奋进号航天飞机即为 ENDEAVOR
考　同义　endeavor = attempt；endeavor = effort

　　类比　endeavor→strive　（同义）
　　　　　努力　　努力

　　　　　defiance→opposition ⇒ exertion→endeavor　（同义）
　　　　　违抗　　反对　　　　努力　努力

endeavor

inhabit
[ɪnˈhæbɪt] v. 居住，栖息

- 记 我周末的习惯（habit）就是宅（inhabit）在家里不出去
- 考 同义 dwell = inhabit；inhabit = occupy

dissolve
[dɪˈzɒlv] v. 溶解，分解

- 记 dis- + solve：问题无法（dis）解决（solve），只能把它溶解（dissolve）在问题之中
- 考 类比 clot 凝块 to dissolved 溶解的 ⇒ crowd 人群 to dispersed 分散的 （修饰）
  fossil 化石 to petrified 石化的 ⇒ solution 溶液 to dissolved 溶解的 （修饰）

pensive
[ˈpensɪv] a. 沉思的

- 记 这个东西的价格有点贵（expensive），是否购买使他陷入沉思（pensive）
- 考 同义 pensive = thoughtful
  类比 demonstrative 感情外露的 to feeling 感情 ⇒ pensive 沉思的 to serious 严肃的 （修饰）
  （这个题的思路有些复杂：Demonstrative means showing feeling openly while pensive means involved in or reflecting serious thought.）

enlighten
[ɪnˈlaɪtn] v. 启发，启蒙

- 考 同义 enlighten = educate；illuminate = enlighten
  类比 appease 安抚 to anger 生气 ⇒ enlighten 启发 to ignorance 无知 （动宾）
  theater 剧场 to entertain 娱乐 ⇒ classroom 教室 to enlighten 启发 （事物及其用途）

blaze
[bleɪz] n. 火焰

- 变 blazing a. 燃烧的
- 记 小孩因为玩火（blaze），所以遭到大人的谴责（blame）
- 考 同义 blazing = fiery
  类比 ignite 点燃 to blaze 火焰 ⇒ trim 修剪 to decrease 减少 （因果）
  trickle 涓流 to flow 水流 ⇒ flicker 闪烁 to blaze 火焰 （<程度）
  drizzle 毛毛雨 to downpour 暴雨 ⇒ kindle 点燃 to blaze 火焰 （<程度）

comply
[kəmˈplaɪ] v. 顺从

- 变 compliant a. 顺从的
- 记 com- (come) + -ply (play)：大家来（come）一起玩（play），要遵守（comply）规则
- 考 同义 acquiesce = comply；compliant = amenable

类比 comply to requirement ⇒ accept to invitation （动宾）
顺从　　　要求　　　　接受　　　邀请

contradict to opposition ⇒ comply to obedience （同义）
矛盾　　　相反　　　　顺从　　　听话

compliant to servile ⇒ trusting to gullible （＜程度）
顺从的　　奴性的　　　信任的　　易受骗的

注 关于"顺从的"单词在 SSAT 的习题中有很多，如：docile, submissive, obedient, amenable。

★ jack

[dʒæk] *n.* 千斤顶

记 杰克（Jack）拿着千斤顶（jack）

考 类比 hammer to pound ⇒ jack to raise （事物及其动作）
锤子　　猛击　　　千斤顶　提升

★ coy

[kɔɪ] *a.* 腼腆的，害羞的

记 他是一个害羞的（coy）男孩（boy）
考 同义 coy = shy

★★★ extrovert

['ekstrəvɜːt] *n.* 外向的人

变 introvert *n.* 内向的人；extroverted 外向的

记 内向的人（introvert）好还是外向的人（extrovert）好，这是个有争议的（controversy）话题

考 同义 extroverted = outgoing

类比 vain to humble ⇒ extroverted to shy （反义）
自负的　谦虚的　　　外向的　　内向的

superscript to subscript ⇒ introvert to extrovert （反义）
上标　　　　下标　　　　内向者　　外向者

perfectionist to exacting ⇒ extrovert to outgoing （人物及其特点）
完美主义者　　苛求的　　　外向者　　外向的

convex to depressed ⇒ introvert to extrovert （反义）
突出的　陷入的　　　内向者　　外向者

（depressed 这个单词的英文释义为：having the central part lower than the margin）

List | **88** words　　　　　　　　　　　★ 复习一下学过的单词！

☐ analyze	☐ doleful	☐ moderate	☐ submerge
☐ barley	☐ extol	☐ morose	☐ tirade
☐ callous	☐ jest	☐ perpetual	☐ vend
☐ coil	☐ kitten	☐ persistent	☐ verge
☐ devour	☐ legend	☐ sketch	☐ wane

☆ jack　　　☆ coy　　　☆ extrovert

SSAT词汇 List 90

★ fret
[fret] v. 烦恼，焦躁

- 变 fretful a. 焦躁的，烦躁的
- 记 女孩子脚（feet）太大，她很烦恼（fret）
- 考 同义 fretful = worried；fret = worry

类比 $\dfrac{\text{amuse}}{\text{娱乐}}$ to $\dfrac{\text{divert}}{\text{娱乐}}$ ⇒ $\dfrac{\text{vex}}{\text{使烦恼}}$ to $\dfrac{\text{fret}}{\text{使焦躁}}$ （同义）

★★ benign
[bəˈnaɪn] a. 良性的，和蔼的

- 记 恶性肿瘤开始（begin）变为良性（benign）
- 考 同义 benign = gentle

类比 $\dfrac{\text{sanitation}}{\text{卫生}}$ to $\dfrac{\text{contamination}}{\text{污染}}$ ⇒ $\dfrac{\text{evil}}{\text{邪恶的}}$ to $\dfrac{\text{benign}}{\text{亲切的}}$ （反义）

$\dfrac{\text{pernicious}}{\text{有毒的}}$ to $\dfrac{\text{benign}}{\text{良性的}}$ ⇒ $\dfrac{\text{obligatory}}{\text{必需的}}$ to $\dfrac{\text{optional}}{\text{可选择的}}$ （反义）

★★★ antagonistic
[ænˌtæɡəˈnɪstɪk] a. 敌对的，对抗的

- 变 antagonize v. 敌对，对抗；antagonist n. 敌手
- 记 ant- 相反 + agoni-（agony）痛苦 + stic：孩子总是和父母反着来（ant），和父母处于敌对状态（antagonistic），让父母很痛苦（agony）
- 考 同义 antagonize = make an enemy；hostile = antagonistic

类比 $\dfrac{\text{hero}}{\text{主角}}$ to $\dfrac{\text{villain}}{\text{坏人}}$ ⇒ $\dfrac{\text{protagonist}}{\text{主角}}$ to $\dfrac{\text{antagonist}}{\text{敌手}}$ （反义）

$\dfrac{\text{happiness}}{\text{快乐}}$ to $\dfrac{\text{sadness}}{\text{悲伤}}$ ⇒ $\dfrac{\text{amiable}}{\text{和蔼可亲的}}$ to $\dfrac{\text{antagonistic}}{\text{对抗的}}$ （反义）

★★ cushion
[ˈkʊʃn] n. 垫子

- 记 现在买个瑜伽垫（cushion）练习瑜伽很时尚（fashion）
- 考 类比 $\dfrac{\text{saddle}}{\text{马鞍}}$ to $\dfrac{\text{horse}}{\text{马}}$ ⇒ $\dfrac{\text{cushion}}{\text{垫子}}$ to $\dfrac{\text{chair}}{\text{椅子}}$ （空间）

☆ fret　　☆ benign　　☆ antagonistic　　☆ cushion

| truck 卡车 | to | wheel 轮子 | ⇒ | sofa 沙发 | to | cushion 垫子 | （空间） |

★★★ stable

['steɪbl] *a.* 稳定的；*n.* 马厩

变 unstable *a.* 不稳定的

记 稳定的（stable）桌子（table）

考 同义 stable = steadfast

类比
apiary 蜂房	to	bees 蜜蜂	⇒	stable 马厩	to	horses 马	（空间）
stable 马厩	to	horse 马	⇒	kennel 狗窝	to	dog 狗	（空间）
hover 盘旋	to	airborne 空中的	⇒	totter 蹒跚	to	unstable 不稳定的	（同义）
allergic 过敏的	to	sneeze 打喷嚏	⇒	unstable 不稳定	to	collapse 倒塌	（动作及其情感）

★ insomnia

[ɪnˈsɒmnɪə] *n.* 失眠症

记 这个词来自罗马睡眠之神修普诺斯（Somnus）

考 类比
| insomnia 失眠症 | to | sleep 睡眠 | ⇒ | amnesia 健忘症 | to | memory 记忆 | （缺乏） |

SOMNUS
insomnia

★★★ imitation

[ˌɪmɪˈteɪn] *n.* 模仿，模拟

变 imitate *v.* 模仿，模拟

记 可以模仿（imitation）别人的作品，但一定要有限制（limitation）

考 同义 emulate = imitate；imitate = mirror；mimic = imitate

类比
| imitate 模拟 | to | copy 复制 | ⇒ | originate 起源 | to | invent 发明 | （同义） |
| cooperation 合作 | to | collusion 勾结 | ⇒ | imitation 模仿 | to | forgery 伪造 | （同义：正反向） |

★ surge

[sɜːdʒ] *n.* 汹涌，飙升

记 一个外科大夫（surgeon）被大浪（surge）冲了起来

考 同义 surge = upwelling

★★ brash

[bræʃ] *a.* 无礼的，傲慢的，仓促的

记 工人用刷子（brush）很无礼（brash）地在别人家门口贴小广告

考 同义 brash = bold

☆ stable   ☆ insomnia   ☆ imitation   ☆ surge   ☆ brash

slander

★

['slɑːndə] *v.* 诽谤

- 记 肥胖的人喜欢诽谤（slander）苗条的（slender）人不够健康
- 考 同义　malign = slander

quandary

★

['kwɒndəri] *n.* 困境

- 记 quan 圈 + dary：困境（quandary）即为陷入圈套
- 考 同义　quandary = puzzlement
- 注 关于"困境"的单词在 SSAT 的习题中有很多，如：dilemma, predicament, uncertainty, perplexity。

clog

★

[klɒg] *n.* 木屐

- 记 木屐（clog）当然是由木头（log）制成的
- 考 类比　clog 木屐 to shoe 鞋子 ⇒ beret 贝雷帽 to hat 帽子　（种属）

lever

★

['liːvə] *n.* 杠杆

- 记 用杠杆（lever）来衡量你的水平（level）
- 考 类比　megaphone 扩音器 to speak 说 ⇒ lever 杠杆 to pry 撬　（事物及其用途）
  clamp 夹钳 to hold 控制 ⇒ lever 杠杆 to lift 提升　（事物及其用途）

thrive

★★

[θraɪv] *v.* 繁荣，兴旺

- 记 注意区分"努力"（strive）和"繁荣"（thrive）
- 考 同义　flourish = thrive；thrive = prosper

masticate

★

['mæstɪkeɪt] *v.* 咀嚼

- 记 mast-（must）+ ic + ate 吃：食物必须（must）通过咀嚼（masticate）才能吃（ate）下去
- 考 类比　masticate 咀嚼 to chew 嚼 ⇒ gesticulate 用手势表达 to gesture 示意　（同义）

authentic

★★★

[ɔːˈθentɪk] *a.* 真正的

- 变 authenticity *n.* 真实性；authenticate *v.* 证明……的真实性
- 记 这是一本货真价实的（authentic）带有作者（author）签名的书
- 考 同义　trustworthy = authentic；authentic = genuine；verify = authenticate
  类比　nature 自然 to nurture 养育 ⇒ authentic 真正的 to artificial 人工的　（反义）

spurious —to→ authenticity ⇒ laughable —to→ serious （反义）
假的   真实性   可笑的   严肃的

artificial —to→ authentic ⇒ gorgeous —to→ dreary （反义）
人工的   真实的   华丽灿烂的   枯燥的

★ facetious   [fə'siːʃəs] a. 诙谐的

记 就算是诙谐（facetious）也要给人留面子（face）
考 同义　facetious = jocular

★ sly   [slaɪ] a. 狡猾的

记 表面害羞（shy）实则狡猾（sly）
考 同义　crafty = sly

rue   [ruː] v. 后悔

记 她后悔（rue）自己当初没说实（true）话
考 同义　regret = rue；lament = rue

★ heinous   ['heɪnəs] a. 可憎的，可恶的

记 he + in + ous（ours）：他在我们家一住就是一年，真是太可恶（heinous）了
考 同义　heinous = atrocious；heinous = wicked

List | **89** words ★复习一下学过的单词！

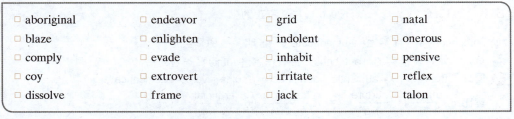

□ aboriginal	□ endeavor	□ grid	□ natal
□ blaze	□ enlighten	□ indolent	□ onerous
□ comply	□ evade	□ inhabit	□ pensive
□ coy	□ extrovert	□ irritate	□ reflex
□ dissolve	□ frame	□ jack	□ talon

☆ facetious　　☆ sly　　☆ rue　　☆ heinous

SSAT词汇 List 91

intern
[ɪnˈtɜːn] n. 实习生

记 他是英特尔（Intel）公司的实习生（intern）
考 类比：royalty 版税 to author 作者 ⇒ stipend 薪金 to intern 实习生（人物及其对象）

diamond
[ˈdaɪəmənd] n. 钻石；菱形棒球场地

考 类比：
carat 克拉 to diamond 钻石 ⇒ calories 卡路里 to heat 热度（修饰）
sprint 快跑 to track 跑道 ⇒ baseball 棒球 to diamond 棒球场（空间）
picture 图画 to frame 框架 ⇒ diamond 钻石 to setting 放钻石的支架（空间）
golf 高尔夫 to course 高尔夫球场 ⇒ baseball 棒球 to diamond 棒球场（空间）

threat
[θret] n. 威胁

变 threaten v. 威胁；threatening a. 威胁的
记 被人威胁（threat），命悬一线（thread）
考 同义：ominous = threatening
类比：
threat 威胁 to insecurity 不安全 ⇒ horror 恐惧 to fear 害怕（因果）
minatory 威胁的 to threaten 威胁 ⇒ laudatory 赞美的 to praise 表扬（同义）
brandish 挥舞 to threat 威胁 ⇒ browbeat 恫吓 to intimidate 威胁（动作及其目的）
extortionist 勒索者 to threaten 威胁 ⇒ zealot 热心者 to patronize 资助（人物及其动作）

novice
[ˈnɒvɪs] n. 初学者，新手

记 nov- 新 + ice
考 同义：novice = neophyte；beginner = novice；novice = fledgling

☆ intern　　☆ diamond　　☆ threat　　☆ novice

(fledgling 这个单词的英文释义为: a young bird that has its feathers and is learning to fly)

receptacle ★

[rɪˈseptəkl] *n.* 容器

- 记 这个慈善机构的大容器 (receptacle) 接受 (receive) 任何新旧程度的衣物
- 考 同义 receptacle = container

trifling ★

[ˈtraɪflɪŋ] *a.* 微不足道的

- 记 旅行 (travelling) 途中不要因为微不足道的 (trifling) 的事而烦恼
- 考 同义 trifling = negligible; trifling = paltry; trifling = trivial

carpenter ★★★

[ˈkɑːpɪntə] *n.* 木匠

- 记 著名乐队"卡朋特兄妹"(Carpenter) 的代表作有 *Yesterday Once More* 等
- 考 类比
  - hammer to carpenter ⇒ knife to butcher
    锤子　　木匠　　　刀　　屠夫 (人物及其工具)
  - saw to carpenter ⇒ scissors to tailor
    锯　　木匠　　　剪刀　　裁缝 (人物及其工具)
  - hammer to carpenter ⇒ awl to cobbler
    锤子　　木匠　　　锥子　　补鞋匠 (人物及其工具)
  - saw to carpenter ⇒ plow to farmer
    锯　　木匠　　　耙子　　农民 (人物及其工具)
  - welder to metal ⇒ carpenter to wood
    焊接工　金属　　木匠　　木头 (人物及其对象)
  - farmer to cook ⇒ lumberjack to carpenter
    农民　　厨师　　伐木工　　木匠 (因果)

  (这个题的思路有些复杂：因为农民 (farmer) 种庄稼, 厨师 (cook) 才可以去做东西, 而因为伐木工 (lumberjack) 伐木, 木匠 (carpenter) 才可以去做东西)

carpenter

stimulate ★★

[ˈstɪmjuleɪt] *v.* 刺激

- 变 stimulus *n.* 刺激, 刺激物
- 记 注意区分"刺激"(stimulate) 和"模仿, 假装"(simulate)
- 考 类比
  - accident to carelessness ⇒ response to stimulus
    事故　　粗心　　　回应　　刺激 (因果)
  - evoke to hot-headed ⇒ stimulate to petulant
    引起　　急躁的　　刺激　　脾气不好的 (纵向)

prosecute ★★

[ˈprɒsɪkjuːt] *v.* 检举, 起诉

- 变 prosecutor *n.* 检察官, 公诉人
- 记 先检举 (prosecute) 后执行 (execute)

考 类比 plaintiff/原告 to defendant/被告 ⇒ prosecute/起诉 to defend/辩护 （纵向）
accuse/控告 to prosecutor/公诉人 ⇒ search/调查 to inspector/检察员 （人物及其动作）

brazen
['breɪzn] *a.* 厚颜无耻的

记 因为厚颜无耻（brazen），所以被冻死（frozen）
考 类比 brazen/厚颜无耻的 to tact/机智 ⇒ lethargic/无生气的 to energy/精力 （缺乏）
insolence/无礼 to brazen/厚颜无耻 ⇒ obedience/顺从 to dutiful/顺从的 （同义）

ominous
['ɒmɪnəs] *a.* 恶兆的

变 omen *n.* 恶兆
记 我们可以通过 omen 来记住 ominous，omen 可以看作 O men，这是一句感叹句，一般是在失望的时候说的
考 同义 ominous = inauspicious; portentous = ominous; ominous = threatening
ominous = sinister; ominous = baneful; ominous = forbidding
类比 auspicious/吉利的 to ominous/恶兆的 ⇒ timely/及时的 to inopportune/不适当的 （反义）

seed
[si:d] *n.* 种子

考 类比 fire/火 to smoke/烟 ⇒ seed/种子 to flower/花 （因果）
sprout/发芽 to seed/种子 ⇒ hatch/孵化 to egg/鸡蛋 （事物及其动作）

deteriorate
[dɪ'tɪərɪeɪt] *v.* 恶化，变坏

记 病人决定（determine）放弃治疗，任由病情恶化（deteriorate）
考 同义 crumble = deteriorate

excess
[ɪk'ses] *n.* 超过，过量

变 excessive *a.* 过多的
记 ex- 朝外 + cess 走路：走向外边，走过（excess）了
考 同义 excess = plethora; exorbitant = excessive

pint
[paɪnt] *n.* 品脱

考 类比 day/日 to week/周 ⇒ pint/品脱 to liter/升 （同类）
pint/品脱 to quart/夸脱 ⇒ week/周 to year/年 （同类）

distance 距离 to yard 码 ⇒ volume 容积 to pint 品脱 （事物及其对象）

★ collie ['kɒli] n. 柯利牧羊犬

考 类比 dog 狗 to collie 柯利牧羊犬 ⇒ lizard 蜥蜴 to chameleon 变色龙 （种属）

collie 柯利牧羊犬 to dog 狗 ⇒ dinghy 无篷小船 to boat 船 （种属）

★★ rigid ['rɪdʒɪd] a. 严格的，僵硬的

记 在寒冷的（frigid）哈尔滨，手脚都冻僵硬（rigid）了

考 同义 rigid = not flexible

类比 fractious 易怒的 to obedience 听话 ⇒ rigid 死板的 to adaptability 适应性 （缺乏）

★ indigenous [ɪnˈdɪdʒɪnəs] a. 本土的，土著的

记 本土人（indigenous）一般会比较天真朴实（ingenuous）

考 同义 indigenous = native born

类比 indigenous 本土的 to native 本地人 ⇒ foreign 外国的 to alien 外国人 （同义）

★ coarse [kɔːs] a. 粗糙的

记 粗糙的（coarse）煤炭（coal）

考 同义 rough = coarse；coarse = crude

类比 irrigate 灌溉 to dry 干 ⇒ smooth 使光滑 to coarse 粗糙的 （反义）

★ genesis ['dʒenəsɪs] n. 发生，起源

记 来自《圣经》中的"创世纪"，讲述的是人类的起源和宇宙的起源

考 同义 genesis = origin

List | 90 words　　　　　　　　　　　　　　　　　　★ 复习一下学过的单词！

- antagonistic
- authentic
- benign
- brash
- clog
- cushion
- facetious
- fret
- heinous
- imitation
- insomnia
- lever
- masticate
- quandary
- rue
- slander
- sly
- stable
- surge
- thrive

SSAT词汇 List 92

★ concrete
['kɒnkriːt] *a.* 具体的；*n.* 水泥

记 用水泥（concrete）来连接（connect）两个物体

考 类比 abstract 抽象的 to concrete 具体的 ⇒ stubborn 倔强的 to flexible 灵活的 （反义）

sidewalk 人行道 to concrete 水泥 ⇒ coat 外套 to cloth 布 （事物及其用途）

★ indignation
[ˌɪndɪɡ'neɪʃn] *n.* 愤慨

变 indignant *a.* 愤慨的

记 in- 否定 + -dign（dignity）尊严 + -ation：没有（in）尊严（dignity），所以愤慨（indignation）

考 类比 ravenous 狼吞虎咽的 to hunger 饥饿 ⇒ furious 狂怒的 to indignation 愤慨 （>程度）

★ illicit
[ɪ'lɪsɪt] *a.* 违法的，不正当的

记 在伊利诺伊州（Illinois）不要做违法的（illicit）事情

考 同义 prohibited = illicit；improper = illicit

★★ impulse
['ɪmpʌls] *n.* 冲动

变 impulsive *a.* 冲动的

记 曾经看到过一句非常浪漫的话：At least we should have two impulses in life. One is for the love regardless of all consequences; another is for the travel we can leave anytime.

考 同义 impulse = urge；whim = impulse

类比 impulsive 冲动的 to calculated 计算好的 ⇒ concrete 具体的 to subjective 主观的 （反义）

cautious 谨慎的 to impulsive 冲动的 ⇒ secretive 秘密的 to proverbial 众所周知的 （反义）

☆ concrete   ☆ indignation   ☆ illicit   ☆ impulse

migrate

[maɪˈgreɪt] v. 移动，移居

- **变** migration n. 移动，移居；immigrant n. 移民
- **记** 这个单词的形容词形式为 migrant，我们常说的"农民工"的英文即为 migrant workers
- **考** 同义 migrate = travel

类比
- bird (鸟) to migration (迁徙) ⇒ bear (熊) to hibernation (冬眠)　（事物及其特点）
- migrate (迁徙) to swallow (燕子) ⇒ hibernate (冬眠) to ground hog (土拨鼠)　（事物及其特点）
- immigrant (移民) to country (国家) ⇒ convert (皈依者) to religion (宗教)　（人物及其对象）

timid

[ˈtɪmɪd] a. 胆小的

- **记** Kimi 很胆小（timid）
- **考** 同义 mousy = timid

类比
- courage (勇气) to craven (胆小的) ⇒ valor (勇猛) to timid (胆小的)　（缺乏）
- reluctant (不情愿的) to eager (渴望的) ⇒ timid (胆小的) to courageous (勇敢的)　（反义）
- fearless (无所不惧的) to timid (胆小的) ⇒ ascending (上升的) to falling (下降的)　（反义）
- dauntless (无畏的) to timid (胆小的) ⇒ remorseful (后悔的) to unrepentant (不悔的)　（反义）

chaff

[tʃɑːf] n. 糠，谷壳，无价值的东西

- **记** 大厨（chef）做饭前得先去掉谷壳（chaff）
- **考** 同义 chaff = waste

euphoria

[juːˈfeɪrɪə] n. 兴高采烈，欢愉

- **记** 将 euphoria 更换字母顺序稍作添加即为 European，欧洲人无论何时总是很兴高采烈
- **考** 同义 ebullience = euphoria

类比
- utopia (乌托邦) to location (地点) ⇒ euphoria (兴高采烈) to sensation (感觉)　（事物及其特点）

lava

[ˈlɑːvə] n. 岩浆

- **记** 用 Java 程序来模拟岩浆（lava）喷出
- **考** 类比
- lava (岩浆) to volcano (火山) ⇒ water (水) to geyser (喷泉)　（事物及其部分）
- water (水) to spring (喷泉) ⇒ lava (岩浆) to volcano (火山)　（事物及其部分）

humus ★

['hju:məs] *n.* 腐殖土

- 记 腐殖土（humus）很潮湿（humid）
- 考 同义 humus = topsoil

belly ★

['beli] *n.* 肚子

- 记 我的肚子（belly）里仿佛有个铃铛（bell），一到饭点就响
- 考 类比 snake 蛇 to belly 肚子 ⇒ person 人 to feet 脚 （事物及其部分）

chide ★★

[tʃaɪd] *v.* 责备

- 记 对孩子（child）的责备（chide）要稍微轻一点
- 考 同义 berate = chide；chide = scold；chide = reprimand
- 注 关于"批评"的单词在 SSAT 的习题中有很多，如：censure, reproach, disparage。

hiatus ★

[haɪ'eɪtəs] *n.* 裂缝

- 记 hi + at + us：他对（at）着我们打了个招呼（hi）之后，就站在我俩之间，致使我俩之间有了裂缝（hiatus）
- 考 同义 hiatus = gap

constellation ★

[ˌkɒnstə'leɪʃn] *n.* 星座，星群

- 记 con- + stell-（star）+ ation：一群星星（star）在一起即为星群（constellation）
- 考 类比 constellation 星群 to stars 星星 ⇒ range 山脉 to mountains 山 （组成）
  constellation 星群 to stars 星星 ⇒ cattle 牛群 to cow 牛 （组成）

pry ★★

[praɪ] *v.* 刺探，撬动

- 记 侦探（spy）都好打听（pry）
- 考 类比 megaphone 扩音器 to speak 说 ⇒ lever 杠杆 to pry 撬 （事物及其用途）

pupil ★

['pju:pl] *n.* 学生

- 考 类比 tutor 老师 to pupil 学生 ⇒ coach 教练 to athlete 运动员 （人物及其对象）
  pupil 学生 to professor 教授 ⇒ apprentice 学徒 to master 师傅 （人物及其对象）

predict ★★★
[prɪˈdɪkt] v. 预测

- 变 prediction n. 预测；unpredictable a. 难以预测的
- 记 pre- 提前 + -dict 说话
- 考 同义 erratic = unpredictable；prediction = forecast；prophecy = prediction

类比
- juror 陪审团 —to→ judge 判断 ⇒ soothsayer 算命者 —to→ predict 预言 （人物及其目的）
- erratic 不可预测的 —to→ predictable 可预测的 ⇒ exorbitant 过高的 —to→ reasonable 合理的 （反义）
- evolve 进化 —to→ dismantle 拆除 ⇒ predict 预测 —to→ withhold 保留 （反义）

（dismantle 这个单词的英文释义为：to put an end to in a gradual systematic way）

sentimental ★
[ˌsentɪˈmentl] a. 感伤的

- 变 sentiment n. 感情，情绪
- 考 同义 sentiment = emotion；maudlin = sentimental

trivia ★★★
[ˈtrɪviə] n. 琐事

- 变 trivial a. 琐碎的，不重要的
- 记 tri- 三 + via：一件事情分三次完成，说明不重要（trivia）
- 考 同义 trivia = minutia

类比
- kernel 核心 —to→ central 中心的 ⇒ trivia 琐事 —to→ unimportant 不重要的 （同义）
- glorious 荣耀的 —to→ exalted 赞扬的 ⇒ trivial 琐碎的 —to→ unimportant 不重要的 （同义）
- trivial 琐碎的 —to→ consequential 重要的 ⇒ robust 强健的 —to→ lethargic 无生气的 （反义）

注 关于"琐碎的"单词在 SSAT 的习题中有很多，如：trifling, negligible。

nib ★
[nɪb] n. 笔尖

- 记 钢笔的笔尖（nib）坏了，直接丢进垃圾箱（bin）里
- 考 同义 nib = point

List | **91** words ★ 复习一下学过的单词！

☐ brazen	☐ diamond	☐ novice	☐ rigid
☐ carpenter	☐ excess	☐ ominous	☐ seed
☐ coarse	☐ genesis	☐ pint	☐ stimulate
☐ collie	☐ indigenous	☐ prosecute	☐ threat
☐ deteriorate	☐ intern	☐ receptacle	☐ trifling

SSAT词汇 List 93

★★ plight
[plaɪt] n. 困境
记 因为陷入困境（plight），所以没有丝毫希望之光（light）
考 同义 plight = impasse; plight = predicament; plight = difficulty

★ pursue
[pəˈsjuː] v. 追
记 谐音：怕羞：尽管怕羞，但是还是要追（pursue）女孩
考 同义 pursue = follow; aspire = pursue

★ jumbo
[ˈdʒʌmbəʊ] a. 巨大的
记 这个词最初是一只大象的名字，由 P. T. Barnum 带去全世界巡演的一只大象。由于这只大象体态巨大，所以之后就有了 jumbo 表示"大"的意思。巧合的是，荷兰著名的大超市也叫 JUMBO，除此之外，新概念 2 第 65 课描述的也是一只大象的故事，题目就叫 *Jumbo V. S. the Police*
考 同义 jumbo = huge

★★★ mock
[mɒk] v. 愚弄，嘲笑；a. 虚假的
变 mockery n. 嘲笑，嘲弄
记 好莱坞电影 *The Hunger Games: Mockingjay* 翻译为《饥饿游戏：嘲笑鸟》
考 同义 travesty = mockery; feint = mock attack; mock = make fun of; jeer = mock
类比 mock 嘲笑 to derision 嘲笑 ⇒ despise 鄙视 to contempt 鄙视 （同义）

★ speculate
[ˈspekjʊleɪt] v. 思考
记 思考（speculate）光谱（spectrum）的组成
考 同义 speculate = think

★★ demonstrate
[ˈdemənstreɪt] v. 显示，展示
变 demonstrative a. 说明的，演示的

☆ plight ☆ pursue ☆ jumbo ☆ mock ☆ speculate
☆ demonstrate

考 同义　demonstrate = show；elaborate = demonstrate

类比　demonstrative/擅表达的 to feeling/感情 ⇒ pensive/沉思的 to serious/严肃的 （修饰）

（这个题的思路有些复杂：Demonstrative means showing feeling openly while pensive means involved in or reflecting serious thought.）

★ seer

[sɪə] *n.* 预言家

记　see + er：能看（see）到未来的人（er）即为预言家（seer）

考 类比　seer/预言家 to prophecy/预言 ⇒ sage/圣人 to wisdom/智慧 （人物及其特点）

★ accrue

[əˈkruː] *v.* 获得，积累

记　谐音 a cruel：这件事情让你获得（accrue）了一个残忍的（a cruel）教训

考 同义　accrue = accumulate

★★★ school

[skuːl] *n.* 学校；鱼群

考 类比
school/鱼群 to fish/鱼 ⇒ flock/鸟群 to birds/鸟 （组成）
pride/狮群 to lion/狮子 ⇒ school/鱼群 to fish/鱼 （组成）
school/鱼群 to fish/鱼 ⇒ pack/狼群 to wolf/狼 （组成）
school/鱼群 to fish/鱼 ⇒ crowd/人群 to people/人 （组成）
school/鱼群 to fish/鱼 ⇒ herd/牛群 to buffalo/水牛 （组成）
gaggle/鹅群 to goose/鹅 ⇒ school/鱼群 to fish/鱼 （组成）
exile/放逐 to country/国家 ⇒ expel/驱逐 to school/学校 （空间）
librarian/图书管理员 to library/图书馆 ⇒ teacher/老师 to school/学校 （空间）
surgery/手术 to hospital/医院 ⇒ lessons/课程 to school/学校 （空间）
sovereign/君主 to monarchy/君主国 ⇒ principal/校长 to school/学校 （空间）

★ tarnish

[ˈtɑːnɪʃ] *v.* 使……失去光泽

记　因为新鞋被弄脏（tarnish），所以受到妈妈的惩罚（punish）

考 类比　tarnish/失去光泽 to silver/银器 ⇒ sully/玷污 to reputation/名声 （动作及其对象）

☆ seer　　☆ accrue　　☆ school　　☆ tarnish

chef
★★★
[ʃef] *n.* 大厨

记 这是我们饭店的首席（chief）大厨（chef）

考 类比
waiter 服务员 to chef 主厨 ⇒ restaurant 餐馆 to kitchen 厨房 （纵向）
chef 主厨 to cook 做饭 ⇒ waitress 服务员 to serve 服务 （人物及其动作）
cartographer 地图编辑者 to map 地图 ⇒ chef 主厨 to meal 饭 （人物及其对象）
sociologist 社会学家 to behavior 行为 ⇒ chef 主厨 to meal 饭 （人物及其对象）

syntax
★
[ˈsɪntæks] *n.* 句法

记 syn-（same）+ tax：从句法（syntax）上分析，这两个句子说的内容相同（same），都在讨论税收（tax）问题

考 类比
syntax 句法 to sentence 句子 ⇒ blueprint 蓝图 to building 建筑 （事物及其用途）
syntax 句法 to sentence 句子 ⇒ dissection 解剖 to specimen 标本 （事物及其用途）

pompous
★
[ˈpɒmpəs] *a.* 自大的，浮夸的

记 教皇（Pope）说这个人非常自大（pompous）
考 同义 pompous = pretentious

heritage
★
[ˈherɪtɪdʒ] *n.* 遗产

记 韩国电视剧《继承者》的英文为 *Heir*，而 heritage 也是这个单词的变体
考 同义 heritage = inheritance

faction
★★
[ˈfækʃn] *n.* 派别，内讧

变 factious *a.* 党派之争的
记 各党派（faction）之间最近动作（action）很大
考 同义 factious = divisive
类比 faction 小派别 to union 联盟 ⇒ cold 冷的 to heat 热的 （反义）

album
★
[ˈælbəm] *n.* 专辑

记 类比 album 专辑 to song 歌 ⇒ menu 菜单 to dish 菜 （组成）

★ irreversible

[ˌɪrɪˈvɜːsəbl] *a.* 不可逆转的

记 ir- 否定 + revers-（reverse）反转 + -ible
考 同义 irreversible = irrevocable

★★ deluxe

[dəˈləks] *a.* 高级的，豪华的

记 很多歌手在发布新专辑时，经常会再多出一个 deluxe 的版本

考 类比 ultimate 最终的 to first 起始的 ⇒ inferior 下等的 to deluxe 高级的 （反义）

house 房子 to palace 宫殿 ⇒ regular 普通的 to deluxe 豪华的 （<程度）

deluxe版本

deluxe

★ intricate

[ˈɪntrɪkət] *a.* 错综复杂的

记 错综复杂的（intricate）阴谋诡计（intrigue）
考 类比 intricate 错综复杂的 to design 设计 ⇒ carbonated 碳酸的 to beverage 饮料 （修饰）

★ access

[ˈækses] *n.* 进入，接近

考 同义 admittance = access

类比 barricade 路障 to access 接近 ⇒ bind 捆绑 to movement 运动 （缺乏）

List | 92 words   ★ 复习一下学过的单词！

□ belly	□ euphoria	□ indignation	□ pry
□ chaff	□ hiatus	□ lava	□ pupil
□ chide	□ humus	□ migrate	□ sentimental
□ concrete	□ illicit	□ nib	□ timid
□ constellation	□ impulse	□ predict	□ trivia

SSAT词汇 List 94

attain
[ə'teɪn] v. 达到，实现

- 记 放弃（abstain）娱乐，实现（attain）梦想
- 考 类比 strive 力争 to attain 达到 ⇒ sidestep 回避 to avoid 避免 （同义）

loquacious
[lə'kweɪʃəs] a. 话多的

- 变 loquaciousness n. 多话
- 记 loqu- 说话 + acious：loquacious 这个单词于 1656 年进入英语，一开始多被诗人引用，是一个很文艺的词
- 考 同义 loquacious = talkative；loquacious = garrulous
  类比 vivacious 活泼的 to lively 活跃的 ⇒ loquacious 话多的 to talkative 话多的 （同义）

evaporate
[ɪ'væpəreɪt] v. 蒸发

- 变 evaporation n. 蒸发
- 记 e- 朝外 + vapor 蒸汽 + -ate
- 考 类比 evaporate 蒸发 to condense 压缩 ⇒ thaw 融化 to freeze 冷冻 （反义）
  evaporation 蒸发 to water 水 ⇒ erosion 腐蚀 to soil 土壤 （事物及其属性）

cull
[kʌl] v. 挑选

- 记 挑选（cull）出一只好奶牛（cow）和好公牛（bull）
- 考 同义 cull = select

profusion
[prə'fjuːʒn] n. 丰富，充沛

- 变 profuse a. 丰富的，大量的
- 记 和这个案件相关的东西太多（profusion），搞得我一头雾水（confusion）
- 考 同义 profusion = abundance；profusion = wealth
  （wealth 这个单词的英文释义为：abundant supply）

palette
[ˈpælɪt] n. 调色板

记 调色板（palette）中有白色（pale）
考 类比　palette/调色板 to colors/颜色 ⇒ collage/剪贴画 to images/图像 （组成）

rudimentary
[ˌruːdɪˈmentri] a. 基本的，初步的

考 类比　enormous/巨大的 to colossal/巨大的 ⇒ fundamental/基础的 to rudimentary/基础的 （同义）

bizarre
[bɪˈzɑː] a. 奇怪的

记 我吃了一个味道很奇怪的（bizarre）比萨（pizza）
考 同义　bizarre = odd；peculiar = bizarre

opaque
[əʊˈpeɪk] a. 不透明的

记 op- 相反 + -aque 水：不像水那样清澈透明即为不透明的（opaque）
考 同义　opaque = unclear
　　类比　fluid/液体 to impermeable/难以渗透的 ⇒ light/光 to opaque/不透明的 （缺乏）
　　　　　transparent/透明的 to translucent/半透明的 ⇒ translucent/半透明的 to opaque/不透明的 （>程度）

accelerate
[əkˈseləreɪt] v. 加快，加速

变 accelerator n. 油门
记 芹菜（celery）的价格加速（accelerate）上涨
考 同义　hasten = accelerate
　　类比　stem/堵住 to accelerate/加速 ⇒ curb/抑制 to develop/发展 （反义）
　　　　　expedite/加快 to process/过程 ⇒ accelerate/加速 to pace/步伐 （动宾）
　　　　　accelerator/油门 to motion/动作 ⇒ catalyst/催化剂 to change/改变 （事物及其对象）

ledger
[ˈledʒə] n. 账本

记 把账本（ledger）放在桌子边（edge）
考 类比　table/表格 to data/数据 ⇒ ledger/账本 to transactions/交易 （空间）
　　　　　bookkeeper/记账员 to ledger/账本 ⇒ maestro/大师 to orchestra/管弦乐队 （人物及其对象）

☆ palette　　☆ rudimentary　　☆ bizarre　　☆ opaque　　☆ accelerate
☆ ledger

precipitate
[prɪˈsɪpɪteɪt] v. 促进；降雨

- 变 precipitation n. 降雨
- 记 站在悬崖（precipice）边看降雨（precipitate）
- 考 同义 precipitate = expedite
- 类比 coal 煤 to heat 热 ⇒ cloud 乌云 to precipitation 降雨 （事物及其对象）

dismay
[dɪsˈmeɪ] v. 沮丧，惊慌

- 变 dismaying a. 惊慌的；dismayed a. 惊慌的
- 记 我不喜欢（dis）五月（May），所以一到五月份我就感到沮丧（dismay）
- 考 同义 dismay = dishearten
- 类比
  - grin 露齿笑 to delight 高兴 ⇒ frown 皱眉 to dismay 沮丧 （动作及其情感）
  - intimidate 恐吓 to daunt 恐吓 ⇒ dismay 使惊慌 to horrify 使恐惧 （同义）
  - ravenous 贪婪的 to famished 饥饿的 ⇒ dismayed 难过的 to distressed 痛苦的 （同义）
  - alarming 令人担忧的 to appalling 可怕的 ⇒ dismaying 惊慌的 to frightful 可怕的 （程度）

gullible
[ˈgʌlɪbl] a. 易受骗的，轻信的

- 记 gull 易受骗之人 + -ible
- 考 同义 gullible = easily deceived；credulous = gullible
- 类比
  - compliance 服从 to servile 奴性的 ⇒ trust 相信 to gullible 轻信的 （<程度）
  - taciturn 不太说话的 to quiet 安静的 ⇒ trusting 信任的 to gullible 易受骗的 （<程度）

abstain
[əbˈsteɪn] v. 自制，避免

- 变 abstinent a. 禁欲的，有节制的
- 记 谐音：不 stay：不 stay 在外面玩耍，而是很自制（abstain）地在家做功课
- 考 同义 refrain = abstain；abstinent = avoiding

hilarious
[hɪˈleəriəs] a. 滑稽的

- 记 希拉里（Hilary）说这个小丑真够滑稽的（hilarious）
- 考 同义 hilarious = humorous
- 类比
  - humorous 幽默的 to hilarious 滑稽的 ⇒ sad 伤心的 to maudlin 极其伤感的 （<程度）
  - funny 好笑的 to hilarious 滑稽的 ⇒ hot 热的 to sweltering 大汗淋漓的 （<程度）
  - funny 好笑的 to hilarious 滑稽的 ⇒ sprinkle 喷洒 to drop 水滴 （<程度）

humorous 幽默的 to hilarious 极其搞笑的 ⇒ warm 温暖的 to parched 烧焦的 （＜程度）

herd ★

[hɜːd] *n.* 兽群

记 听到（heard）兽群（herd）的叫声
考 类比 wolf 狼 to pack 狼群 ⇒ cow 牛 to herd 牛群 （组成）
　　　hive 蜂房 to swarm 蜂群 ⇒ corral 畜栏 to herd 兽群 （空间）

soar ★

[sɔː] *v.* 高飞

记 谐音：嗖：嗖的一声，远走高飞（soar）
考 同义 hover = soar
　　类比 seal 海豹 to float 漂浮 ⇒ bird 鸟 to soar 高飞 （动物及其动作）

earnest ★★

[ˈɜːnɪst] *a.* 认真的

变 earnestness *n.* 认真
记 赚钱（earn）的事一定要做到最（-est）认真（earnest）
考 类比 sanitary 卫生的 to clean 干净 ⇒ earnest 认真的 to serious 严肃认真的 （同义）
　　　earnestness 认真 to seriousness 认真 ⇒ contradiction 矛盾 to opposition 反对 （同义）

jabber ★

[ˈdʒæbə] *v.* 快而含糊地说话

记 英语中的 jabber 和 gabble 不仅长得像，意思也一样
考 同义 jabber = blather incessantly
　　类比 jabber 快而含糊地说 to talk 说话 ⇒ skitter 快走 to walk 走路 （种属）
　　　　jabber 快而含糊地说 to talk 说话 ⇒ skitter 快走 to move 移动 （种属）

List | **93** words　　　　　　　　　　　　　★ 复习一下学过的单词！

- access
- accrue
- album
- chef
- deluxe
- demonstrate
- faction
- heritage
- intricate
- irreversible
- jumbo
- mock
- plight
- pompous
- pursue
- school
- seer
- speculate
- syntax
- tarnish

SSAT词汇 List 95

depart
★★
[dɪˈpɑːt] v. 离开，出发

考 类比：leave 离开 to stay 停留 ⇒ depart 出发 to remain 留下 （反义）
bestow 授予 to withdraw 收回 ⇒ arrive 到达 to depart 出发 （反义）

despondent
★
[dɪˈspɒndənt] a. 沮丧的，泄气的

记 对方拒绝回答（respond）你的问题，让你觉得沮丧（despondent）
考 同义：despondent = depressed
类比：despondent 极度沮丧的 to sad 伤心的 ⇒ furious 狂怒的 to angry 生气的 （＞程度）

shrewd
★★★
[ʃruːd] a. 精明的，狡猾的

记 注意 shrewd 这个单词是"精明的"，不要和"泼妇"(shrew) 搞混
考 同义：astute = shrewd；cagey = shrewd
类比：shrewd 精明的 to foolish 愚蠢的 ⇒ heroic 英雄的 to villainous 邪恶的 （反义）
shrewd 精明的 to unintelligent 不聪明的 ⇒ subdue 抑制 to aggravate 加重 （反义）

trail
★★
[treɪl] n. 小路

考 同义：trek = trail
类比：trail 小路 to hikers 步行者 ⇒ highway 高速路 to motorists 开车者 （人物及其对象）

extract
★★
[ɪkˈstrækt] v. 取出，提出

变 extracting a. 拔出的
记 ex- 朝外 + trac- 拉 + t
考 同义：extract = remove；excerpt = extract

☆ depart ☆ despondent ☆ shrewd ☆ trail ☆ extract

类比 exacting(苛求的) to demanding(苛求的) → extracting(拔出的) to removing(移动的) （同义）

steer ★★★
[stɪə] v. 驾驶，行驶

变 steering n. 操纵；steering wheel 方向盘
记 我驾驶（steer）着车，行驶在崎岖的（steep）山路上
考 类比 rudder(船舵) to steer(行驶) → raft(筏子) to float(漂浮) （事物及其动作）
rudder(船舵) to steering(操纵) → razor(剃刀) to shaving(刮胡子) （事物及其动作）
switch(开关) to light(灯) → steering(方向盘) to wheel car(车) （事物及其对象）

eclectic ★
[ɪˈklektɪk] a. 可多选的

记 这个单词在大部分的双语词典里给出的中文释义都是"折中的"，但是其本意是 diverse or heterogeneous 而不是 compromised
考 同义 eclectic = selective

residual ★
[rɪˈzɪdjʊəl] n. 剩余，残渣

记 残渣（residual）即为剩下的（rest）东西
考 同义 residual = leftover

eager ★★★
[ˈiːɡə] a. 渴望的

变 eagerness n. 渴望
考 同义 agog = eager；avid = eager；eagerness = alacrity；eager = enthusiastic
类比 dauntless(无畏的) to fear(恐惧) → eager(渴望的) to reluctance(勉强) （反义）
reluctant(不情愿的) to eager(渴望的) → timid(胆小的) to courageous(勇敢的) （反义）
eager(渴望的) to fervent(强烈的) → pleased(开心的) to ecstatic(狂喜的) （<程度）

contour ★
[ˈkɒntʊə] n. 轮廓

记 con + tour 旅游：现在很多人跟团游（tour）其实就只能逛一个地方的大概（contour）
考 同义 contour = outline

excerpt ★★
[ˈeksɜːpt] v. 摘录，引用；n. 摘录，引用

记 除了（except）这部分原创，其余都是摘录（excerpt）别人的
考 同义 excerpt = extract

类比　clip 电影一部分 → to movie 电影 ⇒ excerpt 摘录 → to novel 小说　（事物及其部分）
　　　movie 电影 → to close-up 特写镜头 ⇒ book 书 → to excerpt 摘录　（事物及其部分）
　　　excerpt 摘录 → to story 故事 ⇒ prologue 序幕 → to concert 音乐会　（事物及其部分）

capsize ★

[kæpˈsaɪz] *v.* 翻船

记 cap 头 + size 型号：船头（cap）型号（size）太大，容易翻船（capsize）

考 同义　capsize = turn over

　类比　capsize 翻船 → to ship 船 ⇒ crash 车祸 → to car 车　（动宾）

hose ★★

[həʊz] *n.* 软管；长筒袜

记 把药丸放进软管（hose）里，然后朝马（horse）嘴里吹，以此来给马喂药

考 类比　hose 管子 → to water 水 ⇒ artery 动脉 → to blood 血　（空间）
　　　glove 手套 → to hand 手 ⇒ hose 长筒袜 → to foot 脚　（空间）
　　　button 扣子 → to shirt 衬衫 ⇒ valve 阀门 → to hose 软管　（事物及其部分）

assume ★

[əˈsjuːm] *v.* 假设

考 同义　assume = presume

prevaricate ★

[prɪˈværɪkeɪt] *v.* 搪塞，支吾其词

变 prevarication *n.* 搪塞，支吾

记 pre- 提前 + vari-（vary）变化 + cate：提前（pre）想好变化（vary）之词，以免到时支吾其词（prevaricate）

考 同义　prevaricate = be untruthful

explicit ★★

[ɪkˈsplɪsɪt] *a.* 明确的，详述的

记 在 iTunes 的曲库中，我们都可以看到好多音乐的后面标了 explicit 这个单词，这是在告诉你这首歌里面包含有脏话（由"明确的"引申为"露骨的，直白的"，如果是一个干净的版本，后面会标明 clean）

考 类比　explicit 明确的 → to distortion 扭曲 ⇒ frank 坦率的 → to circumlocution 累赘陈述　（反义）
　　　redundant 多余的 → to necessary 必需的 ⇒ vague 模糊的 → to explicit 明确的　（反义）

egregious 过分的 —to→ minor 次要的 ⇒ implicit 含蓄的 —to→ explicit 明确的 （反义）

docile
★★★
['dəʊsaɪl] *a.* 温顺的，驯服了的

记 被驯服了的（docile）小狗（dog）
考 同义 docile = obedient；docile = controlled；docile = tamed
类比 copious 大量的 —to→ abundant 大多数的 ⇒ docile 温顺的 —to→ meek 驯服了的 （同义）
注 关于"温顺的"的单词在 SSAT 的习题中有很多，如：compliant，submissive，amenable。

conflagration
★
[ˌkɒnfləˈgreɪʃn] *n.* 大火

记 con- + flag + ration：好多红旗帜（flag）摆在一起（con）就像着了火（conflagration）一样
考 类比 tempest 暴风雨 —to→ storm 风暴 ⇒ conflagration 大火 —to→ fire 火 （同义）

solemn
★★
['sɒləm] *a.* 严肃的，庄严的

记 所罗门（Solomon）是个很严肃的（solemn）人
考 同义 grave = solemn；solemn = severe；solemn = serious

refill
★
[ˌriːˈfɪl] *v.* 再装满，续杯

记 re- + fill 填满
考 同义 refill = replenish

List | 94 words ★ 复习一下学过的单词！

☐ abstain	☐ dismay	☐ hilarious	☐ palette
☐ accelerate	☐ earnest	☐ jabber	☐ precipitate
☐ attain	☐ evaporate	☐ ledger	☐ profusion
☐ bizarre	☐ gullible	☐ loquacious	☐ rudimentary
☐ cull	☐ herd	☐ opaque	☐ soar

☆ docile   ☆ conflagration   ☆ solemn   ☆ refill

SSAT词汇 List 96

derision
[dɪˈrɪʒn] *n.* 嘲笑

记 她做了一个荒谬的决定（decision），受到大家无情的嗤笑（derision）
考 类比 mock 嘲笑 to derision 嘲笑 ⇒ despise 鄙视 to contempt 鄙视 （同义）

eternal
[ɪˈtɜːnl] *a.* 永恒的

记 外面的（external）世界永远（eternal）充满诱惑力
考 同义 eternal = unending

fragrant
[ˈfreɪɡrənt] *a.* 芳香的，愉快的

记 北京西郊著名的"香山"英文即为 Fragrant Hills
考 类比 palatable 好吃的 to delicious 好吃的 ⇒ aromatic 芳香的 to fragrant 芳香的 （同义）
　　picture 图片 to representation 表现 ⇒ perfume 香水 to fragrance 香味 （事物及其用途）

Fragrant Hills

fragrant

astrology
[əˈstrɒlədʒi] *n.* 占星术

记 astro- 星星 + -ology 学科：研究星星的学科，旧时称为占星术（astrology）
考 类比 chemistry 化学 to alchemy 炼金术 ⇒ astronomy 天文学 to astrology 占星术 （同义：新旧之称）

tact
[tækt] *n.* 机智，老练

变 tactful *a.* 机制的，圆滑的
记 这个警察行动（act）老练（tact）
考 同义 tact = grace；diplomatic = tactful；tactful = skillful
　类比 copious 大量的 to ample 大量的 ⇒ tactful 机智的 to diplomatic 圆滑的 （同义）

☆ derision　　☆ eternal　　☆ fragrant　　☆ astrology　　☆ tact

brazen 厚颜无耻的 to tact 机智 → lethargic 无生气的 to energy 精力 （缺乏）

diplomat 外交官 to tact 机智 → jester 小丑 to clowning 小丑般的 （人物及其特点）

tact 老练 to diplomat 外交官 → agility 敏捷 to gymnast 体操运动员 （人物及其特点）

refurbish [ˌriːˈfɜːbɪʃ] v. 刷新，再磨光

记 re- + furbish (furnish) 装备：上台前，再次 (re) 打磨 (refurbish) 你的装备 (furnish)

考 类比 refurbish 刷新 to worn 磨损的 → resume 继续 to interrupted 被打断的 （反义）

sob [sɒb] v. 啜泣

记 鲍勃 (Bob) 在哭泣 (sob)

考 类比 sleep 睡觉 to doze 打瞌睡 → wail 哀号 to sob 啜泣 （同义）

subside [səbˈsaɪd] v. 下沉，减弱

记 sub- 往下 + side 边：往下边走，即为下沉 (subside)

考 同义 subside = decrease

raze [reɪz] v. 夷为平地

记 牛吃草 (graze) 之后，草地被夷为平地 (raze) 了

考 同义 raze = tear down; raze = destroy

solitary [ˈsɒlɪtri] a. 孤独的

记 sol- 单独的 + -itary

考 同义 solitary = alone

mimic [ˈmɪmɪk] v. 模仿

变 mimicry n. 模仿

记 这个单词的构成本来就是 mi mi c，两个 mi 好像在为了 C 位而相互模仿

考 同义 mimicry = camouflage; mimic = copy; mimic = imitate

类比 emulate 仿效 to person 人 → mimic 模仿 to gesture 姿势 （动作及其对象）

petulant [ˈpetjʊlənt] a. 脾气不好的

变 petulance n. 易怒，生气

记 谐音 pet u lent：The pet you lent to me made me petulant.
考 同义　petulant = ill-tempered；irritable = petulant
　类比　evoke / 引起 — to — hot-headed / 急躁的 ⇒ stimulate / 刺激 — to — petulant / 脾气不好的　（纵向）
注 关于"脾气不好的"单词在 SSAT 的习题中有很多，如：cantankerous，irascible，sullen，sulky，wrathful，surly，grumpy，irate，enraged。

elucidate ★★　[ɪˈluːsɪdeɪt] v. 阐明，说明

记 e- 朝外 + lucid 明晰的 + -ate
考 同义　elucidate = make clear；elucidate = clear up

congregation ★　[ˌkɒŋgrɪˈgeɪʃn] n. 会众

记 先聚集（congregation）起来，再按照健康程度进行隔离（segregation）
考 类比　congregation / 会众 — to — worshippers / 崇拜者 ⇒ galaxy / 银河 — to — stars / 星星　（组成）
注 关于"召集，集合"的单词在 SSAT 的习题中有很多，如：muster，assemble，convene。

regal ★　[ˈriːgl] a. 帝王的，皇室的

记 皇室的（regal）人无论做什么事情都是合法的（legal）
考 同义　regal = royal

monument ★　[ˈmɒnjʊmənt] n. 纪念碑

记 美国有华盛顿纪念碑（The Washington Momument），中国有人民英雄纪念碑（Monument to the People's Heroes）
考 同义　monument = memorial

monument

stiff ★★　[stɪf] a. 僵硬的

记 虽然在屋子里暖和半个小时了，但是他依然（still）浑身僵硬（stiff）
考 类比　viscous / 黏性的 — to — flow / 流动 ⇒ stiff / 僵硬的 — to — bend / 弯曲　（反义）
　　　 starch / 淀粉 — to — stiff / 僵硬的 ⇒ bleach / 漂白剂 — to — white / 白色的　（事物及其用途）

clam ★　[klæm] n. 蛤

记 即使见到活的蛤蜊（clam）你也要保持冷静（calm）
考 类比　clam / 蛤 — to — mollusk / 软体动物 ⇒ spider / 蜘蛛 — to — arachnid / 蛛形纲动物　（种属）
　　　 clam / 蛤 — to — mollusk / 软体动物 ⇒ kangaroo / 袋鼠 — to — marsupial / 袋状类动物　（种属）

☆ elucidate　　☆ congregation　　☆ regal　　☆ monument　　☆ stiff
☆ clam

controversy
[ˈkɒntrəvɜːsi] *n.* 争论

记 To be an introvert guy or an extrovert guy, that is a controversy.
考 同义 debate = controversy

foal
[fəʊl] *n.* 小马驹

记 她的新年目标（goal）是养一只小马驹（foal）
考 类比 foal/小马驹 to horse/马 ⇒ kitten/小猫 to cat/猫 （种属）

List | 95 words   ★ 复习一下学过的单词！

☐ assume	☐ despondent	☐ explicit	☐ residual
☐ capsize	☐ docile	☐ extract	☐ shrewd
☐ conflagration	☐ eager	☐ hose	☐ solemn
☐ contour	☐ eclectic	☐ prevaricate	☐ steer
☐ depart	☐ excerpt	☐ refill	☐ trail

SSAT词汇 List 97

★ defiance [dɪˈfaɪəns] n. 蔑视
- 记 de + fiance (fiancé)：她蔑视 (defiance) 她的未婚夫 (fiancé)
- 考 同义 defiance = rebellion
  类比 defiance 蔑视 to opposition 反对 ⇒ exertion 努力 to endeavor 努力 （同义）

★★★ divert [daɪˈvɜːt] v. 转移；使快乐
- 变 diverting a. 有趣的；diversion n. 消遣
- 记 因为经常转移 (divert) 自己的兴趣爱好，所以有各种各样的 (diverse) 快乐
- 考 同义 divert = amuse
  类比 amuse 使欢娱 to divert 使快乐 ⇒ vex 使烦恼 to fret 使烦恼 （同义）
  dull 无聊的 to insipid 清淡的 ⇒ diverting 有趣的 to entertaining 娱乐的 （同义）
  conundrum 谜 to perplex 使困惑 ⇒ entertainment 娱乐 to divert 使快乐 （同义）
  diversion 消遣 to boredom 无聊 ⇒ assurance 保证 to uncertainty 不确定 （反义）

★★ melodious [mɪˈləʊdɪəs] a. 悦耳的
- 记 melodious 的名词形式即为我们熟悉的 melody
- 考 类比 florid 绚丽的 to prose 散文 ⇒ melodious 悦耳的 to music 音乐 （修饰）
  delicious 美味的 to taste 品尝 ⇒ melodious 悦耳的 to sound 声音 （修饰）

★ ostrich [ˈɒstrɪtʃ] n. 鸵鸟
- 记 不要把鸵鸟 (ostrich) 驱逐 (ostracize) 出去
- 考 类比 ostrich 鸵鸟 to bird 鸟 ⇒ lion 狮子 to cat 猫科 （种属）
  ostrich 鸵鸟 to bird 鸟 ⇒ tiger 老虎 to cat 猫科 （种属）

☆ defiance   ☆ divert   ☆ melodious   ☆ ostrich

extort ★★ [ɪkˈstɔːt] v. 敲诈，勒索

- 变 extortionist n. 勒索者
- 记 注意区分"劝告"（exhort）和"勒索"（extort）
- 考 类比 extortionist 勒索者 to threaten 威胁 → zealot 热心者 to patronize 资助 （人物及其动作）

  extortionist 勒索者 to blackmail 敲诈 → kleptomaniac 偷窃癖 to steal 偷 （人物及其动作）

veal ★ [viːl] n. 小牛肉

- 记 抓紧解决（deal）出问题的小牛肉（veal）事件
- 考 类比 sheep 羊 to mutton 羊肉 → calf 牛 to veal 小牛肉 （事物及其部分）

script ★★★ [skrɪpt] n. 脚本

- 记 听力材料中常见的"听力文本"的英文即为 listening script 或者 audio script
- 考 类比 director 导演 to script 脚本 → conductor 指挥家 to score 乐谱 （人物及其对象）

  actor 演员 to script 剧本 → musician 音乐家 to score 乐谱 （人物及其对象）

  playwright 剧作家 to script 剧本 → choreographer 舞编 to dance 舞蹈 （人物及其对象）

soak ★★★ [səʊk] v. 浸泡，湿透

- 记 先把双手浸泡（soak）在水中，然后抹上肥皂（soap）
- 考 同义 douse = soak; saturate = soak; drench = soak

  类比 knead 捏 to dough 面团 → soak 浸泡 to beans 豆子 （动宾）

affinity ★★ [əˈfɪnəti] n. 亲密关系；相似

- 记 因为友好（affable），所以关系亲密（affinity）
- 考 同义 affinity = affection; affinity = liking; affinity = similarity

cling ★ [klɪŋ] v. 坚持，依附

- 记 坚持（cling）要穿闪亮亮（bling bling）的东西
- 考 同义 cling = fasten upon

undermine ★★ [ˌʌndəˈmaɪn] v. 破坏

- 变 undermining a. 破坏的
- 考 同义 undermine = weaken

类比　irk (使烦恼) to soothing (安慰的) → support (支持) to undermining (暗中破坏的)　（反义）

★ valid
['vælɪd] *a.* 有效的，合法的

变 validate *v.* 证实，验证
记 信用卡上的 valid from 就是"从……开始生效"的意思
考 同义　validate = affirm；tenable = valid

★★ epic
['epɪk] *n.* 史诗

记 用史诗（epic）这个词来描绘（depict）这个壮观的场面
考 类比
- limerick (五行打油诗) to epic (史诗) → ditty (小曲) to opera (歌剧)　（＜程度）
- epic (史诗) to haiku (俳句) → symphony (交响乐) to song (歌曲)　（＞程度）
- epic (史诗) to haiku (俳句) → symphony (交响乐) to ditty (小曲)　（＞程度）

★★ criticize
['krɪtɪsaɪz] *v.* 批评

考 同义　berate = criticize；criticize = disparage
　　类比
- berate (批评) to criticize (批评) → goad (激励) to urge (督促)　（同义）
- exalt (表扬) to criticize (批评) → compliment (赞美) to offend (冒犯)　（反义）
- credulous (轻信的) to believe (相信) → censorious (吹毛求疵的) to criticize (批评)　（＞程度）

★★★ excavate
['ekskəveɪt] *v.* 挖掘

变 excavation *n.* 挖掘
记 ex- 朝外 + cav-（cave）洞穴 + -ate：朝外挖掘（excavate）产生了洞穴（cave）
考 类比
- salvage (营救) to wreck (失事船只) → excavate (挖掘) to ruin (废墟)　（动宾）
- erosion (侵蚀) to gully (水沟) → excavation (挖掘) to mine (矿)　（动宾）
- excavate (挖掘) to dig (挖掘) → avenge (复仇) to revenge (复仇)　（同义）
- excavate (挖掘) to dig (挖掘) → evacuate (疏散) to empty (清空)　（同义）
- scissors (剪刀) to cut (切) → shovel (铁铲) to excavate (挖掘)　（事物及其用途）

★★★ poetry
['pəʊɪtri] *n.* 诗歌

变 poem *n.* 诗；poet *n.* 诗人

考 类比

- poetry(诗歌) to prose(散文) ⇒ sonata(奏鸣曲) to etude(练习曲) （同类）
- prose(散文) to paragraph(段落) ⇒ poetry(诗歌) to stanza(诗节) （组成）
- journal(期刊) to article(文章) ⇒ anthology(诗集) to poem(古诗) （组成）
- song(歌曲) to playlist(播放列表) ⇒ poem(古诗) to anthology(诗集) （组成）
- limerick(五行打油诗) to poem(诗) ⇒ lampoon(讽刺文) to satire(讽刺文学) （种属）
- skit(滑稽短剧) to play(戏剧) ⇒ limerick(五行打油诗) to poem(诗) （种属）
- stanza(诗节) to poem(诗) ⇒ act(幕) to opera(歌剧) （组成）
- poem(诗) to words(词) ⇒ drawing(画) to lines(线) （组成）
- stanza(诗节) to poem(诗) ⇒ paragraph(段落) to essay(散文) （组成）
- poem(诗) to rhyme(节奏) ⇒ novel(小说) to plot(情节) （事物及其特点）
- symbolic(象征性的) to poetry(诗歌) ⇒ paranormal(超常的) to fiction(小说) （事物及其特点）
- poem(诗) to novel(小说) ⇒ backyard(后院) to meadow(草地) （程度）

（这个题的思路有些复杂：Poem is shorter than novel as backyard is smaller than meadow.）

- limerick(五行打油诗) to poem(诗) ⇒ catch(上口的小调) to song(歌曲) （种属）

（catch 此处的英文释义为：a canonic, often rhythmically intricate composition for three or more voices）

- obituary(讣告) to article(文章) ⇒ elegy(挽歌) to poem(诗歌) （种属）

（elegy 这个单词的英文释义为：a sad poem or song, especially about someone who has died）

- virtuoso(行家) to music(音乐) ⇒ bard(游吟诗人) to poetry(诗) （人物及其对象）

（virtuoso 这个单词的英文释义为：a virtuoso is someone who is extremely good at something, especially at playing a musical instrument）

List | 96 words   ★ 复习一下学过的单词！

- astrology
- clam
- congregation
- controversy
- derision
- elucidate
- eternal
- foal
- fragrant
- mimic
- monument
- petulant
- raze
- refurbish
- regal
- sob
- solitary
- stiff
- subside
- tact

类别词

演出开始

prologue	开场白，序言	preamble	序文	preface	序言，前言
prelude	序曲，序幕	overture	序曲，前奏	foreword	前言，序

幕间休息

interlude　幕间休息

演出结束

epilogue	收场，尾声	coda	尾声，终曲	encore	加演的节目
conclusion	结论	addendum	附录	peroration	结束语，结论
finale	终曲	postscript	附言，补充说明	appendix	附录

-ology 学科

anthology	诗集，文选	mythology	神话学	astrology	占星术
psychology	心理学	seismology	地震学	pathology	病理学
archaeology	考古学	terminology	术语学	anthropology	人类学

人的触觉

taste 品尝	to	gustatory 味觉的	sound 听	to	audible 听觉的
smell 闻	to	olfactory 嗅觉的	listen 听	to	auditory 听觉的
touch 触摸	to	tactile/tangible 有触觉的	see 看	to	visual 视觉的
drink 喝	to	potable 可饮用的			
eat 吃	to	edible 可饮用的			

恐惧症

phobia = hatred 恐惧，厌恶	acrophobia	恐高症	arachnophobia	蜘蛛恐惧症
agoraphobia 广场恐惧症	xenophobia	老外恐惧症	arithmophobia	数字恐惧症
claustrophobia 幽闭恐惧症	hydrophobia	恐水病		

走路类

prance	昂首阔步	saunter	闲逛	amble	缓行
stalk	跟踪	trudge	长途跋涉	ramble	漫步
strut	昂首阔步地走	scurry	急跑	canter	慢跑
scud	疾行	trot	小跑，慢跑	stroll	漫步，闲逛

人与工具

surgeon 外科医生	to	scalpel 手术刀	butcher 屠夫	to	cleaver 切肉刀
barber 理发师	to	razor 剃刀			

dentist 牙医	drill 钻子	golfer 高尔夫球手	club 棍棒	conductor 指挥	baton 指挥棒
carpenter 木匠	saw/plane/hammer 锯/刨/锤	batter 击球手	bat 棍棒	farmer 农夫	plow 犁
artist 艺术家	brush/palette 画笔/调色板	boxer 拳击手	glove 手套	photographer 摄影师	camera 相机
cobbler 补鞋匠	awl 锥子	knitter 编织的人	needle 针	potter 陶艺家	kiln 窑
sculptor 雕刻家	chisel 凿子				

人与产品

baker 面包师	cake/bread 蛋糕/面包	cartographer 地图制造者	map 地图	architect 建筑师	blueprint 蓝图
potter 陶艺家	pot 壶	choreographer 编舞者	dance 舞蹈	jeweler 珠宝商	pendant 吊坠
tailor 裁缝	clothes 衣服	composer 作曲家	score 乐谱	cooper 制桶工人	barrel 木桶
cobbler 补鞋匠	shoes 鞋子	playwright 剧作家	script/play 剧本/剧	sculptor 雕刻家	statue/sculpture 雕塑/雕塑

工具与功能

scissor 剪刀	snip/trim/cut 剪/修剪/切	file 锉刀	smooth 使光滑	blender 搅拌机	mix 混合
shovel 铁铲	dig/excavate 挖/挖	tape 磁带	record 记录	stove 炉子	cook 煮饭
blade 刀片	cut 切	chisel 凿子	carve 雕刻	scales 天平	weigh 称重
loom 织布机	weave 纺织				

组成关系

poem 诗	stanzas 诗节	anthology 文选	works 作品	nation 国家	citizen 公民
play 戏剧	scenes/acts 场/幕	congregation 集会	worshipper 做礼拜者	choir 合唱队	singers 歌手
symphony 交响乐	movements 乐章	orchestra 管弦乐队		medley 混合曲	songs 歌曲
glacier 冰川	ice 冰	musicians/instrumentalist 乐手/乐器演奏家		collage 拼贴画	pictures 图片
deck/pack 一副牌/一副牌	card 卡片	molecule 分子	atoms 原子	mosaic 马赛克	tiles 瓷砖
galaxy 星系	stars 星星	cast 卡司	actors 演员	tapestry 挂毯	threads 线
lexicon 词典	words 词	troupe 剧团	performers 表演者	ladder 梯子	steps 梯子的档

chain 锁链	to	links 链环		corolla 花冠	to	petals 花瓣	
bouquet 花束	to	flowers 花		sampler 刺绣样品	to	stitch 针脚	

性别对比

warlock 男巫	to	witch 女巫		patriarch 家长	to	matriarch 女家长
sorcerer 男巫	to	sorceress 女巫		tailor 裁缝	to	seamstress 女裁缝
enchanter 男巫	to	enchantress 女巫				

个体和整体

school 鱼群	to	fish 鱼		swarm 一群虫子	to	bees/insects/wasps 蜜蜂/昆虫/黄蜂
flock 羊群	to	sheep/goat 羊/山羊		colony 种群	to	ants/bacteria/artists 蚂蚁/细菌/艺术家
gaggle 鹅群	to	goose 鹅		herd 兽群	to	pigs/horses/cows/sheep 猪/马/牛/羊
pack 狼群	to	wolves 狼		throng 人群	to	people 人
pride 狮群	to	lions 狮子				

动物的不同阶段

caterpillar 毛毛虫	to	moth/butterfly 蛾子/蝴蝶		goat/buck goat 公/母/山羊	to	goatling/kid 小山羊
cub 幼兽	to	fox/bear/wolf/lion/tiger 狐狸/熊/狮子/老虎		stallion/mare 公/母马	to	pony/foal/colt 小马
tadpole 蝌蚪	to	frog 青蛙		stag/buck doe 公/母鹿	to	fawn 小鹿
piglet 小猪	to	pig 猪		boar/sow 公/母猪	to	piglet 小猪
cygnet 小天鹅	to	swan 天鹅		buck/doe 公/母兔	to	bunny 小兔
sapling 小树苗	to	tree 树		gander/goose 雄/雌鹅	to	gosling 小鹅
joey 小袋鼠	to	kangaroo 袋鼠		rooster/cock hen 公/母鸡	to	chick/chicken 小鸡
bull cow 公/母牛	to	calf 小牛		drake duck 公/母鸭	to	duckling 小鸭
ram ewe 公/母绵羊	to	lamb 小绵羊		cat 猫	to	kitten 小猫

动物及其声音

声音		动物		声音		动物		声音		动物
croak 呱呱叫	to	frog/crow 青蛙/乌鸦		meow 喵喵叫	to	cat 猫		hoot 猫头鹰叫	to	owl 猫头鹰
quack 嘎嘎叫	to	duck 鸭子		bark 犬吠	to	dog 狗		hiss 嘶嘶声	to	snake 蛇
gaggle 嘎嘎叫	to	goose 鹅		bray 驴叫	to	donkey 驴		howl 嚎叫	to	wolf 狼
moo 哞哞叫	to	cow/bull 牛/公牛		bleat 咩咩叫	to	sheep 羊		chirp 喳喳声	to	bird 鸟
whinny 马嘶	to	horse 马								

动物和动作

kangaroo 袋鼠	to	hop 跳		duck 鸭子	to	waddle 摇晃着走		bird 鸟	to	soar 飞翔
snake 蛇	to	slither 滑行		frog 青蛙	to	jump 跳		baby 小孩子	to	crawl 爬

动物和形容词

wolf 狼	to	lupine 似狼的		eagle 老鹰	to	aquiline 似鹰的		bird 鸟	to	avian 鸟类的
bear 熊	to	ursine 似熊的		dog 狗	to	canine 犬科的		ox 牛	to	bovine 似牛的
horse 马	to	equine 似马的		cat 猫	to	feline 猫科的		fish 鱼	to	piscine 似鱼的

动物和肉

sheep 羊	to	mutton 羊肉		deer 鹿	to	venison 鹿肉		calf 牛	to	veal 小牛肉

动物和毛

porcupine 豪猪	to	quill 刚毛		sheep 羊	to	fleece 羊毛		lion/horse 狮子/马	to	mane 鬃毛
pig 猪	to	bristle 猪鬃								

度量单位

fathom 英寻	⇒ a unit of depth
lumen 流明	⇒ a unit of brightness
decibel 分贝	⇒ a unit of volume
liter/gallon/quart/pint 升/加仑/夸脱/品脱	⇒ a unit of volume
pound 镑	⇒ a unit of weight
mile/meter/yard/inch/feet 英里/米/码/英寸/英尺	⇒ a unit of length/height/distance

gram 克	→	a unit of mass	calories 卡路里	→ a unit of heat
carat 克拉	→	a unit of diamond		

球类和运动场所

court for volleyball/basketball/tennis court 球场
course for golf course 高尔夫球场
diamond for baseball diamond 棒球场
rink for hockey rink 溜冰场，冰球场
lane/alley for bowling 保龄球场

物体和外壳

bark 树皮	→ outside of tree	shuck 壳 → outside of shellfish /oyster
peel/rind 外皮	→ outside of fruit	skin/hide 兽皮 → outside of animal
husk 外壳	→ outside of corn	membrane 薄膜 → outside of cell
pod 豆荚	→ outside of pea	hull 果实外壳 → outside of seed
crust 面包皮	→ outside of bread	chaff 谷壳 → outside of wheat
shell 硬壳	→ outside of nut/shellfish/egg	rind 橘子皮 → outside of orange

物体和边缘

circumference 圆周	→ border of circle	border 边境 → border of country
perimeter 周长	→ border of figure	shoreline 海岸线 → border of ocean
outline 轮廓	→ border of object	outskirt 郊区 → border of town
shoulder 路肩	→ border of road	levee 堤岸，码头 → border of river
margin 边缘	→ border of page	

乐器类

brass 铜管乐器 to cornet 短号　　woodwind 木管乐器 to clarinet 单簧管　　percussion 打击乐器 to cymbal 铙钹

测量类

odometer 里程表 to distance/mileage 距离/英里数　　thermometer 温度计 to temperature 温度
barometer 气压计 to pressure 压力　　altimeter 测高仪 to height 高度

405

speedometer 测速仪	to	velocity 速度	scale 秤	to	weight 重量
ruler 尺子	to	length 长度			

宝石类

aquamarine	海蓝宝石	emerald	绿宝石	jade	玉
amber	琥珀	ruby	红宝石	turquoise	绿松石
sapphire	蓝宝石	topaz	黄宝石	amethyst	紫水晶

偏离

digression 离题	to	topic 主题	veer 转向	to	course 跑道
digress 离题	to	subject 主题	detour 绕道	to	itinerary 行程表
discursive 离题的	to	focus 集中			

索引

A

abandon / 357
abash / 287
abate / 139
abbreviate / 63
abdicate / 100
abduct / 195
aberration / 17
abhor / 18
abjure / 177
abode / 279
abolish / 226
aboriginal / 365
abortive / 145
abridge / 164
abrupt / 255
abscond / 305
absolve / 182
abstain / 387
abstract / 318
abstruse / 164
abundant / 294
abyss / 345
accede / 14
accelerate / 386
accentuate / 45
access / 384
acclaim / 349
accomplish / 352
accord / 191
account / 153
accrue / 382
acknowledge / 186
acquiesce / 275
acrid / 237
acumen / 204
adage / 233
adamant / 315
address / 345
adept / 225
adhere / 208
adjacent / 56
adjoin / 77
administrator / 53
admonish / 341
adorn / 113
adroit / 328
adulterate / 158
advance / 60
advent / 113
adversary / 349
advertise / 290
advocate / 254
aesthetic / 338
affable / 45
affectation / 108
affection / 324
affiliation / 290
affinity / 398
affluent / 291
agenda / 264
aggrandize / 299
aggregate / 261
aghast / 52
agile / 85
agitation / 13
agnostic / 42
agog / 246
agony / 313
album / 383
alchemy / 46
alcove / 207
alias / 226
alien / 162
align / 281
allude / 166
aloof / 321
alp / 355
altar / 126
alter / 315
altercation / 232
altimeter / 88
altruism / 47
amalgamate / 260
ambience / 141
ambiguous / 279
ambivalent / 164
ambulatory / 213
ameliorate / 234
amend / 181
amiable / 339
amnesia / 164
amnesty / 246
amorphous / 187
amphibian / 360
ample / 230
amplify / 230
amulet / 73
amuse / 27
analyze / 362
anarchy / 119
anecdote / 281
anesthetic / 260
anguish / 10
animate / 109
animosity / 45
annihilate / 297
annotation / 311
announce / 119
annoy / 142
annul / 312
anomalous / 321
anonymous / 56
antagonistic / 369
anthology / 296
antibiotic / 284
antidote / 188
antiseptic / 227
antithesis / 56
anxiety / 57
apathy / 18
aplomb / 269
apogee / 57
appeal / 310
appease / 301
appendix / 131
applause / 138
appliance / 324
apprehend / 350
appropriate / 64
approve / 103
apron / 139
apt / 214
aptitude / 260
aqueduct / 5
arable / 84
arachnid / 227
arbitrator / 185
arboreal / 149
archaeologist / 158
archaic / 247
archipelago / 314
ardor / 50
arduous / 71
arena / 103
aria / 134
arid / 47
aroma / 340
arrogant / 218
articulate / 33
artificial / 52
aspire / 109
assault / 35
assemble / 39
assert / 325
asset / 59
assignment / 114
assimilate / 13
assist / 234
assortment / 287
assume / 391
assure / 112
astronomy / 393
astronomy / 10
astute / 38
asylum / 245
athlete / 2
atone / 310
attain / 385
atypical / 176
audacious / 27
auditorium / 308
auditory / 224
augment / 5
auspicious / 81
austere / 293
authentic / 371
authorize / 121
autobiography / 89
automatic / 140
automobile / 302
autonomous / 133
avarice / 208
aversion / 120
avocation / 89
avoid / 40

B

babble / 149
badger / 90
bake / 31
balk / 129
banal / 59
banish / 299
bankrupt / 186
bard / 327
barley / 364
barometer / 10
barrage / 333
barrel / 32
barren / 151
bassinet / 72
baton / 18
batter / 265
beam / 238
bellicose / 73
belligerent / 209
bellow / 331
belly / 379
beneficial / 298
benevolent / 273
benign / 369
berate / 313
beseech / 36
bewilder / 200
bias / 337
bibliography / 34
bigoted / 100
biology / 110
bizarre / 386
blade / 106
bland / 31
blanket / 212
blatant / 293
blaze / 367
bleak / 229
blemish / 64
blender / 302
blight / 131
bliss / 212
blithe / 282
blizzard / 60
bloom / 81

blossom / 164
blueprint / 161
boast / 104
boisterous / 179
bolster / 6
bombard / 55
bond / 215
boon / 294
border / 196
bore / 22
botany / 140
boulder / 84
boundary / 5
bouquet / 79
bowling / 27
brash / 370
brave / 237
brawl / 111
brazen / 375
breach / 187
breed / 45
breeze / 119
brief / 236
broach / 174
brook / 309
browse / 244
brush / 173
brusque / 97
buffer / 163
buffoon / 341
bulb / 209
bulwark / 351
bungle / 117
burgeon / 134
butcher / 151

C

cache / 216
cacophony / 94
cactus / 166
cagey / 163
cajole / 263
calamity / 295
calculate / 240
calendar / 142
calligrapher / 305
callous / 362
callow / 260
calorie / 185
camouflage / 217
canal / 346
canary / 262
candid / 155

canine / 353
canoe / 346
cantankerous / 310
canter / 316
canvas / 86
canvass / 327
capital / 348
capitulate / 309
caprice / 28
capsize / 391
captain / 258
captivate / 142
capture / 154
cardiologist / 190
caress / 93
cargo / 276
caricature / 145
carpenter / 374
cartographer / 178
cast / 76
castle / 155
casualty / 315
catastrophe / 9
caterpillar / 343
caucus / 283
caustic / 271
caution / 187
cavern / 7
celestial / 138
cello / 96
censor / 37
ceremonious / 68
chaff / 378
chagrin / 358
chain / 253
champion / 199
chandelier / 73
chaotic / 136
chapter / 146
characterize / 61
chasm / 100
chassis / 244
chauffeur / 107
cheat / 303
chef / 383
chemist / 80
cherub / 14
chide / 379
chill / 204
chisel / 22
choir / 197
choreography / 120
chronic / 325
churlish / 253

circumference / 243
circumlocution / 117
circumspect / 84
cistern / 274
citadel / 118
clam / 395
clamor / 284
clandestine / 55
clarinet / 51
clarity / 155
claw / 84
clay / 112
cleft / 216
cling / 398
clog / 371
clumsy / 326
cluster / 343
coarse / 376
coat / 11
coax / 239
cobble / 176
cocoon / 231
coerce / 93
cogent / 218
cognizant / 33
coil / 362
collaboration / 135
collage / 143
collapse / 292
collide / 137
collie / 376
collusion / 213
colossus / 79
combative / 90
command / 70
commencement / 124
commend / 14
commiserate / 244
commission / 143
commotion / 235
communicate / 359
compassion / 169
compel / 55
compensation / 269
compete / 215
complacent / 258
complete / 289
compliment / 152
comply / 367
composer / 220
composure / 133
comprise / 145
compromise / 282
conceal / 343

concede / 183
conceited / 160
conciliate / 348
concise / 284
concord / 62
concrete / 377
concur / 35
condense / 105
condescend / 302
condole / 308
condone / 231
conductor / 97
confer / 15
confidential / 311
confine / 53
confirm / 315
conflagration / 392
conflate / 128
conform / 272
confront / 170
congeal / 156
congenial / 50
congenital / 142
congregation / 395
conjecture / 48
conscientious / 113
consecrate / 28
consensus / 113
consequence / 193
console / 32
conspicuous / 65
constant / 147
constellation / 379
contagious / 159
contain / 270
contemporary / 6
contempt / 333
contend / 165
content / 124
continent / 216
contort / 197
contour / 390
contradict / 297
contrite / 138
controversy / 396
convention / 209
convert / 95
convince / 6
convoluted / 257
coop / 141
cooper / 11
cooperation / 200
coordination / 32
copious / 168

cork / 8
coroner / 356
corporal / 263
corpulent / 227
corral / 305
correspond / 178
corridor / 25
corrupt / 252
counsel / 178
counterfeit / 18
court / 69
covert / 74
covet / 258
coward / 232
coy / 368
crafty / 302
crass / 226
craven / 195
crawl / 129
creditable / 259
creed / 330
crest / 177
criminal / 141
cringe / 116
criticize / 399
crouch / 256
crucial / 264
crust / 128
crutch / 328
cuff / 196
culinary / 342
cull / 385
culpable / 170
cultivate / 28
cupidity / 301
curator / 179
curd / 248
cursory / 273
curtail / 165
curve / 103
cushion / 369
cyclical / 134
cylinder / 201

D

dam / 276
daunt / 95
dawdle / 337
dawn / 183
deadlock / 288
dearth / 269
debilitate / 79

debris / 328
debunk / 52
decay / 36
deceive / 269
decibel / 152
deciduous / 69
deck / 306
decode / 19
decorate / 61
decree / 231
dedication / 6
deduce / 111
default / 85
defiance / 397
deficient / 203
deft / 82
dejected / 346
delectable / 249
deliberate / 107
delight / 344
dell / 129
deluge / 295
deluxe / 384
demolish / 99
demonstrate / 381
depart / 389
deplete / 85
deplore / 108
derision / 393
derogatory / 146
descend / 256
desecrate / 99
desert / 192
desire / 48
desist / 305
desolate / 272
despondent / 389
despot / 337
destitute / 329
destroy / 168
detain / 321
deter / 284
deteriorate / 375
detest / 45
devastate / 175
devious / 20
devise / 98
devour / 363
dexterous / 93
diagnose / 256
diamond / 373
digress / 26
dilate / 278
dilettante / 19

diligent / 92
dim / 162
diminish / 46
diplomat / 213
direct / 356
disarray / 197
disburse / 254
discard / 317
discern / 91
discipline / 205
disconcert / 137
discord / 212
discourse / 236
discreet / 149
discursive / 307
disdain / 286
disguise / 158
dismantle / 205
dismay / 387
dismiss / 323
disparage / 233
disperse / 57
disposition / 345
disprove / 349
dispute / 217
dissemble / 75
disseminate / 183
dissociate / 104
dissolve / 367
dissonance / 9
distinct / 130
distort / 285
distress / 66
ditty / 199
divert / 397
divulge / 148
docile / 392
dock / 46
document / 25
doleful / 364
domestic / 140
domicile / 221
dominate / 57
dormant / 269
dough / 230
douse / 115
downpour / 356
doze / 93
drab / 72
drastic / 325
drill / 268
drivel / 262
droll / 135
drought / 305

drudgery / 45
dubious / 357
dune / 273
duplicate / 345
durable / 201
dwell / 245
dynamic / 307

E

eager / 390
earnest / 388
eavesdrop / 69
eccentric / 292
eclectic / 390
ecstatic / 83
edible / 122
editor / 271
eerie / 65
efficient / 71
egress / 181
elaborate / 14
elegant / 1
elegy / 98
elevator / 350
elongate / 233
elucidate / 395
elude / 349
emaciated / 40
embellish / 1
embezzle / 212
embrace / 172
eminent / 272
emissary / 17
empathy / 289
emphatic / 315
emulate / 40
enclose / 215
encroach / 37
encumber / 6
endeavor / 366
endow / 263
endure / 63
enervate / 215
engage / 41
enhance / 108
enigma / 267
enlighten / 367
enmity / 249
enormous / 299
ensemble / 244
enthrall / 323
entice / 67
entreat / 49

enumerate / 191
envious / 324
ephemeral / 346
epic / 399
epilogue / 148
epiphany / 358
episode / 116
equable / 270
equal / 62
equitable / 5
erect / 37
erratic / 19
error / 288
erudite / 145
essential / 284
esteem / 277
etch / 118
eternal / 393
ethos / 293
etiquette / 337
eulogy / 205
euphoria / 378
evacuate / 280
evade / 365
evaporate / 385
evict / 330
evident / 333
ewe / 153
exacerbate / 256
exact / 347
exaggeration / 87
exalt / 246
excavate / 399
excerpt / 390
excess / 375
exclude / 257
excursion / 166
exemplify / 254
exhaust / 161
exhort / 8
exile / 275
exorbitant / 145
expedite / 231
expel / 15
explicit / 391
exploit / 54
expropriate / 84
expunge / 7
expurgate / 278
exquisite / 267
extend / 220
extol / 361
extort / 398
extract / 389

extraneous / 283
extraordinary / 16
extravagant / 210
extricate / 143
extrovert / 368
exuberant / 338

F

façade / 277
fabric / 246
fabricate / 122
facet / 301
facetious / 372
facile / 97
facsimile / 251
faction / 383
fake / 56
fallacy / 171
fallow / 332
falter / 186
famine / 187
fanatic / 221
fascinate / 7
fastidious / 150
fathom / 24
fatigue / 51
feasible / 56
fecund / 84
federal / 203
feeble / 69
feign / 179
feint / 115
felon / 62
feral / 303
fiasco / 237
fickle / 332
fierce / 244
filament / 208
filch / 359
finale / 344
firmament / 72
fission / 219
fitness / 93
flagrant / 279
flammable / 307
flaw / 234
fledgling / 4
flee / 289
fleet / 155
flippant / 129
flock / 21
flounder / 209
flour / 222

flourish / 56
fluctuate / 311
flurry / 253
flute / 103
foal / 396
fodder / 211
foe / 239
foible / 1
foment / 183
foolhardy / 85
forbid / 158
forgery / 280
forlorn / 255
formidable / 4
forswear / 64
fortify / 308
fortuitous / 243
foster / 130
foundation / 96
fraction / 316
fragile / 169
fragment / 184
fragrant / 393
frame / 366
frank / 109
fraud / 312
frenetic / 177
fret / 369
friction / 3
frivolous / 276
frown / 235
frugal / 8
fulfill / 297
furious / 277
furl / 81
furnace / 105
furnish / 7
fussy / 197

G

gaggle / 292
gala / 144
gallop / 102
galvanize / 170
gangly / 174
garble / 50
garment / 336
garnish / 150
gaunt / 222
gauntlet / 339
gem / 303
generous / 240
genesis / 376

genre / 271
genuine / 266
geriatrics / 70
ghastly / 126
gimmick / 10
glance / 65
gloomy / 76
glove / 153
gluttony / 340
goad / 169
gong / 2
gown / 68
grace / 222
grand / 163
grant / 355
gratis / 40
gratuitous / 217
grave / 261
gregarious / 141
grid / 365
grief / 290
grimace / 291
grizzly / 1
groove / 359
guarantee / 164
guffaw / 49
guile / 175
gulf / 280
gullible / 387
gully / 316
gyrate / 217

H

habit / 354
hackneyed / 133
hag / 20
haiku / 205
haphazard / 329
hapless / 139
harass / 22
harbinger / 287
harmonious / 132
harsh / 41
hasten / 156
haughty / 55
haunt / 116
headstrong / 78
headway / 243
heap / 253
hedonist / 99
heinous / 372
helix / 121
helmet / 64

henchman / 26
herculean / 49
herd / 388
heritage / 383
heterogeneous / 262
hexagonal / 154
hiatus / 379
hibernate / 185
hide / 203
highwayman / 300
hilarious / 387
hinder / 188
hinge / 225
hint / 257
hoax / 271
hockey / 60
hoe / 165
hoist / 254
homily / 49
horde / 37
horn / 321
hose / 391
hostile / 242
hover / 250
hue / 67
humid / 41
humus / 379
husk / 228
hutch / 242
hybrid / 296
hydrate / 331
hyperbole / 320
hypocrisy / 327
hypothesis / 31

I

iconoclast / 6
identical / 48
idle / 33
igneous / 91
ignite / 166
illicit / 377
illiterate / 318
illuminate / 317
illusion / 128
imagination / 213
imbibe / 161
imitation / 370
immaculate / 54
imminent / 230
immobile / 65
immunity / 207
impact / 336

impair / 147
impart / 223
impasse / 111
impassive / 351
impeccable / 280
impede / 297
imperative / 168
imperious / 312
impervious / 75
impetus / 92
implement / 19
imply / 235
impregnable / 19
impromptu / 48
impudent / 16
impulse / 377
inadvertently / 248
incendiary / 173
incensed / 132
incentive / 97
incessant / 192
incidental / 72
incipient / 200
incision / 11
incite / 348
inconsistent / 313
incorrigible / 206
incumbent / 108
indefatigable / 279
index / 247
indicate / 2
indifferent / 112
indigenous / 376
indignation / 377
indolent / 365
induce / 182
indulge / 51
inept / 19
infamous / 73
infection / 321
infirmary / 312
ingenuity / 201
ingenuous / 240
inhabit / 367
inhospitable / 192
initiate / 221
injustice / 165
ink / 81
inkling / 75
innate / 179
innocuous / 231
innovation / 70
inscribe / 137
insect / 3

insinuate / 307
insipid / 309
insolent / 12
insomnia / 370
inspire / 327
instigate / 316
instruction / 77
insulate / 309
insult / 147
insurgent / 191
intact / 323
integrity / 104
intellect / 109
inter / 80
interfere / 330
interloper / 116
intern / 373
intersect / 336
intimate / 337
intimidate / 313
intransigent / 342
intrepid / 243
intricate / 384
intrigue / 55
introspection / 199
intrude / 133
invade / 201
inventory / 149
investigate / 5
invisible / 113
irascible / 320
irate / 93
irk / 12
iron / 10
irreversible / 384
irrigate / 50
irritate / 366
isolate / 14
itinerary / 44

J

jabber / 388
jack / 368
jail / 203
jargon / 274
jaunt / 202
jeer / 354
jeopardize / 203
jest / 362
jewel / 339
jog / 220
joggle / 133
jollity / 81

jovial / 89
jubilant / 28
jubilee / 101
judicious / 265
juggler / 21
jumbo / 381
jury / 350
juvenile / 172
juxtapose / 67

K

keen / 86
kennel / 125
kiln / 118
kindle / 211
kinetic / 322
kitten / 364
knack / 297
knot / 121

L

labyrinth / 134
lacerated / 336
lackluster / 43
laconic / 4
lament / 37
lamp / 49
lapel / 309
lapse / 230
laud / 173
lava / 378
lavish / 296
lawn / 329
leather / 108
ledger / 386
leery / 23
legend / 363
legible / 333
legislate / 170
legitimate / 162
lenient / 314
lens / 87
lessen / 352
lethal / 67
lethargic / 25
levee / 195
lever / 371
levity / 17
lexicon / 216
liaison / 76
libel / 225
liberate / 39
limb / 242

limber / 308
limerick / 20
limpid / 102
listless / 219
litigant / 216
livid / 77
loathe / 73
locomotion / 183
locomotive / 42
loom / 30
loquacious / 385
lubricant / 291
lucid / 146
lull / 274
lung / 18
lunge / 36

M

magnitude / 358
malady / 6
malfunction / 248
malice / 137
malign / 22
malinger / 154
mammal / 193
manager / 23
mangle / 277
mania / 157
manifest / 179
manufacture / 56
mar / 26
marathon / 323
marble / 188
marquee / 278
marsupial / 279
marvel / 142
mash / 206
mask / 191
masterpiece / 311
masticate / 371
material / 25
maudlin / 200
maxim / 12
mayhem / 285
meager / 254
meander / 190
meddle / 323
meditation / 264
medley / 347
meek / 261
melodious / 397
melt / 358
mendacity / 196

mendicant / 138
merchandise / 70
mercy / 94
merit / 28
metal / 337
meteorology / 24
meticulous / 196
migrate / 378
mileage / 63
milk / 277
mimic / 394
mineral / 268
mingle / 187
mire / 172
mirror / 300
mischievous / 43
miserly / 53
mob / 59
mock / 381
moderate / 363
modify / 259
mogul / 169
moist / 286
molecule / 92
molt / 32
monarch / 173
monologue / 304
monsoon / 358
monument / 395
mope / 226
morgue / 23
morose / 364
mortify / 328
motif / 155
mourn / 281
movement / 152
mow / 92
muddle / 72
muffle / 149
mumble / 236
mundane / 81
munificent / 319
murder / 255
murky / 174
muscle / 52
muster / 122
myriad / 240
mystery / 273
myth / 101

N

nadir / 217
nail / 186

napkin / 293
narrate / 182
natal / 366
navigate / 218
nebulous / 74
negligible / 117
nemesis / 291
neophyte / 58
nib / 380
nimble / 11
noble / 136
nocturnal / 238
nomad / 317
nonchalant / 281
note / 340
nourish / 101
novel / 250
novice / 373
nuance / 247
nudge / 126
nugget / 261
nullify / 165
nurture / 345

O

oasis / 288
oath / 75
obdurate / 304
obedient / 300
object / 325
oblige / 355
obliterate / 68
oblivious / 79
oboe / 104
obscene / 208
obsequious / 182
observe / 109
obsess / 306
obsolete / 355
obstinate / 136
obstruct / 114
obvious / 316
odious / 115
odometer / 69
odor / 354
offense / 319
officious / 102
olfactory / 130
ominous / 375
omniscient / 186
onerous / 366
onslaught / 99
ooze / 260

opaque / 386
opera / 238
opinionated / 357
oppress / 174
optimize / 269
opulent / 339
orator / 257
orbit / 359
orchestra / 194
ordinance / 21
ornament / 174
ornery / 89
ostentation / 134
ostracize / 272
ostrich / 397
ounce / 311
outline / 283
overbear / 268
overture / 168
overwhelm / 237
owl / 341

P

pacify / 259
painstaking / 154
palatable / 223
palette / 386
pallid / 151
paltry / 88
pane / 324
panicky / 2
panorama / 117
paradox / 332
paragon / 137
paramount / 54
parch / 144
pardon / 174
pariah / 258
parody / 346
parry / 146
partial / 226
partisanship / 191
passion / 65
patent / 276
paternalism / 259
patient / 274
patronize / 151
pauper / 210
pause / 96
peacock / 262
peak / 210
pebble / 14
peculiar / 165

pecuniary / 255
pedagogue / 173
pedantic / 294
pediatrics / 200
peel / 125
pellucid / 214
penitent / 267
pensive / 367
penury / 165
perceive / 272
perilous / 284
permanent / 219
permeate / 23
pernicious / 298
perpetual / 361
perplexed / 160
persevere / 328
persistent / 363
perspire / 84
pertinent / 40
peruse / 261
pest / 344
petal / 205
petition / 141
petrify / 145
petulant / 394
phenomenon / 300
philanthropist / 100
phlegmatic / 83
phonetics / 326
physician / 206
pigment / 230
pilfer / 68
pilot / 2
pinnacle / 67
pint / 375
pious / 267
pit / 308
pith / 159
placate / 53
placid / 264
plagiarize / 31
plain / 338
planet / 287
plant / 166
platform / 31
plaudit / 295
plausible / 199
plead / 104
pledge / 316
plethora / 91
plight / 381
plow / 36
pluck / 117

plumage / 150
plummet / 160
plunder / 264
poacher / 174
poetry / 399
poignant / 353
poise / 303
poison / 312
poll / 304
pompous / 383
ponder / 130
ponderous / 314
poodle / 33
portentous / 162
portray / 119
posthumous / 169
postpone / 239
postscript / 158
potable / 350
potent / 320
poultry / 112
pounce / 150
poverty / 46
pragmatic / 209
prance / 288
preamble / 93
precarious / 300
precaution / 97
precede / 115
precipice / 183
precipitate / 387
predicament / 182
predict / 380
predominant / 272
preface / 204
prehensile / 265
prejudice / 156
premonition / 98
prerogative / 299
prescription / 95
president / 181
prestige / 337
presumptive / 163
pretext / 38
prevail / 309
prevaricate / 391
previous / 149
prey / 122
prickly / 282
pride / 126
primate / 285
principal / 278
pristine / 50
process / 212

proclivity / 236
procure / 237
prod / 11
prodigal / 289
profane / 219
proficient / 265
profit / 22
profound / 288
profusion / 385
progeny / 121
prohibit / 281
proliferate / 23
prologue / 220
prolong / 312
prominent / 178
prompt / 208
proof / 225
propel / 280
propensity / 329
property / 77
prophesy / 176
propose / 108
prose / 35
prosecute / 374
prosper / 216
prototype / 73
proverb / 324
provoke / 141
proximity / 48
prudent / 252
prune / 175
pry / 379
psychiatrist / 124
psychology / 110
puck / 116
puerile / 126
pugilist / 297
pugnacious / 341
punch / 265
puncture / 146
pungent / 76
pupil / 379
pure / 36
purloin / 128
pursue / 381
putrid / 124

Q

quake / 349
qualm / 273
quandary / 371
quantity / 102
quarry / 85

quart / 227
quell / 105
quench / 108
querulous / 238
query / 51
quill / 90
quiver / 15

R

racket / 68
radiant / 98
ramble / 13
rancid / 4
ransack / 125
rational / 332
raucous / 351
ravenous / 74
raze / 394
razor / 41
rebel / 26
recalcitrant / 294
recall / 61
recede / 318
receptacle / 374
recess / 41
recipe / 4
reciprocal / 64
recital / 190
reckless / 132
recluse / 299
recoil / 134
recollect / 88
recompense / 200
recruit / 238
rectangle / 151
rectify / 157
recurrent / 172
reduce / 161
redundant / 106
refill / 392
refine / 123
reflex / 365
refractory / 275
refrain / 269
refrigerator / 245
refurbish / 394
refuse / 35
refute / 191
regal / 395
rehearse / 232
reimbursement / 106
reiterate / 106

related / 191
relieve / 38
relinquish / 85
relish / 326
reluctant / 83
reminisce / 91
remiss / 111
remonstrate / 335
remuneration / 178
rend / 60
rendezvous / 125
renounce / 208
renovation / 293
renowned / 196
repeal / 78
replete / 104
replica / 80
represent / 13
repress / 249
reprimand / 94
reproach / 9
reptile / 298
repudiate / 281
repugnant / 77
reputable / 100
required / 100
rescind / 171
reserved / 207
residual / 390
resilient / 64
resist / 306
resolution / 135
respite / 244
restore / 263
restraint / 166
restrict / 221
retaliation / 148
retard / 289
reticent / 331
retreat / 335
reveal / 233
reverence / 183
revitalize / 266
revival / 332
revoke / 138
rickety / 219
ridiculous / 35
rife / 302
rigid / 376
riot / 348
rival / 293
roar / 80
robust / 252
roe / 30

rooster / 270
rotate / 60
rotten / 66
rouse / 329
royalty / 156
ruddy / 102
rudimentary / 386
rue / 372
rummage / 200
ruse / 72
rust / 162
rustle / 244
ruthless / 292

S

saddle / 212
safeguard / 15
saga / 295
sage / 60
salutary / 85
salutation / 247
salvage / 89
sanctimonious / 293
sandal / 152
sanguine / 109
sap / 354
sapling / 285
sapphire / 321
sartorial / 304
satiate / 90
satire / 156
sauce / 141
savory / 204
scale / 107
scatter / 345
schedule / 214
schism / 313
school / 382
scissor / 28
scold / 215
scoop / 49
score / 86
scoundrel / 113
screw / 176
scribble / 266
script / 398
scrutinize / 61
sculpture / 157
scurry / 313
seal / 303
secure / 310
sedentary / 249
seed / 375

seer / 382
semantics / 16
seminar / 275
sensitive / 233
sentence / 7
sentimental / 380
sentry / 250
serene / 248
servile / 214
severe / 127
shard / 68
shell / 354
shelter / 44
shove / 148
shovel / 160
shrewd / 389
shroud / 283
shun / 358
shuttle / 193
sidestep / 52
silence / 276
sincere / 287
sink / 216
siren / 167
skeleton / 335
skeptic / 51
sketch / 362
skit / 55
skitter / 96
skunk / 213
skyscraper / 352
slander / 371
slippery / 78
sluggish / 296
sly / 372
smite / 322
snack / 198
sneak / 248
snoop / 43
snout / 270
soak / 398
soar / 388
sob / 394
sober / 329
sojourn / 89
solar / 159
solemn / 392
solicit / 279
solitary / 394
solo / 307
solution / 79
solvent / 318
somber / 54
somnolent / 227

soothe / 304
soothsayer / 322
sophisticated / 163
sour / 234
sow / 352
spark / 71
sparse / 40
spear / 326
spectator / 188
spectrum / 129
speculate / 381
sphere / 39
spicy / 125
split / 37
spoil / 145
sporadic / 285
spouse / 298
spring / 243
sprinkle / 226
sprint / 251
sprout / 252
spurious / 66
spurn / 289
squalid / 230
squall / 205
squander / 102
square / 48
stab / 220
stable / 370
stadium / 277
stag / 170
stagnant / 268
stain / 257
stanza / 3
stare / 157
stark / 162
static / 121
stature / 54
steadfast / 260
steady / 80
stealth / 301
steel / 41
steer / 390
stench / 133
sterilize / 39
stern / 154
stiff / 395
stifle / 232
stimulate / 374
stingy / 224
stipend / 195
stipulate / 211
stomp / 146
stool / 89

stove / 21
stratify / 115
stream / 182
strenuous / 120
string / 322
strive / 334
stroll / 238
stubborn / 47
stymie / 273
submerge / 363
submissive / 105
subsequent / 235
subside / 394
substantial / 257
subtle / 212
subtract / 38
succinct / 97
succumb / 91
sufficient / 225
suffocate / 128
suffuse / 296
sullen / 317
sully / 30
summary / 267
summit / 264
sunder / 52
superficial / 319
superimpose / 335
supervisor / 349
supplant / 295
supplement / 11
supreme / 62
surge / 370
surgeon / 229
surly / 111
surmount / 235
surrender / 136
surreptitious / 101
sustenance / 256
swarm / 283
sweatpants / 59
swelter / 44
swivel / 34
sword / 305
symmetry / 161
sympathy / 123
symphony / 342
synchronize / 325
syntax / 383
synthesis / 40

T

taciturn / 129

tact / 393
tactile / 169
taint / 171
talkative / 198
talon / 365
tangible / 206
tarnish / 382
taunt / 104
tawdry / 195
tear / 196
tedious / 261
temperate / 144
tenacious / 80
tenuous / 185
tepid / 170
terminate / 256
terrain / 332
terrestrial / 30
terrier / 118
terse / 88
theme / 224
therapeutic / 335
thermometer / 21
thesis / 334
thicket / 353
thorn / 198
thread / 26
threat / 373
thrifty / 154
thrive / 371
throne / 247
throng / 121
thwart / 356
tile / 57
timid / 378
tirade / 361
toady / 27
tobacco / 153
token / 124
tolerate / 300
tongue / 181
tornado / 43
torpid / 242
torque / 239
torrent / 186
torrid / 333
torsion / 16
torturous / 22
tournament / 92
tower / 32
tracery / 137
track / 150
tractable / 253
tractor / 76

trail / 389
trample / 346
tranquil / 192
transcribe / 207
transmit / 134
transplant / 120
travesty / 286
treachery / 334
trek / 57
tremendous / 207
trial / 125
triangle / 179
tribute / 66
trickle / 357
trifling / 374
trigger / 181
triplets / 95
trite / 190
trivia / 380
trophy / 78
tropical / 139
trot / 189
truce / 17
trumpet / 359
truncate / 44
trust / 63
tumult / 229
turbulent / 345
turmoil / 207
tutor / 201
tweak / 158

U

ulcer / 343
umbrella / 351
undermine / 398
understate / 80
unflinching / 288
ungainly / 305
unicorn / 11
uniform / 159
universe / 82
unkempt / 331
unrealistic / 130
unscrupulous / 340
uprising / 330
uproar / 320
urbane / 122
urgency / 17
utilize / 112

V

vaccination / 229
vacillate / 39
vacuous / 234
vacuum / 352
vague / 202
valediction / 2
valet / 71
valid / 399
valley / 350
valor / 211
vanity / 159
varnish / 172
vary / 43
vault / 204
veal / 398
vegetarian / 17
veil / 110
velocity / 96
vend / 364
venerate / 320
veracious / 263
verbose / 65
verdict / 322
verge / 361
verify / 46
versatile / 143
vertical / 344
vessel / 110
veto / 88
vex / 348
vibrate / 140
victory / 292
vie / 112
vigilant / 319
vigor / 193
villain / 1
vine / 104
violate / 248
violin / 353
virtually / 59
visage / 9
vital / 95
vivacious / 317
volume / 177
voracious / 347
vow / 130

W

wail / 22
waiter / 275
waive / 353
wan / 2
wane / 361
warlock / 331
warn / 138
warrant / 9
wary / 117
wave / 341
waver / 13
wax / 284
weary / 329
weave / 14
weep / 202
wheedle / 355
whim / 88
whip / 133
whisper / 222
widespread / 332
wily / 131
wing / 197
winsome / 24
wire / 184
wisdom / 239
wispy / 323
withdraw / 180
wither / 78
witness / 87
wood / 251
worm / 234
wrap / 71
wrath / 121
wreak / 124
wreath / 147
wreck / 27
wretched / 243
wrist / 114
writhe / 197

X

xenophobia / 336

Y

yacht / 154
yawn / 168
yearn / 62
yield / 265

Z

zany / 246
zeal / 198
zenith / 75